Cryptography for Internet and Database Applications

Cryptography for Internet and Database Applications

Developing Secret and Public Key Techniques with Java™

Nick Galbreath

Wiley Publishing, Inc.

Publisher: Bob Ipsen
Editor: Carol A. Long
Developmental Editor: Adaobi Obi
Managing Editor: Micheline Frederick
New Media Editor: Brian Snapp
Text Design & Composition: Wiley Composition Services

This book is printed on acid-free paper. ♾

Published by Wiley Publishing, Inc., Indianapolis, Indiana

Published simultaneously in Canada

Library of Congress Cataloging-in-Publication Data:

ISBN: 0-471-21029-3

Printed in the United States of America

10 9 8 7 6 5 4 3 2 1

Contents

Preface

I wrote this book for software engineers with little or no exposure to cryptography. Most other books fall into one of two categories, the encyclopedia and description or the purely API descriptive. The goal was try and bridge the two by providing a solid introduction to cryptography while providing solid examples and uses. In addition, many books focus overwhelmingly on public key techniques. In my experience the most common uses for public key ciphers are handled by third-party applications (VPNs, Emails) or off-the-shelf protocols such as SSL and SSH.

While there are a number of excellent cryptographic libraries in C and C++, Java serves as the reference since:

- It's very popular for new business and server applications.
- Memory management is automatically done, eliminating entire classes of bugs (stack smashing and buffer overflows).
- It provides a standard cryptographic API that, while not perfect or complete, is about as "universal" as we can get.

The cryptographic API for Java is scattered among several packages. Instead of listing classes by packages as is commonly done, Appendix A lists the classes alphabetically. I found this to be much more useful than flipping between different package sections.

I've tried to limit source code to examples that are relatively simple or that demonstrate main points or self-contained utilities. More complicated (and perhaps more useful) examples were excluded simply because the error and exception handling for a security application can be quite long and tedious and didn't really add much value. I have always disliked

CD-ROMs glued into books and likewise, never found chapters and chapters of source code to be very useful. Instead, full source code and more examples are presented at the companion Web site at `www.wiley.com/compbooks.galbreath`.

Unfortunately, time and space didn't permit examination of many topics. In particular:

- XML key management, encryption, and signature scheme
- Privacy Issues, including privacy "seals," Gramm-Leech-Biley Act of 1999 and HIPPA privacy rule.
- More detailed database tips and techniques.

Perhaps these will be detailed in future editions. Until then, I hope you find this book useful.

Finally, this book would not have been possible without the many fruitful conversations and support from Dave Andre, Jeff Bussgang, Ann Calvit, Roy Dixit, Jim Finucane, Bill French, Venkat Gaddipati, Nabil Hachem, Sam Haradhvala, Adam Hirsch, Steve Morris, Jack Orenstein, Rich O'Neil, and Matt Rowe, and many others from Upromise, SightPath and Open Market. Special thanks to my family and friends that had to put up with my social hiatus while working on this book. Thank you all.

Nick Galbreath
Plum Island, MA
June 2002

Introduction

The goal of the book is to present the systems programmer with a full introduction into the science and the application of cryptography using Java. Unlike many texts, this book does *not* focus on cryptography for *transmission* (allowing two parties to communicate securely). For most applications, those requirements are handled by the SSL or SSH protocols, or a third-party application. Instead this book focuses on cryptography for storage, message integrity, and authentication, (the so-called "single-point" techniques) which is more common with custom applications. Beside pure cryptography, many "auxiliary" techniques are covered that make cryptography useful.

The first chapter covers basic logical and numeric operations, both at the theoretical level and with the specifics of the Java numeric model. While it may be a review to many readers, I've found that many system programmers just do not have exposure to these low-level details. Either they never learned, or more likely, because it just isn't normally used in day-to-day work, it's been forgotten. Those readers who are more familiar with C or C++, should find this chapter especially useful for translating code one way or another from Java.

The next two chapters introduce the reader to science, mathematics, and standards of both secret key and public key cryptography. Here you'll learn why the algorithms work and the various tradeoffs between them. While the mathematics aren't essential in day-to-day programming tasks, the goal was to teach the reader to be familiar with the terminology that is often tossed around to be able to make informed decisions.

Chapter 4 discusses random numbers and random number generators. While not technically *cryptography*, random numbers are essential to it. Those readers developing gaming systems should find this section especially interesting. Java is used for examples of algorithms, but it could be easily converted to any other programming language.

Finally, in Chapter 5 we introduce Java's cryptographic APIs. The Java SDK already comes with some excellent documentation, but I've tried to pull it together consolidating the JCA and JCE into a coherent format. Likewise, I made Appendix A the Java cryptography reference I wanted when I'm programming. Instead of listing classes by package, I list them all alphabetically. You'll find you'll do a lot less page flipping this way and get a much better understanding of the API with this organization.

Chapter 6 is on small message encoding, and like Chapter 4, isn't technically cryptography, but it's always an issue when using cryptography. Here you'll learn how to convert binary data (perhaps encrypted) into various ASCII formats. This is critical when embedding data in a URL, creating passwords and cryptographic tokens.

Chapter 7 pulls everything together and discusses many topics: application and database design, working the passwords and tokens, key management, and logging.

Numerous source code examples are used, and the source itself can be found at the companion Web site www.modp.com. Many of the examples in the book will require a little reworking for production use. You'll want to modify the error handling to suite your needs. In some cases, if the code is especially long and not particularly illuminating, I decided not to list it and instead just refer to the Web site. I find page after page of printed source code in a book to not be particularly useful.

Unfortunately, due to time and space requirements a lot of important topics are not covered. Digital signatures are only mentioned and they deserve more, but I've found for basic application work, they just aren't that useful. Either, most people won't use them or there is already a trust relationship in place eliminating their usefulness, or encryption with a hash or MAC is preferable. And finally, when I do need to use them, the process is normally handled by a third party application. Other topics not given their due are the new XML and SAML standards for creating documents that contain encrypted data, and embedding cryptography *within* the database (instead of the application), such as the newer Oracle database can do. A lot more could be said for key management and database design as well. Perhaps future editions will remedy this.

Bits and Bytes

Before getting into the details of cryptographic operators, we'll review some basics of working with bits and number bases. For those of you who have worked on operating systems, low-level protocols, and embedded systems, the material in this chapter will probably be a review; for the rest of you, whose day-to-day interactions with information technology and basic software development don't involve working directly with bits, this information will be an important foundation to the information contained in the rest of the book.

General Operations

Most cryptographic functions operate directly on machine representation of numbers. What follows are overviews of how numbers are presented in different bases, how computers internally represent numbers as a collection of bits, and how to directly manipulate bits. This material is presented in a computer- and language-generic way; the next section focuses specifically on the Java model.

Number Bases

In day-to-day operations, we represent numbers using base 10. Each digit is 0 through 9; thus, given a string of decimal digits $d_n d_{n-1} \cdots d_2 d_1 d_0$, the numeric value would be:

$$10^n d_n + 10^{n-1} d_{n-1} + \cdots + 10^2 d_2 + 10 d_1 + d_0$$

This can be generalized to any base x, where there are x different digits and a number is represented by:

$$x^n d_n + x^{n-1} d_{n-1} + \cdots + x^2 d_2 + x d_1 + d_0$$

In computer science, the most important base is base 2, or the binary representation of the number. Here each digit, or bit, can either be 0 or 1. The decimal number 30 can be represented in binary as 11110 or 16 + 4 + 2. Also common is hexadecimal, or base 16, where the digits are 0 to 9 and A, B, C, D, E, and F, representing 10 to 15, respectively. The number 30 can now be represented in hexadecimal as 1E or 16 + 14. The relationship between digits in binary, decimal, and hexadecimal is listed in Table 1.1.

Table 1.1 Binary, Decimal, and Hexadecimal Representations

BINARY	DECIMAL	HEXADECIMAL
0000	0	0
0001	1	1
0010	2	2
0011	3	3
0100	4	4
0101	5	5
0110	6	6
0111	7	7
1000	8	8
1001	9	9
1010	10	A
1011	11	B
1100	12	C
1101	13	D
1110	14	E
1111	15	F

When you are working with different bases, the base of a number may be ambiguous. For instance, is 99 the decimal or the hexadecimal 99 ($= 9 \times 16+9$)? In this case, it's common to prefix a hexadecimal number with 0x or just x (e.g., 99 becomes 0x99 or x99). The same confusion can happen with binary numbers: Is 101 the decimal 101 or the binary 101 ($4 + 1 = 5$)? When a number in binary may be confused, it's customary to add a subscript 2 at the end of a string of binary digits, for example, 101_2.

Any number can be represented in another base *b* if it is positive; however, doing the conversion isn't necessarily easy. We'll discuss general-purpose base conversion in a later section, but it's useful to note that conversion between two bases is especially easy if one of the bases is a power of the other. For instance, the decimal number 1234 has the canonical representation in base 10 as $1 \times 1000 + 2 \times 100 + 3 \times 10 + 4$. However, 1234 can also be thought as two "digits" in base 100: (12) and (34), with a value of $12 \times 1000 + 34 \times 100$. It's the same number with the same value; the digits have just been regrouped. This property is especially useful for base 2. Given a binary string, it's possible to convert to hexadecimal by grouping 4 bits and computing the hexadecimal value:

```
10011100 = 1001 1100 = 9C
```

Bits and Bytes

A *bit* is the smallest unit of information that a computer can work on and can take two values "1" and "0," although sometimes depending on context the values of "true" and "false" are used. On most modern computers, we do not work directly on bits but on a *collection* of bits, sometimes called a *word*, the smallest of which is a *byte*. Today, a byte by default means 8 bits, but technically it can range from 4 to 10 bits. The odd values are from either old or experimental CPU architectures that aren't really in use anymore. To be precise, many standards use *octet* to mean 8 bits, but we'll use the more common *byte*. Modern CPUs operate on much larger word sizes: The term *32-bit microprocessor* means the CPU operates primarily on 32-bit words in one clock cycle. It can, of course, operate on 8-bit words, but it doesn't mean it happens any faster. Many CPUs also have special instructions that sometimes can operate on larger words, such as the SSE and similar instructions for multimedia, as well as vector processing, such as on the PowerPC.

A byte has a natural numeric interpretation as an integer from 0 to 255 using base 2, as described earlier. Bit *n* represents the value $2n$, and the value of the byte becomes the sum of these bits. The bits are laid out exactly as expected for a numeric representation, with bit 0 on the right and bit 7 on the left, but the layout is backward when compared to Western languages.

$$(b_7b_6b_5b_4b_3b_2b_1b_0) = 2^7b_7 + 2^6b_6 + 2^5b_5 + 2^4b_4 + 2^3b_3 + 2^2b_2 + 2^1b_1 + 2^0b_0$$

or using decimal notation

$$(b_7b_6b_5b_4b_3b_2b_1b_0) = 128b_7 + 64b_6 + 32b_5 + 16b_4 + 8b_3 + 4b_2 + 2b_1 + b_0$$

For example, 00110111 = 32 + 16 + 4 + 2 + 1 = 55.

Bits on the left are referred to as the *most-significant bits,* since they contribute the most to the overall value of the number. Likewise, the right-most bits are called the *least-significant bits.* This layout is also known as *Big-Endian,* which we'll discuss later.

Signed Bytes

Negative numbers can be represented in a few ways. The simplest is to reverse one bit to represent the sign of the number, either positive or negative. Bits 0 through 6 would represent the number, and bit 7 would represent the sign. Although this allows a range from –127 to 127, it has the quirk of two zeros: a "positive" zero and a "negative" zero. Having the two zeros is odd, but it can be worked around. The bigger problem is when an overflow occurs—for instance, adding 127 + 2 is 129 in unsigned arithmetic, or 1000001. However, in signed arithmetic, the value is –1.

The most common representation is known as *two's complement.* Given *x*, its negative is represented by flipping all the bits (turning 1s into 0s and vice versa) and adding 1, or computing –1 –*x* (the same value). For example, note in Table 1.2 that adding 1 to 127 makes the value –128. While this method is a bit odd, there are many benefits. Microprocessors can encode just an addition circuit and a complementation circuit to do both addition and subtraction (in fact, many CPUs carry around the complement with the original value just in case subtraction comes up). The other main benefit is when casting occurs, or converting a byte into a larger word, as described in the following section.

Bitwise Operators

The usual arithmetic functions such as addition and multiplication interpret words as numbers and perform the appropriate operations. However, other operations work directly on the bits without regard to their representation as numbers. These are *bitwise* or *logical* operations. While examples shown in the next sections use 8-bit bytes, they naturally extend to any word size.

Table 1.2 Two's Complement Representation

UNSIGNED VALUE	SIGNED VALUE	HEXADECIMAL REPRESENTATION	BINARY REPRESENTATION
0	0	00	00000000
1	1	01	00000001
2	2	02	00000010
126	126	7d	01111110
127	127	7f	01111111
128	-128	80	10000000
129	-127	81	10000001
130	-126	82	10000010
253	-3	fd	11111101
254	-2	fe	11111110
255	-1	ff	11111111

As shown in Table 1.3, the operations are represented by different symbols depending if the context is programming or typographical. When required, this book will use the programming notations, with the exception of XOR, since the caret symbol (^) is used to denote exponents in some systems.

Table 1.3 Bitwise Operations and Notation

OPERATION	C-STYLE NOTATION	C-STYLE SELF-ASSIGNMENT	TYPOGRAPHICAL
NOT *a*	`~a`	n/*a*	$\neg a$
a AND *b*	`a & b`	`a &= b`	$a \wedge b$
a OR *b*	`a	b`	`a |= b`	$a \vee b$
a XOR *b*	`a ^ b`	`a ^= b`	$a \oplus b$
Shift *a* left by *n* bits	`a << n`	`a <<= n`	$a \ll n$

(continues)

Table 1.3 Bitwise Operations and Notation *(Continued)*

OPERATION	C-STYLE NOTATION	C-STYLE SELF-ASSIGNMENT	TYPOGRAPHICAL
Shift *a* right by *n* bits, preserve sign of *a*	`a >> n`	`a >>=n`	None; all shifts and words are assumed to be unsigned
Shift *a* right by *n* bits, unsigned	`a >>> n`	`a >>>=n`	$a \gg n$
Rotate *a* right by *n* bits; w is number of bits of *a*	`(x >>> n) | (x << w-n)`	*n/a*	$\mathrm{ROTR}^n(a)$
Rotate *a* left by *n* bits; w is the number of bits of *a*	`(x << n) | ( x >>> w-n)`	*n/a*	$\mathrm{ROTL}^n(a)$
Concatenating *a* and *b*	`(a << shift) | b`	*n/a*	$a \parallel b$
Take *n* least-significant bits of *a*	`a & mask`	`a &= mask`	$\mathrm{MSB}_n(a)$
Take *n* most-significant bits of *a*	`a & mask >>> shift`		$\mathrm{LSB}_n(a)$

Complementation or Bitwise NOT

The simplest bit operation is complementation or the *bitwise NOT*. This simply flips bits within a word, where 0s become 1s and 1s become 0s—for example ~11001 = 00110. Cryptographically, this operation is not used much, primarily for implementing basic arithmetic in hardware.

Bitwise AND

AND is useful in bit testing and bit extraction. It's based on the usual truth table for logical AND, as shown in Table 1.4. You can remember the truth table by observing that it's the same as binary multiplication—anything times zero is zero.

Table 1.4 Bitwise AND

AND	0	1
0	0	0
1	0	1

To test if a bit is set, create a mask with 1s in positions you wish to test and perform the logical AND operation. If the result is nonzero, the bit is set; otherwise, the bit is not:

```
    01011101
AND 00001000
    --------
    00001000 // not == 0, bit 4 is set
```

It's also useful for bit clearing. A mask is created with 1s in positions to preserve and 0s where you want to clear. For instance, to clear the four least-significant bits in a byte, use the mask `11110000`:

```
    11011101
AND 11110000
    --------
    11010000
```

Bitwise OR

Bitwise OR extends the logical OR to a series of bits. In English, *or* means one or the other but not both. The bitwise version means one or the other or both (the same as the logical OR). See Table 1.5.

Logical OR is useful in joining nonoverlapping words. The following example joins two 4-bit words together:

```
   11010000
OR 00001111
-----------
   11011111
```

In this case, the same effect could be done by using regular addition; however, it's pretty standard to use OR instead to make it clear that addition is not the point of the operation and that you are doing bit operations.

Table 1.5 Bitwise OR

OR	0	1
0	0	1
1	1	1

Table 1.6 Bitwise XOR

XOR	0	1
0	0	1
1	1	0

Bitwise Exclusive OR (XOR)

Exclusive OR is abbreviated as XOR, and its operation is denoted by ⊕. It is less common in normal programming operations but very common in cryptographic applications. Table 1.6 shows the Bitwise XOR table. This table is easy to remember, since it is the same as addition but without any carry (this is also known as addition modulo 2). It's also equivalent to the English usage of *or*—one or the other but not both.

XOR tests to see if two bits are different: If the bits are both 0s or both 1s, the result is 0; if they are different, the result is 1. XOR is useful in cryptographic applications, since unlike AND and OR, it's an invertible operation, so that A ^ B ^ B = A:

```
    11010011
XOR 10101010
------------
    01111101
XOR 10101010
------------
    11010011
```

Left-Shift

As its name implies, the left-shift operator shifts the bits within a word to the left by a certain number of positions. Left-shifts are denoted by $a << b$, where a is the value and b denotes the number of positions to shift left. Zeros are filled in on the least-significant positions:

```
11111111 << 1 = 11111110
11001100 << 3 = 01100000
```

Mathematically, each shift left can be thought of as multiplication by 2:

```
 3 x 2   = 00000011 << 1 = 00000110 = 4 + 2 =  6
 3 x 4   = 00000011 << 2 = 00001100 = 8 + 4 = 12
-3 x 2   = 11111101 << 1 = 11111010 = -6
-128 x 2 = 10000000 << 1 = 00000000 = 0 (overflow)
```

When you are working with large word sizes (such as 32-bit integers), left-shifts are used to compute large powers of 2, since $2^n = 1 << n$. A trick to test to see if only one bit is set (or rather the value is a power of 2) is using `x & -x == x`. In many cryptographic operations, we need to extract a certain number of the least-significant bits from a word. Normally you are working with word sizes much bigger than a byte. However, say you needed to extract the six least-significant bits from a byte *B*. You could perform *B* & 0x3f (*B* & 0011111). Computing this for larger word sizes is a bit clumsy, and worse, some algorithms may extract a variable number of bits, so the mask has to be dynamic. Hardwiring a hexadecimal mask is also prone to errors, and someone reading your code would have to think about how many bits you are extracting. How many bits are in 0x7fffff? The answer is 23, but it's not automatically clear, and staring at a computer monitor all day where the text is in a small font makes the task harder. Instead, a left-shift can be used, since $2^n - 1$ or $(1 << n) - 1$ has binary representation of with $(n - 1)$ digits of "1." Instead of 0x7fffff, we can use ((1 << 24) – 1), which will be perfectly clear to someone familiar with bit operations. Even better, you can make your intentions clearer by making the mask a constant:

```
public static final int mask23lsb = (1<<24) -1; // 23-bit mask
```

Right-Shift

Not surprisingly, right-shifts, denoted by >>, are the opposite of left-shifts, and positions are shifted to the right. However, there is another significant difference. In left-shift notation, zeros are placed in the least-significant position. With right-shift, the value of the most-significant bit is used to fill in the shifted positions. For example, 1000000 >> 2 = 1100000, but 0100000 >> 2 = 00100000. This is designed so that the sign is preserved and the right-shift is equivalent to division by 2 (dropping any fractional part), regardless of the sign. For example, we'll "undo" the previous left-shift examples:

```
   6 / 2  = 00000110 >> 1 = 00000011 =   3
  12 / 4  = 00001100 >> 2 = 00000011 =   3
  -6 / 2  = 11111010 >> 2 = 11111101 =  -3
-127 / 2  = 10000001 >> 1 = 11000000 = -64
```

This works well when you are treating the byte as a number. In cryptographic applications, the bits are just treated as bits without any numerical interpretation. In every case, it is assumed the byte or word is unsigned (e.g., unsigned long in C). If you are using a signed type (such as Java), you'll want to use the *unsigned* right-shift, denoted by >>> (three less-than symbols). This just shifts the bits to the right and fills in zeros for the most significant bits. All cryptographic papers assume the shift is unsigned and normally use the plain >>. When coding an algorithm using signed types, make sure you convert >> to >>>.

Special Operations and Abbreviations

The previous operations, while useful, are fairly basic and typically directly implemented in hardware. By combining and composing them, you can create new higher-level bit operations. For cryptography, the most useful operations are rotations, concatenation, and extraction of most- and least-significant bits.

Rotations

Bit rotations are fairly self-explanatory: Bits are shifted either left or right, and the bits that "fall off the edge" roll over onto the other side. These are commonly used in cryptography, since this method provides an invertible operation that can aid in scrambling bits. The problem is that they aren't used for much else, so many CPUs do not have rotation instructions, or if they do, they are frequently slow. Even if they have a fast rotation, the only way to access them is by writing assembly language, since rotations do not have a standard operator like the shifts do. Common programming rotations can be accomplished with a combination of shifts and logical operators, which is the slowest method of all. In its most general case, a rotation will take one subtraction, two shifts, and a logical OR operation. Remember to use the unsigned right-shift operator:

```
(x >>> n) | (x << 32-n);    // rotate right n positions, x 32-bit int
(x << n) | (x >>> 32-n);    // rotate left n position, x 32-bit int
```

There is no special typographical symbol for rotations; we normally use the abbreviations ROTR or ROTL, although certain technical papers may define their own symbols in their work.

Bit Concatenation

Bit concatenation is the process of simply joining together two sets of bits into one word. If *b* is *n*-bits long, then a || b is `a << n | a`:

```
a = 101
b = 0011
a || b = 11 << 4 | 0011 = 1010000 | 0011 = 1010011
```

MSB and LSB operations

Two other common operations are extracting a certain number of most-significant bits (MSB) or least-significant bits (LSB). We'll use the notation $MSB_n(a)$ to denote extracting the n most-significant bits. Likewise with $LSB_n(a)$. These operations are accomplished by making the appropriate mask, and in the MSB case, by shifting appropriately:

```
MSB3(10111111) = (10111111 & 11100000) >>> 5 = 101
LSB2(11111101) = 11111111 & 00000011 = 00000001
```

Packed Words

Shifts are useful in creating *packed words*, where you treat the word as an array of bits rather than as a number, and where the bits represent anything you like. When doing this, you should use an unsigned numeric type. Unfortunately, Java and many scripting languages do not have unsigned types, so you must be extremely careful. As an example, suppose you have two variables that are numbers between 0 and 15. When transmitting or storing them, you might want to use the most space-efficient representation. To do this, you represent them not as 8-bit numbers from 0 to 255, but as two numbers each with 4 bits. For this example, we'll use pseudocode and use the type `int` to represent an unsigned 8-bit value:

```
int a = 5; // 00000101
int b = 13; // 00001101
int packed = a << 4 | b; // = 00000101 << 4 | 00001101
                         // = 01010000 | 00001101
                         // = 01011101
```

To undo the operation:

```
b = packed & 0x0F; // 01011101 & 00001111 = 00001101
a = packed >>> 4;  // note unsigned right-shift
                   // 01011101 >>> 4 = 00000101
```

Likewise, you might wish to view the byte as holding eight true/false values:

```
int c = b0 | (b1 << 1) | (b2 << 2) | (b3 << 3) | (b4 << 4)
           | (b5 << 5) | (b6 << 6) | (b7 << 7);
int mask = 0x01;
b0 =  c & mask
b1 = (c >>> 1) & mask;
b2 = (c >>> 2) & mask;
```

and so on. If you were using an array, you could do this dynamically in a loop as well.

```
for (int i = 0; i < 8; ++i)
    b[i] = (c >>> i) & mask;
```

It's quite easy to make mistakes, especially when the packed word has a complicated structure. If you are writing code and the answers aren't what you'd expect:

- Check to make sure you are using the unsigned right-shift operator >>> instead of the signed version >>.
- Check that the language isn't doing some type of automatic type conversion of signed values (e.g., turning bytes into integers before the shift operation happens).
- Check to make sure your masks are correct.
- If you are using dynamic shifts, make sure the shift amount isn't larger than the word size. For instance, if you are shifting a byte, make sure you aren't doing >> 9. How this is interpreted depends on the environment.

Integers and Endian Notation

Endian refers to how a string of bytes should be interpreted as an integer, and this notation comes is two flavors: *Little-Endian* and *Big-Endian*. The names come from Jonathan Swift's *Gulliver's Travels*, where the tiny people, Lilliputians, were divided into two camps based on how they ate eggs. The Little-Endians opened the eggs from the small end, and the Big-Endians opened theirs from the big end. As you might expect with that reference, there are pros and cons to Big-Endian and Little-Endian representations, but overall it doesn't make any difference except when you have to convert between the two formats. A comparison of the two is shown in Table 1.7.

Table 1.7 Comparison of Little-Endian versus Big-Endian Representation

ENDIAN TYPE	$B_0B_1B_2B_3$ = 0XAABBCCDD	SAMPLE MICROPROCESSORS
Little-Endian	aa bb cc dd	Intel x86, Digital (VAX, Alpha)
Big-Endian	dd cc bb aa	Sun, HP, IBM RS6000, SGI, "Java"

Big-Endian, also know as most-significant byte order (MSB) or network order, puts the most-significant or highest byte value first. This is equivalent to how we write decimal numbers: left to right. The downside is that many numerical algorithms have to work backward starting at the end of the array and working forward (just as you would manually with pencil and paper).

The Little-Endian, or least significant byte (LSB), format is the opposite. This makes it harder for humans to read hex dumps, but numeric algorithms are a little easier to implement. Adding capacity (or widening conversions) is also easier, since you just add bytes to the end of the array of bytes (i.e., 0xff becomes 0xff00).

Fortunately, regardless of what the byte Endian order is, the *bits* within bytes are always in Big-Endian format. For instance, 1 is always stored in a byte as 00000001_2 no matter what platform.

The Endian issue becomes critical when you are working with heterogeneous systems—that is, systems that use different Endian models. When shipping bytes between these machines, you must use a standard Endian format or an ASCII format. In many other programming languages, you must determine in advance what the Endian architecture is and adjust subsequent bit operations appropriately. For cryptographic applications this becomes critical, since you are often manipulating bits directly.

With Java, the underlying architecture is hidden and you program using a Big-Endian format. The Java virtual machine does any Endian conversion needed behind the scenes.

For C and C++ programmers, normally a `BIG_ENDIAN` or `LITTLE_ENDIAN` macro is defined by the compiler or from an include file. If not, you can use code similar to this for testing. It sets raw memory and then converts it to an integer type. The value will be different depending on the CPU's Endian type. This C code assumes an `int` is a standard 4 bytes or 32 bits, but you may wish to generalize:

```
int isBigEndian() {
  static unsigned char test[sizeof(unsigned int)] = {0, 0, 0, 1};
  unsigned int i = *(unsigned int) test;
  if (i == 0x0000001) return 1; // true, big-endian
  return 0;                     // false, little-endian
}
```

Java Numerics

We'll now apply the information in the previous section to the Java numeric model. While notation is similar to the C or C++ model, there are

Java-specific issues with using signed and unsigned types—specifically, byte arrays. Java also provides class wrappers around the native types, as well as an unlimited-capacity integer arithmetic.

Basic Types

Java provides the standard basic numeric types—integers with 8, 16, 32, and 64 bits, and floating-point types with 32- and 64-bit representations. Unlike C and other languages, all the types are signed—there are no native unsigned types. Table 1.8 shows Java's primitive numeric types.

For integer types, a literal integer can be expressed in decimal or hexadecimal formats (using lower- or uppercase letters for hex digits):

```
int i1 = 1000;
int i2 = 0x3e8; // == 1000 decimal
int i3 = 0x3E8; // same
```

For literal long values, a prefix of L or l should always be used, even if it appears unnecessary:

```
long l1 = 1000;           // compiles but is not recommended
long l1 = 1000L;          // recommended
long l2 = 0xfffffffff;    // won't compile, error
long l2 = 0xfffffffffL;   // correct
```

Table 1.8 Primitive Numeric Types in Java

NAME	TYPE	LOGICAL SIZE	RANGE
byte	signed integer	8 bits	−128 to 127
short	signed integer	16 bits	−32768 to 32767
int	signed integer	32 bits	−2,147,483,648 to 2,147,483,647 (2.1 billion)
long	signed integer	64 bits	−9,223,372,036,854,775,808 to 9,223,372,036,854,775,807 ($\pm 9.2 \times 10^{18}$)
float	ANSI/IEEE 754 floating point	32 bits	$\pm 1.4 \times 10^{-45}$ to $\pm 3.4028235 \times 10^{38}$ (6–7 significant decimal digits)
double	ANSI/IEEE 754 floating point	64 bits	$\pm 4.9 \times 10^{-324}$ to $\pm 1.7976931348623157 \times 10^{308}$ (15 significant decimal digits)

Specifying literal values for bytes can be tricky because a byte is signed from –128 to 127, while very often you'll be using constants specified from 0 to 255. If the value is within –128 to 127, the code will compile. If the value is from 128 to 255, you can either convert it to its negative equivalent or use a cast operation. The same principles apply to the `short` type:

```
byte b1 = 10;
byte b2 = 189;                    // error, out of bounds
byte b3 = -67;                    // = 189, ok
byte b4 = (byte) 189;             // ok
byte b4 = (byte) 0xbd;            // ok
```

Floating-type literals are assumed to be a `double` type unless suffixed by an `f` for `float`. Floating types can also be representing using scientific notation using `valEscale` = val × 10^{scale}.

```
float  f1 = 0.1;     // compiler error
float  f2 = 0.1f;    // by default "0.1" is a double type
double d1 = 0.1;
double d2 = 1.0E2    // == 100
```

In practice, the `short` type is rarely used because it almost always is converted into an `int` type before anything else is done. The `float` type also isn't used because it doesn't provide enough precision for most applications.

Type Conversion

Conversions between types can either be widening or narrowing. A *widening conversion* is where the new type can represent larger numbers and can "contain" the old type. For an integer-to-integer type conversion (i.e., `short` to `long`), this just means putting the same number in a larger container. Integer-to-floating-point conversions are also considered as widening, but some of the least-significant digits may be scrambled or zeroed due to how floating point numbers are presented. These types of conversion happen automatically and silently either at compile time or at run time. For example:

```
int    i1 = 123;
long   l1 = i;          // ok -- l = 123
float  f1 = i;          // ok -- f = 123

int    i2 = 123456789;
float  f2 = i;          // ok, but f = 123456792
```

Narrowing conversions may result in a loss of magnitude and precision. Any conversion from floating-point to an integer type is considered narrowing and is clearly a larger integer type to a smaller integer type. Java will *not* automatically do narrowing conversions, and a compiler error will be issued if the compiler detects such a conversion. To do these conversions, you must explicitly declare them with the cast operator.

Converting floating point to integers drops or truncates any digits to the right of the decimal point:

```
float  f1 = 0.123456;
int    i0 = f1;          // compiler error -- requires a cast.
int    i1 = (int) f1;    // == 0

float  f2 = 0.99999;
int    i2 = (int) f2;    // == 0

float  f3 = 100.9;
int    i3 = (int) f3;    // == 100

float  f4 = -100.9;
int    i4 = (int) f4;    // == -100

int    i5 = 0xffL;       // compiler error;  long to int conversion
```

For narrowing conversions from one integer type to another, the least-significant bits (or bytes) form the larger type:

```
int    i1 = 0xffffff01;
byte   b1 = (byte) b;     // b = 0x01;
```

These rules are summarized in Table 1.9, with *N* representing a narrowing conversion, *W* for a widening conversion, and *W** for a widening conversion that may result in a loss of precision.

Table 1.9 Primitive Type Conversion

	BYTE	SHORT	INT	LONG	FLOAT	DOUBLE
byte		W	W	W	W	W
short	N		W	W	W	W
int	N	N		W	W*	W
long	N	N	N		W*	W*
float	N	N	N	N		W
double	N	N	N	N	N	

Unsigned to Signed Conversions

There are no unsigned types in Java; however, you can still use the signed types as an unsigned *container*. Even though a `byte` is signed, it still has 8 bits and can represent an integer from 0 to 255 even if Java thinks otherwise. To use the unsigned value, it must be converted into a larger type using an AND mask.

To convert a unsigned byte:

```
byte  c = (byte) 254;           // b = -2 in Java.
short c = (short)(x & 0xff);    // c = 254
int   c = x & 0xff              // c = 254
long  c = x & 0xffL;            // c = 254, must put L at end of 0xffL
```

Unsigned short values are converted by the following:

```
int  c = x & 0xffff;
long c = x & 0xffffL;
```

Finally, the unsigned `int` is converted into a signed `long` by the following:

```
long c = x & 0xffffffffL
```

It's critical to put an `L` at the end of the mask when working with `long` types. Without it, Java will respond as if you are doing an `int` computation, then doing a widening conversion to a `long`:

```
byte b = (byte)0xff;

long b = (b & 0xff) << 56;                  //  Wrong.  b = 0
long b = (long)((int)(b & 0xff) << 56); //  same as previous

long b = (b & 0xffL) << 56; // Correct. b = 0xff00000000000000
```

Overflow

When a computation exceeds an integer type's bounds, the value is "rolled over" *silently;* no exception is thrown:

```
byte b = (byte) 127;  // b = 0111111
b++;                  // b = 1000000, but b has the value of -128
```

While the silence may seem disturbing, in practice overflow is rarely a problem. For floating-point computations overflow is still silent, but the result is not rolled over. Instead, the type takes on a special `Infinity` value that can be checked using normal comparison operators or by using the `Double.isInfinite` method. Also note that Java does not think 0.0 is the same as 0 (zero). Instead, 0.0 is treated as a number that is very close to zero, so division by 0.0 results in an infinite value. Keep in mind, however, that Java throws an exception if you try to divide by the *integer* 0. In the event that a computation doesn't make sense, the value is `NaN`, which stands for "not a number." If you wish to see if a value is `NaN`, then you *must* use the `Double.isNaN` method. Various examples of manipulating double types are shown as follows:

```
double d1 = 1.7E308 * 2.0;          // overflow = Infinity
double d2 = 1.0/0.0;                // =  Infinity
double d3 = -1.0/0.0;               // = -Infinity
int i = 1 / 0;                      // throws a DivisionByZero exception
double d4 = 0.0/0.0                 // = NaN
boolean b = (d4 == d4);             // = false,  always
boolean b = Double.isNan(d4);       // true;
boolean b = Double.isInfinite(d3); // true
```

Arrays

In Java, native-type arrays are treated and created as if there were objects created using a constructor with the `new` operator. Arrays can also be set with initial values, as shown in the following code snippet.

```
int[] a= new int[3]; // all three elements set to zero
int[] a = {1, 2, 3}; // a pre-set 3 element array.
```

Once constructed, an array is *not* resizable. If dynamically allocated storage is needed, you should use one of the collections in the `java.util` package. The index to arrays is with `int` types, and the first element starts at 0 (as in C). Small types will have widening conversions done to them, and the `long` type cannot be used without a cast operation. Thus, single dimensional arrays cannot be larger than 2^{31}, or roughly 2.1 billion, entries. Hopefully, this will be sufficient for your needs.

Since arrays are objects, assignment is done by *reference*, as shown in the following:

```
int[] a = {1,2};
int[] b = a;
b[0] = 100; // modifies the object that both a and b point too.
System.out.println(a[0]); // will print 100, not 1
a = null; // b is null, but a is intact.
```

In addition, they can be copied using the `clone` method. To use this, cast the result to the correct array type:

```
int[] a = {1, 2};
int[] b = (int[]) a.clone(); // b is a "deep copy" of a
```

The `System.arraycopy` method is extremely useful for copying parts of an array or concatenating arrays. It makes a native system call to copy memory directly instead of copying each element individually and is much faster than writing a custom `for` loop:

```
System.arrayCopy(Object input, int inputOffset,
                 Object output, int outputOffset, int length)
```

Even though the method has `Object` in its signature, this method only works on array types. Other useful methods for manipulating native arrays can be found in the class `java.util.Arrays` and are summarized in Table 1.10.

Table 1.10 Summary of Methods from `java.util.Arrays`

JAVA.UTIL.ARRAYS METHOD	DESCRIPTION
`static boolean equals(type[] a, type[] b)`	Returns true if and only if the arrays are the same length and every element is equal.
`static void fill(type[] a, type val)`	Fills an array with a single value.
`static void sort(type[] a)`	Performs a fast numeric sort. Array is modified.
`static void sort(type[] a, int fromIndex, int toIndex)`	Sorts only part of an array.
`static int binarySearch(type[] a, type val)`	Performs a binary search of a sorted array. Returns the array index if a match is found and –1 if no match. Arrays must be sorted first.

Numeric Classes

Each numeric type has a matching class that acts as an object wrapper, as shown in Table 1.11.

These classes do not have any support for mathematical operations—you can't add two integer objects directly. Instead, these classes are primarily used to allow numeric types to be used in methods that expect an `Object` type, such as in collections from the `java.util` package (e.g., `ArrayList`, `HashMap`). The wrapper classes also provide basic string formatting and parsing from strings for numbers. Since they are objects, they can also be `null`. Likewise, objects are always pass-by-reference.

```
public void changeInt(Integer i) {
     i = new Integer("1");
}
Integer I = new Integer("0");
changeInt(i);     // i is now 1
```

All of the classes share some common traits (examples are just shown for `Integer` and `Long`):

- Two public fields, `MAX_VALUE` and `MIN_VALUE`, in case you don't want to memorize the previous table.
- `byteValue`, `doubleValue`, `floatValue`, `intValue`, and `longValue` methods that return the underlying number in a native type.
- A static method valueOf that accepts a string and an optional radix to parse a string and return an object. The radix can be 2 to 32.

  ```
  static Integer Integer.valueOf(int val)
  static Integer Integer.valueOf(int val, int radix)
  static Long Long.valueOf(long val)
  static Long Long.valueOf(long val, int radix)
  ```

- A static method `parseClass` (where `Class` is the name of the class, such as `Byte` or `Integer`) that also accepts a string, and an optional radix to parse a string returns the *native type* instead of an object.

  ```
  static int Integer.parseLong(int val)
  static int Integer.parseFloat(int val, int radix)
  static long Long.parseLong(long val)
  static long Long.parseLong(long val, int radix)
  ```

- `toString` that returns the number as unformatted decimal number.

Table 1.11 Java Class Wrappers for Native Types

NATIVE TYPE	MATCHING JAVA.LANG CLASS
`int`	`Integer`
`byte`	`Byte`
`double`	`Double`
`float`	`Float`
`long`	`Long`
`short`	`Short`

The `Long` and `Integer` classes have a few other useful static methods that provide an *unsigned* representation of the number in binary, hex, or octal formats as shown:

```
static String Integer.toBinaryString(int val)
static String Integer.toHexString(int val)
static String Integer.toOctalString(int val)
static String Long.toBinaryString(long val)
static String Long.toHexString(long val)
static String Long.toOctalString(long val)
```

Binary representation is especially useful for debugging bit fields. These objects do not add any "leading zeros" to the output, so `new Integer(16).toHexString()` just returns `F` and not `0F` or `0x0F`.

Booleans and BitFields

Java provides a native `boolean` type that can either be `true` or `false`. Unlike C and C++, it is not a numeric type and does not have a numeric value, and it is not automatically cast. Like the numeric types, there is also a boolean class wrapper. If you want to create an array of boolean values, you could use `Boolean` with one of the collection classes (e.g., `ArrayList`). However, there is a special class `java.utl.BitField` specially designed for use with boolean types that provides a huge performance increase and memory savings. More specialized applications will convert a native type or byte array into a bit field directly.

Chars

Java has another native type `char` that represents a Unicode character and is used by `String` and `StringBuffer` internally. It is represented by an *unsigned* 16-bit integer, but it is not a numeric type. It is automatically cast to an integer in situations when needed, such in mathematical or bitwise operations, but it's not automatically cast to any other type. However, you can explicitly convert a char to another type by using a cast operator.

Since it's unsigned, it might be tempting to use `char` in places for mathematical purposes and for raw bit fields. In practice, there is not much point, since `char` types are automatically converted into an `int` before any operation is done, eliminating any advantage

Working with Bytes

Because the Java `byte` type is signed and because of the automatic conversion rules, working with bytes and byte array can be frustrating. Following are some tips and tricks to simplify byte manipulation.

Sign Problems

It's always easiest to specify a constant byte value by using a cast (later in this chapter you will see tricks on making byte arrays):

```
byte b = 0xff;          // Compiler error.  0xff is an 'int' type
byte b = (byte) 0xff; // right
```

Bytes range from –127 to 128, and not 0 to 255. Setting a byte with the value 128–255 and a cast is fine—the byte contains the correct bits. The problem is when you want to retrieve the unsigned value or when you perform a computation with bytes and ints. For instance:

```
byte b = 127;
int  i = 3;
System.out.println((i+b));  // Prints -126 and not 130
```

results in –127 being printed, not 129. In the addition step, byte *b* is automatically converted to an `int` type, including the sign. While b was set with 128, internally it's really –1, and this is its value when converted.

The key point to remember is that all bitwise and arithmetic operators work on `int` and `long` types only. All other types are automatically cast. If you are using a byte as an unsigned value, you must manually convert the type to an `int` or `long` *before* the operation using `val & 0xFF` or `val & 0xFFL` respectively.

The problem is more mysterious with the shift operators. Let's say you want to do a right-shift on 0xFF. In binary, this is 11111111, so you'd expect an unsigned right-shift to be 0111111, or 0x7F. The natural way to write this is:

```
byte b1 = (byte) 0xff;
byte b2 = b >>> 1;       // compiler error
```

However, this results in a strange error from the javac compiler, and the problem isn't clearly defined:

```
aprogram:java.6: possible loss of precision
found: int
required: byte
      byte b2 = b >>> 1;
                ^
```

You might try and fix this by casting the result:

```
byte b1 = (byte) 0xff;
byte b2 = (byte)(b >>> 1);  // error #2
```

This performs the compile operation; however, the result is still wrong. The value of `b2` is *not* 0x7f, but strangely remains at 0xff or –1. Again, Java is converting the byte into an integer *before* the shift. Since bytes are signed, it converts the byte value of –1 into an `int` value of –1, which is 0xffffffff. *Then* it performs the shift, resulting in 0x7fffffff. Finally, the cast takes the least bits, or 0xff, and converts them to a `byte`. The step-by-step details are listed in Table 1.12. The correct solution is to treat the `byte` as an unsigned value, then convert to an `int`, and then do the shift and cast back down to a `byte`:

```
byte b1 = (byte) 0xff;
byte b2 = (byte)((b & 0xff) >>> 1); // correct:
```

Table 1.12 Comparison of Bit-Shifting a Byte Type

STEPS	INCORRECT	CORRECT
Initial value	`0xff` = –1	`0xff` = –1
Convert to `int`	`0xffffffff` = –1	`0x000000ff` = 255
Right-shift `>>>`	`0x7fffffff` = large int	`0x0000007f` = 127
Cast down to `byte`	`0xff` = –1	`0x7f` = 127

To convert a `byte` back to its unsigned value, you have to do a little trick; you must bitwise AND the `byte` with 0xff, that is, `b & 0xff`. For example:

```
byte b = 128;
int i = 1;
int unsignedByteValue = b & 0xff
System.out.println((i + unsignedByteValue);  // 129
System.out.println((i + (b & 0xff));         // combined
```

This trick works by observing that the least-significant bytes in an `int` match exactly with the `byte` type, as shown in Table 1.13.

Conversion of Integral Types to Byte Arrays

Java does not have any easy way of converting integral types into raw bytes. There are the serialization methods, but these involve a lot of work for something that should be relatively simple. For example:

```
public static byte[] intToByteArray(int i) {
     byte[] buf = new byte[4];
     b[0] = (byte) (i >>> 24);
     b[1] = (byte) (i >>> 16);
     b[2] = (byte) (i >>>  8);
     b[3] = (byte) i;
}

public static int byteArrayToInt(byte[]) {
     If (buf.length != 4)
          throw new RuntimeException("Bad Length");
     return ((b[0] & 0xff) << 24) | ((b[1] & 0xff) << 16) |
  (b[2] & 0xff) << 8) | (b[3]);
}
```

Table 1.13 Comparison of Representation between `int` and `byte` Types

UNSIGNED VALUE	SIGNED VALUE	BYTE REPRESENTATION	INT REPRESENTATION
0	0	00	00000000
1	1	01	00000001
2	2	02	00000002
126	126	7d	0000007e
127	127	7f	0000007f
128	-128	80	00000080

Table 1.13 *(Continued)*

UNSIGNED VALUE	SIGNED VALUE	BYTE REPRESENTATION	INT REPRESENTATION
129	-127	81	00000081
130	-126	82	00000082
253	-3	fd	fffffffd
254	-2	fe	fffffffe
255	-1	ff	ffffffff
256	256	00	00000100

We could do the same thing for longs. Instead, we'll demonstrate a different technique that builds the result by incrementally shifting the value in question:

```
public static byte[] longToByteArray(long I) {
     byte[] buf = new byte[8];
     for (int j = 7; j >= 0; ++j) {
          buf[j] = (l & 0xffL); // !! must use 0xffL, not 0xff !!
          l >>>= 8;           // l = l >>> 8;
     }
}

public static long byteArrayToLong(byte[] buf)
{
     long i = 0;
if (buf.length != 8)
          throw new RuntimeException("Bad Length");
     for (int j = 0; j < 8; ++j) {
          i |= buf[j];
          i <<= 8;      // l = l << 8;
     }
     return i;
}
```

Converting to Hex Strings

Converting an array into a hexadecimal string is a fairly common task for printing, data interchange, and debugging. A naive way to do hex conversions is by using one of the previously mentioned byte `array-to-long` methods followed by `Long.toHexString`. However this is very slow and is limited to arrays smaller than 8 bytes. Even worse would be using `BigInteger` (discussed later in the chapter). For example:

```
byte[] mybytes = ...;
BigInteger a = new BigInteger(1, mybytes);
return a.toString(16);
```

While mathematically correct, most programs operate on printing two hex digits per byte; for example, decimal 16 is converted to 0F, not F. The other problem is that this method is horrendously slow.

While these methods are useful in a pinch, for high performance applications they won't do. If one is willing to use a little memory, performance can be doubled or tripled. The conversion itself is fairly simple, but an implementation that uses tables has some important benefits:

- Provides typically higher performance (at the expense of some minor setup and memory costs).
- Allows using different alphabets instead of the standard. These issues are further detailed in Chapter 4.
- Typically allows simpler coding.

The conversion class starts out defining the hexadecimal alphabet (in our case, the standard one). The `hexDecode` table is the inverse mapping; for instance, character A is mapped to 10. Characters that are invalid are set to –1. For example:

```
public class Hexify
{
    protected static char[] hexDigits = {'0', '1', '2', '3', '4',
           '5' '6', '7', '8', '9', 'A', 'B', 'C', 'D', 'E', 'F'},
     protected static int[]  hexDecode = new int[256];
    static {
     for (int i = 0; i < 256; ++i) hexDecode[i] = -1;
     for (int i = '0'; i <= '9'; ++i) hexDecode[i] = i - '0';
     for (int i = 'A'; i <= 'F'; ++i) hexDecode[i] = i - 'A' + 10;
     for (int i = 'a'; i <= 'f'; ++i) hexDecode[i] = i - 'a' + 10;
    }
```

Encoding is fairly straightforward. Each byte is split into two sections, and the table is used to determine the appropriate character:

```
public static String encode(byte[] b) {
 char[] buf = new char[b.length * 2];
 int max = b.length;
 int j = 0;
```

```
    for (int i = 0; i < max; ++i) {
        buf[j++] = hexDigits[(b[i] & 0xf0) >> 4];
        buf[j++] = hexDigits[b[i] & 0x0f];
    }
    return new String[buf];
   }
```

Decoding is more interesting. First, a function, given a hexadecimal character, returns the integer value. This is done via a table lookup, and the result is verified to make sure it's valid. It's always important to check the input for validity, especially if you don't have control of what the input is. You could easily add or inline these checks into the main decode routine for a minimal improvement in execution time, as follows:

```
protected static int getHexDecode(char c) {
 int x = hexDecode[c];
 if (x < 0) throw new RuntimeException("Bad hex digit " + c);
 return x;
}
```

While the encode function always encodes two characters per byte, you may receive a hexadecimal string that doesn't conform to this rule. If you are only processing strings that you created, you could check that the number of input characters is even and that an exception is thrown if it's not. The following implementation handles full generality. The string is checked to see if it has an odd number of characters, by computing `max & 0x01` (or, equivalently, `max % 2`), which just looks at the least-significant bit. If it's set, then the value is odd.

```
public static byte[] decode(String s) {
 char[] input = s.charArray[];
 int max = input.length;
 int maxodd = max & 0x01;
 byte b;
 byte[] buf = new byte[max/2 + odd];
 int i = 0, j = 0;
 if (maxodd == 1) {
     buf[j++] = getHexDecode[input[i++]]
 }
 while (i < max) {
     buf[j++] == (byte)(getHexDecode[input[i++]] << 4 |
      getHexdecode[input[i++]]);
 }
 return buf;
}           //end of class Hexity
```

BigInteger

The `BigInteger` class in the `java.math` package provides a way of doing computations with arbitrary large integer types. Unlike C++, Java does not overload operators, so to do basic math, you have to call methods to perform mathematical operations such as addition. All of the operations create new `BigInteger` objects as results. The objects used in the operations remain untouched. For instance:

```
BigInteger b1 = new BigInteger("1");
BigInteger b2 = new BigInteger("2");
BigInteger b3 = b1.add(b2);
```

At the end, `b1` is still 1, `b2` is still 2, and `b3` is what you'd expect it to be, 3. Modifying an object requires explicit code. For instance, if we wanted `b1` to contain the result of the addition, we would use self-assignment like this:

```
b1 = b1.add(b2); // b1 is now 3
```

While the notation is different, the behavior is no different than using normal operators. Adding 1 + 2 doesn't change the original values of 1 or 2.

All of the usual arithmetic operations are available: `add`, `subtract`, `multiply`, `divide`, and `remainder`. Another method, `divideAndRemainder`, returns a two-element `BigInteger` array where element 0 is the division result and element 1 is the remainder. A complete list and comparison of BigInteger operations is given in Table 1.14.

Table 1.14 BigInteger Arithmetic Operators

ARITHMETIC OPERATION	NATIVE TYPE NOTATION	BIGINTEGER NOTATION
Addition	`a + b`	`a.add(b)`
Subtraction	`a - b`	`a.subtract(b)`
Multiplication	`a * b`	`a.mult(b)`
Integer division	`a / b`	`a.divide(b)`
Remainder	`a % b`	`a.remainder(b)`
Division with remainder	`int[] result = { a / b, a % b }`	`BigInteger[] result = a.divideAndRemainder(b)`
Negation	`-a`	`a.negate()`

Table 1.14 *(Continued)*

ARITHMETIC OPERATION	NATIVE TYPE NOTATION	BIGINTEGER NOTATION
Exponentiation	`Math.pow(a,b)`	`a.pow(b)`

Random value	`Random r = new Random();`
	
	`a = r.getInt();`
		`Random r = ...`
		`int bits = ...;`
		`BigInteger a =`
		`new BigInteger(bits, r);`

Absolute value	`(a >= 0) ? a : b` *or* `Math.abs(a)`	`a.abs()`
Minimum of a, b	`(a < b) ? a : b` *or* `Math.min(a,b)`	`a.min(b)`
Maximum of a, b	`(a > b) ? a : b` *or* `Math.max(a,b)`	`a.max(b)`

Likewise, all the usual bit operations are available, as described in Table 1.15. There is no need for a special unsigned right-shift operator, since `BigInteger` has unlimited capacity; the result of shifting n places to the right is the equivalent of dividing by 2^n, regardless of sign. In addition are a few new methods that simplify working with bits: `testBit`, `setBit`, and `flipBit`. Two others called `bitCount` and `bitLength` need a bit more explaining. For positive integers the results are what you'd expect: `bitLength` returns the minimal number of bits required to represent the integer, and `BitCount` returns the number of one-bits in the representation. For negative numbers, `bitLength` gives a minimal length *excluding* the sign bit, and `bitCount` returns the number of zeros in the representation.

Creating and Converting

`BigInteger` objects can be converted by using a string representation of a number, a native type, or with a byte array. Using a native type, a string, or a byte array representation of a number creates `BigInteger` objects.

Strings

You can create `BigInteger` objects by using a construction that takes a string representation of a number. By default, the constructor expects the string representation to be in decimal (base 10) form. However, you can also use the standard base 16 representations, as follows:

```
BigInteger(String base10Rep)
BigInteger(String representation, int radix)
```

Table 1.15 BigInteger Bit Operations

BIT OPERATION	NATIVE TYPE NOTATION	BIGINTEGER NOTATION
AND	`a & b`	`a.and(b)`
ANDNOT	`a & ~b`	`a.andNot(b)`
NOT (complement)	`~a`	`a.not(b)`
OR	`a	b`	`a.or(b)`
XOR	`a ^ b`	`a.xor(b)`
Shift left *n* bits, signed	`a << n`	`a.shiftLeft(n)`
Shift right *n* bits, signed	`a >> n`	`a.shiftRight(n)`
Test bit *n*	`(a & (1 << n) != 0)`	`a.testBit(n)`
Set bit *n*	`(a	(1 << n))`	`a.setBit(n)`
Flip bit *n*	`(a ^ (1 << n))`	`a.flipBit(n)`

Conversely, you can retrieve a string representation in an appropriate base by using the `toString` method:

```
String toString()
String toString(int radix)
```

Numeric Types

The `BigInteger` class can be created from a long by using the static method:

```
Long val = 123456789123;
BigInteger bi = BigInteger.valueOf(val);
```

Once you have the `BigInteger` object, it can be converted directly into a numeric type by using `intValue`, `longValue`, `floatValue`, or `doubleValue`. Not that we'll mind, but there is no method to directly convert into a `short` or `char` value. If the value is too large to fit into the numeric type, a silent narrowing conversion is done (the high bits are chopped off).

Byte Arrays

Generating byte arrays and constructing byte *a*. Assuming you have a `BigInteger` object, a byte array can be generated with:

```
byte[] toByteArray()
```

And the results of this output can be used to create a new `BigInteger` object:

```
BigInteger(byte[] array)
```

However, because of signing issues, typically this format is not used for cryptographic purposes. If the bit length is a multiple of 8, and it always is for cryptographic applications, the byte array starts with an extra byte indicating the sign (0 for positive). Either your application can deal with a leading zero, or you can strip it away, as in the following:

```
byte ba[] = bi.toByteArray();
if (ba[0] == 0) {
     byte[] tmp = new byte[ba.length - 1];
     System.arraycopy(ba, 1, tmp, 0, tmp.length)
     ba = tmp;
}
```

A lower-speed option is to use strings as the common medium:

```
Byte ba[] = Hexify.decode(bi.toString(16);
```

Since `BigInteger` expects a sign-bit, you'll need to use a special constructor and manually indicate the sign by passing in 1, –1, or 0 for positive, negative, or zero:

```
BigInteger(int signum, byte[] magnitude)
```

BigInteger and Cryptography

`BigInteger` has a few special methods specifically designed for cryptography, listed in Table 1.16. These operations are discussed fully in Chapter 3.

Secret Methods in BigInteger

For Sun Microsystems to effectively test for primality, many generic methods and algorithms had to be implemented; however, they are *not* part of the public API. For people working in numbers theory or who are developing more advanced cryptographic algorithms, these "hidden" methods may be useful. Unfortunately, they are declared private; but with a few modifications to the source code, you can create your own enhanced `BigInteger` variant.

Table 1.16 BigInteger Operations Useful in Implementing Cryptographic Algorithms

OPERATION	BIGINTEGER NOTATION
Create a random nonnegative integer uniformly distributed from 0 to 2^n-1	`BigInteger (int numBits, Random r)`
Create a random integer that is prime with certainty $1 - 2^n$	`Random r = ...;` `int bitLength = ...;` `BigInteger a = BigInteger(bitLength, r)`
Check if prime with certainty using IEEE standard of $1 - 2^{100}$	`a.isProbablePrime()`
a mod b	`a.mod(b)`
a^n mod b	`a.modPow(b, n); // n is an int, not BigInteger`
find a^{-1}, such that $aa^{-1} = 1$ mod b	`a.modInv(b)`
Greatest common denominator of a, b	`a.gcb(b)`

The most interesting of these are the following methods:

```
int jacobiSymbol(int p, BigInteger n); // this is "package protected"
private boolean passesMillerRabin(int iterations)
private boolean passesLucasLehmer()
private static BigInteger lucasLehmerSequence(int z,
                                               BigInteger k, BigInteger n)
```

In addition, there is an implementation of sieve for testing primality of small numbers in the class `BitSieve`.

To "free" them:

1. Copy all the source files from this directory into a new directory.
2. Edit each file and change the package name from `sun.math` to one of your own choosing.
3. Make the `BitSieve` class "public."
4. Change the desired methods and classes to public. Note that the method `jacobiSymbol` in `BigInteger` and the class `BitSieve` do not have an access modifier, so you have to add `public` in front of the method.
5. Compile.

This code is copyrighted by Sun Microsystems. For commercial use and distribution, refer to the license agreement distributed with the source code.

Now that we have a full understanding of bit operations and the Java model, we'll discuss secret and public key cryptography.

Secret Key Cryptography

Secret key cryptography is based on cryptographic functions that rely on a single key that must be kept confidential. Secret key ciphers perform encryption and decryption using the same key, and cryptographic hashes must be computed and verified using the same key.

Symmetric Block Ciphers

In general, a *cipher* is a function that maps a message, known as *plaintext*, into an unreadable form, known as *ciphertext*, by use of a key. This is known as *encryption*. Without the key, you cannot do the inverse transformation, the *decryption*, or turning the ciphertext back into its original plaintext form. In lay terminology *code* is often used interchangeably with *cipher*. However, they have different meanings. A *code* is translation of a message by use of a dictionary, without any key being used.

Modern *block ciphers* operate on a fixed number of bytes in a single pass, for instance, transforming 8 bytes plaintext into 8 bytes ciphertext. Messages larger than the block must be chopped into pieces, and if the message isn't a multiple of the block size, the message must be *padded* appropriately.

Cipher Properties

To be useful a cipher must be secure and must be usable. What makes a cipher secure? For ciphers that have stood the test of time (i.e., those in common use and have not been cracked), a rough estimate of security is key length, with the longer the key being more secure. A cipher is deemed secure if there is no attack that is significantly better than brute force. However, clearly this by itself is not enough, and the notion of security is tied to current or contextual computation resources available to an attacker. An algorithm may be structurally secure, but if the key is too small, brute-force attacks can easily break the cipher by directly recovering the key.

Security Properties

The fundamental property of an encryption algorithm is that the output be effectively random, regardless of what the input or key is. From this property, many notions emerge regarding how well the algorithm performs:

Semantically secure, polynomially secure, or "indistinguishably of encryptions." There are many variants of this idea, but the simplest is that, given two plaintext messages and their ciphertext equivalents, it is impossible to determine which plaintext matches the correct encrypted version with a probability greater than .5. In other words, the ciphertext does not reveal any information about the plaintext.

Nonmalleability. Given a ciphertext, it is impossible to manipulate the ciphertext to produce related plaintext. In other words, a 1-bit change to a ciphertext should result in a very different plaintext.

Plaintext-aware. It is computationally infeasible to produce a valid ciphertext without knowing the corresponding plaintext. For instance, you should be able to generate ciphertext that decrypts to 7-bit ASCII, unless you are encrypting the original plaintext. This is useful to prevent the generation of false messages.

Lack of algebraic structure. It's very important that a cipher doesn't have certain algebraic properties that might allow multiple encryption or multiple keys to negate each other. In particular, it is important that the cipher does not form a *group* where:

- Each key has an inverse key.

- Encrypting something twice with different keys is equivalent to encrypting it once with another key.
- The result of encrypting with one key and decrypting with another key is the same as encrypting with one key. This would be very useful for attack purposes.

Ideally, you don't even want a subset of keys and messages to form a group; however, proving that is quite tricky. You also don't want "fixed points," that is, messages that encrypt to themselves.

Brute-Force Attacks

Brute-force attacks are the simplest attack, and for symmetric ciphers, this means trying each key, one after another, until the message decrypts properly. In decryption, there is no inherent flag saying "this is the right key" or "decryption occurred correctly." For instance, a ciphertext with one key might decrypt to *cat*, while the *same* ciphertext decrypted with a *different* key might decrypt to *dog*. Another way of looking at this is if you encrypted a random number or binary data, an attacker using the brute-force technique would be unable to determine if the resulting plaintext was the original number without using some additional context.

Typically, you do not encrypt random binary data, but rather something with more structure. During brute-force attacks, the decrypted result is checked to see if the structure exists. For instance, English text is encoded using ASCII where only 7 bits in each byte are used. During a brute-force attack, every output that is only 7 bits is stored in a "candidates" file, which will need to be checked by an actual human to determine what the correct result is. False-positive results are extremely rare for language texts.

Even with small key sizes, such as DES (for Data Encryption Standard), there are 2^{55}, or approximately 3.6×10^{16}, keys to check. When measuring cryptographic security, you can't be afraid of large numbers. While 2^{55} sounds out of reach, in fact, it's quite doable. Brute-force algorithms are easily parallelizable, and with the Internet, tens of thousands of computers are easily pooled for such attacks, thereby enabling trillions of keys to be tested per second.

Other Attacks

Brute-force attacks can easily be thwarted by using a larger key, so a full key-space scan becomes impossible. The following attacks attempt to find weaknesses in the cipher and provide shortcuts to a brute-force attack. If a significant attack occurs, the cipher is said to be broken and thus insecure.

Ciphertext-only attack. This is probably the most non-networked application. The adversary here has a ciphertext message and that's it. In the vast majority of cases, this attack indicates brute force, where every key is checked.

Chosen plaintext. Here the attack has a bulk list of plaintexts and receives the corresponding ciphertext and through analysis can determine the key.

Adaptive chosen plaintext. Similar to the previous except the process is more interactive. Plaintext may depend on the results of the previous plaintext and ciphertexts.

Chosen ciphertext. The attack selects ciphertext, which is then decrypted.

Related key. The attack requires the plaintext and the ciphertext from different keys.

Partial known plaintext attack. This attack is one of my own devising. I haven't seen anything in literature of this. Here the attacker has the ciphertext and *some* of the plaintext. This potential attack turns out to have applications for database security.

Power attack. This only applies to smartcard-like devices. An attacker can actually measure the radiation and time of the cryptographic computation and estimate the key or size of the key.

Many of these attacks come in the form of linear or differential (or some combination) analysis. Knowing the algorithm being used and with many pairs of text (plaintext and/or ciphertext), an attacker can determine the internal structure and thus extract the key or limit the key space.

Many might be wondering what the point is of the attacks if the attacker already has plaintext-ciphertext pairs. The trick is that the text pairs are chosen by the attackers and by themselves are not interesting (the values are more or less random or generated by an algorithm). The plan is to use these pairings to recover the key and thus decrypt ciphertexts that *do* contain useful information. Still, the attacks may seem odd, yet many network protocols allow many of these types of attacks since they echo back. For common ciphers most of these attacks require a lot of (at least 2^{40}) pairings, which would certainly be noticed by even the most primitive network monitoring. Another way these attacks can be exploited is by an attacker having access to either the encryption or decryption functions of a system. A hacker breaking into a system might not have access to the keys but will have access to system calls to do encryption. Then the attack might only generate a modest strain on the system's resources and not be noticeable.

Common Block Ciphers

There are dozens of block ciphers; however, you really only need to consider a small handful (see Table 2.1). Block ciphers come in two flavors: 64-bit block and 128-bit block.

Data Encryption Standard (DES)

The Data Encryption Standard, first developed in the 1970s, is the most widely used cipher. It was the first industrial-strength algorithm that was fully specified to the public, in Federal Information Processing Standard, or FIPS, 46-2. (FIPS are the standards used by the U.S. federal government for information processing.)

DES keys are specified as a 64-bit value; however, only 56 bits are used as part of the key. For each byte, the 8th bit is a parity bit that causes bytes to have an odd number of one-bits in them (other wise known as "odd-parity"). This is left over from the early days of computing.

Table 2.1 Selected Secret-Key Ciphers

ALGORITHM	YEAR	BLOCK SIZE BITS	KEY SIZE BITS	REASON
DES	1977	64	56	Standard
Triple DES	1985	64	168	Standard
Blowfish	1993	64	40–442	Popular, fast
RC5	1996	64 standard, but supports 32 and 128	0–2048	Popular, supported
IDEA	1992	64	128	Popular
Rijndael	1998	128, 192, 256	128, 192, 256	Standard, fast
Twofish	1998	128, 192, 256	128, 192, 256	Popular
RC6	1998	128, 192, 256	128, 192, 256	Popular, supported

It's worth looking at the inner workings of DES, since the ideas are used in many ciphers and the concept is actually fairly simple. First, the key is expanded. Although the key itself is only 56 bits, internally the key is expanded into sixteen 48-bit values. Likewise, various stages in the pipeline also expand data from 32 bits to 48 bits. Later, these expanded values get contracted as well. While, theoretically, expanding a key into larger values doesn't make a key longer than it really is, it does have the benefit of allowing more complicated functions to be constructed with simpler code.

The basic structure of DES is reused in many other ciphers and is what is known as *Feistel structure*. The plaintext block is split into left and right sections, and then the following is iterated:

$$L_{n+1} = R_n$$
$$R_{n+1} = L_n \oplus \mathrm{f}(R_n, K_n)$$

where K_n is a subkey of the main key and f is a mixing function. This mixing function is really what makes DES successful. It uses what are called S-Boxes, which are maps from a 6-bit input to a 4-bit output (the contraction) based on a lookup table. In DES (and other ciphers) the map is nonlinear and normally specified by using tables. The security of DES depends entirely on the values in the S-Boxes and exactly how they were constructed is a mystery to this day.

DES Security

As of this writing, DES has had no attacks that are significantly better than brute force. So in structure DES is solid and secure. However, the problem of short key size and vulnerability to brute-force attacks remains. Nowadays DES can be cracked either by specialized hardware or by distributed networks in a few hours. (See `www.eff.org/descracker/` for full details.) What's interesting is that various modifications have been proposed to enhance DES. It has been shown that just about any tampering or enhancements to the S-Box structure results in a much weaker cipher. These days there really is no reason to use DES except in legacy applications.

Triple DES

While DES appears to have a solid design, the key space is just too short and is susceptible to brute-force attacks. To help fix the problem, an interim solution was proposed that effectively performs multiple iterations of DES on the message using different keys. What's known as Triple DES, TDES, DES-EDE, or 3DES can provide 168 bits of security using three DES keys. A less common version is a two-key version providing 112 bits of security where three operations are done, but where one key is used twice. It does this by composition of three DES operations, as shown in Table 2.2.

Table 2.2 Triple DES Operations

OPERATION	3 KEYS	2 KEYS
Encryption	$E_{k3}(D_{k2}(E_{k1}(m)))$	$E_{k1}(D_{k2}(E_{k1}(m)))$
Decryption	$D_{k3}(E_{k2}(D_{k1}(m)))$	$D_{k1}(E_{k2}(D_{k1}(m)))$

In software this is a bit slow, but for basic networking (100 megabit), the speed limitations aren't much of a problem, since the algorithm can be implemented in hardware fairly efficiently. Triple DES is not a FIPS but instead is specified under the ANSI X.9.52 standard and NIST SP 800-20 (ANSI stands for American National Standard Institute, NIST for National Institute of Standards and Technology).

Triple DES Security

Providing 168 bits of security, Triple DES is by far the most studied, strongest algorithm available. When in doubt, DES is probably the best choice. Despite more modern ciphers, nobody suggests that Triple DES is less secure than others.

Why Not "Double DES"

Using two keys, or "Double DES," isn't done because the key size of 112 is too small; moreover, it isn't much more secure than a single iteration of DES. Given a plaintext-ciphertext pair, an attacker could extract the key using a brute-force attack requiring up to 2^{112} computations. However, the attacker can trade computation costs for memory storage by using a "meet-in-the-middle" attack. There are many variations, but the simplest is to compute 2^{56} different encryptions of the plaintext and store them, then begin decrypting the ciphertext using keys and compare the result to the table. The attacker will likely get multiple matches and would need another plaintext-ciphertext pair to verify that is the correct key. The worst case is that the attacker would need to perform 2^{56} decryptions, but even then that's only 2^{57} total operations.

There is nothing specific to DES in this; any doubled-cipher will have this problem. The attack extends to the two-key version of Triple DES as well, but it's generally less feasible, since the storage requirements become quite large.

Blowfish

In 1994, 56-bit DES was becoming obsolete and Triple DES was still very slow. Every other secure encryption algorithm was classified, incompletely specified (GOST, a Soviet algorithm was known, but the critical S-Boxes were classified), or known but unusable, since they were patented (Khufu, REDOC II, IDEA) or crippled for legal export (RC2, RC4).

In late 1993, Bruce Schneier presented the Blowfish cipher, a free, non-patented, drop-in replacement for DES with a 64-bit block size but a variable key length of up to 448 bits [Schneier1994]. In today's world awash with cryptologists and a healthy open-source movement, it's easy to forget how revolutionary this was—strong cryptography for anyone who wanted it. Even better, the Blowfish cipher is still secure.

The block size is the same as DES with 64 bits. However, Blowfish can have a variable key size in multiples of 8 bits, from 40 to 442 bits (56 bytes). During initialization, a key regardless of length is expanded to an internal structure of 4,168 bytes. The setup costs are expensive, since it does 521 iterations of encryption to generate the key schedule. However, after this, the key size has no effect on performance—in other words, the speed using a 442-bit key is the same as with a 56-bit key. This allows key choice to be based purely on security, storage, and protocol requirements instead of on performance. The initialization penalty can somewhat be avoided by directly specifying the internal array instead of having it generated (of course, then a key of 4168 bytes instead of at most 56 bytes must be saved and stored).

In overall structure, it's not that different from DES. The subkey array is eighteen 32-bit subkeys (compare to DES with sixteen 48-bit subkeys). There are four S-Boxes, each with 256 entries (compare to DES, which has eight S-Boxes with 64 entries). The most important difference is that Blowfish dynamically creates S-Box values during initialization, while DES uses fixed values. Notice that in Blowfish, all data is a nice round number of 32 and 8 bits, all designed to fit into machine registers with minimal amount of bit extractions and shifts. This gives Blowfish its speed.

Cryptographically, Blowfish has been deemed strong and has been quite well received. The algorithm has been included in dozens of free and limited commercial products. There have been no significant faults found with the algorithm. In a reduced eight-round version (not the standard 16 rounds), roughly 1 in 2^{14} keys are weak [Vau1996]. The weakness allows an attacker to know if a weak key is being used or not, but not what the specific key is (and it also allows some other more abstract attacks). The weak keys come about because Blowfish dynamically creates S-Boxes. Apparently, in some cases Blowfish generates some stinkers where some of the S-Box values are duplicated. There is no way of knowing which key is weak in advance; you have to go through the iteration and then check the S-Box values to see. Again, no weak keys have been found for the full-strength 16-round version.

IDEA

The IDEA cipher also operates on 64-bit blocks but uses a fixed-size 128-bit key length [LaMa1990, LaMaMu1991]. It is generally regarded as a very well-designed cipher and has experienced no known cryptographic attacks better than brute force. It is covered by patents owned by the Swiss firm Ascom, but they have allowed free noncommercial use, provided permissions are first obtained. Because of this licensing, IDEA became popular in the email encryption program PGP (Pretty Good Privacy). Today it seems to still be quite popular in the Perl community, partially since it is a very secure cipher and has received a positive recommendation from Bruce Schneier in *Applied Cryptography* (at the time Schneier had just developed Blowfish and it was still too new to be recommended). However, IDEA, like Blowfish, generates some nonlinear aspects of the cipher based on the key; because of this there are classes of weak keys [DaGoVn1993]. Fortunately, the odds of using one of the weak keys is 2^{-77}, so it's not considered a grave threat.

While IDEA is fairly easy to implement in software, it's also very slow because of generous use of expensive multiplication operations. A naïve implementation is typically about the same speed as DES, if not slower. Those same multiplications allow it to speed up significantly on 64-bit machines, or if someone hand-codes an assembly version that uses some microprocessors' extensions such as MMX (Intel and AMD processors), SSE2 (Intel's Pentium 4), or AltiVec (IBM/Motorola's PowerPC). In these cases, it's about twice as fast as DES. See [Lipmaa1998] for a discussion of using the MMX extension with IDEA.

RC5

RC5 was presented by Ron Rivest (coinventor of the RSA, for Rivest-Shamir-Adelman, algorithm) in 1995 [Rivest1995]. It is also fully specified in RFC 2105; however, it is patented (U.S. Patent 5,724,428) and is proprietary to RSA Security. It is fully parameterized in terms of block size, key size, and security represented as RC5-$w/r/b$, where:

- w = Word size in bits—16, 32, and 64—which results in a block size of $2w$. The standard is 32.
- r = Number of rounds, which, in turn, provides security. The appropriate number depends on w.
- b = Number of bytes in secret key; can be 0 to 255.

Internally, the key expansion stage takes a key and turns into an internal array S of $r \times w/8$ bytes. Following that, encryption is amazingly short and simple:

```
A = A + S[0]; // A is first half of plaintext block
B = B + S[1]; // B is second half of plaintext block
for (i = 1 .. r)
     A = ((A ⊕ B) << B) + S[2i]; // <-- data-dependant rotations
     B = ((B ⊕ A) << A) + S[2i+1] ;
```

The matching decryption algorithm is equally terse. As you can see, like Blowfish, RC5 uses data-dependant rotations.

RC5 is typically used with 64-bit blocks, 16 rounds, and keys being at least 128 bits (e.g., RC5-32/16/128+). While you can use larger blocks, you might consider using the newer ciphers like Rijndael or RC6 (discussed in the following sections). Using these guidelines, the most effective attacks are brute force, and the security is based on the size of the key. There is no reason not to use at least 128 bits, since after key setup, the cipher runs at the same speed independent of key size.

Rijndael and the Advanced Encryption Standard (AES)

In 2001, the NIST selected Rijndael as the replacement for DES (FIPS 197). Flemish for *XYZ* and pronounced "rain-doll," Rijndael is an interesting cipher, since it works in a completely different way from the previous ciphers.

The algorithm is in some ways similar to shuffling and cutting a deck of cards. The interstate is laid out in a square, and the rows and columns are shifted, mixed, and added in various ways. The entries themselves are also substituted and altered. It has a lot of parallel and symmetric structure because of the mathematics, which provides a lot of flexibility in how it is implemented. However, some have criticized it as having too much structure, which may lead to future attacks. Apparently that didn't bother the NSA (National Security Agency) or the NIST. No known cryptographic attacks are known, and it works well on a wide variety of processors, doesn't use bit shifting or rotation, and is very fast.

The AES Competition

How Rijndael was selected is also interesting. Knowing that DES had outlived its useful lifetime, the NIST issued an open call for replacements. Anyone was welcome to submit a cipher. The general requirements were:

- Must be a symmetric block cipher.
- Must support a block size of 128 bits.
- Must support key sizes of 128, 192, and 256 bits.
- Should be at least as fast Triple DES.
- Should run on a variety of hardware and should have "good" characteristics for implementation in hardware.
- If selected as the winner, the submitter relinquishes all intellectual property claims such as patents and trademarks.

Out of 15 semifinalists, 5 were selected:

- Rijndael, the eventual winner.
- MARS, from IBM.
- RC6, from RSA Labs (similar to RC5).
- Serpent, from Ross Anderson, Eli Biham, and Lars Kundsen.
- Twofish, from Bruce Schneier, John Kelsey, Doug Whiting, David Wagner, Chris Hall, and Niels Ferguson. It is the successor to the previously mentioned Blowfish algorithm.

How did they rate? Table 2.3 presents summaries from the conference reports from the Third Advanced Encryption Standard Candidate Conference.

The rankings are extremely relative, and a last-place finish does not mean the algorithm was unacceptable. Each algorithm author had his or her own interpretation of what the NIST selection process called for. Serpent, for instance, was extremely conservative in security, and this shows in its performance, while RC6 focused on 32- and 64-bit processors.

That the four other ciphers were not selected does not imply they are insecure. To the contrary, the NSA said any of the final candidates would make a good standard from a security standpoint (the speed with which they made their decision would seem to imply that the NSA has much more sophisticated methods of cipher analysis than the public has). In addition, the NIST has not specifically excluded them from being used. Since the NIST wanted a "generalist" cipher, these alternates may find their way into other more specialized standards and applications. However, Twofish and RC6 are particularly noteworthy because they have strong corporate or independent support and are likely to be used in future applications.

Table 2.3 Evaluation of AES Finalists on Various Platforms

PROCESSOR ARCHITECTURE	RELATIVE RANKING BETTER				WORSE
FGPA (programmable logic)	Rijndael Twofish	Serpent	RC6	MARS	
DSP TMS320C62x	RC6	Rijndael Twofish			
Toshiba T6N55 (smart card)	Rijndael	RC6 Twofish			
Pentium II	Rijndael	RC6	MARS Twofish	Serpent	
Itanium / PA-RISC (HP)	Rijndael	RC6 Twofish	MARS	Serpent	
Alpha 21264 Twofish	Rijndael RC6	MARS	Serpent		
ASIC hardware, worst case	Rijndael	Serpent	Twofish	MARS/RC6	
"Parallelism" (feedback modes)	Rijndael	Twofish	Serpent	MARS	RC6
Memory usage	RC6	Serpent	MARS	Twofish	Rijndael
Software (summary, Whiting)	Rijndael Twofish	MARS RC6	Serpent		
Software (summary, Bassham)	RC6	Rijndael	MARS	Twofish	Serpent
Java (speed)	Rijndael RC6	MARS			
Java (throughput)	RC6	MARS Rijndael Twofish			
Java (key setup)	Rijndael	Serpent	RC6	MARS	Twofish

Twofish

The successor to Blowfish, Twofish has already been widely deployed in many open-source and minor commercial projects. Twofish is meticulously constructed and well documented, and the submission paper is an excellent reference and bibliography on cryptanalysis. The developers even published a book on its design [ScKeWhWaFe1999]. In some ways, Twofish is a very traditional design that isn't dissimilar to DES: it's based on a Feistel design using expanded keys and S-Boxes for nonlinearity. The big difference is how each part was designed and how each part interacts with the others. Many components were found by an exhaustive search for a mapping that provided an optimal result using the smallest number of machine operations. While each piece of Twofish separately is fairly straightforward, the final result is hard to understand and analyze. One description of it is "a collection of patches which fix various problems" [Baudron1999]. That said, no one is suggesting it is insecure and currently the best attack is brute force.

RC6

RC6 builds upon the success of RC5 and is modified to handle 128-bit block sizes using four 32-bit registers. Like RC5, the algorithm is completely parameterized and specified as RC6-$w/r/b$. As submitted to the AES, RC6 uses $w = 32$ and $r = 20$. The length of the key may be any multiple of 8; however, it is most common to use $b = 16$, 24 or 32 bytes (128, 192, and 256 bits). The key scheduling function is almost identical to the one used in RC5, except that RC6 generates more bytes from the key. It is fast—and in many cases faster than Rijndael—and Java performance is excellent. RSA Security has submitted RC6 to various other standard bodies, so you can be sure you will be seeing more of it. They also have trademarked the name "RC6" and received a patent on its design (U.S. Patent 6,269,163).

Ciphers You Shouldn't Use

This section lists ciphers that are insecure and should not be used. Oddly, they keep turning up in supposedly high-security applications such as authentication tokens (see [FuSiSmFe2001] for examples). The ciphers are most likely used because they are simple to implement in a few lines of code and visually appear to do a good job obscuring the underlying data.

Password XOR Schemes

In this type of scheme, the user takes a password and repeatedly uses it to XOR against the message. This has been used in various forms, including file protection. It is also common in protecting machine code where the program starts to decrypt the machine code and then jumps into the newly decrypted code. However, this is a weak scheme, and it can be easily cracked, especially if there is any knowledge about what the plaintext looks like (such as common headers or ASCII). It can be used to *obscure* data to make it *visually* unreadable, but not for anything that is susceptible to an attack:

```
// same function to encode and decode
public static void xorData(byte[] data, byte[] key) {
      for (int i = 0, j = 0; i < data.length; i++) {
            data[i] ^= key[j++];
            if (j == key.length) j = 0;
      }
}
```

Classical Cryptography

Classical cryptography involved simple ciphers that typically worked on letters or characters as opposed to bytes. More advanced classical cipher operated on blocks, but typically blocks of letters instead of blocks of bytes. These are now primarily of historical interest and useful as examples for more advanced concepts.

Interestingly, some of the work of classical cryptography is still classified. From 1938 to 1941, William Friedman wrote a four-volume series titled *Military Cryptanalysis*. In 1984 the first two volumes were declassified. A more modern series from Lambros Callimahos included three volumes written from 1959 to 1977. Again only the first two are declassified. In 1992, an attempt to declassify the remaining volumes using the Freedom of Information Act was rejected. According to the NSA (*Gilmore v. NSA*: 10-02-93 letter, available at: `www.eff.org/Privacy/Key_escrow/ITAR_export/ITAR_FOIA/Gilmore_v_NSA/10-02-93.letter`

> *The documents are classified because their disclosure could reasonably be expected to cause serious damage to the national security . . . . In addition, this Agency is authorized by various statutes to protect certain information concerning its activities. We have determined that such information exists in these documents.*

In other words, 45 years later, World War II cryptography is still essential to national security. One can only speculate as to why this would be. To my knowledge no further attempts have been made to release the material since 1992, but maybe someone will try again.

Regardless of what is hidden in those texts, classical cryptography has no place in your security solution.

Aegean Park Press (www.aegeanparkpress.com/) is the place to go for reprints of declassified military material regarding cryptography.

ROT 13

ROT 13 is really a primitive classical cipher and is an abbreviation for "rotation by 13 places." Encoding transforms a letter by rotating 13 places in the alphabet, so *a* becomes *n*, *b* becomes *o*, and so forth. Decoding is done similarly to performing a reverse rotation. It does not encode spaces, digits, or symbols, and its primary use is for posting messages in a public forum, such as newsgroups, that others may not want to intentionally read such as jokes, movie endings, and potentially offensive material. The difference between encoding and decoding is just adding or subtracting:

```
char p = .. .; // plaintext char
char c;        // output ciphertext char
if (p >= 'a' && p <= 'z') c = (char)((p - 'a' + 13) % 26 + 'a');
else if (p >= 'A' && p <= 'Z') c = (char)((p - 'A' + 13) % 26 + 'A');
else c = p;
return c;
```

Padding

Block ciphers work on fixed-sized input. If a message doesn't end on a block boundary, it needs to be padded with additional data to make it fill an entire block.

Fixed-Value Padding

Fixed-value is the simplest form of padding. A constant byte is added to the end of the message to make it fit a block boundary. Somehow the length of the message must be known in order to correctly remove the padding. The most common value used is simply 0x00. Another common scheme is to first add 0x80, then add zeros, or alternate ones and zeros. Less common is using 0xFF. However, the value used doesn't really make much difference. This scheme needs to be used with care when the message is always a fixed length and has a particular structure. For instance, assume you are just encrypting "true" or "false" with the bytes 0x00 or 0x01. Using a fixed-value padding scheme, the two messages encrypt to two different values, thus leaking some information. An attacker examining multiple messages will know the plaintext is one of two values, even if he or she doesn't know what the message is. Using this information, the attacker can generate legitimate messages or replace a message in transit with the other value. Worse, using some context an attacker might be able to determine which value is "true" even without knowing the key, or using some optimizations, the attacker might even be able to recover the key.

Random Padding

Another common technique is to use random bits as padding. As with fixed-value padding, a message length is required to remove the padding. Here the same message is (probably) encrypted to different ciphertext and thus solves the weaknesses mentioned with fixed-value padding. However, this now causes problems in databases when a uniqueness constraint, indexing, or searching is required. This issue is discussed in detail in Chapter 7.

PKCS Padding

This padding scheme is known as PKCS #5 (most common) or PKCS #7 padding, since it was originally defined in PKCS #7 in Section 10.3, Note 2, then generalized in PKCS #5. (PKCS stands for Public Key Cryptography Standard.) Unlike the previous schemes, the message length is encoded into the padding scheme itself. You don't need to know the length of the message in advance in order to strip off the padding.

If you need 1 byte of padding, you would add byte 0x01 to the end of the block, if you need two, you would add 0x0202, and so on. If the message ends on a block boundary, you add a new block filled with the value of block length (i.e., if the block has a length of *B* bytes, the new block is filled with *B*). Formally, this can be described as:

```
int b = // block size in bytes, b < 256
int n = // number of bytes in message, n I< b
int k = n % b ;
if (k > 0)
     // add k bytes with value k to message
else if (k == 0)
     // add k bytes with value k
```

The addition of an extra block to the message isn't normally a problem; however, it must be considered when sizing database fields. If the message can be a maximum of nB bytes, you will need a database field of $(n+1)B$, or you'll have to reduce your maximum by 1 so the extra padding block is not generated.

Modes of Operations

So far we examined ciphers that map a plaintext "block" to ciphertext. If we could only encrypt messages a few bytes long, then modern cryptography would not be very useful. Using various modes of operations, we encrypt longer messages by stringing together blocks.

There are four significant characteristics of a mode:

Parallelization. Can blocks be encrypted or decrypted without depending on the previous block? This has become especially important with TCP/IP transmissions, since packets may arrive out of order.

Initialization vector. Many modes require an initialization block (also known as an initialization vector or salt) to get started. This generally adds security but at a cost for both storage and speed.

Error propagation. Does a 1-bit error in a block affect subsequent blocks?

Self-synchronizing. Can the mode recover from a "bit slippage," where a bit gets lost? If not, the rest of the transmission will be gibberish. This mostly applies to radio-type transmissions.

Table 2.4 summarizes the various modes of the operations. RBE stands for *random bit errors*, or in other words, complete corruption. SBE is for *single-bit errors*, where a single bit is altered.

Initialization Vectors

Most modes require an initialization vector (IV)—that is, a random byte array with the length of the cipher's block. Depending on how the mode works, this vector is used as an alternate start to the message or as a dummy ciphertext block. Following are some guidelines for using IVs:

- The same IV must be used in the decryption as was used for the encryption.
- The IV does not have to be generated by a secure random source (although it certainly can be); timestamps or other semi-unique sources can be used.
- The IV is not a key and can be transmitted or stored in the clear.
- The same IV can be used for multiple messages, although for transient messages a different IV should be used.
- The null IV—that is, an IV with all zeros—is commonly used to minimize bookkeeping, storage, or transmission costs, especially in database applications.

Table 2.4 Modes of Operation Summary

MODE	SUGGESTED USE	REQUIRES IV	BIT ERRORS IN BLOCK	BIT ERRORS IN IV	MESSAGE	SECURITY ISSUES
ECB	Single block (small data) highest speed	No	RBE in block	Not applicable	Yes	Susceptible to dictionary attacks
CBC	Most common for general use	Yes	RBE in block SBE in next block	SBE in first block only	Yes, but optional first block with random bit will prevent this	
CFB	To change ciphers' block size into another (stream ciphers)	Yes	SBE in block RBE in subsequent block	RBE of first few blocks		Not to be used with public key ciphers
OFB	Minimize bit errors	Yes	SBE in block	RBE in every block		Not to be used with public key ciphers
CTR	Out-of-order decryption	Yes	SBE in block	No IV, but bit error in counter block will result in RBE		Not to be used with public key ciphers

Electronic Codebook Mode (ECB)

Electronic Codebook is the simplest mode. As shown in Figure 2.1, the message is chopped up into block-sized chunks, and each block is encrypted independently. In this way, the cipher can be thought of as a code; each plaintext block has a corresponding ciphertext block (with respect to a given key). If you had a large enough codebook, you could actually do away with the cipher algorithm and just refer to it. This simplicity also provides a useful method for attack, however. With long messages or with many short messages, an attacker might be able to determine the value of one block (as in the case of our fixed-value padding example). Then using that block, the attacker might be able to determine the value of another block, and so on. This is most applicable to messages that have a lot of structure, such as a human or computer language. For instance, in this chapter the eight-letter string " cipher " (*cipher* with a space before and after) appears very frequently. If we encrypted this chapter with a cipher using an 8-byte block and ECB mode, we'd certainly see that block frequently (depending if it aligned correctly).

Because it's vulnerable to the dictionary attack, ECB mode is normally not used unless there is a specific reason *to* use it. On the plus side it's the fastest of any mode.

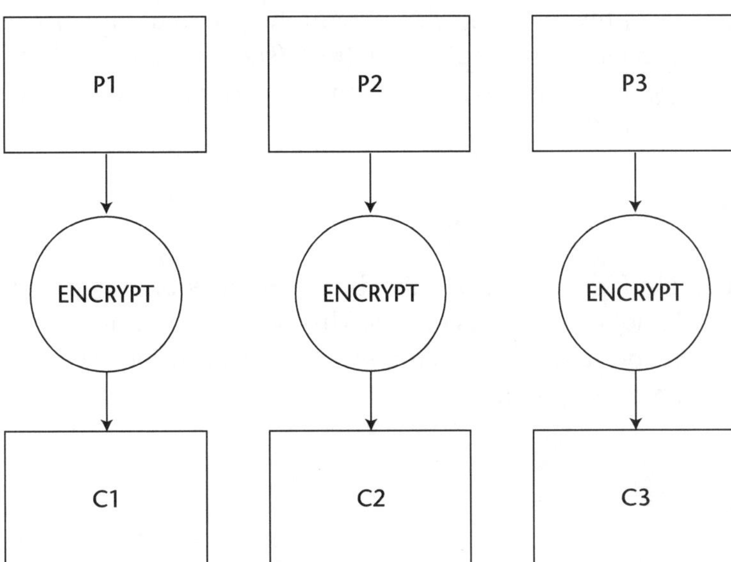

Figure 2.1 ECB encryption.

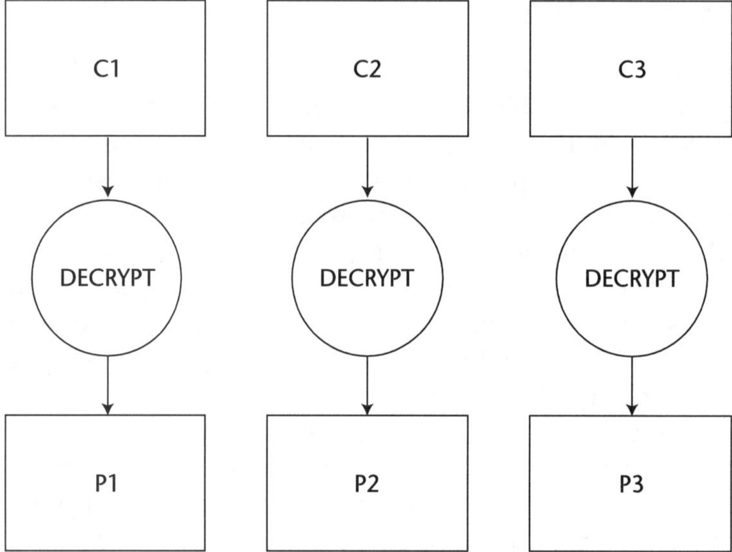

Figure 2.2 ECB decryption.

Cipher Block Chaining Mode (CBC)

Cipher Block Chaining mode eliminates the dictionary attack by using the contents of the previous block to encrypt the current block. This extra overhead adds about 20 to 30 percent to the running time over ECB mode. During encryption, each plaintext block is XORed with the previous ciphertext block, and the IV is used as the first ciphertext block (see Figure 2.3). In this way the last block depends on all blocks previous to it. The following code shows encryption using CBC:

$$C_1 = E_k(P_1 \oplus IV)$$
$$C_n = E_k(P_j \oplus C_{n-1})$$

Decryption, shown in Figure 2.4, is similar, but each block only depends on the previous block, not *all* previous blocks. This way decryption can be done in parallel, possibly making it much faster than encryption. The following code shows CBC decryption:

$$P_1 = D_k(C_1) \oplus IV$$
$$P_n = D_k(C_n) \oplus C_{n-1}$$

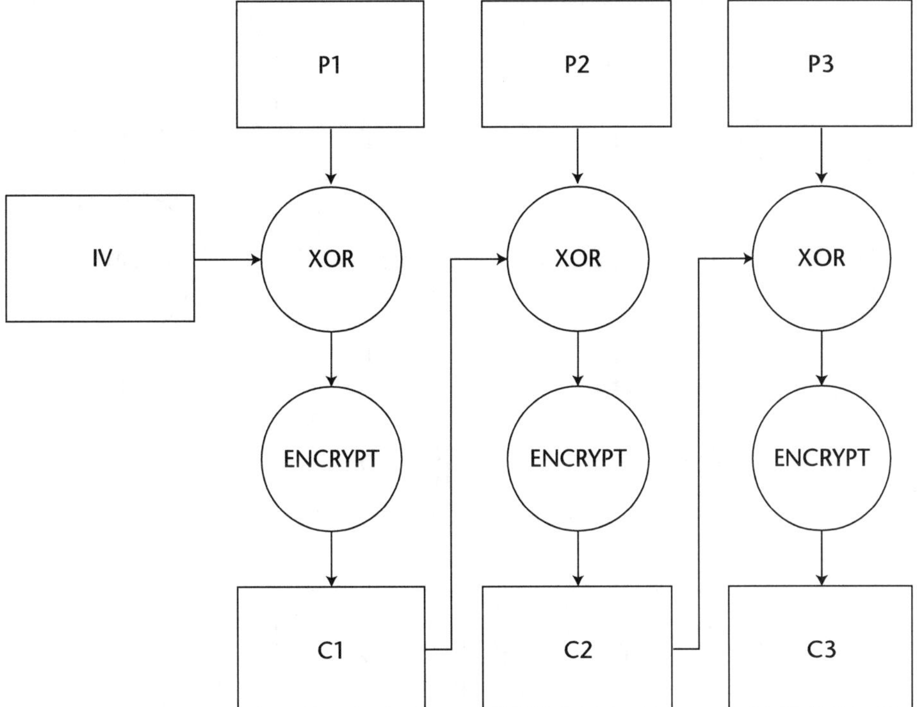

Figure 2.3 CBC encryption.

CBC mode has some interesting error properties. First, it's self-synchronizing: A dropped block or a block with errors will result in only two plaintext blocks being corrupted. However, this doesn't extend to bits. If a bit is dropped, the remaining message will be completely corrupted. The other property is that a single bit error will corrupt the current block but will only change the corresponding bit in the *next* block; thereafter the message is intact. Finally, the first block is vulnerable to manipulation of the IV. Changing the IV will result in the plaintext modified in the corresponding bits. Therefore, it's advisable to keep the IV secret. If message integrity is a prime concern, a different mode or the use of a hash (see the next chapter) is recommended.

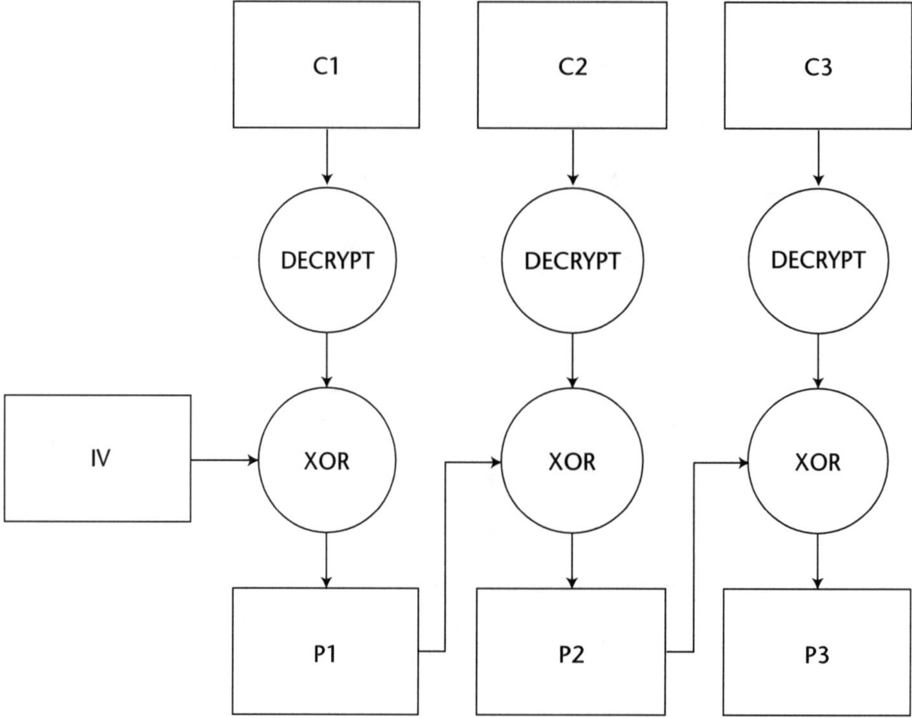

Figure 2.4 CBC decryption.

Cipher Feedback Mode (CFB)

This mode is designed to be used when some application can process data in a block size that is different from the underlying cipher block size. Most common is processing data as single bytes, while the cipher block is 8 or more bytes. If the block size is *b* bits and CFB mode processes *s* bits, the throughput is decreased by *b/s* times when compared to CBC mode.

The following code shows CFB encryption (also illustrated in Figure 2.5):

$$I_1 = IV$$
$$I_n = (I_{n-1} << (b - s)) \mid C_{n-1}$$
$$O_n = E_k(I_n)$$
$$C_n = MSB_s(P_n \oplus O_n)$$

This code shows CFB decryption (also illustrated in Figure 2.6):

$$I_1 = IV$$
$$I_n = (I_{n-1} << (b - s)) \mid C_{n-1}$$
$$O_n = E_k(I_n)$$
$$P_n = C_n \oplus MSB(O_n)$$

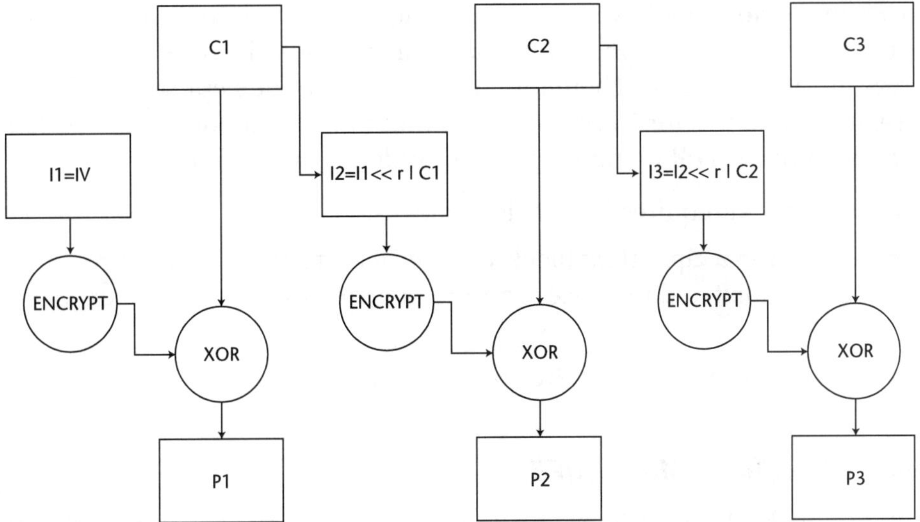

Figure 2.5 CFB encryption.

Notice how the encryption and decryption steps are virtually identical and that the cipher is only used to encrypt. The cipher algorithm is only used to generate a sequence of pseudorandom bits to XOR against the plaintext. Since encryption is only used, this mode cannot be used with public key ciphers, because this would allow anyone to decrypt in this mode.

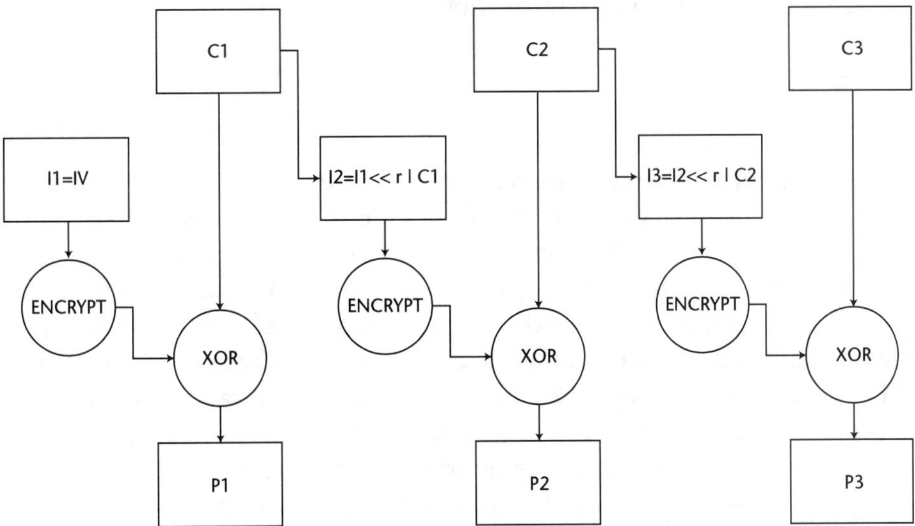

Figure 2.6 CFB decryption.

CFB mode does not have the same sensitivity to the initialization vector that CBC mode has. A single bit change in the IV will cause random bit errors in the first block. Therefore, the IV need not be kept secret. Otherwise, the properties for CFB mode are similar to CBC mode, except scaled by a factor of *b/s*. Following are further guidelines for CFB mode:

- Decryption requires *b/s* previous blocks.
- Bit error in a ciphertext block will cause corresponding bit errors in the plaintext and produce random bit errors in the subsequent *b/s* blocks.
- CFB can recover from a dropped block in *b/s* blocks.

Output Feedback Mode (OFB)

Output Feedback mode is used if there is a requirement that a single bit error in the ciphertext causes a single bit error in the corresponding plaintext to occur (i.e., no error propagation). Formally, OFB is specified using *s*-bit chunks as in CFB mode, instead of the full block size. However, for security reasons this should not be done. OFB mode should only use the native block size (like ECB and CBC modes).

The following code shows OFB encryption (also illustrated in Figure 2.7):

$$O_1 = IV;$$
$$O_n = E_K(O_{n-1})$$
$$C_n = P_n \oplus O_n$$

The following shows OFB decryption (also illustrated in Figure 2.8):

$$O_1 = IV$$
$$O_n = E_K(O_{n-1})$$
$$P_n = C_n \oplus O_n$$

Again, the encryption and decryption steps are identical; the underlying cipher is only used to decrypt, and thus OFB mode cannot be used with public key. The initialization vector, along with the key, completely determines the bytes used to XOR the plaintext; there is no feedback of the message (plain or ciphertext) used in computing subsequent blocks. The drawback of the scheme is that while the IV need not be kept secret, it cannot be used with same key, since there are some cryptographic attacks than can recover the key. Rather, you need a new IV for every message. The good news is that sophisticated implementations can precompute the masks (i.e., O_j) while waiting for input, resulting in high throughput.

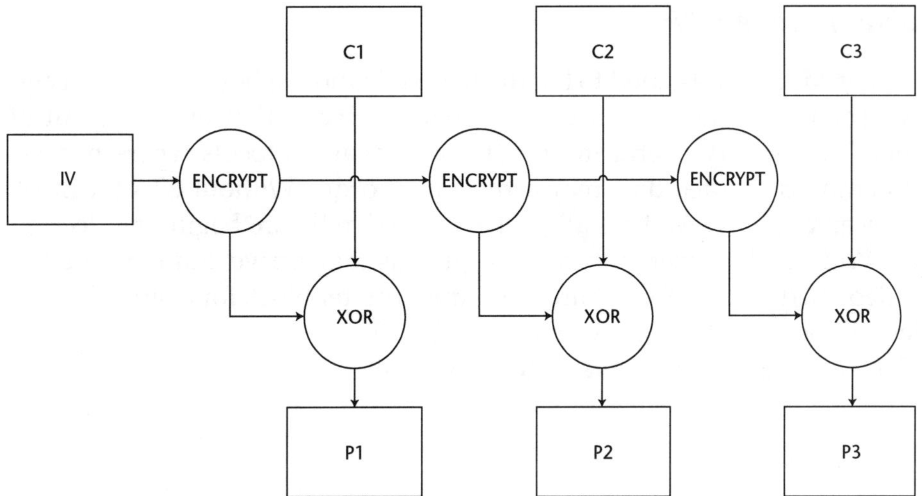

Figure 2.7 OFB encryption.

Unlike CBC and CFB, this mode is not self-synchronizing. Any dropped bits or blocks will result in the rest of the message being corrupted.

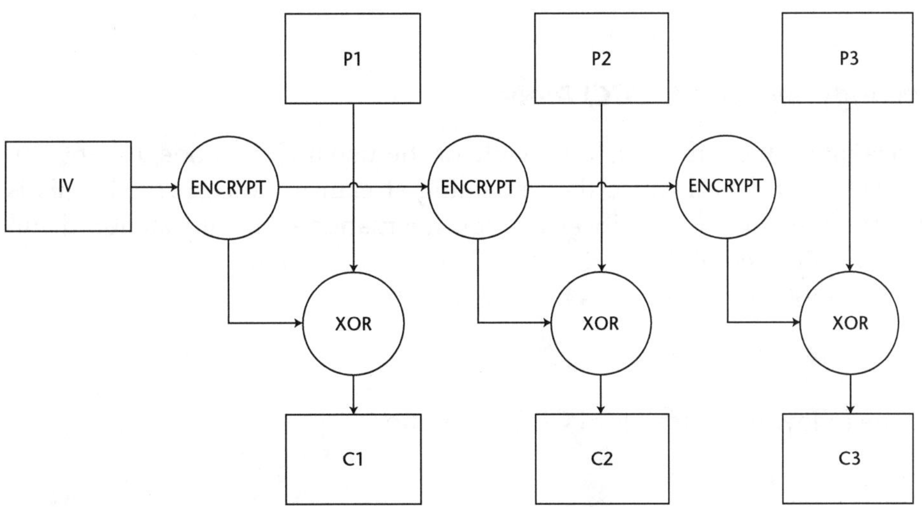

Figure 2.8 OFB decryption.

Counter Mode (CTR)

Counter Mode is designed to handle parallelization of both encryption and decryption operations, as well as to handle decryption of blocks out of order. This is very useful in TCP/IP or similar protocols where packets containing encrypted data may arrive out of order. Without CTR (or ECB), the receiver has to wait for all packets to arrive before beginning decryption. With CTR, packets can be decrypted as they arrive and reordered as needed. To do this, CTR requires a unique counter block for every plaintext block, denoted in the following code as $T_1 \ldots T_n$.

The following code shows CTR encryption:

$$O_n = E_k(T_n)$$
$$C_n = P_n \oplus O_n$$

Following is the code used for CTR decryption:

$$O_n = E_k(T_n)$$
$$P_n = C_n \oplus O_n$$

The issue then becomes generated counter blocks. If a counter block with a key is reused, the block is at risk of attack. The NIST recommendation (in Special Publication SP800-38A) only presents guidelines in how the counter blocks should be generated. It is up to protocol designers to specify the exact method of generating counter blocks, including how two parties agree on what the first counter block is.

Propagating CBC (PCBC) Mode

Propagating CBC mode is a variable of the usual CBC mode, except any single-bit error will cause the remaining stream to be corrupted. This is designed to quickly identify errors. It is not mandated by any standard and is primarily used in the Kerberos authentication system.

The following code shows PCBC encryption:

$$C_n = E_k(P_n \oplus P_{n-1} \oplus C_{n-1})$$

The following is used for PCBC decryption:

$$P_n = D_k(C_n) \oplus C_{n-1} \oplus P_{n-1}$$

Key Wrapping

One problem with the previous modes of operation is that it's not clear how to encrypt a key (that is, not how to encrypt using a key but rather encrypting a key itself). The modes of operation are really designed for longer messages. Typically, the last message depends on every previous block, but the second block only depends on the first block and not on any subsequent blocks. Since keys are only a few blocks long, it doesn't seem right that one block is protected while the first block isn't. You certainly would want to use a stronger key or cipher to encrypt an underlying key as well. Key wrapping solves this problem. It's somewhat of a cross between a specialized mode of operation and a new cipher.

Triple DES KEY Wrapping

The following key wrapping technique is from RFC 3217 and is designed for Triple DES and other symmetric ciphers. The strategy is to repeat encrypt the key and perform various alterations of the result. In particular, the algorithm is as follows:

1. `MESSAGE` = the Triple DES key, 128- or 192-bit, parity-adjusted.
2. `CHECKSUM` = Perform a SHA-1 hash of the key and use the first 8 bytes (64 bits) as a checksum.
3. `IV` = Generate 8 random bytes (64 bits) as the IV.
4. `TEMP1` = Encrypt `MESSAGE || CHECKSUM` using CBC mode using the IV from the previous step.
5. `TEMP2` = `IV || TEMP`.
6. `TEMP3` = `TEMP2`, but the order of bytes is reversed.
7. Encrypt `TEMP` using CBC mode using an IV of 0x4adda22c79e82105.

This same method is specified for RC2 keys, except Step 1 is replaced with the following:

1. Key must be multiple of 8 bits.
2. `LENGTH` = One byte containing the key length in bytes.
3. `MESSAGE` = `LENGTH || KEY || PAD`, where PAD is the least number of random bytes so that the final result is multiple of 8 bytes.

Decryption is fairly clear, as it's just the reverse process. Be sure to verify the final key is correct by recomputing the CHECKSUM value and comparing it with what was received.

AES Key Wrapping

A new AES key wrapping algorithm has been proposed but not formally published by the NIST (see `http://csrc.nist.gov/encryption/kms`). It's defined to use AES but will of course work with any 128-bit block cipher. Although the cipher is 128-bit block, the wrapping algorithm operates on 64-bit blocks. Given $n > 2$ plaintext blocks (which contain the key), this outputs n+1 ciphertext blocks. Using five rounds, the algorithm splits each plaintext block and mixes it with other functions and then encrypts the output. This function is relatively expensive—wrapping 128-bit key makes 10 calls to the underlying cipher function.

The following code shows the key wrap process:

```
IV = 0xA6A6A6A6A6A6A6A6; // 64-bit value
a = 64-bit value
b = 128-bit value
r = new array of n 64-bit values;
for (i = 0...n-1)
     r[i] = p[i];

for (j = 0...4)
     for (i = 0...n-1)
          b = AES_k(a | r[i]);
          a = MSB_64(b) ^ ((n * j)+i+1)
          r[i] = LSB_64(b);

c = new array of n+1 64-bit values
c[0] = a;
for (i = 0..n-1) c[i+1] = r[i];
return c
```

The following code shows the key unwrap process:

```
IV = 0xA6A6A6A6A6A6A6A6; // 64-bit value
a = c[0]
for (i = 0..n-1)
     r[i] = c[i+1];
for (j = 5...0)
     for (i = n-1 ...0)
          b = AES_k^-1((A ^ ((n*j)+i+1)) | r[i])
          a = MSB_64(b)
          r[i] = LSB_64(b)
```

```
if (a != IV) error

p = new array of n 64-bit values
for (i = 0..n-1)
     p[i] = r[i]
return p
```

The initial value of A6 repeated is used. According to the specification, the chance that a random input will unwrap and produce the initial value correctly is less than 2^{-64}. In this case, the IV functions as a checksum for data integrity.

Turning Passwords into Keys

Keys of more than a few bytes aren't easily memorizable. A common technique is to use a password or passphrase that is used to generate a key. An obvious technique is to hash or MAC the password bytes in order to generate new bytes to use as a key. This certainly works; the problem is that the number of possible passwords is *much* smaller than the possible number of keys. If the password is nine characters made from the set of upper- and lowercase letters, digits, and symbols for a total of 72 symbols, you have at best $72^9 \approx 2^{55}$ possible passwords, which means you really only have a 55-bit key. Instead of trying to brute-force the key, an attacker would find it easier to try every password instead. For AES where the key might be 255 bits long, this is a huge optimization.

You can solve this problem by making the password longer, but humans have a limited capacity for this. So instead of adding more bits to the password, the trick is to make the computational cost of brute-forcing the password to be higher.

To make this work, you need a salt value and an iteration count. The *salt* is a random number to be associated with the password. It can be from a random source (either cryptographic or not) or from a few bytes of the hash of it. The salt is normally 64-bits, and it doesn't have to be strictly random values. You can add other parameters to it to distinguish what the key is for, how long it is, and any other parameters you may have. The point is just not to duplicate salt values. The goal is make the salt uniformly distributed so duplicates don't occur very often.

Then you compute the key by:

```
T1 = Hash(password || salt);
T2 = Hash(T1);
...
Tcount = Hash(Tcount -1)
```

or in programming notation:

```
tLast = hash( password || salt); // concatent password and salt
for (int i = 1 ; i < iterationCount; ++i) {
     t = Hash(tLast);
     tLast = t;
}
```

The output *t* contains the final hash value whose bytes can be used as a key. The iteration count is also at least 1000.

This system can also be used as a MAC value. Instead of storing an encrypted password or using a MAC that requires a key, you can store the recursive hash in the database. During login, the user looks up the salt and iteration count, generates a new recursive hash, and compares it to what was stored. If they are a match, the user is logged in. This technique works best on systems where login is an infrequent event, as opposed to Web server applications. In this case, it's a nice system, since you don't have to worry about keys.

Performing a few thousand hash operations shouldn't be an issue for noninteractive programs, initialization steps, or when password matching isn't a common occurrence. For an attacker, it's a big problem, since it multiplies the work of brute-forcing passwords by 1000*x* or more. If it took one month to brute-force the list, it now takes 83 years. And the work only applied to one salt value (or rather one key).

Hashes

A *hash*, or *message digest*, is a function that takes an arbitrary-sized message and returns a deterministic number based on the contents of the message. These are most commonly used in the basic data structures such as hash tables or hash maps. In general, a hash has the following properties:

Compression. It "compresses" an arbitrary sized message into a number, typically one with a fixed number of bits.

Ease of computation. A hash needs to be fast; otherwise, the purpose is defeated.

Uniform distribution of values. On average, a set of inputs will be uniformly distributed among the possible outputs. This means a hash function that just returns 1 for any input is not a good hash function. In addition, a hash that can return 10 possible values but that has a preference for 1, 2, and 3 isn't particularly useful.

A full discussion of general-purpose hashes can be found in [Knuth1998]. For our purposes, hashes need to be more specialized and come in two different flavors: noncryptographic hashes, which are used for testing against accidental or spurious errors in the message, and cryptographic hashes, which are used for testing for messages with malicious or intentional alteration (among many other uses).

Cryptographic Hashes

Cryptographic hashes are different from checksum hashes, since they guard against malicious alteration of a message. For instance, you wouldn't want "Please send me $10" to have the same hash as "Please send me $10,000 jkjs," with the junk at the end of the last message added to make the message have the correct checksum.

To formalize, a cryptographic hash has the following requirements:

One-wayness. Given a hash value, it is computationally infeasible to find a message that hashes to that value.

Weak collision resistance. Given x and $H(x)$, determine y so that $H(x) = H(y)$. This is an extension of the previous condition. Before, you just had a hash value; now you have that and the original message.

Strong collision resistance. You couldn't find *any* two messages x, y such that $H(x) = H(y)$. Here you are not interested in what the hash value is, only that you can find two messages that hash identically.

Near-collision resistance. It is hard to find two messages x and y such that difference (in bits) between $H(x)$ and $H(y)$ is "small." This property is only desired since it's common to use part of the output of a hash instead of the whole value.

Independence or noncorrelation. The hash value is not dependant on the input message — a single-bit change in the input should on average cause about half the output bits to change (i.e., the same as a random string). In other words, the hash is a randomizer of the input. Yet another way to say this is that every output bit depends on every input bit.

Leakage resistance or "locally one-way." This is almost a corollary to the previous condition. The hash should not leak information about the message. Even stronger, given a hash and part of the message, the hash should not leak any information on the remaining part of the message. If the input bits are unknown, it should take on average 2^{t-1} hash operations to recover those bits.

Collisions

Since a hash can take a message of *any* length and compute a fixed-size number, overlaps or collisions will happen. The question is how often? The answer is smaller than you might expect because of the so-called birthday paradox. This is most commonly described as "how many people do you need in a room to expect (or with 50-percent probability) that two will have the same birthday (or to have a birthday collision)?" The answer is only 23! The key point in understanding is that it is for *any* two people having common birthday, not two people having a specific birthday, and not anyone else having your birthday. There are a lot more possible combinations when the choice of birthday is unspecified. See Figure 2.9.

The standard approximation for the birthday problem is given k distinct random (i.e., people) elements out of n possibilities (i.e., days); the probability of one collision is given by:

$$p = 1 - e^{\frac{-k(k-1)}{2n}}$$

The basis for attack is knowing how many hash values you need before two are identical or when a collision occurs. Cryptographic hashes have 2^{128} to 2^{512} different possible outputs (the variable n), so using the formula as presented is quite unwieldy. Since we know the number of attempts is also going to be large, we can simplify the formula by changing the $k - 1$ into plain k, resulting in:

$$p = 1 - e^{\frac{-k^2}{2n}}$$

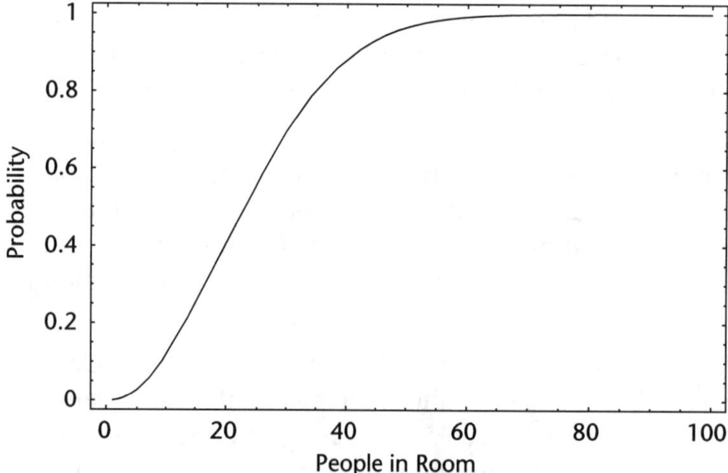

Figure 2.9 Probability of a matching birthday.

The expected number of hashes needed before a collision occurs is when the probability is 50 percent. Solving for k by using logarithms, we find that $k \approx 1.7741\sqrt{n}$. Since n is also going to be very large, the rule of thumb is just using $\sqrt{n}$. Or given a hash with 2^x outputs, you can expect a collision after collecting $2^{x/2}$ outputs.

If we assume that both k and n are powers of 2, we can make a change of variables that is much easier computationally to work with:

$$n = 2^h, k = 2^n$$

$$p = 1 - e^{-(2^{2x-h-1})}$$

With this, h now represents the bit length of the hash, while x is logarithm (base 2) of the number of hashes collected. Using a 160-bit hash as an example, the odds of collision are extremely low until you collect 2^{76} hashes (see Figure 2.10). This is what gives a hash its resistance. After that, however, the odds rocket upward; by 2^{82} the odds of collision are greater than 99.95. The behavior is even more extreme using larger hash sizes.

Attacks

Collisions can be used to attack the hash either by determining its contents or by generating fraudulent messages. Two of the most common are the dictionary attack and the birthday attack.

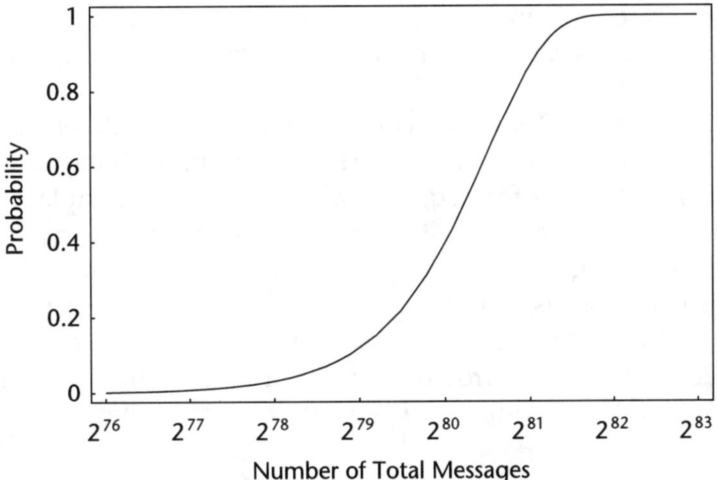

Figure 2.10. Collisions probability for 160-bit hash.

Dictionary Attacks

The most basic attack is the dictionary attack. Here the attacker has some idea of what the message being hashed is and compiles a dictionary of hashes to message. For instance, assume the message is just the ASCII representation of your bank account balance. Let's assume it's less than $100,000.00 and not negative, so there are only 10,000,000 possible values. An attacker could easily just compile a 10-million entry dictionary mapping a balance to a hash. When the attacker sees a hash, he or she just looks in the compiled hash dictionary and immediately knows the value.

A more realistic example is using a hash to store a password. When the user types in a password, you'd compute the hash of what he or she typed in to one in your password list. This sounds secure, since an attacker looking at the password file will see only hashes, which don't leak any information of the original password. However, the attacker computes a dictionary of common passwords to hashes. If the attacker finds a match between the compiled dictionary and an entry in password file, the attacker immediately knows what the password is.

Yuval's Birthday Attack

This attack can be considered a brute-force attack since it's computationally intensive. Assume you have a message you wish to forge, it's hash n bits long. You generate $2^{n/2}$ "benign" changes to the original message, such as adding spaces and junk to the end of the message, compute the hash, and store the result. Then with the fraudulent message you do the same thing: compute a benign change to the message, hash it, and compare it with the previous list of hashes. You should generate a collision quickly. There is a slightly more complicated version that doesn't require as much storage, but the result is the same. After this you have two messages that both hash to the same value.

So what are the implications? Say you send one version of a contract that states, "I promise to pay $100,000.00" for some service, along with the hash to the victim. The service is performed, and when the victim complains about getting paid, you pull out your "alternate" version of the message: "I promise to pay $100.00." This is a rather silly example, but you get the idea.

For a 128-bit hash, this means generating 2^{64} or 1.85×10^{19} different messages. That's a lot, but as we saw in the DES case, this is in the realm of reason, and today 128-bit hashes are frowned upon for high-security work. Stepping up to a 160-bit hash requires the generation of 2^{80} hashes, which involves at least 60,000 times more effort than the 128-bit case. Today this is secure, but some are worried about the security of very long term applications, and even longer hashes have been produced.

Clearly this attack works well with messages that can be altered or appended to and still make sense. This attack doesn't apply if the message is of a fixed size, but regardless, because of this attack (and because of general collision properties) a hash with n bits is said to have $n/2$ bits of security.

Algorithms

While there are quite a few cryptographic hash algorithms, in practice, you use one from one of three families: MD, SHA, or RIPE-MD. And all the algorithms derive from a common ancestor, MD4. The hash dynasty is summarized in Figure 2.11.

Table 2.5 summarizes the structure of the hash dynasty. The internal buffer size is the size of one iteration of the hash. The internal buffer is then broken down into words, and each word has a number of steps performed on it. Computing the word size (bits) × the number of words × the number of steps gives us a rough "complexity" score and is a relative estimate of performance. SHA-512, with a score of 40960, is about four times slower than SHA-1, with a score of 12800. The only catch is that RIPE-MD 160 actually is much faster than its complexity score would indicate. In the field, it's only about 20 percent slower than SHA-1.

Table 2.5 Comparison of Hash Algorithms

FUNCTION	INTERNAL BUFFER SIZE	HASH SIZE	ENDIAN PREFERENCE	COMPLEXITY WORDSIZE/ WORDS/STEPS
MD4	512	128	Little	32×4×48=6144
MD5	512	128	Little	32×4×64=8192
SHA-1	512	160	Big	32×5×80=12800
RIPE-MD 160	512	160	Little	32×10×80=25600
SHA-256	512	256	Big	32×8×64=16384
SHA-384	1024	384	Big	64×8×80=40960
SHA-512	1024	512	Big	64×8×80=40960

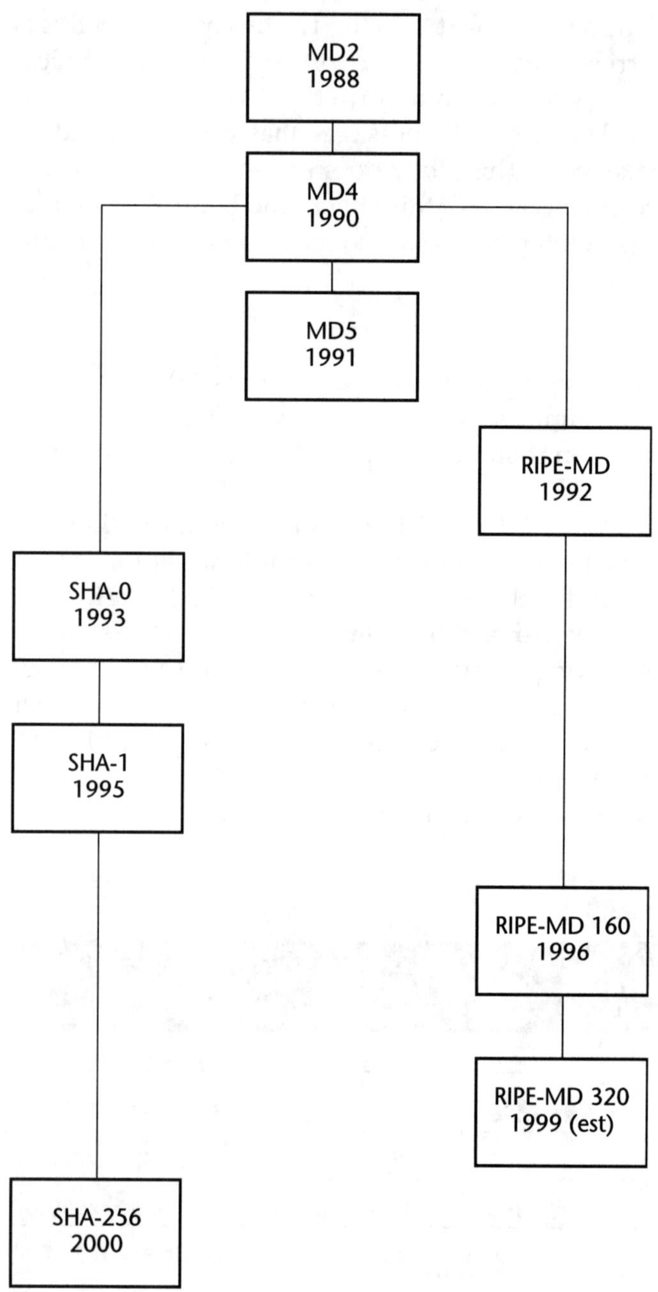

Figure 2.11 Hash family tree.

The MD Family

Ronald Rivest (whom we've met before) is the father of the MD (for Message Digest) family. First of the series, MD2 was used in early secure email systems and produced a 128-bit hash. It operates on byte arrays instead of larger word arrays (such as 32-bit integers) and is quite slow. While it's more or less still secure, it's just about never used because of its performance and the availability of other algorithms.

To help remedy the performance problem, Rivest introduced MD4 in 1992. MD4 was more an experiment in producing a fast hash rather than a fast *secure* hash. However, because of its speed, it had a rapid uptake. While no defects were initially found, Rivest was concerned about its security and therefore decommissioned RC4 and issued a more conservative replacement, MD5, in 1991. A wise move, since MD4 was subsequently shown to be broken [Dobbertin1995].

MD5 uses a 512-bit block size (only 448 are from the actual message, however; the rest is internal padding) and produces a 128-bit hash. More details and a sample C implementation can be found in RFC 1321. No collisions have been found; however, some of the internal functions have shown some minor problems [DeBo1994]. The real problem with MD5 is that, with only 2^{64} messages, the resulting hash is too small and susceptible to the birthday attack problem. That may still sound like a lot of values to test, but it is computationally feasible and thus not recommended for high-security applications, especially those with a long time span. MD4 and MD5 both favor Little-Endian architectures.

However, that does not mean that MD5 is useless—far from it. It's currently used in many Internet protocols, and the small hash size is actually better for many applications, as it requires less storage. In addition, MD5 is the fastest of all hashing algorithms presented. Many Unix and Linux systems have a built-in command, `md5sum`, that hashes a file using MD5. This can be used to verify file integrity and for many other applications.

The SHA Family

In 1993 the NIST introduced the Secure Hash Standard (SHS) as the federal standard for cryptographic hashes. This algorithm, creatively named "Secure Hash Algorithm," is an NSA-designed modification of MD4, but the rationale behind the changes has not been made public. Two years later, the original algorithm, now known as SHA-0, was recalled and replaced with SHA-1 because of security concerns, and again, the exact details of what the problems were and why the added 1-bit rotation would fix it were not made public. Independently, only theoretical problems have been found with SHA-0 [ChJo1998], so it's clear the NSA knows a lot more about construction hash functions than the public does. Today, "SHA" and "SHS" refer to "SHA-1."

Like MD4 and MD5, SHA-1 operates on 512-bit block; however, it is optimized for Big-Endian (e.g., Intel) architectures and produces a 160-bit hash. The added security and larger output size makes SHA-1 run at half the speed of MD5.

Although a 160-bit algorithm would seem secure, because of the birthday attack, it only produces 80 bits of security. In addition, many applications of hashes are for generating keys, and many algorithms now take keys that are much longer than 160 bits. To address these problems, in 2000 the NIST announced three new extensions of the SHA-1 that generate hashes of 256, 384, and 512 bits: SHA-256, SHA-384, and SHA-512.

SHA-256 is a natural extension of SHA-1. It operates using the same internal block size, but it uses more words but with a few less rounds. Even though the standard is not officially approved (as of this writing), SHA-256 is appearing in cryptographic software and hardware.

SHA-512 is a bit different. It works on a 1024-bit buffer and works on eight 64-bit blocks internally. Partially since it uses 64-bit blocks and operates on twice as much data, the performance takes a hit on 32-bit machines. Roughly, one iteration takes five times as long as SHA-1.

SHA-384 is a bit of an oddball. It's basically SHA-512 with different initialization vectors and just truncates the result to give 384 bits. Unless you have some need for exactly 384 bits, you might as well use SHA-512, since the running time is the same.

The RIPE-MD Family

The RIPE-MD family got its start as part of the RIPE (Race Integrity Primitives Evaluation) project, which was a European project to produce standardized cryptographic primitives based on open design processes. Not surprisingly, this algorithm has wide use in Europe.

In 1993, RIPE-MD was updated with RIPE-MD 160, which generates a 160-bit hash and was based on input form MD4, MD5, and the original algorithm. The final result was roughly two modified versions of MD4 running in parallel. It's a very conservative design that to date has no known flaws. However, this added security comes at a cost: It runs approximately 20 percent slower than SHA-1. Like MD4 and MD5, it favors Little-Endian architecture.

In addition to RIPE-MD 160, a smaller version, RIPE-MD 128, was produced as a secure drop-in replacement for the original RIPE-MD algorithm. More recently, the inventors of RIPE-MD 160 designed RIPE-MD 256 and RIPE-MD 320, which extend the algorithms to produce larger hash sizes. Unlike the extended SHA variants, these versions *do not* provide extra security; the expected number of messages before a collision occurs for RIPE-MD 256 is roughly the same as RIPE-MD 128. They are only designed to produce more bits, which can be useful for generating keys and random values. These algorithms were only published on the inventors' Web site and have not been used in any standards.

Hash Standards and Practices

Which hash function to use? In some cases you might not have a choice; the receiving party may only accept MD5, for instance. But for new applications, here are some basic guidelines:

- Use MD5 for basic file integrity checks as a checksum replacement. It's also useful for generating cryptographic tokens that have a low value or a short lifetime, as well as in cases where extreme speed or performance is a real concern. Do not use MD5 for digital signatures.
- SHA-1 is the de facto standard as a general cryptographic hash. It's the standard hash for digital signatures and other cryptographic applications.
- RIPE-MD 160 is a perfectly acceptable alternative to SHA-1. It's listed in virtually every standard, such as IEEE, ANSI, and ISO (except FIPS, of course).
- SHA-256, 384, 512 are still quite new and as of this writing have not officially been made into a FIPS. For generating keys for symmetric ciphers, they should work fine right now, although there are other methods. For use in digital signatures, I'd wait until the standard becomes official and algorithms have had some time to be optimized. Check with the NIST's Secure Hash Standard Web site at `csrc.nist.gov/encryption/tkhash.htm` for further details.
- Because 128-bit hashes are on their way out, RIPE-MD 128 is not recommended for new applications. If MD5 becomes broken, this will be a good drop-in replacement. However, using MD5 is much faster.

- RIPE-MD 256 and RIPE-MD 380 should not be used for digital signatures. While these are well designed, I wouldn't recommend them. They aren't part of any standard, and they don't offer more security, only more bits. If you need to generate more bits, there are better ways of doing so.
- Do not use MD2, MD4, SHA-0, or RIPE-MD (the original) unless you have some legacy application that requires them.

Hashed Message Authentication Codes (HMACs)

In general, a Message Authentication Code (MAC) is a device that allows the receiver to know the author sent the message and that it is intact. Originally, MACs were based on using DES in CBC mode as described in the FIPS 81 standard. But cipher-based MACs are out of favor now, and the current standard is to use Hashed Message Authentication Codes (HMACs). Here, a secret key is added to the message and then hashed normally. This will thwart any dictionary attacks, since the attacker will not know the key.

HMACs are commonly used for message integrity (is the message received the same as the message sent?) and authentication (did the right party send this message?). If the message is stored or transmitted with a HMAC, the receiver with the secret key can verify the message's integrity. If the message has been altered in any way, a different hash will be computed. Depending on the HMAC used, it can also help indicate or verify whom the message came from.

Given that the original message is frequently known either in its entirety or is an educated guess, and since the original message is frequently quite short—for instance, a control code or a price—there is great concern that the HMAC doesn't leak any information about the secret key. While the underlying hash algorithms are not supposed to leak any information of the original message, they have not been *proven* leakproof. Given the security and applications, there are many guidelines on key selection, padding around the message and keys, and the use of multiple iterations of the hash algorithm.

The Standard HMAC

The standard HMAC is specified in ANSI X9.71 and RFC2104 and in a forthcoming FIPS. It computes, in effect, a hash of a hash by using two different keys. While this may seem excessive, this scheme has proven sound

[BeCaKr1996]. Simpler schemes, on the other hand, that don't use nested hashing have been shown to have flaws.

Schematically, the HMAC can be represented by:

```
H((k0 ⊕ opad) || H((k0 ⊕ ipad) || m)
```

where:

- `H` is a hash function that has an internal block size of B bytes (e.g., MD5 and SHA-1 uses 512 bits, or 64 bytes).
- `opad` is a byte array of length B filled with value 0x5c.
- `ipad` is a byte array of length B filled with value 0x36.
- k_0 is a key of length B based on a original key k, such that:
  - If $k \leq B$, then pad $k_0 = k$ with zeros at the end so it's B bytes.
  - If $k > B$, then pad $k_0 = H(k)$ with zeros so it's B bytes.

This technique ensures that each hash computation requires at least two internal blocks to be processed, further scrambling the bits. This scheme can be implemented very efficiently. The values $k_0 \oplus$ ipad and $k_0 \oplus$ opad can be precomputed, but they must be treated as if they are the actual key k.

Legacy Concatenation Schemes

You would expect that, given the wonderful properties of a cryptographic hash, you could just append or prepend a key with the message, then take the hash:

```
K = key
M = message
H = cryptographic hash function
HMAC = H(k || m)
```

A more secure approach is the so-called padded envelope, where you make sure the internal hash algorithm is iterated more than once by adding padding after the first key:

```
HMAC = H(k || p || m || k)
```

It turns out that these systems are *not* architecturally sound, but an attack on them is impractical [PrVa1996].

It's conceivable (but I'm having a hard time thinking of a case) that you might find one of these schemes useful for low-security (meaning the message has low value; if it's forged or extracted from the hash, little is lost) but extremely performance-sensitive applications that use small messages. In this scenario, you'd want the length of `k||m` to be less than the hash's internal block size (typically, 448 bits) so the hash only iterates once. In every other case, forget everything I've said here and use the standard HMAC.

HMAC Standards and Practices

As mentioned, the current standard HMAC algorithm is RFC 2107 using MD5, SHA-1, or RIPE-MD 160. There are a few other requirements regarding the key size and how many bytes of the hash to use:

- Keys must be $\geq L/2$, where L is the size of the hash output.
- Keys $\geq L$ do not increase security.
- If Key > B (block size), transform the key by talking the hash of the key. This results in a new key of L bytes.

Summary

While a lot of material was covered, it can be summarized quite compactly:

- AES/Rijndael is the new standard and is recommended for new applications. The other AES finalists are all acceptable as well. All of these algorithms are based on a 128-bit block size and can handle at least key sizes of 128 bits and beyond.
- Block ciphers that are 64 bits are useful in many applications when encrypting small messages. In this case, Triple DES is the most secure but also the slowest. Blowfish is commonly used as a faster alternative.
- Use CBC-mode when possible.
- For padding, PKCS is the most common, although fixed padding (with zeros) is fine for smaller messages.
- For hashes, SHA-1 is the most common, while MD5 is useful for a smaller, faster hash in certain applications.

Public Key Cryptography

Public key cryptography is based on a system using *two* keys: one for encryption and another for decryption. One of the keys is deemed "private," meaning it must be kept secret, while the other is deemed "public" and can freely be distributed. That may not sound like much of an improvement over secret key cryptography, but it is. The big problem with secret key cryptography is how two parties will share keys. Somehow, in advance of the communication, the secret keys need to be shared. With public key cryptography, this problem doesn't exist. Instead, one party looks up the other's public key and performs encryption. Only the receiver, using his or her private key, can decrypt the message.

These systems work by using "trapdoor" mathematical problems. These problems are typically easy to compute but very hard to invert, such as to do multiplication is relatively easy when compared to long division (at least when using pencil and paper).

Public Key Ciphers

The most common application of public key cryptosystems is for encryption. While public key, or asymmetric, ciphers can operate in the same way secret key, or symmetric, ciphers do, which use various modes of operation to encrypt the message, in practice this is rarely if ever done, since the performance is just too slow. To work around this problem, a public key cipher is only used to encode one block that contains a key for a symmetric cipher. The symmetric cipher performs the actual encryption of the plaintext. This scheme is sometimes referred to as *enveloping*. Table 3.1 shows a comparison of symmetric and asymmetric ciphers.

Since Public Key Cryptosystems (PKCS) are based on "hard" problems and not specific functions that scramble and scatter bits, virtually all systems require the plaintext message to be transformed into a different format before being encrypted in order to be secure. These transformations are known as all or nothing transformations (AONT), since the original message can't be recovered unless you know the entire encoded message. They are somewhat similar to a reverse-hash function. With AONT functions you can't recover the original message unless you have every bit of the AONT encoding. The need can be demonstrated with a simple function such as $m^2 \bmod n$. Clearly, if the message is "1," then the encryption algorithm doesn't do very much, since the ciphertext is also "1."

Brute-force attacks against public key ciphers are very different than with symmetric ciphers. With public key ciphers, the keys themselves may be *thousands* of bits long, which makes it completely impractical to try every value. Instead, the brute-force attack works on the underlying mathematical problem, which when solved, will allow the keys to be recomputed.

Table 3.1 Comparison between Symmetric and Asymmetric Ciphers

SYMMETRIC	ASYMMETRIC
One key to encrypt and decrypt.	One key to encrypt, another key to decrypt.
Key is array of bytes.	Key is typically one or more integers (represented as bytes).
Block size is small and fixed; key size may be variable.	Block size may be large and depends on key size.
Specifically designed to scatter bits.	Designed around a "hard" mathematical problem.
Brute-force attacks try keys.	Brute-force attacks "decompose" a parameter to recover keys.
Message can be encrypted as is.	Message requires transformation before being encrypted.
Faster.	Slower.

Other Systems

Either by using encryption and decryption in novel ways or by reusing the underlying mathematics, various new types of cryptographic *primitives* have been devised. These new primitives, outlined in the following sections, provide new functionality that was previous unobtainable using traditional secret key techniques.

Digital Signatures

Digital signatures function like a normal signature; they provide proof that a message came from the signer. At its simplest, a signature algorithm works in reverse of public key encryption. Given a message, it's hashed and the hash is encrypted using the *private* key (this is reverse of normal encryption where the public key is used for encryption). Someone wishing to verify the signature recomputes the hash and then using the *public* key decrypts the signature and compares the two. If they match, then the signature is valid, since only the person that held the matching private key would be able to create this signature. The catch here, and it's a big one, is the verification step must have some way of knowing the public key actually matches with the corresponding private key; in other words, it must ensure the public key actually belongs to the person in question. To solve this problem, public keys are issued in the form of a *certificate*, which is the public key signed again, by a trusted third party.

Key Agreements

Key agreements allow two unknown parties to simultaneously derive a common secret value without actually sending the value over the wire. This is enormously useful since it allows communicating securely by using the secret value as a key for a symmetric cipher. This is the basis for the Secure Sockets Layer (SSL) protocol used for secure communication on the Web. Key agreements can also be used as a basis for public key encryption.

Zero-Knowledge Schemes

Zero-knowledge schemes operate like reverse secret-sharing schemes. With key agreements two parties agree on a common unknown value without sending it "in the clear." With zero-knowledge schemes, two parties have the same value but wish to verify that they both have the same value without actually sending the value. By zero-knowledge, each party can verify they have the secret but without leaking *any* information about the value itself. While very interesting technically, in practice, this scheme hasn't found much use, since leaking a little information is normally acceptable.

Secret Sharing

Secret sharing splits a secret value into parts so that each part or combination of parts doesn't leak any information of the underlying secret. The pieces can be combined (in any order) to retrieve the secret.

Public Key Security Classification

The notions of security are categorized by a property or goal of the cipher, and an attack model it withstands. The standard goals are as follows:

One-way (OW). The most basic principal in cryptography is whether, given a ciphertext, the attack can produce the original plaintext. In practice this means can the attacker successfully complete a brute-force attack.

Indistinguishability (IND). As mentioned in the secret key case, if a system has indistinguishability, an attacker is unable to determine by inspection which plaintext belongs with its matching ciphertext.

Nonmalleability (NM). One cannot alter the ciphertext so that the decrypted text is meaningfully or closely related to the original plaintext.

The standard attack models are variations of:

Chosen plaintext. Using the public key, an attacker can generate ciphertext for arbitrary plaintext. The attacker would then use the plaintext-ciphertext pairing to determine the key.

Nonadaptive chosen ciphertext (CCA1). In addition to the public key, the attacker also has access to a "decryption oracle" or "decryption API," where arbitrary ciphertext can be decrypted, but only before the challenge is issued. This means, for example, an employee can use the oracle but then be fired. Could the employee have cracked the key?

Adaptive chosen ciphertext (CCA2). Similar to the preceding, except the attacker has access to the decryption oracle, and the only restriction is he or she can't use it on the challenge text itself. This is a bit more artificial, but perhaps the attacker has access to some protocol that can decrypt only certain-sized text. Given a cipher, you can say it is "OW-CCA1 secure" if the cipher was designed to have a one-way property and resists chosen-plaintext attacks.

As you might expect, ciphers typically meet many of the goals and resist multiple types of attacks, and the different notions of security are interrelated. As shown in Figure 3.1, an arrow between two boxes means implications, while the lack of an arrow normally means there are provable counterexamples and thus no implication (for instance, NM-CCA2 implies NM-CCA1, but the reverse is provably not the case).

Not surprisingly, CCA $\Rightarrow$ CCA1 $\Rightarrow$ CPA, since in each case the attacker is given more tools and information. Likewise, NM $\Rightarrow$ IND $\Rightarrow$ OW. Onewayness is a very basic property of any cipher, while indistinguishability prevents leakage and nonmalleability prevents corruption.

NM-CCA2 and IND-CCA2 are equivalent, and they are "strongest" notions of the security. If the cipher is NM-CCA2 or IND-CCA2 secure, then all other notions of security are implied. As shown in Figure 3.2, we can roughly rank the different types of security by how many other notions they imply. This is a bit artificial, since for public key ciphers anything less than NM-CCA1 is deemed insecure.

Oddly, many public key ciphers out of the box aren't particularly secure. Before the encryption step, the input needs to be preprocessed, or how the encryption process is altered must be specified, in order to make it at least NM-CCA1. If the final algorithm results in a security of anything less that NM-CCA, it is typically deemed insecure and is not used.

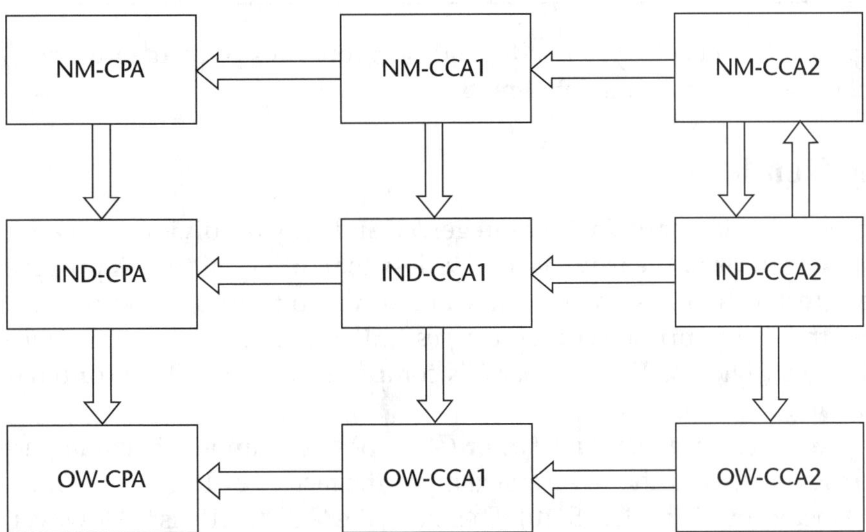

Figure 3.1 Relationship between different security notions.

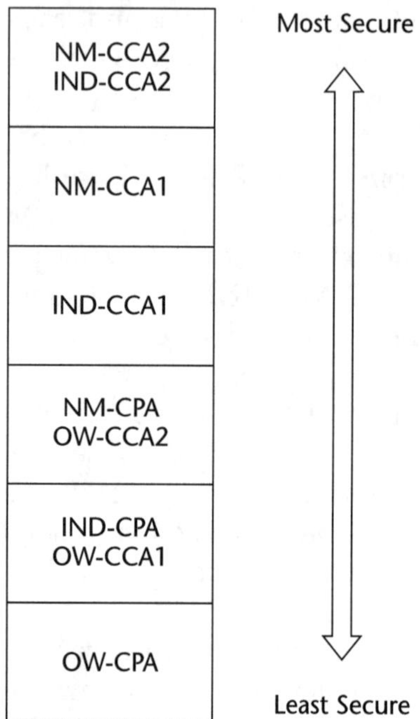

Figure 3.2 Relationship and ranking of security categories.

Fundamental Mathematics

Most public key cryptosystems depend on properties of prime numbers, and all heavily use modular arithmetic.

Prime Numbers

An integer a is a factor of another integer b if and only if a divides b (evenly, with no remainder). Clearly, a is always less than or equal to b. A positive integer greater than 1 is *prime* if there are only two factors, 1 and itself. A number that is not prime is called *composite*. For instance, 5 is prime since only 1 and 5 divide 5. The number 6 is composite since $6 = 2 \times 3$ (or 6 has two factors, 2 and 3).

The *greatest common denominator*, or GCD, of two numbers is the largest shared factor between them. As an example, the factors of 15 are (1, 3, 5, 15) and the factors of 10 are (1, 2, 5, 10). Therefore, the GCD(10,15) is 5. However, there are much more efficient ways of computing the GCD of two numbers other than computing every factor. See [Knuth98.3] for details. Since a prime number only has two factors, the GCD of a prime and another number other than itself is always 1.

The Distribution of Prime Numbers

A Prime number can only be divided trivially by 1 and itself. Many popular public key cryptographic systems depend on prime numbers and a related aspect of factoring: decomposing a number into its prime components. In the case of the RSA system, two random prime numbers of approximately the same size are needed for every key pair.

A fair question to ask then is this: How many primes are there? And how rare are they? Fortunately, Euclid proved 2,300 years ago that there are infinitely many prime numbers. (In short, say there are only n primes, and let $x=, p_1 p_2 ... p_{n},$. Then $x + 1$ isn't divisible by any of the previous primes; therefore, x is prime.)

This is all well and good; however, it does not tell us anything about the distribution of prime numbers. Certain ranges of numbers might not have any primes at all. Another way of looking at the distribution of primes is by considering the functioning $\pi(x)$ defined to be the number of prime numbers less than x. The prime number theorem states that $\pi(x)$ is asymptotic (or roughly similar when x is large) to $x/\ln x$. Using this formula we can estimate the number of primes that can be represented by a certain bit size:

Number of primes with n-bit representation =

$$\pi(2^n) - \pi(2^{n-1}) \approx 1.447 \times 2^{n-1}/n.$$

Table 3.2 shows the number of primes for each n-bit prime.

Table 3.2 Approximate Number of Primes that Are n-Bits Long

N-BIT PRIME	APPROXIMATE NUMBER OF PRIMES
128	1.9×10^{36}
256	3.3×10^{74}
512	1.9×10^{151}
1024	1.3×10^{305}
2048	1.4×10^{613}

In other words, there are *many* primes and this is very important for cryptography, since large primes (512-bit and up) are used for keys or for generating keys. In particular:

- It's infeasible that two parties will randomly pick the same prime number. The odds are even lower for the same people picking *two* identical prime numbers.
- It's infeasible to generate a list of all primes with 512-bit or higher representation.
- Even if you had that list, it's so long, it's infeasible to iterate through all of them (and perform some operation using them).

One other condition should be that it's not too hard finding a prime number. Fortunately, the prime number theorem has an interesting corollary: Given a "large" random number x, the odds of it being a prime number is approximately $1/\ln x$. Given an n-bit random string and setting the least-significant bit to 1 so it's always an odd number, the probability of it being prime is $1/\ln 2^n$ or $1/n\,(\ln 2)$. For a 1024-bit prime, the odds are about 1 in 700, which isn't bad, provided we have some quick way of testing to see whether a number is prime.

Prime Testing

Given a number n, how can you tell if it is prime? The naïve approach would be to try and divide every value between 2 and $\sqrt{n}$. This certainly works but is quite slow.

For reasonably small numbers an ancient technique called the Sieve of Eratosthenes can be used. This involves simply making a list of integers from 2 to n. Starting at the leftmost at 2, cross out all multiples of 2. Now move to 3 and cross out all of its multiples. Multiples of 4 have been crossed out already, so move to 5, and so on. At the end, if n has survived, it is a prime (and you have a nice list of all primes less than n). This can be implemented surprisingly fast, since it doesn't require any division, which is typically the slowest integer operation on a computer.

Using trial division with small primes is a very efficient way of weeding out obviously composite numbers. It works well since half of the integers are divisible by 2, a third divisible by 3, a fifth divisible by 5—in other words, most numbers are divisible by small primes. This can certainly be extended by downloading prime tables that are available on the Internet (or you can compute them yourself), but at some point the cost of division is going to be excessive. However, trial division using small primes is so useful and fast that this is normally done before using any of the more advanced tests.

True Primality Tests for Large Numbers

There are many more tests for numbers with certain forms, but currently there are only two main algorithms for testing general numbers. The fastest is the APR-CL, which runs in $O((\ln n)^{c \ln \ln \ln n})$ bit operations. This means large numbers of cryptographic interest can be checked in under a minute. Sometimes this is known by the name of the Jacobi sum test or APR.

The other algorithm is the Elliptic Curve Primality Proving (ECPP) or Atkin's test. With a running time of a bit more than $O((\ln n)^6)$, it's not as fast as the previous algorithm; however, it has the advantage that it produces a *certificate of primality*. Without having to go though the entire test, the verifier can quickly check the certificate and know that the number in question is prime.

Both algorithms are quite complicated. I won't present the details here, since they involve too much work for cryptographic purposes anyway.

Probabilistic Tests

A probabilistic test for primality tests "partial primality." The more you run the test with a pass, the more likely it is the number is prime, but the test can never prove that a number is prime. On the other hand, if a test fails, the number is surely composite.

The main advantage of probabilistic tests is that they are radically faster than their absolute counterparts. This is crucial when we look at generating a prime number in the next section, since we may need to make many checks for primality of very large numbers.

This would be useless if it wasn't that *absolutely* knowing the primality of a number is not necessary for cryptographic purposes. Specifically:

- Numbers that are "nearly prime" work just as well as "truly prime" in many algorithms.
- Conversely, algorithms that attack the mathematics of encryption will run just as slow with a near prime as with a true prime.
- No cryptographic system, end to end, is 100 percent secure. The weak link is highly likely to be something else.

Strong Probable Prime Test

The strong probable prime test is the basis for a number of other tests. It requires a particular base or test value *a*. If the test fails, the number is definitely composite, and sometimes the number *a* is called a "strong witness" for *n* being composite, since it provides a quick way of testing for compositeness. If the test succeeds, the number is called a "base-*a* pseudoprime" or a "strong pseudoprime to base *a*." It could be a composite, in which case it's a called a "base-*a* strong liar." And finally, if the number is truly prime, the test will always pass, but the test by itself can't tell you with certainty.

```
n = 1 + 2^s r; // r is odd
a = , 2 ≤ a ≤ n-2; // base

y = a^r mod n
if (y == 1 or y == n-1) then "strong pseudoprime to base a"
for (j = 1; j < r-1; j++)
  y = y^2 mod n
  if y = n-1 then "strong pseudoprime to base a"
return "composite"
```

The base $a = 2$ is especially useful because it can be optimized by using shift operations instead of using modular exponentiations and modular squarings.

Miller-Rabin

The Miller test states that if given $n>17$ and if n passes the strong probable prime test with every base from 2 to $2 \ln^2 n$, then n is prime (*or* a famous mathematical conjecture, the Riemann hypothesis, is false, but for practical purposes this can be safely ignored).

While interesting, computationally it involves too much work. The Miller-Rabin extends the basic Miller test by converting it into a probabilistic algorithm, by testing using random bases. An odd composite number will pass t iterations of the strong probable prime test with a random base with probability $1/4^t$ (and this is a conservative upper bound too).

Current standard practice as set forth in IEEE 1363-2000 mandates a confidence level of 2^{-100}, or rather, 25 iterations, of Miller-Rabin when you are testing an *arbitrary* number. However, if you are attempting to generate a *random* prime, you can also take into account the distributions of prime numbers and dramatically reduce the number of iterations. Given a random k-bit number, the probability it is composite after t rounds is given by [DaLaPo1993]:

$$P_{k,t} = 2^{t+4} k \left(2^{-\sqrt{tk}}\right) \sqrt{\tfrac{k}{t}}$$

Solving for the standard tolerance of 2^{-100} gives us the data in Table 3.3.

Table 3.3 Iterations of Miller-Rabin Algorithm Required for 2^{-100} Confidence

BITS	NUMBER OF ITERATIONS
160	34
192	25
256	17
512	8
768	5
1024	4
> 1854	2

If you do the math, for large numbers only one iteration is necessary, but it's common practice to always do two rounds, especially using the test with base $a = 2$, since it's very fast. This table does not include the effect of using trial division first. Doing so will only increase the confidence level of the Miller-Rabin test.

It's very important to note the difference between testing an arbitrary number versus a random number. A *random number* is one you have generated using a "secure random source"—you know it's random. An *arbitrary number* is one where you don't know the origin. It might be random, it might be claimed to be random, or it might be a specially constructed composite number that a very strong liar specifically designed to fool you.

Sequence-Based Tests

You may recall the Fibonacci sequence that starts with $x_0 = 0$ and $x_1 = 1$ and has the recurrence relationship of $x_n = x_{n-2} + x_{n-1}$ (e.g., 0, 1, 1, 2, 3, 5, 8,...).There is an interesting result that if n is prime, then if:

$n \equiv 2 \bmod 5$, or $n \equiv 3 \bmod 5$, then $x_{n-1} \equiv 0 \bmod n$
$n \equiv 1 \bmod 5$, or $n \equiv 4 \bmod 5$ then $x_{n+1} \equiv 0 \bmod n$
$n \equiv 0 \bmod 5$, then $x_n \equiv 0 \bmod n$

As in the case of the strong probable prime test, there are composites that are liars; however, this situation appears to be rare. While it would seem that generating the nth Fibonacci number would be difficult, you can use specialized algorithms for generating it in approximated $\log_2 n$ steps using basic integer multiplication and addition. There are also generalizations of the Fibonacci test, including the Lucas test and the newer Frobenius test, which provide even better results.

Elementary Number Theory

I intend this book to be essentially nonmathematical and do not set out to formally prove any of the results. However, for clarification, I must occasionally make use of some basic abstract algebra and number theory.

Modular Arithmetic

This book will make heavy use of modular arithmetic. The most common use of modular arithmetic is in time, where minutes and seconds "roll over" after 59. Mathematically, two numbers a and b are said to be *congruent* under a *modulus* n, or $a \equiv b \bmod n$, if they only differ by a multiple of modulus. For example, $61 \equiv 1 \bmod 60$ and $15 \equiv 3 \bmod 12$. This works for negative numbers as well: $-1 \equiv 59 \bmod 60$.

Given $a \equiv b \bmod n$, we have the properties shown in Table 3.4.

Division works a bit differently. First, you can't just use normal division like you do for real numbers, since that will probably result in a noninteger. To divide by $a \pmod{n}$, you need to find a *multiplicative inverse* for a, such as $aa^{-1} \equiv 1 \bmod n$. The process of finding a^{-1} is often called a *modular inversion*, and in many cases, a^{-1} will not exist. For instance, there is no number $a \pmod{10}$ such that $2a \equiv 1 \bmod 10$. However, given $3 \pmod{10}$ we know its inverse is 7, so we are to divide by 3 (or 7) in this case.

Computational Modular Arithmetic

Many times in cryptography, we'll be raising numbers to very high powers: $a^b \bmod n$. Fortunately (and in fact essential) for cryptography, there exist many very efficient algorithms for doing this. We won't go into detail, but the essential point is that you can do repeated modular squarings. For instance:

$$a^5 \bmod n = a\,(a^2 \bmod n)^2 \bmod n$$

is only two modular squarings and one multiplication, and more importantly, it only requires that you can store a number n^2 in size, instead of n^5. There are many more tricks, including efficient modular algorithms for:

- Using modular inversion.
- Using modular squaring.
- Using modular exponentiation.
- Solving simultaneous congruences $x = a_1 \bmod n_1 = a_2 \bmod n_2$.... (This is the Chinese remainder theorem when certain conditions are met.)
- Performing mod n on an arbitrary number without using division.

For a more detailed account see [CrPo2000] or [Knuth1998].

Table 3.4 Properties of Modular Arithmetic, given $a \equiv b \bmod n$

Reflexive	$b \equiv a \bmod n$
Additive	$a + c \equiv b + c \bmod n$
Multiplicative	$ac \equiv bc \bmod n$
Distributive	$a(b + c) \equiv ab + bc \bmod n$

Additive Groups

Just as physicists examine the world to distill relevant properties, so do mathematicians, except they examine common mathematical objects. One simple observation is that when adding any two integers, the sum is another integer, as opposed to a fractional number or floating-point number. In other words, adding two items produces another item of the same type. This property also shows up in many places—rational numbers, real numbers, solutions to equations, polynomials—and is very useful, since it means there are no "special cases." When a set of objects (integers, solutions, etc.) and an operation (in this case addition) has this property, it's called an *additive group* and can more formally be described in terms of the following properties:

Closure. Any two elements added together is another element of the group.

Identity. There is an identity element so that for every element in the group, $a + 0 = a$.

Inverse. Every element a has an inverse element $-a$, such that $a + (-a) = 0$.

Clearly, looking at the rules for modulo arithmetic, the number [0, 1, ..., n–1] forms an additive group under addition. This set is denoted Z_n.

In general, a group need not have the communitive property where $a + b = b + a$. Some groups do not have this property, but those that do are called *abelian groups*.

Multiplicative Groups

Another obvious property of integers is that two integers multiplied together is again an integer, and this type of behavior shows up in many places in mathematics. Functionally this is just the same as additive groups, but in this case you would be using a different operation, and the notation is different. Formally, a multiplicative group has the following properties:

Closure. Any two elements multiplied together is another element of the group.

Identity. There is an identity element so that for every element in the group, $1 \times a = a$.

Inverse. Every element a has an inverse element a^{-1}, such that $aa^{-1} = 0$.

When using nonzero real numbers, $a^{-1} = 1/a$, but under modulo arithmetic, there might not be an inverse. Recall that you can divide only if the greatest common divisor of the modulus and the divisor is 1. If the divisor is a prime number, then this is true for any number (mod n), and thus $[0,...n-1]$ is a group under multiplication if and only if n is prime. This is denoted by Z^{*}_{n}.

Fields

Based on the preceding, the numbers $[0, 1, 2, \ldots, p-1]$ can be thought of as: An additive group Zn using normal addition, the multiplicative group $Z_n{}^*$ using normal multiplication rules, or a field, GF(p) of F_p, the general field of order p.

If you read the cryptographic literature, any of the notions may be used. Frequently, it doesn't matter and it's just shorthand for saying $[0, 1, 2,..., p-1]$.

Rings

Finally, you might have noticed that $[0, ..., n-1]$ form an additive group, and if n is prime, they form a multiplicative group and together form a field. However, if n is not prime, you still have an additive group, and you have 2 out of the 3 requirements for a multiplicative group. In this case, the set is called a *ring*.

In fact, the set of integers by themselves is a ring, since regular division of two integers is frequently not an integer and it's denoted by a plain Z (and is the origin of the other symbols used).

Orders and Generators

The order of an element in an additive group is how many times do you need to add itself so that the result is zero:

$$ax \bmod n = 0$$
$$ax \bmod n = 1$$

A generator is an element that has a $o(a) = n$. In other words, the entire group (or field) can be generated by successive additions or multiplication. For instance, 3 is a generator in Z_{10}, since successively adding 3 results in 10 elements 0, ..., 9: 3, 6, 9, 2, 5, 8, 1, 4, 7, 0.

Public Key Encryption and Major PKCS Categories

Three major categories of public key cryptosystems (PKCS) are used. The first, RSA, originally patented and marketed by RSA Security (www.rsasecurity.com) is by far the most common and the easiest to understand, because it only uses basic modular arithmetic. The ElGamal and similar schemes became popular, since the patent covering the system expired in 1997, four years before the RSA in 2001 and could be integrated without paying any licensing fees. To the end user, both ElGamal and RSA are more or less equivalent in terms of security, and typical security parameter is 1024 bits. The final scheme, the Elliptic Curve Cryptosystem (ECC) translates the mathematical problems from the ElGamal system into a different domain. The result is that the same level of security can be achieved using 160 bits. While it is not patented, ECC has been developed and marketed primarily by Certicom (www.certicom.com) and today is a popular choice for embedded and resource constrained systems. See Table 3.5 for a comparison of the major algorithms for public key encryption.

Table 3.5 Comparison of Major Public Key Encryption Algorithms

	RSA	ELGAMAL (DIFFIE-HELLMAN)	ELLIPTIC CURVE
Patent status	Expired in 2001	Expired in 1997	Not patented, but many low-level optimizations are
Mathematical problem	Integer factorization	Discrete logarithm over a finite field	Discrete logarithm of elliptic curve
Best known attack	Subexponential	Exponential	Exponential
Average key size	1024 bits	1024 bits	160 bits
Corporate "champion"	RSA Security	None	Certicom

RSA and Integer Factorization

The RSA cryptosystem was first publicly presented in 1976 by Ron Rivest (whom we met before with the RC ciphers and MD series of hash function), Adi Shamir, and Leonard Adleman [RiShAd1978]. They went on to patent the system (U.S. Patent 4,405,829) and to form a company of the same name—RSA Security.

RSA has proven popular because the underlying algorithms are quite simple (even memorizable) and because it lends itself to study and implementation in both software and hardware. Other factors in its popularity include commercial-grade implementation and corporate support. In addition, the RSA system is self-contained, in that the keys contain all the information needed to use the system. No additional parameters are needed. The RSA algorithm derives its strength from the trapdoor function of factoring. Multiplying is easy, but decomposing a number into its original components is much more time-consuming,

The patent expired in 2001; however, RSA does hold a patent on a particularly efficient method of doing the computations required (see *MultiPrime RSA Algorithm* coming up in the chapter).

Factoring

Closely related to prime number verification and generation is the issue of taking a number and decomposing it into its prime factors. Every integer can be decomposed in this manner. It turns out that given an arbitrary number, factoring it is a computationally intensive process.

Most algorithms for factoring are really splitting algorithms. Instead of full factorization, they will just return two factors, $n = ab$. Each can be then tested for primality using the preceding algorithms. If either is composite, it is resplit. The process continues until a full factorization continues. This recursion is needed in cryptographic applications, since most composite numbers have a special form: They are just the product of two primes.

To factor an arbitrary number, you typically start with one of Pollard's algorithms and if they fail, progress to more complicated methods (see Table 3.6). However, factoring an RSA number is a little different because we already know the underlying structure has two very large prime factors.

Using the standard notation for complexity, it's a bit hard to see if the new algorithms offer any improvement. It's even hard to see why the latter three algorithms are known as subexponential. They certainly *look* exponential. The differences can be reconciled because in cryptographic literature, you determine complexity by using the number of *bits* of n (or the

Table 3.6 Comparison of Factoring Algorithms

ALGORITHM	FIRST INTRODUCED	COMPLEXITY FOR $N=PQ$	COMPLEXITY FOR $N = 2^M$
Lehman Method	1974	$O(n^{1/3}\ln \ln n)$	$O(2^{m/3} \ln 0.69m) > O(e^{0.232m})$
Pollard's rho	1975	$O(n^{1/4})$	$O(2^{m/4}) = O(e^{0.173m})$
Pollard's p-1	1974	$O(n^{1/4})$	$O(2^{m/4}) = O(e^{0.173m})$
Elliptic Curve	1987	$O(e^{\sqrt{2 \ln n \ln \ln n}})$	$O(e^{\sqrt{1.39m \ln 0.69m}}) < O(e^{cm})$
Quadradic Sieve	1987	$O(e^{\sqrt{\ln n \ln \ln n}})$	$O(e^{\sqrt{0.69m \ln 0.69m}}) < O(e^{cm})$
Number Field Sieve	1994	$O(e^{1.92 (\ln n)^{1/3} (\ln \ln n)^{2/3}})$	$O(e^{1.7m^{1/3} (\ln 0.69m)^{2/3}}) < O(e^{cm})$

length of n), not the actual number n. Converting the estimates using the length of n, it's clear to see that the first three algorithms are exponential, but the latter three still aren't clear. The trick is to see that the exponent is actually less than m. No matter how small c is, the function e^{cm} grows faster when compared to these functions. Therefore, it's subexponential.

Normally, the functions in the Big-O notation are just estimates, since they can be off by either very large or very small constants. However, in this case, they work quite well. Visually one can see the amount of work needed to factor numbers using different algorithms in Figure 3.3.

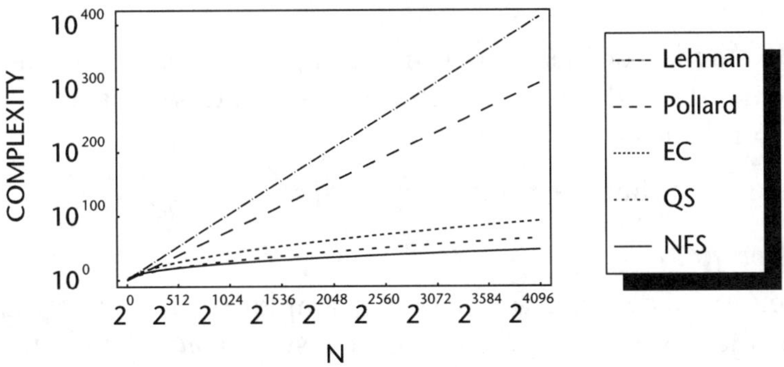

Figure 3.3 Comparison of factoring algorithms.

The RSA Problem

The RSA cipher doesn't directly use factoring to provide security. Instead, it uses a similar problem that, to date, is based on factor. Given n, a composite number, and a value e, compute the eth root of c mod n; in other words, find m such that $m = c^e \bmod n$. The value e is specially constructed from the factors of n such that this root actually exists and is unique. There is no known efficient algorithm for computing this root, and the only real way of computing such a root is to factor n so that one can recompute e and some related parameters. So while related to factoring, no one has proven that RSA Problem is equivalent to factoring. There are some hints that it's not equivalent, but even so, it's unlikely to be significantly weaker than factoring.

The Algorithm

RSA uses (indirectly) the trapdoor function of multiplication/factoring. Multiplication is easy, but given a number, determining what its factors are is very time-consuming. However, factoring by itself doesn't directly provide a useful way for making a cryptosystem. Instead, RSA uses the factoring problem to construct another related problem that has good properties.

Key Generation

The first step in using RSA is setting up a key pair:

1. Generate two large and distinct primes p, q roughly the same size (same bit length representation).
2. Compute $n = pq$, and $\phi = (p - 1)(q - 1)$.
3. Optionally, choose e such that the GCD(e, ϕ) =1, or, instead, choose a prime number and skip the computation of the greatest common denominator (this is easier in practice).
4. Using the extended Euclidean algorithm, compute the unique value d, such that $ed \equiv 1$ (mod ϕ with $1 < d < \phi$. These conditions ensure that given e or d, the other *uniquely* exists.

The public key is (n, e), and the private key is (n, d).

Encryption and Decryption

Once keys are set up, using them is remarkably simple. The message m to encrypt is represented by an integer $[0, n{-}1]$. The result $c = m^e \bmod n$ is the encrypted message. This is where the RSA problem comes in. If it were easy to compute the eth root of c, then you could extract the original message.

The decrypt process is similarly simple. Computing $m = c^d \bmod n$ recovers the original message. This works because by using some basic number theoretic results, we know that:

$$c^d \equiv (m^e)^d \equiv m^{ed} \equiv m \bmod n$$

Chinese Remainder Theorem Implementation

The standard format works, but it is inefficient because it doesn't leverage the knowledge of the factorization of n. The RSA system derives its strength because it's impractical for an attacker to factor the modulus; however, the private key holder does (or can) know the factorization and use it to speed up decryption. This system works well, since on average, each modular exponentiation requires L^3 number of steps in computation. By using the factorization of n and using the Chinese remainder theorem (CRT), the same computation can be done by performing two $L/2$ modular exponentiation operations. In the optimal case, this requires $2\ (L\ /\ 2)^3 = 2\ (L^3\ /\ 8)$ or $L^3/4$ steps, or a saving of four. If done in hardware or using threads on multiple CPUs, the two steps can be done simultaneously, theoretically providing for eight-fold performance improvement.

You convert the regular private key (n,d) into the CRT form by:

$$\begin{aligned} d_1 &= d \bmod (p-1) \\ d_2 &= d \bmod (q-1) \\ c &= q^{-1} \bmod p \end{aligned}$$

Then you use the following decryption step:

$$\begin{aligned} j_1 &= m^{d1} \bmod p \\ j_2 &= m^{d2} \bmod p \\ h &= c(j_1 - j2) \bmod p \\ \text{Plaintext} &= j_2 + hq \end{aligned}$$

Using the public key is no different, and anyone inspecting the public key has no knowledge of whether the decryption step is done using the standard or CRT methods.

MultiPrime RSA Algorithm

The MultiPrime RSA algorithm is a patented (U.S. Patent 5,848,159) extension of the CRT method that uses more primes in the modulus n. The public key is still the same, but n is now made of three or more primes. Decryption is done using a natural extension of the CRT method: Each additional prime p_i requires an exponent $d_i = d \bmod p$ and a coefficient $c_i = p_i^{-1} \bmod p$.

The security of this system relies on the fact that the factoring algorithms listed earlier are actually splitting algorithms; they only return one (or perhaps two) factors per iteration. If n is 2048 bits composed of four 512-bit primes, then the factoring algorithm will have do three iterations to produce a factory once on 2,048, which results in a 1536-bit number and one of the factors. Reapplying the algorithm results in a 1024-bit number and another factor, and a final iteration is needed to get the remaining two factors. Care has to be taken not to make the primes numbers too small.

It's patented, but if you have access to an RSA toolkit or another licensed implementation, then the only reason *not* to use it is if you wish to change toolkits. Encryption is still the same and the decryption process is invisible (i.e., you don't know if you are using the slow method, CRT, or MultiPrime).

Message Representation and OAEP

Mathematically, the message to be encrypted can be any number from 0 to n–1. However, n does not take up an exact number of bits, so breaking up a message to this size is a bit tricky. Typically, the message value can range from 0 to the largest power of 2 less than n, $0 < m < 2^k < n < 2^{k+1}$. This means the message can be k bits long. Even then, it is typically truncated to a multiple of 8 so it can fit in a byte boundary.

However, the RSA algorithm by itself is not secure for arbitrary messages. The problem occurs when the message is very short relative to the block size of the algorithm, and most of the message block is zero value. In these cases, they are attacks to recover the message that are significantly better than brute force. A good summary can be found in [BoJoNg2000] [Boneh2001].

This problem can be solved by padding the original message. Originally, a simple padding scheme was used. Given a length BL of the block length, the following scheme was used:

0×02 || PS || 0×00 || Message

where PS was enough nonzero random bytes with a minimum of 8 to fill out the block. The size of the message was communicated out-of-band or based on the protocol. This scheme works well; however, it's not *proverbially* secure.

The current standard uses an algorithm known as Optimal Asymmetric Encryption Algorithm (OAEP):

- *bLen* is the size in bytes of the key (for RSA this is the length of (in bytes).
- H is hash function with hLen output bytes, normally SHA-1, but in some cases RIPE-MD 160 is also allowed.

- P is a parameter list (standardized).
- *m* is the message, with mLen in bytes.
- MGF(seed, length) is a function that computes a *mask generation function*, which is basically a pseudorandom byte generator that takes a seed and outputs *l* bytes.

This scheme requires that mLen <= blockLength – messageLength – 2 × hashLength –1:

1. messageLength > zero bytes (may be zero length)
2. parameterHash = Hash(Parameters), of length hashLength
3. dataBlock = parameterHash || PS || 01 || message
4. seed = RNG(hashLength)
5. dataBlockMask = MGF(seed, emLen- hLen)
6. maskedDataBlock = dataBlock ⊕ dataBlockMask
7. seedMask = MGF(maskedDataBlock, hLen)
8. maskedSeed = seed ⊕ seedMask
9. encodedMessage = maskedSeed || maskedDataBlock

For example, if the RSA key size is 1024 bits, the symmetric cipher is 128 bits, and using SHA-1 as the hash function, the layout of the message to be encrypted is as given in Table 3.7.

To decode EOAEP, the reverse operations are used:

1. maskedSeed = encodedMessage[0, hashLength –1]
2. maskedDataBlock = encodedMessage[hashLength, end]
3. seedMask = MGF(maskedDataBlock, hashLength)
4. seed = maskedSeed ⊕ seedMask
5. dataBlockMask = MGF(seed, encodedMessageLength - hashLength)
6. dataBlock = maskedDataBlock ⊕ dataBlockMask
7. parameterHash = Hash(parameters)
8. Confirm that:
   a. dataBlock[0, hashLength] = parameterHash
   b. dataBlock[hashLength, XYZ] are all zeros
   c. dataBlock[XYZ, 1] = 0x01
9. Return message = dataBlock[XYZ, 20]

Table 3.7 Example of EOEAP

CONTENTS	LENGTH	TOTAL
Masked seed	20	20
Hash of parameter file	20	40
0x00 bytes	71	111
0x01	1	112
Message	16	130

In Practice and Standards

The main standard for this is RSA's PKCS #1, which specifies the standard for the RSA algorithm but focuses on encoding and interoperability. As in many cases, each standards organization puts out identical standards. Some use bit lengths, others use bytes.

RSA is typically used with p and q being at least 256 bits each. This produces an RSA composite of approximately 512 bits. This means the message block (as defined, a number less than n) is at least 80 *bytes*, which is typically 10 times larger than symmetric ciphers' block sizes. RSA is also typically 10 times slower than symmetric ciphers. Because of this, RSA is typically not used directly; instead, one block contains a key for another symmetric cipher. This allows the best of both worlds: the speed of a symmetric algorithm along with public/private properties of RSA.

The message m is normally not the original plaintext message broken up into blocks but actually is a key for a symmetric cipher that will encode the rest of the message. This has the advantage of computing only one block using the expensive algorithm and a fast cipher for the rest of the message.

Choice of Parameters

Because of the relative simplicity of the RSA algorithm, it is susceptible to poorly chosen parameters.

Choice of Primes, p and q

There is quite a large amount of literature on how to select the primes p and q for optimal security. The most common is on generating special prime numbers that have additional structure to resist factoring algorithms.

These *strong primes* have various definitions; most include that $p - 1$ or $p + 1$ has a large prime factor. Strong primes used to be helpful in protecting against Pollard's factoring algorithms. However, today, better algorithms exist, such as the Number Field Sieve, that are faster than Pollard's algorithms and work equally well if the prime is "strong" or not. The other problem with using strong primes is that most of the algorithms for creating them are probabilistic in nature anyway, meaning you aren't 100 percent sure that the result is even a prime number.

Another requirement is that the difference between p and q is large. If the difference is small, then p and q are approximately $\sqrt{n}$. An attacker could start factoring tests around $\sqrt{n}$ until they bump into p or q. However, the odds of two randomly chosen primes having the same values for the first k bits matching is 2^{1-k}. In other words, it's highly unlikely. The most likely cause of this happening would be a faulty random generator. However, it is quite trivial to check against this when generating the primes.

Finally, while it is technically possible to generate new encryption keys by reusing the modulus n and selecting a new encryption exponent, this should not be done and a fresh modulus using new primes should be used for every key pair. If two parties are using a key generated from the same set of primes, they can easily determine the other's private key.

Choice of Public Exponent e

Rather than actually trying to compute the greatest common denominator of ϕ, you typically choose the encryption exponent e as a prime number. Popular prime choices are those with a low "hamming weight," or a low number of 1s in a binary string representation, since on properly implemented systems, multiplication is very fast. Common choices are 3, 17, and $2^{16} - 1 = 65{,}537$, since they all only have two one-bits in them.

However, there have been some attacks when using a low exponent. In particular, $e = 3$ is troublesome. For instance, if the same message is encrypted using three different public keys $(3, n_1)$, $(3, n_2)$, $(3, n_3)$, and an attacker has access to the three encrypted messages, the message can be retrieved quite easily.

For simplicity, you should use $e = 65{,}537$. This only requires 17 multiplications to compute, while a random "large" e might take 1,000 multiplications.

Choice of Private Exponent *d*

You might expect there to be some conditions on the private exponent d, since if it's a small value, a simple brute-force method of trying small values of d would be an effective attack. It has been shown that if $d < N^{0.25}$ [Wiener1990], then an attacker can break RSA quite easily using continued fractions. This has been improved to d < $N^{0.282}$ using *Lattice Basis Reduction* [BoVe1998]. And although the authors were unable to prove it, they suspect the actual bound is $N^{0.5}$, or in other words, d should be roughly the same bit size as the original primes p and q.

If you choose e first, you do not a have a choice in d, since it is uniquely determined. But if you choose e to be small, like 65,537 as suggested previously, then d will be much larger than $N^{0.5}$ anyway, and this attack is of no concern.

Discrete Logarithm Systems

Cryptosystems based on discrete logarithms were first proposed by ElGamal in 1985 [ElGamal1985]. Unlike RSA, the ElGamal system never had a strong corporate parent commercializing it, and it is not as well known. However, it is a secure system. As mentioned, it was especially popular in early free cryptography packages, since its patent expired four years before the RSA patent did.

Underlying Mathematics

The ElGamal and related systems are based on computing the discrete logarithm over a finite field. The discrete logarithm is equivalent to a normal logarithm. Recall that given two numbers a and b, the logarithm x is defined to the value that makes the following equation true:

$$a = b^x$$

Computationally, in real numbers this is not particularly difficult; many pocket calculators can do this without difficulty. The discrete version is exactly similar except that a, b are integers and the operations of multiplication are not in GF(p), or rather under modulus p:

$$a = b^x \bmod p$$

For cryptographic purposes this problem is ideal, since modular exponentiation can be done very quickly. However, the reverse operations, the discrete logarithm, is hard.

This is a little bit different than the RSA problem. It too considered taking roots; however, in the case of RSA, the modulus was a composite number and there were conditions on the exponent. Here the modulus is prime, and mathematically, that makes quite a bit of difference.

Generators

A *generator* of a field is an element under exponentiation that produces each value of the field. Every field of order n has at least six ln ln n generators. Table 3.8 shows an exponentiation chart for GF(7).

Here 3 and 5 are generators, while 2, 4, and 64 are not. Notice how other elements that are not generators "roll over" (i.e., are 1) at the exponents with multiples of 2 or 3, which happen to be prime factors of 6 = 7 – 1. This observation holds true for any field and provides an efficient algorithm for testing to see if an element is a generator:

1. Let $n = p_1^{e1} p_2^{e2} \ldots p_k^{ek}$.
2. Choose a random element a in g.
3. For i = 1 to k. compute $b = a^{np_i}$
4. If b =1, go to Step 1.
5. Return a.

Discrete Logarithms

Since a generator "generates" every value in the field, this mean that given a generator g and another value a, there exists x such that $a = g^x \bmod p$. That is, the logarithm a relative to g under a modulus p or $\log_p a = x \bmod p$.

As mentioned, given real numbers, computing logarithms is quite easy. However, computing logarithms under a finite field is quite hard, while exponentiation is easy. For finite fields, the only known algorithms are fully exponential.

Table 3.8 Exponentiation Table for GF(7)

	X^1	X^2	X^3	X^4	X^5	X^6
2	2	4	1	2	4	1
3	3	2	6	4	5	1
4	4	2	1	4	2	1
5	5	4	6	2	3	1
6	6	1	6	1	6	1

Generating Safe Primes and Generators

Of course, this algorithm does require a factorization of $(p - 1)$, which normally can be very difficult. However, we will need special primes for the ElGamal system that have a large prime factor to guard against certain factoring attacks. Optimal choices are selecting primes in the form of $p = 2q + 1$, where q is prime (these primes are sometimes referred to as Sophie Germain primes).

Here the factorization of $(p - 1)$ is just $2q$, and the algorithm becomes quite simple and efficient, since it can be shown that a random element has approximately a 50 percent chance of being a generator.

To compute p:

1. Select a random $(k - 1)$ bit prime q by randomly selecting a number, and then test using Miller-Rabin.
2. Compute $p = 2q + 1$ and test to see if p is prime.

To compute generator g:

1. Select a random element g.
2. If $g^q = 1$ or $g^2 = 1$, select a new element g.

The Diffie-Hellman Problem

Like the RSA cryptosystem, the security of the ElGamal cryptosystem does not directly depend on the discrete logarithm, but on a problem very related, called Diffie-Hellman. Here, let a be a generator of Z_p, and given two elements, a^a and a^b, find a^{ab}. Clearly, if you know a and b, this is trivial. The trick here is that you don't know what the exponents are; you are just given two elements of the group x and y. Since we know a is a generator, some values a and b exist such that $x = a^a$ and $y = a^b$, and you could compute a^{ab}.

This is not exactly the same as the discrete logarithm problem, and no one has proven the two are equivalent. There could be some way of computing a^{ab} without taking the discrete logarithm. However, current research suggests if there is, it is not any faster. Currently, only attacks against the Diffie-Hellman problem are algorithms to compute discrete logarithms.

Bit Security

While computing the full discrete logarithm is hard, it turns out that computing the least-significant bit and sometimes other bits can be relatively easy. It's 0 if $b^{(p-1)/2} = 1 \bmod p$ and 1 otherwise. Worse, if $p - 1 = 2^s t$, then it can be shown that computing $L_i(B)$ is $i <= s$.

With this in mind, it's a good idea to pick a modulus where $s = 1$; in other words, $p - 1 = 2t$, where t is not divisible by two. The easiest way of computing this is to see if four (i.e., 2^2) divides p, and if so, throw it out.

The Algorithm

Now that we have a good trapdoor function and a way of generating secure parameters, we can develop a cryptosystem.

Domain Parameters

Unlike RSA, the discrete logarithm requires *domain parameters* — or rather, common parameters describing the system. These are not keys and can be, and in some cases must be, publicly available. Likewise, the domain parameters can be reused. RSA's *domain parameters* are just the set of integers, so it doesn't need to be prescribed. The parameters are as follows:

- p, a prime with a suitable size.
- g, a generator of GF(p) with order r.
- $k = (p - 1) / r$, defined from the preceding parameters. In some circumstances a further requirement is that GCD(r, k) = 1, or rather, r does not divide k.

Many times you are given a set of parameters (p, g, r) to use. In these cases, you must *validate* the parameters to make sure they are secure and valid. Basically this means checking every issue listed previously:

1. You are reasonably sure that p is prime.
2. g is in fact a generator of GF(p) with order r.
3. Possibly checking that GCD(r, k) = 1.

Key Generation

Given a set of domain parameters, (p, g, r) , you can generate keys very quickly. Given any value x, a value less than p, you can then compute y using the relationship $y = g^x \bmod p$, where the public key is y and the private key is x. Keys are inherently tied to the domain parameters, so sending a key requires sending the domain parameters (if they aren't previously agreed to).

Key Agreements (Secret Sharing)

Given a set of domain parameters, you can very quickly generate key pairs. One trick to this is *key-agreements*, or *secret-sharing algorithms*. Two strangers can agree on a secret value without explicitly saying what the secret is. An eavesdropper hearing the agreement would be unable to determine what the secret is. When the discrete logarithm problem is used for key agreements, typically it's called the *Diffie-Hellman Key Exchange Protocol.* Under this scheme the secret ranges from 0 to $r - 1$.

In particular, two parties agree upon a common domain parameter p, g, r. Then each side generates a key pair (x, y) (or has an existing key pair) and gives the other side its public key. Then each side simply computes $z = pub^x$ mod p. After this step, each side will have the same value. More formally, given two sets of key pairs (x_1, y_1) and (x_2, y_2), the first party receives the second party's public key and computes $z = y_2^{x_1}$. Then (or simultaneously) the second party receives the first party's public key and computes $z = y_1^{x_2}$. Assuming both sides have properly generated keys and domain parameters, the secret value is the same for both parties, since:

$$y_1 \equiv g^{x_1} \bmod p$$
$$y_2 \equiv g^{x_2} \bmod p$$
$$y_2^{x_1} \equiv \left(g^{x_2}\right)^{x_1} \equiv g^{x_1 x_2} \equiv \left(g^{x_1}\right)^{x_2} \equiv y_1^{x_2}$$

In both cases, this requires that at least one side is using a valid public key—that is, the key actually belongs to the sender. In many protocols, one side is just a server waiting for someone to initiate a request. One attack is to send particular values in order to see what the response is and thus be able to compute the server's private key. This type of chosen-plaintext attack in called the *small-subgroup attack.*

One way around this is to slightly modify the protocol and make the domain so that GCD(k, r) = 1. Instead of computing $z=y_2^{x_1}$ mod p, you now compute $z=y_2^{kx_1}$ mod p. If the other party's public key was not generated correctly, z breaks down, resulting in a value of 0 or 1, and the process is stopped (under IEEE 1363-2000, this technique is known as DLSVDP-DHC).

Another attack is for someone to hijack the protocol and replace one side's public key with another, or to change the domain parameters, thus causing one side to generate an invalid secret. There are many variations to solve this problem, such as having each side use two sets of key pairs. While this works, when using key agreements in practice, you should modify the existing system so the secret value is used as a seed in a hash function.

ElGamal Encryption

Encryption requires a random value r, relatively prime to $r - 1$. Then you generate two values, both of which are the ciphertext:

$$a \equiv g^k \bmod p$$
$$b \equiv y^k m \bmod p$$

This system has the unfortunate effect of doubling the ciphertext in size compared to the original message. Notice how this requires a random value to be used for encryption. This means that the same message encrypted twice is likely to have different ciphertext values.

Decryption is performed by:

$$m \equiv b/a^x \bmod p$$

This works since $a^x \equiv g^{kx}$ and $b/a^x \equiv y^k m/a^x \equiv g^{xk} m/g^{xk} \equiv m \pmod p$. (Recall that division is really modular inversion.)

DHEAS Encryption

While ElGamal allows you to specify a key for symmetric cipher, DHEAS encryption extends the key agreement system to produce a secure cryptosystem. Instead of using the secret directly for the symmetric cipher, you use it as an input to a hash function to generate *two* keys: one for the symmetric cipher and another for use in HMAC. In particular, you use the hash of *H(zBits | | counterBlock | | pBits* where:

- *zBits* is the shared secret bits.
- *counterBlock* is a 32-bit integer that starts at 0.
- *pBits* is whatever parameters are needed in the domain, and any other parameters needed (such as the type of symmetric cipher).

If the hash doesn't provide enough bits (for instance, if you are generating a 256-bit key using SHA-1 that has a 160-bit output), you increment the counter by 1 and do another hash. Then you feed the final key into a symmetric cipher, which does the bulk encryption. Finally, you produce a MAC using k_2 with the message being $(C \mid\mid P_2)$.

Decryption is similar: Given (C, y_2, mac), you use the private key x_1 and compute the shared secret. The symmetric key k_1 and the mac key k_2 are regenerated using the hashing method, and the symmetric cipher decrypts the message. Message integrity is ensured by recomputing the MAC_{k2} $(C \mid\mid P_2)$ and comparing that it is the same as what is received.

Another option is using k_1 not as a key for a symmetric cipher, but as a mask that is XORed against the message. Otherwise the scheme is identical. This is designed mostly for small messages where the overhead of the cipher is not needed.

Just using this scheme to generate k_1 (of whatever size) is a much more secure way of doing a key agreement when the goal is just having two parties generate a common number.

Standards and Practice

As mentioned, the ElGamal system for *encryption* never really took off and has never been used as a standard. ElGamal is available in a number of free and commercial systems, since for a while it was the only alternative to the patented RSA algorithm. Nowadays there is not much use for it beyond legacy encrypted email.

While the new DHAES style of encryption has been noted since 1998, only until 2001 was it included in a *draft* standard of IEEE 1363a. The IEEE standard only standardizes the algorithms; the actual protocols and usage is left to others. To my knowledge, it's not used in any commercial products (although that may change as the IEEE standard propagates).

As for key agreements, it's been a fundamental building block for SSL, the system that is most commonly used for encryption for HTTP transactions. A variation of it allows an unknown client (i.e., you) to connect to a server and produce an encrypted session.

Elliptic Curves

The Elliptic Curve Cryptosystem (ECC) has the advantage of keys that are much smaller than the RSA or DHAES systems, with a 160-bit key roughly equal to 1,024 modulus in the other systems. The small key size implies that it's much faster as well. Unfortunately, it's primarily used for embedded and wireless systems and not integrated into SSL protocol, although there is no reason why this could not be done. It's also been popular for digital signatures in the financial services industries, because it produces a compact signature. This is important, since the messages are typically very small and using the other schemes produce a signature that is often much larger than the message (size does matter).

Underlying Mathematics: Elliptic Curves

Elliptic curves as functions have been studied for hundreds of years. They were first investigated because they describe arc length of an ellipse; today they are studied as pure mathematical objects. Part of the interest is that solutions to elliptic curves, with appropriate definitions of "addition," can be turned into a group. This means:

- There is a "zero" element, denoted as O, where $P + O = P$
- Every point on the curve has an inverse, such that $P + (-P) = O$
- The addition of any two elements is another solution on the curve, $P + Q = R$

In addition, the solution set on elliptic curves is an *abelian group*, which just means it doesn't matter in what order you do addition: $P + Q = Q + P$.

Elliptic Curves over Real Numbers

Visually it is easiest to understand elliptic curves by looking at how mathematicians saw them hundreds of years ago by using real numbers. Given a point on an elliptic curve $P = (x, y)$, we define its inverse by $-P = (x, -y)$, which is just it flipped on the x-axis.

An additional two points on a curve is made by drawing a line through the points, seeing when it intersects the curve again, and taking its inverse. If this line is vertical (infinite slope), then the result is defined to be zero (see Figure 3.4).

Addition of a point to itself, $P + P = 2P$, is done by taking a line tangent to the point, seeing where it intersects the curve, and then taking its inverse (see Figure 3.5).

Finally, multiplication of two points is not defined.

With these rules, you can see that the points on an elliptic curve form a group. The computations can be made rigorous using algebra; however, for our purposes, we don't need to go into this.

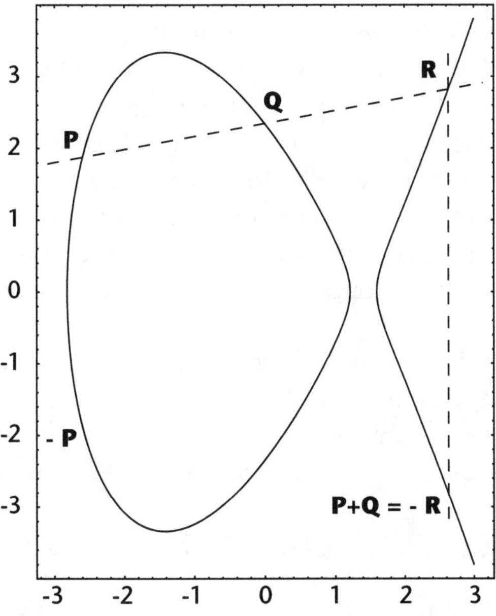

Figure 3.4 Elliptic curve point inversion and point doubling.

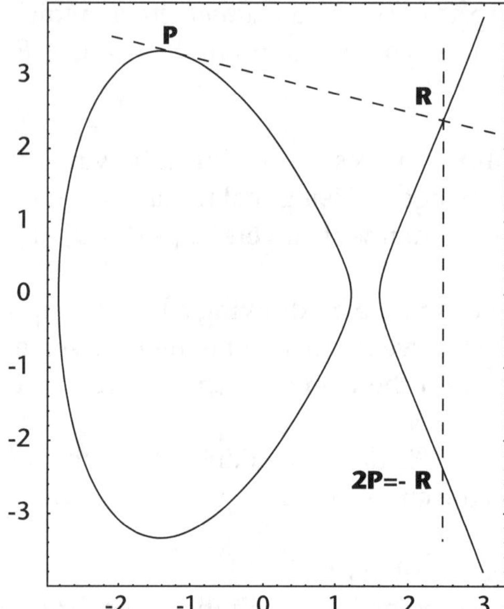

Figure 3.5 Elliptic curve point addition.

Elliptic Curves over Prime Fields

Doing computations over real numbers presents some difficulties for cryptographic applications, since the calculations are inexact and representation of floating-point numbers can be tricky. You don't want to base the security of anything that can be miscomputed due to a rounding error. Integers, on the other hand, are very easy to work with and always exact.

Elliptic curves can also be defined over finite fields instead of real numbers. This means the coefficients of the curve and the x, y values of a point all come from the field. To make this work, some restrictions on the curve are required:

Given a prime field $F_p > 3$, and given a and b are both nonzero and satisfy $4a^3 + 27b^2 \neq 0 \pmod{p}$, the elliptic curve $E(F_p)$ is the set of all points (x, y) in F_p that satisfy the equation $y^3 = x^3 + ax + b$.

Given the simplest curve $y^3 = x^2 + x + 1$ ($a = 1, b = 1$) and the field F_{11} has 14 points:

O, (0, 1), (0, 10), (1, 5), (1, 6), (2, 0), (3, 3), (3, 8), (4, 5), (4, 6), (6, 5), (6, 6), (8, 2), (8, 9)

There is no simple geometric visualization when elliptic curve is defined on a finite field. You cannot really graph them, since they are only a finite number of points and there is no relationship between the same curve under the real numbers and under a finite field.

Just like the real case, we can define rules for the addition of points. All the following formulas are under the field (using modular arithmetic).

Point Inversion Rule

Given $P = (x, y)$, the inverse is just $(x, -y)$

Point Addition Rule

Given two points on $E(F_p)$, $P = (x_1, y_1)$ and $Q = (x_2, y_2)$ such that $x_1 \neq x_2$. Then $P + Q = (x_3, y_3)$ is defined as:

$$x_3 = \lambda^2 - x_1 - x_2$$
$$y_3 = \lambda(x_1 - x_3) - y_1$$
$$\lambda = \frac{y_2 - y_1}{x_2 - x_1}$$

Point Doubling Rule

Given a point $P = (x_1, y_1)$, then $2P = (x_3, y_3)$ is defined as:

$$x_3 = \lambda^2 - 2x_1$$
$$y_3 = \lambda(x_1 - x_3) - y_1$$
$$\lambda = \frac{3x_1^2 + a}{2y_1}$$

a is the coefficient in the elliptic curve. If $iy_1 = 0$, then $2P = O$ (since $P = -P$)

Multiplication of two points is not defined, but using the rules, you define scalar multiplication nP as P added n times, for example, $3P = P + P + P$.

After a certain number of times of a point being added to it, the result will be O. The least number of times r such that $rP = O$ is called the order of the point P. Finally, we can define the trapdoor problem that defines elliptic curve cryptography. If $Q = rP$ on given curve E, but only given P and Q, what is r? This is known as the Elliptic Curve Discrete Logarithm Problem, or ECDLP. It is exactly the same type of problem as the Diffie-Hellman Discrete Logarithm, but it operates on a different field and uses addition notation (using scalar multiplication) instead of multiplication notation. See Table 3.9 for a comparison.

Table 3.9 Comparison between Discrete Logarithm Systems

DISCRETE LOGARITHM	ELLIPTIC CURVE DISCRETE LOGARITHM
Given a field F_p, Given g, y what is x in $Y = g^x \bmod p$	Given a curve E on field F_p. Given points P and Q, what is r? $Q = rP$ (on E)

Elliptic Curves over Binary Fields

So far we have only discussed finite fields with a prime number of elements. However, the important category of fields is known as the Galois fields. These have p^m number of elements where p is a prime number and $m > 1$. Computationally, the form of 2^m is useful, since mod 2^m involves just taking the left-most m bits. These fields are sometimes known as *binary fields,* and the elements are all 2^m-possible binary bit strings. For example, $GF(2^3)$ is {000,001,010,011,100,110,111}.

Addition in this field is very simple; it's the XOR operation (or addition modulo 2). Multiplication is much more complicated and depends on how you wish to view the binary bits. There are roughly three different representations: polynomial, normal, and Gaussian normal. In fact, we could spend the next 20 pages listing algorithms for each of the different methods and ways of converting between them. However, the important point is that the operations are fast.

When using a binary field, you would use a different curve equation. Given a point P, the inverse is bit different but still very easy to compute: $P = (x, x + y) \pmod{2^m}$. Addition and point doubling, on the other hand, become very tricky.

The Algorithm

The Elliptic Curve encryption algorithm does have a fairly complicated set of domain parameters that describe what curve is being used. However, after the parameters are chosen (either generated or selected from a table), the actual algorithm for encryption is very simple. The domain conditions are as follows:

DOMAIN PARAMETERS

1. The field, either p, a large prime, or 2^m. These values can be predetermined and preselected and may be reused. The size of p or m needs to be sufficiently large in order in order allow Condition 3.
2. Curve coefficients a, b that are elements of the field, that define an elliptic curve E.
3. A prime number r that divides the number of points on E.
4. A curve point G of order r. The size of r (in bits) is what determines the strength of the EC family; normally the minimum is 161 bits.
5. If a binary field is used, a parameter specifying the coordinate representation.

6. Optionally, a cofactor k such that $k = o(E)/r$.
7. Additionally, in some cases, $GCD(k, r) = 1$.

The generation for prime fields isn't so bad, but the binary case requires using various tables to aid in computation.

Fortunately, the domain parameters can be reused. If that sounds odd, think of being able to "reuse" integers even though you generated an RSA key pair. However, unlike RSA key pairs, these parameters will need validation.

Using our previous example, we use the $E(\text{field} = F_{11}, a = 1, b = 1, o(E) = 14)$. The point $G = (6, 5)$ has order 7, since $7 \times (6, 5) = O$. And, finally, $k = 14/7 = 2$, and $GCD(7, 2) = 1$.

Key Generation

Once you have the all the domain parameters (either generated or validated), generating keys is very simple:

1. Pick a random integer $0 < s < r$.
2. Compute a point on the curve $W = sG$.

W is the public key, and s is the private key. Key generation is fast once the domain parameters are computed. There are other algorithms for validating public keys to make sure points aren't completely bogus. Using our example again, we'll pick $s = 4$, so $W = 4G = 4\,(6, 5) = (3, 3)$.

Key Agreements and Encryption

Just as in the Diffie-Hellman case, we can define key agreements. Regardless of the representation or field, the process is identical. Given two sets of key pairs (W_1, s_1) and (W_2, s_2), the shared secret value is computed by using:

$$s_2 W_1 = s_1 W_2$$

The shared secret is a point on the curve, and the coordinates are effectively random. However it's traditional to use just the x-coordinate. The bits that make up the x-coordinate can be used as a secret key for a symmetric cipher. Continuing our example using a key of ((3, 3), 4); we'll pick another key ((0, 10), 5) and compute the secret.

$$5\,(3, 3) = (6, 6)$$
$$4\,(0, 10) = (6, 6)$$

Now that we have a secret value, encryption and decryption work identically to the regular discrete logarithm version.

Standards and Practice

As you can see, the operations of addition and multiplication of the field, along with the operations of adding points on the elliptic curve, are powerful mixing functions. This allows a much smaller key size than either RSA or ordinary discrete logarithm systems, and this in turn allows it to run much faster.

The target market for elliptic curve cryptography is embedded systems, especially wireless systems and smart cards. These systems are typically proprietary, so one company, Certicom, provides both the clients and servers. There is no reason why ECC couldn't be integrated into stock Web browsers and servers, but for whatever reason, this has not happened. This is unfortunate, since such a setup could increase the number of connections a server could handle. Nowadays, a heavily loaded server requires a hardware acceleration card to handle the math-intensive parts.

Table 3.10 compares prime and binary fields. The security is the same for both.

For quite some time, RSA (the company) downplayed the usefulness of ECC, but now it also provides toolkits. However, standards for encryption have only come about recently. The only standard to date is in the draft in IEEE 1363a, but this only standardizes the algorithms and not the actual format of many parameters.

Other Public Key Cryptographic Systems

The following systems are fairly new but are being actively developed and put into commercial use.

Rabin Cryptosystem

The Rabin system is based on integer factorization. Unlike RSA, which is thought to be similar in difficulty to factoring, Rabin is provably equivalent and is a remarkably simple algorithm. However, like RSA, by itself it is insecure.

Table 3.10 Comparison between Field Types

	PRIME FIELDS	BINARY FIELDS
Software implementation	Less complicated	More complicated
Software speed	Slower	Faster
Hardware Acceleration	Yes	No (as of yet)

To generate a key using the Rabin cryptosystem:

1. Choose primes p, q that are roughly equal size.
2. Let $p \equiv q \equiv 3 \bmod 4$ (technically this is not necessary, but it makes decryption faster).
3. Determine a and b such that $ap + bq = 1$ using the Euclidean algorithm. Again this is not technically necessary, but it makes decryption easier.
4. Let $n = pq$.

The public key is just n, and the private key is (p, q) or (p, q, a, b).

Recall in RSA the primes were only used in generating a key and could be forgotten. Here the primes *are* the key.

To encrypt using the Rabin system:

1. Represent the message as an integer in Z_n ($[0, n-1]$).
2. Let $c \equiv m^2 \bmod n$.

That's all there is to it.

Decryption is a bit more complicated.

There are generic algorithms for computing the square root of c, given p and q. However, with our requirements on p and q, and previously computing (p, q, a, b), the algorithm simplifies into:

1. $r = c^{(p+1)/4} \bmod p$
2. $s = c^{(p+1)/4} \bmod q$
3. $x = (aps + bqr) \bmod n$
4. $y = (aps - bqr) \bmod n$
5. The four square roots are $x, -x, y, -y$, all mod n.
6. Select (somehow) which of the four roots is the correct message.

In Rabin, decryption is not unique, and you are left with a choice of four results. We'll resolve this problem in a bit, but for now, let's say you randomly pick one of the results.

Performance

For encryption, only one modular squaring is done, which gives it a large advantage over RSA. Decryption is roughly comparable to RSA.

Security

The security of Rabin lies in the fact that computing a square root of a number given n is equivalent to factoring n into its parts p and q. There is no other efficient algorithm.

The problem with Rabin is that it is susceptible to chosen-ciphertext attacks. Suppose you had access to a "decryption machine" that would decrypt any ciphertext sent to it but doesn't provide the primes p and q. For instance, suppose an engineer had to use an API to do decryption. Also suppose that the decryption function just returns randomly one of the four possible messages. Here's how the attack works:

1. Pick a random number x from Zn.
2. Encrypt using the standard mechanism.
3. Send this number to the decryption API.
4. The result will be one of $\pm x$, the original message, *or* $\pm y$, which is the other set of roots.
5. If the result is $\pm x$, repeat the process. If it's the other root, then the $GCD(x - y, n)$ is a prime factor of n. You can quickly recover p and q from this.

Since our engineer already has access to the API, this might not sound like an issue. It's not, as a long as the engineer is honorable. If the engineer leaves employment or publicly posts the secret key, then you have a problem.

NTRU

The NTRU system was introduced in 1996 and uses a completely different trapdoor problem. It doesn't have a snappy summary like the RSA problem does (i.e., factoring); however, a rough idea of the problem is as follows: From linear algebra, you might recall basis vectors and how linear combination of the basis vectors forms a vector space. This is similar, but instead of linear vector spaces, the NTRU basis vectors form a *lattice*, or a discrete version of a vector space. And instead of using real numbers, we are using the ring of truncated polynomials over a field. A NTRU key is only one-half of the basis, and finding the other half without the private parameters is a hard problem.

The beauty of the system is that it's fairly simple to implement, very compact, and high speed. In particular:

- It does not require large integer arithmetic. In NTRU, only 8-bit arithmetic is needed.
- It features rapid key generation that only requires generating a list of random 8-bit numbers and then doing a small computation. The claim is that this can be thousands of times faster than RSA, since no primality checks are needed and no special algorithms are needed to construct a key.

- Sample algorithms for encryption and decryption only take a few dozen lines of code (see www.ntru.com/NTRUFTPDocsFolder/NTRUTech001.pdf).
- Custom chips can implement the algorithms with approximately 1,000 gates (this is very small).
- Claimed performance is 100 times faster than ECC with equivalent security (www.ntru.com/technology/tutorials/techsummary.htm).
- The best brute-force attacks do not parallelize well at all. This is unlike RSA and ECC, where the attacks do parallelize well.

What makes NTRU especially interesting is that it is being commercialized (by a company of the same name), has strong corporate backers, and is well funded. NTRU is currently targeting smart cards, very small embedded systems, and wireless systems. Sony and Macrovision (digital rights management) are investors, so some people expect some type of media-on-demand application to appear.

NTRU had a bumpy start—the original digital signature scheme was revoked—and has experienced a few other growing pains. However, it seems to be maturing quickly. A working group of IEEE 1363 is working on standards (although this seems a bit artificial, since it just formalizes NTRU's patented algorithms).

The NTRU Web site, www.ntru.com, has extensive details on their system, including their mathematics and challenge problems.

Summary

The choice of selecting a public key cipher frequently is determined by who you are communicating with and what their requirements are. However, if you are free to pick the system, the choice boils down to selecting either RSA or Elliptic Curve. The discrete logarithm systems for encryption aren't recommended, since they provide few if any benefits over the more common RSA. The NTRU system is a possible choice for certain applications, but so far, it has not had wide adoption.

RSA has the advantage that it's by far the most popular system, it's fairly easy to implement, and there are many commercial and free versions available. The downside is that it's relatively slow and has an enormous key and block size. Both of these concerns may or may not be an issue with your applications, and in some cases, hardware acceleration can be done to help the performance problem (although it is quite expensive). In general,

RSA is normally selected to be at least 768 bits, and 1024 is commonly used (even at 512-bits, the system will remain secure for all but the most determined adversaries). With computing power at least doubling every 18 months, for long-term storage, it's wise to use the 2048 bit system.

Elliptic Curve has the advantages of a small key size and greater speed than RSA; however, it's also a lot more complicated, and because of this, it's a little harder to find solid implementations. An ECC system of 161- and 224-bits is roughly equivalent to an RSA system of 1024 and 2048 bits. If you are considering a new project or you have an implementation of ECC available, you should at least experiment with it and compare the performance with RSA.

Random Numbers

Random numbers are an essential part of computer science, security, and cryptography. Clearly, we know they are used in generating keys, various parameters, initialization vectors, and passwords. But what is a *random* number? A number by itself isn't random one way or another—is 213 a random number? Instead, the phrase refers to the context where it came from—a random source or process. A random source generates numbers that are independent of all previous numbers before it. If you had an infinite sequence of random bits, you could make the following assumptions:

- There are an equal number of 1s and 0s.
- Every possible subsequence exists.
- Any subsequence of length *n* occurs equally as often as any other subsequence of length *n*.

However, we don't work with infinite sequences. Locally (any finite subset) a random sequence may not follow these rules. Picking any set of bits you are just as likely to find all 1s as you are any other sequence. In fact, you'd actually expect there to be variance. If you asked for 10 sets of bits, and each set has exactly the same number of 1s and 0s, you'd suspect something wasn't right. Therefore, with a finite set, you can never prove that it is random or came from a random source. In statistics there are no absolutes; you can only provide a *probability* that it came from a random source. If this seems a bit odd, consider that even with a truly random source, you still must measure it and get it into the computer. There is only a finite amount of precision, and there are calibration and transcription issues, along with time constraints on how many random numbers you can measure in a time interval. In other words, even with a truly random source, the measurement process may introduce errors and skew. However, the unprovability of randomness is actually useful, since it allows us to simulate randomness using software algorithms.

Randomness is simulated with pseudorandom number generators, abbreviated PRNG, which are deterministic algorithms. Given the same *seed* value or initial input, these algorithms will generate the same numbers. However, the output behaves similarly to what a truly random source would do: It produces similar statistical results. As mentioned, there is no definitive yes/no answer for determining if a sequence is actually random. Instead, a battery of tests have been developed that capture various qualities of randomness. These test are generally in one of the following categories:

Uniform distribution tests. The most basic test of randomness is that each outcome occurs equally. This is only a smoke test to root out the worst cases; overall, it doesn't do much. The only issue becomes how to interpret the bits and bytes from a random stream into numbers.

Runs testing. Given a sequence of binary digits, a *run* is a consecutive sequence of 1s or 0s. For example, 111001011, has five runs: 111 | 00 | 1 | 0 | 11. You could tally up the runs of different sizes against expected values for random sequence. A slightly more complicated version of this test is to measure *monotonic* runs, where the values increase in succession (for instance, allowing for rollover, 8, 9, 0, 1 has a run length of four).

Random walk tests. These tests treat the data as movement instructions, where a one-bit moves up, while a zero-bit moves down. The test then can look at how often the sequence stays above the starting mark, how often each position is hit, and so on.

Poker and monkey tests. Poker tests convert the random sequence into a series of "poker hands" by converting the bits of integers into a card and grouping cards into "hands." For instance, every 4 bits may represent a card with value 0 to 15; then five cards are selected (for a total of 20 bits) for a hand. The distribution of two-of-a-kind, two pairs, and so on is then tested. The monkey test gets its name from the monkeys-typing-at-keyboards theory. Eventually, the monkeys should test every "word" of a certain size. Formally known as overlapping m-tuple tests, these tests are similar to poker tests, except the bits that make up a card (or letter in this case) overlap. The tests vary from large keyboards but short words to small keyboards with long words. There are an enormous number of words that can be created, so instead of doing a frequency count of each word, the tests measure the expected number of word misses.

Rank tests. These tests put random numbers into a particularly sized matrix, typically 6x8, 31x31, or 32x32. Then the *rank* of the matrix is determined, or rather, the number of linearly independent rows. This test is repeated many times, and the statistic measures the frequency distribution of the rank of the matrixes.

Spectral tests. This test converts the data using the discrete Fast Fourier Transformation to determine any periodic elements in the data. A typically random sample should be fairly wideband, with all frequencies occurring equally and without any one frequency dominating.

Compression tests. These tests don't actually do compression; using various techniques, they generate statistics based on how compressible the data is. Maurer's Universal Statistical Test, Lempel-Ziv, and the Linear Complexity Test are examples.

Numerical simulation. These tests perform a simulation of physical phenomenon that should converge to a known value. The most common of these is computing π by probabilistic methods.

A word that is often used in conjunction with *random* is *entropy*. Briefly, entropy is a measure of information. A nonrandom source should have a low amount of entropy, while a random one should have a high amount. Another (simplistic) way of looking at entropy is thinking how well it compresses. Very often you'll see references to "this source contains x bits of entropy per call," or something similar. This means they suspect that only x bits of true information exist, while the rest is just filler, although exactly measuring this is more art than science.

Randomness and Security

One reason there are so many tests for PRNGs is to make sure the generated sequence is unpredictable. Even a slight skew in the long term can have devastating results. For scientific applications, the entire numerical experiment can produce incorrect results. For cryptographic applications, security can be compromised. As a simple example, suppose you needed to generate a 4-bit key and you used a random number generator that always generated an equal number of 1s and 0s.

All 4-bit keys are listed in Table 4.1, and the keys with equal 1s and 0s are highlighted in bold.

Instead of having $2^4 = 16$ possible keys as expected from a truly random source, there are now only six. In other words, an attacker who knows about your random source's flaw now only has six keys to try instead of all 16.

Today, most cryptographic PRNGs are quite good, so this type of attack is not much of a problem. What is a problem is how the initial seed is generated. If an attacker can guess what the seed or internal state of the generator is, then he or she can "predict" all of the output, which means the attacker will know what keys and initialization vectors are, or in gaming applications, what the output of the game will be. This type of attack is documented in the now famous paper "Randomness and the Netscape Browser" by Ian Goldberg and David Wagner, which describes how the seed in a version of the Netscape browser could be recovered with minimal difficulty [GoWa1996].

Testing for Randomness

Many of the previous tests have been coded and packaged in many forms, such as the original random testing package DIEHARD from Dr. George Marsaglia. Unfortunately, it does not appear to be actively maintained; the source is originally in FORTRAN, but there is a converted C version, available at `http://stat.fsu.edu/~geo`. John Walker (of Hotbits fame; see later in the chapter) also has a small testing package called ENT, which should be fairly portable.

Table 4.1 Possible 4-Bit Keys

0000	0100	1000	**1100**
0001	**0101**	**1001**	1101
0010	**0110**	**1010**	1110
0011	0111	1011	1111

The new standard is from the NIST. Recognizing that there really wasn't a standard way of testing for randomness, they produced a 163-page document (NIST SP 800-22), which contains just about everything you'd want to know about randomness testing. It defines 16 different tests and acceptable results for each of them. It's not actively maintained either, but it's written in portable C and should compile and work on most systems.

FIPS 140-2 Requirements

While a statistical test can't give a yes or no answer whether a sequence is acceptable, a standard can. FIPS 180 defines four tests, and their results are required for hardware modules. All tests require 20,000 bits, or 2,500 bytes. Although there are four tests, they can be efficiently implemented as just two tests. Most PRNGs can pass these tests. These tests were originally designed as a smoke test for hardware devices to make sure they are not damaged.

Monobit Test

This test counts the number of one-bits in the stream. The test passes if the value is between 9,725 and 10,275.

"Poker" Test

This is the same test as the monobit, but it operates on 4-bit chunks. The test itself involves counting the frequency of occurrence for each chunk and computing the chi-squared static:

$$X = (16/5000) * \left(\sum_{i=0}^{15} \left[freq(i) \right]^2 \right) - 5000$$

The test passes if $2.16 < X < 46.17$. This test is very different than the poker test described at the beginning of the chapter, where you take a "hand" of five cards and test the distribution of common poker hands (flush, two pairs, four-of-a-kind). The FIPS poker test, on the other hand, just makes sure there is a full deck.

Runs Test

This test measures runs of consecutive 0s or 1s in the bit stream. Any run of 6 or more bits is lumped into one category. The test passes if the length count for both 0s and 1s runs are in the intervals described in Table 4.2.

Table 4.2 Runs Test Requirements

LENGTH OF RUN	REQUIRED INTERVAL
1	2343-2657
2	1135-1365
3	542-708
4	240-384
5	111-201
6 or more	111-201

Long Run Test

This test extends the previous test. The test passes if there are no runs of 26 or more bits.

Pseudorandom Number Generators

Random number generators come in two flavors: cryptographic and noncryptographic. The most commonly used noncryptographic generator by far is the linear congruential type, which comes in the form of the recurrence $X_{n+1} = aX_n + c \bmod m$. This generator is used in most libraries and operating systems. With appropriate values of a, c, and m, it can generate a full period of m before repeating. The random qualities are fairly good. However, these types of generators have a few drawbacks for use in cryptographic applications (not that this stops them for being used that way!).

There are many other noncryptographic generators such as lagged fibonacci generators, linear feedback shift registers (LFSRs), and generators based on cellular automata. All are not suitable for cryptographic work. If you need a general-purpose generator, take a look at the Mersenne Twister [MaNi1998]. It's been shown to yield exceptionally high-quality (but not cryptographic) numbers and has a period of $2^{19927} - 1$, or roughly $10^{6000164}$. (Prime numbers in the form $2^n - 1$ are called Mersenne primes.) It also has the advantage that it can be seeded by a single 32-bit `int`, or by using up to 19,968 bits. Depending on implementation it can also be up to four times faster than using the usual built-in linear congruential generator (LCG) functions (more on LCG later in the chapter). The homepage for the Mersenne Twister is at `www.math.keio.ac.jp/~matumoto/emt.html`.

Cryptographic PRNG

Statistics and entropy don't tell the whole story. For cryptographic purposes, random number sources and generators must also have one other property: unpredictability. From a truly random source, this is a given, but with PRNGs, this condition isn't always met. Given a sequence of previous values, you might be able to predict the next value. Scientific applications typically don't care about predictability, since there is no "adversary" trying to guess what the next random input is. To create cryptographic PRNGS, most software constructions use hash functions, symmetric ciphers, or public key mathematics in new ways. The most commonly used systems are shown below.

SHA-1 PRNG

The SHA-1 PRNG is a generator we've looked at already in Chapter 2. It takes a key and a counter block, and optionally some other data, typically parameters. Random bytes are produced by using a secure hash H(K || CB || P) and successively increasing the counter block. For instance, using SHA-1, H(K || 000001 || p) produces the first 160 random bits, then H(K || 000002 || p) produces the next 160 bits, and so on. The actual format isn't terribly important. Oddly, I have not seen any of the MAC formulations used.

The strength of this system depends on the "uninvertability of SHA-1," which hasn't been (publicly) proven. That said, I haven't seen *any* significant attacks against SHA or this method. If SHA-1 becomes "invertible," all hell will break loose and random numbers will be the least of your concerns.

That said, it's always a good idea to periodically reseed (use a different key), and it's probably not good to use it to generate masks for very long messages.

Cipher-CBC or ANSI X9.17

Before the introduction of SHA-1, a common approach was to use Triple DES in a CBC feedback mode—specifically, $x_{n+1} = E_k(timestamp \oplus x_n)$ with x_0 being a seed value and the timestamp being a 64-bit value. The same concerns apply to this method as with SHA-1.

FIPS 186

FIPS 186 defines a number of different cryptographic PRNGs (CPRNGs) for use with the Digital Signature Algorithm and for other methods. One is similar to the SHA-1 function, and another is a more complicated version of ANSI X9.17.

Blum-Blum-Shub

The previous methods produce cryptographic-quality numbers; however, there is no proof that inverting SHA-1 is "hard"; it's only suspected to be so. There is a class of CPRNGs that are provably secure, in the sense that being able to consistently predict the next output is equivalent to a "hard" problem such as factoring. While that would seem extremely advantageous, there is no evidence that the quality of the random number is any better than the SHA-1 method. The NIST compared both and found them equivalent. There *is* evidence that the provably secure generators are a lot slower.

The most popular of the provable CPRNGs is the Blum-Blum-Shub generator, since it requires the least computational effort and has the strongest assumption [BlBlSh1986]. Here only *1 bit* is generated per modular squaring, and predicting the output is provably equivalent to being able to factor the internal parameter n. In other words, if you developed a fast (i.e., polynomial time) way of predicting the output, you in fact developed a new factoring algorithm.

The algorithm itself is quite simple:

1. Generate two distinct random primes p, q so that both $p \equiv q \equiv 3 \bmod 4$, compute $n = pq$, and discard the original primes. This can be done once, and n can be reused if desired.
2. The seed x_0 is a number between $[1, n - 1]$ such that $GCD(x_0, n) = 1$, for instance x_0 could be a random prime.
3. Compute $x_i = x_{i-1}^2 \bmod n$.
4. Return the least-significant bit of x_i as the random bit.
5. Repeat Steps 3 and 4 as needed.

The efficiency can be improved by extracting $j < c \ln \ln n$ bits per iteration, with c being a constant and using "large n," and still be equivalently secure. Unfortunately, c has not been determined.

While interesting, provably secure generators aren't used very often because of their cost. They are not required by any standards. Implementation in Java is discussed in Chapter 5.

Stream Ciphers

While block ciphers encrypt an entire block at a time, stream ciphers encrypt 1 byte at a time. The theory is quite simple: Generate pseudorandom bytes using the key as a seed. These bytes are XORed against the plaintext to produce an encrypted byte. The same bytes are used to decrypt the stream. A block cipher can be used as a stream cipher by using the OFB and CFB modes discussed in Chapter 2; however, there are some special stream ciphers worth mentioning.

One-Time Pads

One-time pads (OTPs) are special ciphers designed for one-time use and are based on truly random numbers. For business purposes, the concept is more theoretical than practical, but it does provide "perfect" security if done appropriately. The principal behind one-time pads is that the result of XORing *truly* random bytes with an *arbitrary* message is itself completely random. (You might need to consider this for a while before being convinced that it's true.) Using an OTP, each byte of the plaintext is XORed with a random byte from a list, so the "key" is the size of the message. Decryption is done similarly: Each ciphertext byte is XORed with the same "random" byte from the list. The end result is that there is no way of determining what the original plaintext is unless you have the original random bytes, since without them, the original text could have been *anything*. Given a ciphertext of XYZ, the key is just as likely to have been one that produces 123 or ABC.

There are a few conditions to ensure that this all works. First is that the bytes are truly random. There cannot be any structure in how they are generated; otherwise, it provides something that analysis can possibly crack. Second, once a message is encrypted, the bytes used in the process can never be used again. Finally, you have to distribute the random bytes securely. If it's just you and a buddy, you can burn a CD-ROM full of random bytes for this purpose and communicate securely. Otherwise, it's a bit harder to implement.

RC4 or ArcFour

RC4 is one of many ciphers designed by Ron Rivest for RSA Security in 1987. It was a proprietary algorithm and was (is?) deemed a trade secret.

Details were available only by signing nondisclosure agreements. Given the simplicity of the algorithm, it would not have been very difficult to determine the algorithm just by looking at assembly code. In any event, someone anonymously posted the details of the algorithm to a newsgroup, where it has spread precipitously.

Trade secrets have a funny place in United States law: The holder of the secret can do nasty legal maneuverings to prevent the disclosure of the trade secret; however, once the secret has been disclosed, there is not much they can do. RC4 is not patented (to do so would have disclosed the algorithm in public). However, the name RC4 is trademarked by RSA and cannot be used, so the alternate name of ArcFour is commonly used.

RC4 has proven very popular and is used in variety of applications. Commonly used in the SSL protocol, more recently it's been used in the 802.11b specification for wireless LANs.

Using Randomness

Even if you have a good source of randomness, the next step is using it correctly. For initialization vector and searching for prime numbers, there isn't much to do, since the raw bytes are used. However, there are specialized methods using random numbers for searching, sorting, and generating numbers in a range.

Generating Random Numbers for Gaming

For gambling applications, you need lots of "small" random numbers. Of course, it's best to use a true random source. However, it takes time to generate random bits, so using a true source as the only source is limiting.

Since the implementation of `SecureRandom` isn't publicly available, we do know exactly how Sun's implementation works (the `SecureRandom` and `Random` APIs are discussed in detail later in the chapter.). However, doing some quick timing tests, it appears that each call of the `nextInt` performs one hash operation. Given that the SHA-1 hash produces 20 bytes per operation, a lot of "randomness" is wasted. Using the `nextBytes` method and directly extracting random bytes is about five times faster.

One problem with this scheme is that every outcome is predetermined once the `SecureRandom` instance starts. To solve this you need to reseed the `SecureRandom` instance regularly. See the *Java and Random Numbers* section later in the chapter for more on this.

Using noncryptographic PRNGs is not recommended for obvious reasons. Predictability is paramount!

Generating Random Numbers in a Range

While the focus of this book is with Java, a few words about using other programming languages is useful, since it's done wrong so often. Assume you have a function `rand()` that returns a random integer from 0 to `m` (inclusive). The wrong way is to select a random number from 0 to $k - 1$ in order to compute `rand()% k`. This method has some statistical faults that are especially apparent if the random integer generated or the maximum value is close to n. A trivial example is with $m = 8$ and $k = 3$. All possible results are:

$$0 \% 3 = 0$$
$$1 \% 3 = 1$$
$$2 \% 3 = 2$$
$$3 \% 3 = 0$$
$$4 \% 3 = 1$$
$$5 \% 3 = 2$$
$$6 \% 3 = 0$$
$$7 \% 3 = 1$$

Here, the value 1 occurs more frequently than any other value. The quick solution is simply to discard the value 7 when it occurs; then every outcome occurs equally. In general, the random number r should be discarded if $r > m - m \% k$. (An alternate version is to discard if $b < m \% k$, but it's not as intuitive.) A sample implementation might be as follows:

```
static final int n = ... ; // want range 0 .. n-1.  n fixed value
static final int max = RAND_MAX - RAND_MAX % n;   max fixed value

int nextInt(){
     int r;
do {
          r = rand();
while ( r > max);
return r % n;
}
```

If you are writing a generic function where the range can change from one call to the next, the following is an equivalent and slightly faster variation, since it only requires one division:

```
int nextInt(int n) {
int r, result;
do {
```

```
r = rand(); // rand returns 0 ... RAND_MAX
result = r % n;
} while ((bits - result + (n-1)) > RAND_MAX))
return result;
}
```

In Java, this is already done for you in the `Random` and `SecureRandom` `nextInt` method. (*Note:* Here the cutoff test is done using the expression `(bits - val + (n-1)) < 0`. This works since the value of the *m* is the same as the maximum value an `int` type can hold. If the value of the computation is greater than *m*, the value overflows and becomes negative.

If *n* is small (say, under 16,000), it might be better to work with raw bytes or with unscaled values. If your random function returns a 32-bit integer, it's very possible to generate multiple smaller values using this method by chopping up the integer into parts and extracting the random values you need from each part. Besides conserving randomness, it's much faster than making multiple calls to the main random function (especially if you are using a secure random source). This technique should only be used with cryptographic-quality generators, since common noncryptographic generators produce numbers that have strong byte-to-byte correlations. For example, say you wish to get a random number from 0 to 51 (for shuffling cards, for instance). Calling `nextInt` with `SecureRandom` will result in one iteration of the SHA-1 hash function, which is relatively expensive. Instead, by requesting bytes and extracting the values as shown in the following code, you can get a 5× performance boost (of course, you could make a more complicated version that just uses 6 bits):

```
public int getNextCard() {
int b = 0;
do {
        b = getRandByte();
} while (b >= 208);  // note: 208 = 255 - 255%52
return b % 52;
}
```

Following is one example of using a 32-bit `int` to extract 4 bytes:

```
public int randint;             // random 32-bit int
public int index;               // byte position in int.

public int getRandByte() {
     if (index > 4) {
          randint = rand(); // rand() returns 32-bit int
```

```
            index = 0;
        }
        randint = randint >>>= 8;
        index++;
        return (randint & 0xFF);
    }
```

Here's a more Java-centric version that uses bytes from a `SecureRandom` source:

```
    protected SecureRandom rand;
    protected byte[] buffer = new byte[20];
    protected int i = 0;

    public int getRandByte() {
        if (i == buffer.length) {
        rand.nextBytes(buffer);
        i = 0;
        }
        return buffer[i++];
    }
```

There are other ways, but this is foolproof, simple to implement, doesn't require floating point arithmetic, and conserves the random bits (only enough are used).

Shuffling

Given an array of objects, rearranging them in a random order is somewhat counterintuitive when compared to, say, how we shuffle cards. When humans shuffle cards, it's mostly just a fixed number of interchanges, such as:

```
    int max = a.length;
    for (int i = 1; i < max; ++i)  {
        int x = r.nextInt(max);
        int y = r.nextInt(max);
        int tmp = a[x]; a[x] = a[y]; a[x] = tmp;
    }
```

However, this method doesn't do a very good job shuffling, since it produces n^n outputs while there are only $n! = (n)(n-1)(n-2)....(3)(2)$ outcomes, so some results occur more often than others. Using 123 as an example, it produces nine possible outcomes, as shown in Figure 4.1.

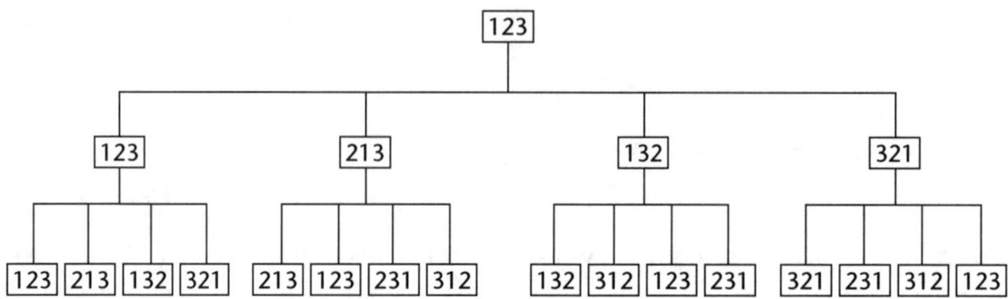

Figure 4.1 Tree of results for incorrect shuffling algorithms.

Here, 123 occurs four times, but 213 only occurs twice. The result is more or less the same if you eliminate the "null swaps" (where $i = j$) or add more iterations. The right solution is to simulate how the factorial operation works. The first element has n choices, the next element can be $n - 1$ possibilities, and so on:

```
for (int i = a.length; i >= 1; --i)  {
     int j = r.nextInt(i);
     int tmp = a[i]; a[i] = a[j]; a[j] = tmp;    // swap a[i] and a[j]
}
```

Using 123, the correct distribution occurs where each outcome occurs equally, as shown in Figure 4.2. One nice aspect about this algorithm is that at each step of the loop, the element `a[i]` is fixed, so you can draw one random element at a time. For some types of games, it's nice to know even the house doesn't know in advance how the cards will be shuffled until it actually receives the cards. A sample implementation follows with the `getNext` randomly selecting a new value on demand:

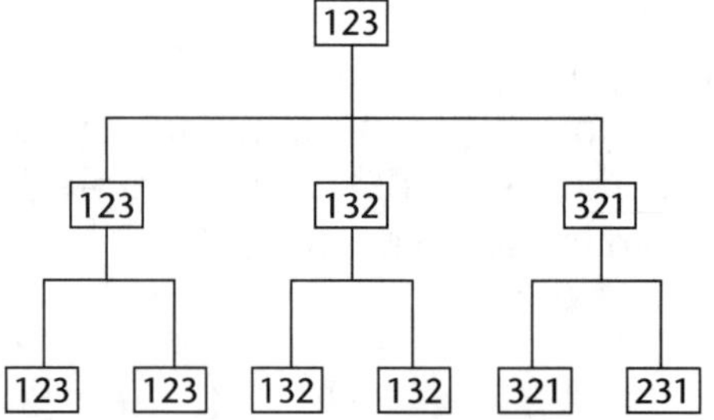

Figure 4.2 Tree of results for shuffling done correctly.

```
public class ShuffleIterator
{
     protected int a[];
     protected int i;
     protected Random r;

     public ShuffleIterator(int a[], Random r) {
     this.a = a;
     this.r = r;
     i = a.length;
     }

     public boolean hasNext() { return (i >= 0); }

     public int getNext() {
          if (i > 0) {
               int j = r.nextInt(i);
                    int tmp = a[i]; a[i] = a[j]; a[j] = tmp;
     }
          i--;
          return a[i];
     }
}
```

In Java, there is no shuffling algorithm in the `java.util.Arrays` class; however, there is a `shuffle` method in `java.util.Collections` that takes a `List` type and, optionally, a source of randomness.

Generating Random Permutations

Instead of shuffling an existing array, you occasionally want to generate random permutations, or a rearrangement of the numbers 0 to $n - 1$ (or 1 to n). There are two types of categories: where n is small and permutations need to be done frequently, and where n is large and you just need one fixed permutation.

Small Permutations

This category is just a small optimization of the shuffling algorithm and is equivalent to shuffling a fresh pack of cards. It doesn't require a temporary variable to do the swapping. You can also modify this to make the generation iterative instead of all at once:

```
int i, j;
for (i = 0; i < n; ++i)
      s[i] = i;
for (i = 0; i < n; ++i) {
      j = r.nextInt[i]
      s[i] = s[j];
      s[j] = i;
}
```

Large Fixed Permutations

Occasionally, you need to generate a single random permutation from 1 to m, where m is large. This is useful when you are generating database sequence numbers (if the database doesn't provide them) but don't want to use sequential numbers. Perhaps you want to disguise the order in which elements were added. Another application is where you want a sampling from a large sorted array but you don't want the output to be sorted and you want to make sure you visit every record. For smaller applications, you could just generate a random permutation, but if m is large, you might not want to generate an array of several hundred thousand or even millions of elements just for quick sampling.

The simplest way of generating a large permutation is to use specially constructed linear congruential generators (LCG). These aren't useful for cryptographic purposes, since the data is predictable and doesn't have particularly good random qualities. But they work fine if you are generating simple sequence numbers.

Recall that an LCG is defined as $x_{n+1} = ax_n + c \bmod m$. The main theorem defines when a, c, and m define a random permutation of length m, if and only if [Knuth1998]:

1. c is relatively prime to m (i.e., $GCD(c, m) = 1$, and c may be 1).
2. $a - 1$ is a multiple of every prime that divides m (and $a < m$).
3. $a - 1$ must be a multiple of 4 if m is a multiple of 4 too.

For a given m, there may not be an LCG that can generate a permutation. For instance, $m = 30$ has a prime factorization of $2 \times 3 \times 5$. However, the smallest multiple of the prime factors is 30, meaning there is no number less than 30 that will satisfy Condition 2. As another example, 60 has the prime factorization of $2^2 \times 3 \times 5$. Again, choosing c is no problem. Choosing $a = 31$ works, since $a - 1 = 30$ and from the previous example 30 is a multiple of every prime ($30 = 2 \times 15 = 3 \times 10 = 5 \times 6$). But this time, Condition 3 fails, since 4 divides 60 but 4 does not divide 30.

Fortunately the most common cases are when m is a power of 2 or 10. Then the conditions are fairly easy to satisfy, as shown in Table 4.3. While sample value generators are given, in practice you should use larger values for a and c so most computations of $ax + c$ exceed m. This way the sequence is not so monotone (e.g., 1, 6, 31, ...).

Table 4.3 LCG Generators for Common Periods

PERIOD SIZE	CONDITION ON *C*	CONDITION ON *A*	SAMPLE
$m = 2^i$	*c* must be odd.	$a = 4^r, + 1\, r > 1$	$x_{n+1} = 21x_n +$ 1 mod 10^n
$m = 10^i$	*c* must be odd, not 5.	$a = 4^r5^s + 1; r, s > 1$	$x_{n+1} = 5x_n +$ 1 mod 2^n

Random Sampling

One final application is random sampling, where given a large set, you wish to take a random sample of *n* elements. Putting them all into memory and selecting a random permutation is either too slow or too expensive. Most common is selecting a sample from the database. The order that is returned is either fixed or is "semirandom" based on some attribute. This section follows directly from [Knuth1998], Section 3.4.2:

```
Random rand = ... ; // random source
int i = 0;          // total records selected
int scanned = 0;    // total records scanned
int max = ... ;     // total available records
int n = ...;        // number of records to select, 0 <= n <= max


Records[] sample = new Records[n]; // the result of n records
Random rand = ...;
while (i < n) {
      Record r = getNextRecord();
      int numberSamplesNeeded = n - i;
      int numberRecordsRemainingPlusOne = max - j;
      if (rand.nextInt(numberRecordsRemaining) < numberSamplesNeeded) {
          sample[i] = r;
          i++;
      }
      j++
}
```

This is a funny algorithm, since at first glance, it might appear that you could scan the entire database and not get *n* records. Looking carefully at the statement:

```
rand.nextInt(numberRecordsRemaining) < numberSamplesNeeded
```

notice that if `numberRecordsRemaining = numberSamplesNeeded`, then every remaining record is selected (recall that `nextInt(x)` returns a random number in the range 0...x – 1). So if the algorithm falls behind, it automatically catches up.

In most database applications, determining the total number of records is a quick calculation and the previous algorithm is all you need. However, if the database is having rapid additions or deletions, or if you are selecting from a stream or variable record-length file where how to determine the number of records isn't automatic, then another technique can be used. Here's one that starts out taking the first n elements and then carefully replaces entries with new records as you scan the database:

```
Random r = ...;                     // random source
Record[] samples = new Record[n]; // result
int i = 0;                          // number of records scanned
for (i = 0; i < n ; ++i)
     samples[I] = getNextRecord();
while (hasMoreRecords()) {
     r = getNextRecord();
     i++;
     m = random.nextInt[i];
     if (m  <  n) { // selection with probability n / i
          samples[m] = r;
     }
}
```

Again, at first glance this algorithm seems a bit odd, since it appears that the last element has much less chance of being selected as the first element. Although this is the case, the earlier elements have a much higher chance of being overwritten. When you compute the odds of being selected with the odds of being overwritten, every element has an equal chance of surviving into the final sample.

Accessing Entropy

For high-volume cryptographic and gaming applications, it's essential to have access to truly random numbers that are not from PRNGs. The more adventurous will wish to try and hook in a physical external source of randomness, described in subsequent sections.

OS Services

Many operating systems have built-in sources of entropy and randomness.

Win32 CryptoAPI CryptGenRandom

Included in Microsoft's CryptoAPI is a function to retrieve random bytes by use of the `CryptGenRandom` function. I have been unable to find hard facts on exactly how randomness is distilled. I do know that the entire provider is based on RSA's BSAFE toolkit, which uses a hash-based system to generate values. And I don't see any specific random service running, so I can assume a hash-based system is used. The question then becomes how does it seed itself?

/dev/random and friends

The `/dev` filesystem exists on many Unix variants, in particular Linux and BSD-based distributions. Internal sources of randomness such as the timing of interrupts and network traffic are added into an *entropy pool* (an array of bytes) that is mixed by multiple uses of hashes. An estimate of the number of bits of entropy that is in the pool is normally kept track of.

Linux

The `/dev/`random system first appeared in Linux. `/dev/random` only returns "truly" random bytes and may block if not enough bytes are available. `/dev/urandom` feeds data from `/dev/random` into a PRNG and thus never blocks. The source for the "random.c" is a good source of information of general entropy pool design (a quick location is `www.cs.berkeley.edu/~daw/rnd/linux-rand`).

NetBSD

NetBSD is designed to run on every possible machine, from small, embedded systems to 64-bit servers. Therefore, it's hard to know in advance what is available to poll and how good the randomness is. You can't monitor disk interrupts if the device doesn't have a disk drive! Because of this, NetBSD has a very generic system that allows registration of various sources to be polled. The user interface provides the ability to poll, probe, and modify the internal entropy state and attach sources for collection and control of the internal processes of entropy collection. See rndctl(8), rnd(9), and rnd(4) man pages for more details.

FreeBSD

FreeBSD has a similar system to NetBSD; you can add or remove various interrupts for polling; however, it's not quite as flexible. FreeBSD allows you to control what interrupt sources are polled with the `rndcontrol` utility (see the man page `rndcontrol 5`).

OpenBSD

OpenBSD has a slightly different model. /dev/random is reserved for direct access to a hardware source, and /dev/srandom works similarly to the "original" /dev/random. /dev/urandom works similarly to other Unix variants.

They also defined a few other /dev/files. /dev/prandom is a simple noncryptographically strong number generator. It provides an interface to the internal posix rand() function.

/dev/arandom is a cryptographically strong pseudorandom number generator. It is seeded by /dev/srandom as needed. When /dev/urandom runs out of the true random bits, this device fills in.

Cygwin

Cygwin provides a Unixlike operating environment in Windows. /dev/random and /dev/urandom *do exist*. The directory /dev/ doesn't appear, but the special device files are there. You just need to specify them explicitly. They are functionally identical to standard Linux. These are wrappers to calls to the default Windows CryptoAPI call. It would not take much to add a new file /dev/arandom to call the Intel RNG:

```
$ ls /dev
ls: /dev: No such file or directory

$ ls -l /dev/random /dev/urandom
crw-rw-rw-    1 Everyone Everyone  21,   8 Dec 26 14:50 /dev/random
crw-rw-rw-    1 Everyone Everyone  21,   9 Dec 26 14:50 /dev/urandom
```

Sun Solaris

Solaris does not provide a cryptographic strength source of randomness; however, a student at the University of Salzburg developed a kernel module by the name of ANDIrand (www.cosy.sbg.ac.at/~andi/) that provides a /dev/random.

Userland Services

The following services were originally desired for Unix systems that did not have a /dev/random or /dev/urandom source. Instead of the polling process being in the kernel, these are "userland" programs that do basically the same service but outside the kernel. They poll various keyboard and mouse timings, timing between interrupts (when the CPU is interrupted

Table 4.4 Comparison of Userland Services.

SYSTEM	COMMENTS
EGD	Perl-based, works best on Unix and not as well on Windows.
PRNGD	Written in portable C; works on many Unixlike systems. Suitable for `inetd` (the Internet services daemon).
Yarrow	Windows only. Based on solid design, but source seems to be abandoned.
EGADS	Works on Unix, and Windows 2000 and XP. Based on Yarrow. Alpha state, but actively worked on.

to do another process), and other system parameters, put them into an entropy pool, and hash the pool to obtain random bits. Unfortunately, most are not polished or are limited to Unix environments.

Table 4.4 provides a comparison of the services discussed.

Entropy Generating Daemon (EGD)

A more localized approach to entropy network services appears as the Entropy Generating Daemon, or EGD. This is a Perl script that can be configured to poll various services by forking off commands and hashing the output. Although it's Perl, it really must run on a Unix machine (Cygwin users can use it, but as of 0.8, it needs some tweaking). Windows doesn't have the system commands to run. Each source can be configured to determine how many bits of entropy it contains. It stores bits, and bits are requested, they are pulled out of the stack. These systems do *not* read randomness from keyboard, mouse, or windowing events, which are likely to be nonexistent anyway on server machines.

EGD can be configured for use with the GNU Privacy Guard (GPG) encrypted email system and the OpenSSL cryptographic library. In addition, it can use Internet-style sockets (e.g., localhost on port 4000) or Unix-style sockets, which are mapped to a filename (`/etc/egd`).

Random bits can be requested and written into the pool using a simple protocol.

Using EGD

The following method is based on version 0.8:

1. Download and unpack.

2. Configure. Configuring the ECG is done by editing the source egd.pl that contains an embedded configuration file. You don't need to know anything about Perl to configure it. First, search for the line $sources <<'EOF'. Right above this line is a description of the configuration file, and right below it is the actual configuration. Each entropy source starts with the line:

```
bpb=float,filter=[1/0],maxbits=max,timeout=n,reuse
```

   - bpb is the number of bits of entropy per byte of the source. How you estimate this is more an art than a science.
   - filter determines if any preprocess of the input is required. If the filter is on (1), then all nondigit values in the input are removed. This is very useful, since it can remove constant text and values in the output of system commands.
   - maxbits is a maximum number of random bits, regardless of what the bpb says.
   - timeout=n means to kill off the process after *n* seconds.
   - reuse=n refers to the number of seconds to wait before reusing this source.

3. Build and install. The next line is the command you wish to run. If a command doesn't exist or doesn't work on your system, EGD ignores it without error. EGD makes use of the standard methods for Perl modules:

```
perl Mafile.pl
make
make test
make install
```

4. Run using any of the following forms:

```
egd.pl /unix/domain/style/socket
egd.pl portNumber
egd.pl address:portNumber
```

   By default, EGD will fork off a new process and run in the background. You can automatically kill off the background process by redoing the command that started it and adding -kill to the command line:

```
>egd.pl 4000        # off and running
>egd.pl -kill 4000  # kill it
```

Alternatively, you can have the process run in the foreground by adding the `-nofork` flag. It will run forever until you terminate it with Ctrl-C or another method. Finally, you can set a self-destruct mechanism to make the EGD stop running after a set number of minutes:

```
egd.pl -quit-after=30
```

5. Test and debug. Make sure all the entropy sources are unique by running `-debug-gather`. This will show what commands are being executed for entropy. Check to make sure the output makes sense. The first time I ran EGD the output of `ps aux` and `ps -el` were used as separate entropy sources, although on my system the output was identical. If you need to make a configuration change, edit the source file again and do a `make install`. The full list of debug options are shown in Table 4.5.
6. Then test the system by using the `egc.pl` (located in the "eg" directory). This is a simple client application that allows interact queries to the EGD. The help file says it all:

```
$ ./egc.pl
Usage: egc.pl <daemon> <command> [<args>]
  daemon: host:portnum or /path/to/unix/socket
  commands:
     get:  returns bits of entropy in pool
     read N: tries to get N bytes of entropy, nonblocking
     readb N: gets N bytes of entropy, blocking
     write N: reads from stdin, adds N bits to entropy pool
     pid: report PID of daemon

$ ./egc.pl localhost:4000 get
 619 bits of entropy in pool

$ ./egc.pl localhost:4000 read 10
got 10 bytes of entropy: 7c3ae8109a81cca16bdc
```

While the configuration system of editing the source file is a bit screwy, it's nice because you can easily add entropy sources.

The EGD Protocol

The protocol to request random bytes is fairly simple (see Table 4.6). The first byte is a control byte determining the function. This is followed by any additional arguments in binary format.

Table 4.5 Debug Options for EGD

EGD DEBUG OPTIONS	DESCRIPTION
`-debug`	Displays basic entropy size and sleeping counts.
`-debug-select`	Displays file descriptors used in `select()` loop.
`-debug-gather`	Prints information on entropy sources.
`-debug-client`	Prints information on client access.
`-debug-pool`	Prints size and contents of the entropy pool.
`-bottomless`	Normally, client requests for entropy reduces the internal pool of random bits. With this flag, the pool size only grows. This is useful for debugging and not for production use.

Table 4.6 EGD Protocol

FUNCTION	REQUEST	RESPONSE
Retrieve number of entropy bits available	0x00	An unsigned 32-bit integer (or 4 bytes) in Big-Endian format, e.g., 1 bit is represented as 4 bytes by 00 00 00 01.
Get random bytes, nonblocking	0x01 0xNN 0xNN unsigned byte value, 0-255, for the number of bytes requested	First byte returns the number of random bytes to follow. If not enough bytes are available, as many are returned.
Get random bytes, blocking	0x02 0xNN 0xNN unsigned byte value, 0-255, for the number of bytes requested	Same as previous. If the full number of bytes is not available, the request will block or wait until it is able to complete the request.
Add random bytes to pool	0x03 0xLL 0xNN NN 0xLL is number of bits of entropy 0xNN is number of bytes to follow NN NN bytes	None; no acknowledgement is provided.
Get process ID (PID) of daemon	0x04	0xMM length of PID string not null terminates. MM ASCII bytes.

Problems with EGD

Unfortunately, EGD is very much a work in progress and has a few problems. As of version 0.8:

- EGD doesn't know that a polled source isn't changing. If a source returns the same value as it did in the last polling session, EGD happily thinks that the data is fine.
- EDG can run out of bits. This can be a huge problem, particularly when many people are starting up applications. When the bits are used up, everything stops. Then you must manually restart the daemon or wait for it to wake up again.
- It is written in Perl and uses system resources to fork off processes.
- The configuration file is embedded in the source file. This is not the most convenient method (but it's also not bad either and works fairly well).

Fortunately, most of the problems are easily fixable, and may even be fixed in the current release already.

PRNGD

As part of an effort to make EGD more robust, PRNGD was developed. It is written in portable C and should work on most Unix-based platforms. It uses the EGD protocol and polls various system sources. Unlike EGD, these values are constantly fed into an internal pseudorandom number generator, so it never blocks and never runs out of values to return. For more details see `www.aet.tu-cottbus.de/personen/jaenicke/postfix_tls/prngd.html`.

Yarrow and EGADS

Yarrow is more a design than an actual product. System data is fed into a pool again, and the system uses both a hash and cipher to generate random bytes. The original paper is must-reading for the design of cryptographic PRNG. Source code is provided, but it's been abandoned. Fortunately, another project, EGADS, picks up where Yarrow left off. It's beta software, but it appears there is active development, and it works on both Windows and Unix. See `www.securesw.com/egads/` for more details.

TrueRand Library

TrueRand is an algorithm developed by a few people from AT&T in 1995 to produce "true random" numbers. It uses *drift* between different clock sources in the computer. Clocks or the oscillators they are based on are fairly stable, but they do drift a bit. The raw output isn't particularly good and needs to be whitened by hashing the result or by other techniques before being used. The estimate is 16 bits of entropy per call. You can write a small wrapper around TrueRand for use in entropy pollers described in the next section. So while this is a software source, it's based on a physical principal. Since computers contain a lot more parts than just two oscillators, this type of technique is very system-specific. However, it may work for you.

Finding the actual TrueRand code is a bit tricky. David Wagner has a large collection of articles on randomness at `http://now.cs.berkeley.edu/~daw/rnd`, which among other things, contains the TrueRand code.

It's also available from the very good article by Gary Mcgraw and John Viega entitled "Make Your Software Behave: Software Strategies," available at `www.106.ibm.com/developerworks/security/library/randomsoft/`. Even here the code is a bit hard to find; to directly get the source code, add indexcode2.html to the URL.

In addition, the Apache mod_ssl module uses a variant of TrueRand. To get the source code, go to `www.modssl.org/` and look for the file truerand.c.

Remote Services

Currently three "live" true random number generators are available on the Web. You can query the bit server and receive fresh random bits that only you will use. Writing a simple client is fairly simple to simulate an HTTP request. However, another very useful way of querying servers is by using the Unix-based `wget`. This application downloads Web pages directly and doesn't use a full graphical interface. The code is as follows:

```
wget -q -O file URL
```

The flag `-q` turns off unnecessary comments. If the file is '-' (a dash character), then the output is sent to the console. Finally, if you are looking for a little random number humor, see `www.noentropy.net/`.

WARNING These random bits are coming over the network in the clear. For cryptographic purposes, you will want to do additional processing before using them as a seed. Ideally, they should only be used for testing.

RAND Corporation

In 1955, the RAND Corporation published the book *A Million Random Digits with 100,000 Normal Deviates*, mostly for use with numerical or probabilistic scientific algorithms. A *normal deviate* is just a random number between 0 and 1, but the New York Public Library didn't know that and filed the book in the psychology section!

The numbers were generated with a random pulse that was blasted through a circuit 100,000 times per second. Every second, a 5-bit number was extracted and converted to decimal. Then just the last digit was fed onto an IBM punch card. The original set of numbers was as random as they hoped, so the final version of each digit is the mod 10 result of adding the original number with another number in the same position but on another page. (Yes, it was proofread, but only every twentieth or fortieth page.)

In 2001 the RAND Corporation reprinted all 628 pages of it as well as making the raw data available for download. See `www.rand.org/publications/classics/randomdigits/` for more details.

HotBits

Everyone would talk about using radioactive sources for randomness, but nobody ever did anything about it. John Walker, coauthor of AutoCAD, decided to fix that by hooking up a Geiger counter and radioactive source to his computer and putting the results on the Web at `www.fourmilab.ch/hotbits/`. To directly download raw binary, use the URL `www.fourmilab.ch/cgi-bin/uncgi/Hotbits?nbytes=n&fmt=bin`. An example using the `wget` utilitity is show below:

```
$ wget -q -O '-'
  'http://www.fourmilab.ch/cgi-bin/uncgi/Hotbits?nbytes=10&fmt=bin'
BJ<d+I?_?A
```

Random.org

Random.org has been up since 1998 serving random bits generated from atmospheric noise. A variety of interfaces are available, but the most useful is Web-based using the following URL:

`www.random.org/cgi-bin/randbyte?nbytes=n&format={f,h,d,o,b}`

The format X can be one of f, h, d, o, or b and determines what format the random numbers should be. The default format is *f*, which is raw bytes. The other values return the data as plaintext using hexadecimal, decimal, octal, or binary encodings, respectively. The values are presented in columns: Below is sample output:

```
$ wget -q -O '-' \
   'http://www.random.org/cgi-bin/randbyte?nbytes=10&format=decimal'
231 191  74 131 137 143  32 136 124 135
```

LavaRnd

While at Silicon Graphics, Landon Curt Noll, Robert G. Mende Jr., and Sanjeev Sisodiya devised a novel system for generating random numbers. Noticing that lava lamps have chaotic (or long-term unpredictable) motion, they pointed a camera at a lamp (or multiple lamps), digitized the result, and put the bits into a hash function. For a while, you could not only view a lamp over the Web but also download the random bits generated by it. However, the parent-company hosting site has since discontinued public access. It's such a good idea that they patented it (U.S. Patent 5,732,138). If the thought of going to prison for pointing a Web cam at a lava lamp scares you, don't worry. The inventors have a new method that they believe is patent-free. A new Web site describing the method, new cam views, and a network download of bits should by up and running in the summer of 2002 at `www.lavarnd.org/`.

Java and Random Numbers

As mentioned earlier in the chapter, Java provides a CPRNG class. The API is quite simple, but the real trick is first getting the truly random seed (or initial) value for the generator and to periodically reseed the generator.

Random and SecureRandom

Java provides two classes for random number generation. `Random` from `java.util` is the general-purpose API that is useful for simple applications, but is completely inappropriate for anything cryptographic. `SecureRandom` from `java.security` extends the `Random` API slightly and produces cryptographic strength numbers.

java.util.random

The Random class provided in the java.util package provides a basic interface for generating random numbers. You can provide a seed; otherwise, it defaults to the current time. The interface is fairly straightforward:

```
boolean nextBoolean(); // next bit
int nextInt(); // next int
int nextInt(n); //return random int between [0, n-1]
int nextLong(); // next long.
float nextFloat(); //return [0, 1)
int nextDouble(); // return [0, 1)
double nextGausian();  Guassian distributions
void nextBytes(byte[] bytes);; fills in array with random bytes
void setSeed(long seed); reset the seed using a long for 8 bytes
```

For cryptographic purposes, you will most likely use the methods that work with bytes or integer types. Oddly there is no nextLong(int n). However, if you are working on an application that needs random real numbers, you have a few options.

The nextFloat and nextDouble methods return a random real number from 0 (inclusive) up to 1 (exclusive). This result can then be scaled to the desired value.

Cracking java.util.random

The Java random number generator uses a modified version of the LCG, where a = 0x5DEECE66D, b = 0xB, and $m = 2^{48} - 1$. However, only the 32 leftmost bits are used for integers (Java int type) and two iterations are used for generating a long type. Since we know the parameters, cracking this one only involves determining the 16 bits that are thrown out. Iterating through all 65,536 possible values is quite simple. This means given any two consecutive integers from Random or just one long value, we can determine the internal state and predict the next value, and every value afterwards. If this doesn't convince you that Random is completely unsuitable for cryptographic work, then nothing will! Source code and sample output is listed below:

```
$ java RandomCracker
x0 = 908910814
x1 = -1510378413
Found match at 27305
x2 = 2012762866 (estimate)
x2 = 2012762866 (actual)
```

```
import java.util.Random;

public class RandomCracker {
    protected static final long a = 0x5deece66dL;
    protected static final long b = 0xbL;
    protected static final long m = (1L << 48 ) -1;

     // given two calls to Random.nextInt(), determine the third
    public static void  crack(int xint0, int xint1)
    {
     long i;
     long seed = -1L;
     // convert unsigned int to long value
     long x0 = (xint0 & 0xFFFFFFFFL) << 16;
     long x1 = (xint1 & 0xFFFFFFFFL);

     for (i = 0; i <= 0xFFFFL; i++) {
         seed = (((x0 + i) * a) + b) &  m;
         if ((seed >>> 16) == x1) {
          // found it
          break;
         }
         seed= -1L;
     }
     if (seed == -1L) {
         throw new RuntimeException("invalid input");
     } else {
         System.out.println("Found match at " + i);
         System.out.println("x2 = " +
                      (int) ((((seed * a) + b) & m) >>> 16));
     }
}

    public static void main(String[] args) {
     Random r = new Random();
     int x0 = r.nextInt();
     int x1 = r.nextInt();
     System.out.println("x0 = " + x0);
     System.out.println("x1 = " + x1);
     crack(x0, x1);
     System.out.println("x2 = " + r.nextInt());
     }
}
```

java.security.SecureRandom

`SecureRandom` inherits from `Random` and provides cryptographic-strength random number generation. It's actually a bit more complicated than that, but I'll defer those issues until the next chapter. The interface is extended by the static method `getSeed` that will generate true random numbers (not pseudorandom ones) and has the option of getting random bytes with `getBytes`. In addition, you can set the internal seed with a long value or with an array of bytes. If you do not provide a seed, the `SecureRandom` instance will go through a self-seeding method to generate truly random numbers.

Standard SHA-1 PRNG Seed

For self-seeding, the stock method collects system entropy from a variety of sources and stores it in a byte array. Then numerous threads are launched that basically just increment a counter for a fixed time period and index an array of values that is XORed against the byte array. When finished, the counters for each thread are mixed and a seed value is produced. This system seems to work well, and the quality of the randomness is quite good; however, it has some drawbacks. It's very system-resource-intensive and therefore slow; it may take 10 seconds for the application to initialize. Java 1.4 seems to have improved this a bit, but it still will max out the CPU. For the most part, this happens once, and it's not a problem. The issue is when developers are constantly starting and stopping applications and are unable to share instances.

URL-Based Seeding

Starting in Java 1.4, the seeding can be done by specifying a URL to read for the seed value. The benefit is that seeding is almost instantaneous and doesn't have any CPU load. The fastest way of specifying the random source is to add `-Djava.security.egd=file:/dev/random` (or another URL) on the command line. To permanently specify a random source URL, edit the file `${java_home}/jre/lib/security/java. security`, and uncomment the line with `securerandom.source` and add the appropriate value. It can be overridden using the `-Djava.security.egd` as well. Even though the letters *egd* are present in the property name, out of the box, Java does *not* know the EGD protocol. You can certainly add your own URL protocol handler. This way you can read (or put) random bytes from the EGD service by using something like `egd://localhost:3000/get?bytes=20`. The process of making a customer URL handler is a bit tricky, and the source code is a bit long, but a good write-up on how to do this can be found in "A New Era for Java Protocol Handlers" by Brian Maso (`http://developer.java.sun.com/developer/onlineTraining/protocolhandlers/`).

Developer Issues

If you use a seeding method that takes a long time or use a `SecureRandom` generator that is slow, developers are sure to complain. One way around this is to swap out seeding or algorithms for a faster one in the development process and put in a strong version in production. In addition, sometimes randomness is not useful in testing for bugs. Such times you want deterministic behavior.

Like initializing providers, initializing `SecureRandom` instances can be done in a separate class. One way is to specify a `-Drandom=devel` on the command line. The danger is that it will be used on the production network. To prevent this, you can check the network and throw an exception if the application is run on the production network:

```
import java.security.SecureRandom;
import java.util.Properties;
public class SecureRandomFactory {

    protected static SecureRandom srand = null;

    public static synchronized SecureRandom getInstance() {
     if (srand == null) {
         srand = new SecureRandom();
         if (NOT_ON_PRODUCTION_NETORK) {
          String prop = System.getProperties().getProperty("random");
          if (prop.equals("fixed")) {
              // always same random numbers
              srand.setSeed(1); // or System.currentTimeMillis();
          } else if (prop.equals("devel")) {
              // random, but not secure
              srand.setSeed(System.currentTimeMillis());
          }
         } else {
          srand.nextInt(); // make seeding happen right away
         }
     }
     return srand;
    }
}
```

Reseeding

For long-lived applications that use lots of random numbers, using `SecureRandom` by itself is problematic, since every output is predetermined at the start of the application. For gaming applications, it's especially disturbing that every outcome is predetermined at the start. It's critical then to inject true randomness into the system. One application is, of course, just using an EGD or hardware-based source. Unfortunately, often these are either slow (network EGD) or unavailable (no direct access to hardware from Java). For occasional use these are just fine (generating long-term keys), but for gaming and other high-volume applications, this may be too slow (or it may not; be sure to check first).

If you have an EGD or `/dev/random` that `SecureRandom` can read, then this system should be very fast. If not, you'll either have to live with the application periodically hanging while the seeding process starts or you'll have to use another technique listed in the next section. The code for reseeding with `SecureRandom` is as follows:

```
import java.security.SecureRandom;
public class SecureRandomReseeder extends SecureRandom implements
Runnable
{
    protected SecureRandom srand;
    protected long sleeptime;
    protected Thread t;
    protected boolean reseed = true;

    public SecureRandomReseeder(SecureRandom r, long sleeptime) {
     this.srand = r;
     this.sleeptime = sleeptime.
     t = new Thread(this);
     t.start();
    }

    public void stopSeeding() {
     reseed = false;
    }

    public void run() {
     while (reseed) {
         byte[] seed = srand.getSeed(20);
         srand.setSeed(seed);
         try {
          t.sleep(sleeptime);
         } catch (InterruptedException e) {
          // nothing
         }
     }
    }
}
```

Collecting Entropy

If you do not have a hardware or OS source for entropy, you'll have to create it yourself using various input and system values in a way similar to how EGD and Yarrow work. An *entropy pool* is a buffer where random or semirandom events are mixed together in order to generate truly random results. The input of events into the pool is done in background so the application doesn't come to a halt. Eventually this pool can be hashed and used as a seed for a `SecureRandom` instance. This can all be done automatically by extending the `SecureRandomReseeder` class to use an entropy pool.

An Entropy Pool Implementation

A simple entropy pool mixer is given in the code that follows. Unlike more advanced systems, there is no running estimate of the total entropy collected or automatic feeding of the result into another PRNG—that's for you to do.

The mixing function is byte-by-byte addition with carry instead of the usual XOR in a ring buffer. XOR certainly would work, but if the same value is passed in twice, they undo each other. Addition with carry is a much more complicated function. It returns a seed value that is the result of hashing the entropy pool. This should then be set into a `SecureRandom.setSeed` method. The seed is then fed back into the pool as well. The pool by itself is pretty simple; it just grinds away on the input bits. There are lots of other tricks you can do, but the real issue is making sure you add good data, or the old motto of "garbage in, garbage out" applies. The code is as follows:

```
import java.security.MessageDigest;

public class EntropyPool
{
    public static final String HASH_NAME = "SHA";
    public static final int    HASH_SIZE = 20;
    public static final int    POOL_SIZE = 512; // bytes
    public byte[] pool = new byte[POOL_SIZE];

    public int index = 0;           // offset in pool
    public int newbytes = 0;        // total bytes added since last
seeding
```

```
    public int carry = 0;          // interal carry value for addition
    public MessageDigest md;

    public EntropyPool() {
     try {
         md = MessageDigest.getInstance("SHA1");
     } catch (Exception e) {
         throw new RuntimeException("Should never happen" + e);
     }
    }
    // add data to the pool
    public void add(byte[] input)
    {
     for (int i = input.length-1; i >=0; --i) {
         int a = pool[(index + i) % POOL_SIZE] & 0xff;
         int b = input[i] & 0xff;
         int sum = a + b + carry;
         int carry = sum >>> 8;
         pool[(index + i) % POOL_SIZE] = (byte)(sum & 0xff);
         index++;
         newbytes++;
     }
    }

    // get a seed value for use in the secure random
    public byte[]  getSeed()
    {
     byte[] seed = md.digest(pool);
     add(seed);
     newbytes = 0;
     index = index % POOL_SIZE; // keep it small
     return seed;
    }

    // retrieve number of bytes added to pool since last seeding.
    public int newPooledBytes() {
     return newbytes;
    }
}
```

Basic System State

While not ideal, you can generate semirandom numbers useful in development purposes from basic values in Java Virtual Machine. The sources are shown in Table 4.7.

Table 4.7 System State Sources

SYSTEM VALUE	DESCRIPTION
java.lang.Runtime.getRuntime().totalMemory()	Total memory available to the VM (long).
java.lang.Runtime.getRuntime().freeMemory()	Total free memory (long).
java.lang.System.currerntTimeMillis()	Current time in milliseconds (long).
new Object.hashCode() new Object.toString()	On the Sun implementation of the VM, `toString, hashCode` produces a reference to memory location. May have a touch of entropy in it.
java.net.getLocalHost().getHostAddress();	The machine's host (Internet) address. Useful for helping applications that are on different machines and starting at the same time to produce different random values.
System properties	System environment and JVM properties.
List of system temporary files	The java property `java.io.tmpdir` holds the name of a system directory where temporary system files are stored. Many times the name of these files are randomly generated and the files themselves are transient.

Gluing string representations of all these and taking a hash will produce reasonable random numbers for *development*, or as part of the input for an entropy pool, even if multiple developers are on the same machine or on different machines. In a production environment on a fresh reboot, every one of these values should be similar (if not identical) values except for the current time, which is not a good seed to use.

Thread Schemes

Thread-based schemes rely on the nondeterministic behavior of the thread scheduler either from Java or from the operating system. If two threads are running, one will have to be picked first. Each thread has some type of counter that is free-running, something similar to the class shown in the following code.

These thread schemes should only be used only after being tested on the target platform using the target VM. Threading is notoriously finicky.

```
public class Counter extends Thread
{
 protected int count = 0;
 protected boolean dorun = true;

 public Counter() {  super(); }

 public byte getCounter() { return (byte)count; }

 public stopCounting() { dorun = false;}

 public void run() {
      while (dorun) {
            count++;
            // optional --  if (count % 1000) yield()
      }
 }
}
```

Then random bytes can be generated by letting the counter run. Exactly how many times the counter is incremented depends on how often the thread yields. The optional comment, which has a yield, may be necessary to prevent lockups on your system:

```
public static byte[] generateBytes(int num) {
 byte[] buf = new byte[num];
 Counter c = new Counter();
 c.start();

 try {
     for (int i = 0; i < num; i++) {
      c.join(100L);  // time to wait.  Adjust as needed
      buf[i] = c.getCounter();
     }
```

```
    } catch (Exception e) {
        buf = null;
    }
    c.stopCounting();
    return buf;
}
```

An alternate approach is using multiple threads simultaneously. Under 1.3, this worked well whether or not the optional yield was in the comment. In Java 1.4 the threading is a bit different and with the comment, the results are not random:

```
public static byte[] generateBytes(int num) {
    byte[] buf = new byte[num];
    Counter c[] = new Counter[num];
    for (int i = 0; i < num; i++) {
        c[i] = new Counter();
        c[i].start();
    }

    try {
        Thread.currentThread().sleep(50*num);
    } catch (InterruptedException e) {
        return null;
    }

    for (int i = 0; i < num; i++) {
        c[i].stopCounting();
        buf[i] = c[i].getCounter();
    }

    return buf;
}
```

Using Race Conditions

Race conditions occur when two threads write to the same memory location, causing corruption because the value has bits from each of the two threads. Normally, race conditions are something you very much want to avoid. However, you can actually use them to your advantage by creating random numbers. The technique outlined in the following is highly system-specific, including CPU type, speed, and load, as well as the operating system being used. It is presented here as an opportunity for further study. This method has a property that you can check to see if corruption occurred. You can add all the values in any order, and the result will be the same. The only way it can be different is when a race condition occurs.

The following program files off 64 threads, each containing a different value to add. What order the threads do their addition and what the corruption is are nondeterministic. After running through a few iterations, the final result is effectively random, at least on the few machines I've tested. Run the result through the random tests. If it works for you, you can either convert the `long` value to a byte array and use it as a seed, or you can use it in the hashing technique previously described. On 32-bit CPUs, the `long` type seems to work very well.

```
//
// A Random seed generator
// using race conditions causing beneficial memory corruption
//
public class RThread extends Thread {
    // read/write
    private static long seed = 0;

    // read only -- total number of iterations per thread
    private static int max = 100;

    // local variables
    private long inc;
    private int count;

    public RThread(long i) {
     inc = i;
     count = 0;
    }

    public void run() {
     try {
         while (!interrupted() && count < max) {
          seed += inc;
          sleep(1);
          count++;
         }
     } catch (InterruptedException e) {}
    }

    public static long generateSeed() {
     for (int i = 0; i < 64; i++) {
          RThread  t= new RThread(1L << i);
          t.setPriority(Thread.NORM_PRIORITY + i % 2);
          t.start();
     }
     return seed;
    }
```

Reading External Sources

An application can read external files and sources just like EGD does and pump them into the entropy pool. While the stock `SecureRandom` can read URL sources, you may wish to manually read those sources instead of relying on system files or command-line flags. And as mentioned, you could install an "egd" URL protocol handler to read EGD sources. Another option is to compress or hash the input data to remove redundancy before passing it to the pool. The program is as follows:

```
public static byte[] getURLEntropy(String urlString, int num)
              throws Exception
{
     URL url = new URL(urlString);
     InputStream is = url.openStream();

     byte[] buf = new byte[num];
     int len;
     try  {
         len = is.read(buf);
     } catch(Exception e) {
         throw new Exception("Random Source:  " + url +
           " generated exception:  " + e.getMessage());
     }

     if (len == -1) {
         throw new Exception("Random Source:  " + url + " EOF")
     } else if (len != buf.length) {
         throw new Exception("Random Source:  " + url + " read failed");
     }

     return buf;
 }
```

Application Events

For server applications, the application itself can produce random values by noting the time when a commonly used function is called or the time between function calls. Adding the least-significant bits into the entropy pool is very easy, very fast, and produces good-quality random data. It's important not to use the actual duration but only the least-significant bits of the time value, since the actual distribution is not uniform. Most events will be approximately evenly spaced apart; however, very short or very long intervals will occur, but with less regularity.

Another option is to use any user input from forms and hash it. It's also conceivable to poll the client's state or start a counter running on the client's machine and use the counter value and pass it (or a hash or low bits) back to the server as fodder for the entropy pool.

User Events

If the application runs with a Java AWT window with frequent user interaction, you can stir into the entropy pool any window, mouse, or keyboard event. The sample that follows is very simple. It extends the entropy pool class with one that adds user events. You might wish to extend the `stirEvent` method to:

- Use actual keyboard, mouse, or window values instead of using a hash code.
- Ignore for repeated values (keyboard) or insignificant values (mouse moved by 1 pixel) by comparing the last event or last several events.
- Use every *n*th event instead of every one.
- Add in a running counter that is incremented every event.

Following is the sample code:

```
import java.awt.Component;
import java.awt.event.*;

public class AwtEventEntropy extends EntropyPool {
    protected long eventCount = 0;

    public EventEntropy() {
     super();
    }

    public void addAsListener(Component c)
    {
     c.addComponentListener(this);
     c.addKeyListener(this);
     c.addFocusListener(this);
     c.addMouseMotionListener(this);
     c.addMouseListener(this);
     c.addMouseWheelListener(this);
    }


    public void componentHidden(ComponentEvent e) { stirEvent(e); }
```

```
    public void componentMoved(ComponentEvent e) { stirEvent(e); }
    public void componentResized(ComponentEvent e) { sitrEvent(e); }
    public void componentShow(ComponentEvent e) { stirEvent(e); }
    public void focusGained(FocusEvent e) { stirEvent(e); }
    public void focusLost(FocusEvent e) { stirEvent(e); }
    public void mouseClicked(MouseEvent e) { stirEvent(e); }
    public void mouseEntered(MouseEvent e) { stirEvent(e); }
    public void mouseExited(MouseEvent e) { stirEvent(e); }
    public void mousePressed(MouseEvent e) { stirEvent(e); }
    public void mouseReleased(MouseEvent e) { stirEvent(e); }
    public void mouseDragged(MouseEvent e) { stirEvent(e); }
    public void mouseWheelMoved(MouseWheelEvent e) { stirEvent(e); }

    public void stirEvent(Object o)
    {
     add(o.hashCode ());     }
}
```

Java Cryptography

In addition to Java's native advantages in portability, it also has a very flexible and portable cryptography architecture. The Java Cryptography Architecture, or JCA, provides standard interfaces to the most common cryptographic operations and has the following goals:

- *Implementation independence.* An application is not tied to a particular implementation of an algorithm.
- *Implementation interoperability*. Different operations should be repeated or reversible regardless of implementation.
- *Algorithm independence.* Applications need not care what particular algorithm is being used.
- *Algorithm extensibility*. New algorithms can be added in a standardized way without any changes to the API.

These aims are achieved in three ways: through the provider architecture, concept engine classes, and key/parameter representation and standardization. Core Java does not actually implement any cryptographic algorithms, only cryptographic interfaces.

The plug-in modules are invoked by *concept* or *engine* classes that handle one type of cryptographic operation, such as `Cipher` or `MessageDigest`.

These classes are completely parameterized to handle most appropriate algorithms (and if not, standardized APIs are provided for the others). After initialization, these classes work identically regardless of the algorithm chosen or provider used. This parameterization keeps the JCA API compact, and it also allows for extensibility. If a new algorithm matches more of the fundamental engine types (e.g., a cipher, a digest, etc.), it can be added in a provider without any changes to the API.

Organization

Cryptography in Java is organized into two logical units. The Java Cryptography Architecture defines digests, digital signatures, and certificate handling and contains classes from `java.security`. The Java Cryptography Extensions (JCE) work with ciphers, Message Authentication Codes (MACs), and key agreements from classes from `javax.crypto`. Details for both are in Table 5.1. The split of common cryptography functions into two packages is for legal and political reasons and not because of architectures. The JCA has been historically and is currently unrestricted from export and import restrictions, while the JCE classes have commonly been restricted. Originally, only JCA was part of the core Java API, since Sun did not want to restrict the usage of Java. The JCE was an *optional standard extension* that could be downloaded (after appropriate licensing) and added on separately. Starting with Java 1.4, the JCE was brought into the core with some tricky usage restrictions.

Throughout this book, no distinction is made between these packages, and they are treated as a unified API. Classes will not be fully qualified; `java.security.MessageDigest` will be referred to as just `MessageDigest`. When writing code, trying to pick the smallest subset of package to import is difficult, since you can easily write four lines of code that reference all seven packages. In all examples, we expect that every package is imported:

```
import java.security.*;
import java.security.spec.*;
import java.security.interfaces.*;
import java.security.certificate.*;
import javax.crypto.*;
import javax.crypto.spec.*;
import javax.crypto.interfaces.*;
```

Table 5.1 JCA and JCE Components

LOGICAL UNIT	PACKAGE	DESCRIPTION
Java Cryptography Architecture (JCA)	java.security	Digital signatures, message digests, and random numbers.
	java.security.certificate	Certificate handling, encoding, and storage.
	java.security.interfaces	Interfaces for accessing parameter and key values.
	java.security.spec	Specification objects that hold parameters for key and algorithms in java.security.
Java Cryptography Extensions (JCE)	javax.crypto	Ciphers, MACs, key agreements.
	javax.crypto.interfaces	Interfaces for accessing parameters and key values.
	javax.crypto.spec	Classes that specify parameters for use in javax.crypto.

Providers and Engine Classes

As mentioned providers are JAR files containing implementations of cryptographic functions. They can be added statically using a configuration file or dynamically during run time, and they can be ranked in preference. Sun provides two providers: SUN for JCA algorithms and SunJCE for JCE algorithms. The algorithms themselves are accessed using one of 14 core generic engine classes that handle everything from basic cipher functionality to key generation and representation. These engine classes, shown in Table 5.2, do not have constructors. Instead, using the `getInstance` method, along with the algorithm name and optionally a provider source, you load the appropriate algorithm and then access it with a standard set of methods. If a provider is not listed, the provider with the highest ranking will be used. For example:

```
MessageDigest md = MessageDigest.getInstance("SHA1");
byte[] d = md.digest("This is a message".getBytes());
```

Table 5.2 Cryptographic Engine Classes

FUNDAMENTAL CLASS	DESCRIPTION
`CertificateFactory`	Transforms encoded certificates into certificate objects.
`Cipher`	Secret or public key ciphers for encryption and decryption. Additionally handles padding and modes of operation.
`ExemptionMechanism`	Provides means of weakening the strength of a cipher or restricting its use by using key escrow, key recovery, or key weakening.
`KeyAgreement`	Key agreement protocols.
`KeyFactory`	Used to translate between internal and external representations of public key pairs.
`KeyGenerator`	Used for secret key generation.
`KeyPairGenerator`	Used for key generation for public/private key pairs.
`KeyStore`	Provides public key storage and management.
`Mac`	Used with Message Authentication Codes.
`MessageDigest`	Used with message digests.
`SecretKeyFactory`	Used to translate between internal and external representations of secret keys.
`SecureRandom`	Provides cryptographic-strength random number generation.
`Signature`	Used with digital signatures.

For algorithm implementers, each engine class has a matching *service provider interface* class with the same name but ending in `Spi` (e.g., `Mac` has matching class `MacSpi`). Providers subclass these `Spi` classes to create there own implementations. In the provider JAR, a configuration file maps algorithm names to `Spi` classes. End users and applications never directly access the `Spi` classes. It is handled for you by the `getInstance` method in the core class.

Parameters, Keys, and Certificates

You can also specify keys in an opaque means by using the `Key` interface, or in a transparent means by objects implementing the `KeySpec` class.

Secret keys are generated by the `KeyGenerator` class, and public/private key pairs are generated by the `KeyPairGenerator`. In addition, keys can write or read from an external format using the `SecretKeyFactory` and `KeyFactory` engine classes.

Parameters that are not part of a key, such as initialization vectors, or parameters used in key generation (for Diffie-Hellman) can also be specified in a transparent or opaque format, but the process works differently than how it's done for keys. The `AlgorithmParametersSpec` is an empty interface that signals the implementing class has a transparent representation and allows for individual access to the parameters. Opaque representations are handled by the `AlgorithmParameter` engine class. The API is a bit rough here. First, only Cipher accepts `AlgorithmParameter` types. Every other class (and Cipher too) accepts `AlgorithmParameterSpecs`. To make matters even more confusing, many of the so-called opaque representations have interfaces that functionally make them identical to the transparent representation.

Certificates are most commonly encoded using the X.509 format with the `CertificateFactory`.

Finally, Java provides two means of storing keys and certificates. The `KeyStore` class provides a way of storing private keys and trusted certificates, while the `CertificateStore` class provides a more "white pages" approach for storing untrusted or public certificates.

Error Handling

With only a few special cases, all exceptions derive from `GeneralSecurityException`. Because the JCA was introduced in pieces, the organization and structure of the exception isn't as tight and uniform as it could be; however, it's not a problem. The complete hierarchy is pictured in Figure 5.1

There are two cases where the exception is not from this base exception and both inherit from `RuntimeException`:

- `IllegalStateException`. This occurs when an object is improperly configured. This case typically indicates a programming error.
- `ProviderException`. This occurs when a specified provider does not exist. This indicates a configuration error.

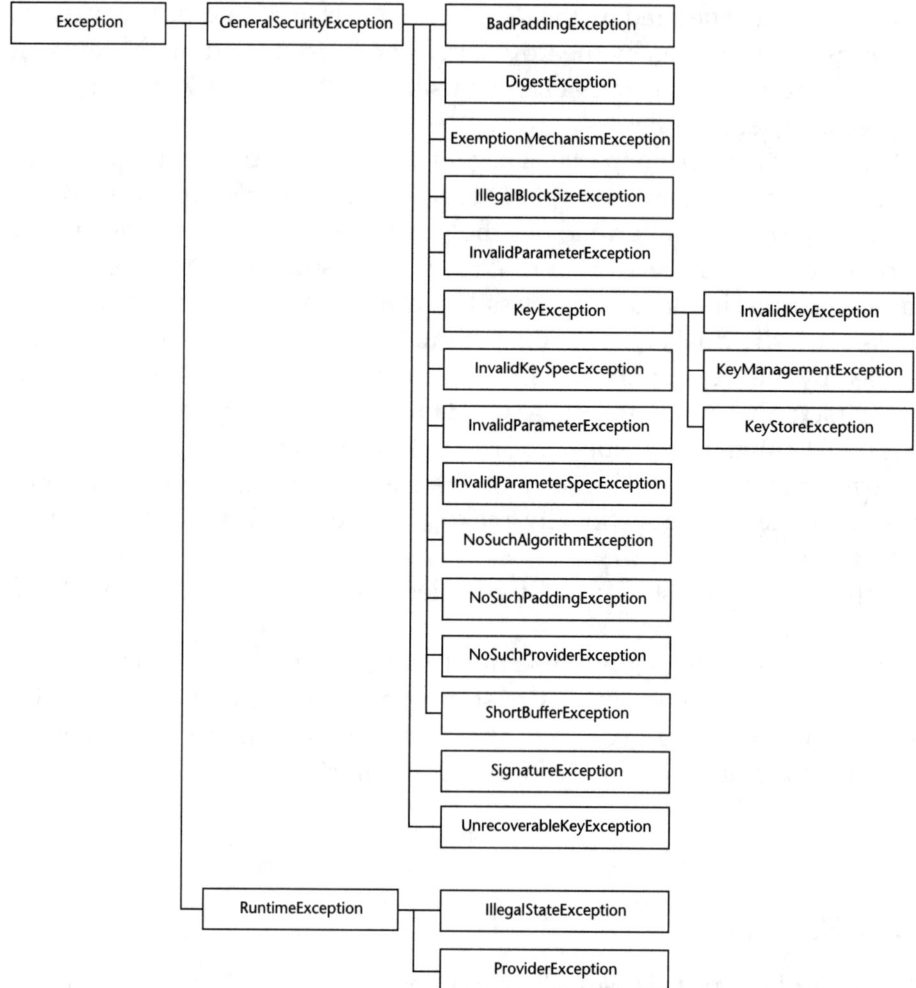

Figure 5.1 Exception hierarchy.

Providers

As mentioned, a provider is a JAR file containing implementations of cryptographic algorithms that can be plugged into the Java Virtual Machine to extend functionality.

Standard Names

To make working with multiple providers easier, Sun has mandated certain standard names for various algorithms and standards. Table 5.3 lists the standard names for main engine classes, while Table 5.4 provides standard names for the supporting engine classes. Standard names are case-insensitive, so the following all create the same object:

```
MessageDigest.getInstance("MD5");
MessageDigest.getInstance("Md5");
MessageDigest.getInstance("md5");
```

Table 5.3 Standard Names for Main Engine Classes

CATEGORY	STANDARD NAME	STANDARD REFERENCE
Ciphers	AES	FIPS 197
	DES	FIPS 81
	Triple DES	NIST SP 800-20
	Blowfish	[Schneier1994]
	PBE	PKCS #5
	RC2, RC5	RFC 2268, 2040
	RSA	PKCS #1
	RC4	RSA Security
Modes of operation (part of cipher specification)	None	
	ECB	FIPS 81
	CBC	FIPS 81
	CFB*n*, with *n* being size of block	FIPS 81
	OFB*n*, with *n* being size of block	FIPS 81
	PCBC	Kerberos

(continues)

Table 5.3 Standard Names for Main Engine Classes *(Continued)*

CATEGORY	STANDARD NAME	STANDARD REFERENCE
Padding (part of cipher specification)	NoPadding	
	PKCS5Padding	PKCS #5
	SSL3Padding	SSL v3.0
	OAEP	PKCS #1
Key agreement	DiffieHellman	PKCS #3
Digests	MD2	RFC 1319
	MD5	RFC 1321
	SHA	FIPS 180-1
	SHA-256, 512	FIPS tbd
	SHA-384	FIPS tbd
MAC	HmacMD5	RFC 2104
	HmacSHA1	RFC 2104
Exemption mechanism	KeyRecovery	
	KeyEscrow	
	KeyWeakening	
SecureRandom	SHA1PRNG	IEEE1363, G7
Signatures	MD2WithRSA	PKCS #1
	MD5WithRSA	PKCS #1
	SHA1withDSA	FIPS186
	SHA1withRSA	PKCS #1

Notes

According to Sun documentation, SHA-384 may be implemented as a truncated version of SHA-512, not what is specified in the future FIPS document.

The general format for signatures is *DIGEST*with*ENCRYPTION* or *DIGEST*with*ENCRYPTION*and*MGF* (MGF stands for mask-generating function).

Table 5.4 Parameter, Key, and Certificate Engine Class Standard Names

ENGINE CLASS	STANDARD NAMES
AlgorithmParameters	Blowfish
	DES
	Triple DES
	DiffieHellman
	PBE
	DSA
	RSA
AlgorithmParameterGenerator	DiffieHellman
	DSA
	RSA
CertificateFactory	X.509
KeyGenerator	Blowfish
	DES
	Triple DES
	DSA
	HMACMD5
	HMACSHA1
	RSA
	DiffieHellman
KeyPairGenerator	DSA
	RSA
KeyStore	SUN (proprietary)
	JCEKS (proprietary)
	PKCS12

(continues)

Table 5.4 Parameter, Key, and Certificate Engine Class Standard Names *(Continued)*

ENGINE CLASS	STANDARD NAMES
SecretKeyFactory	DES
	Triple DES
	PBEWithMD5AndDES

Standard Sun and SunJCE Providers

Sun's implementation of the Java runtime includes the SUN provider, which is installed by default out of the box. Other implementations may use a different provider name or provide different algorithms, but the SUN provider gives the specific implementations of:

- DSA, the Digital Signature Algorithm.
- MD5, SHA-1
- DSA Key Pair Generator
- DSA Parameter Generator and Manager
- DSA Key Factory (read external keys into internal objects)
- A proprietary PRNG called SHA-1 PRNG, which follows the IEEE P1363 standard in section G7
- Certificate factory for X.509 certificates and certificate revocation lists (CRLs)
- Proprietary Key Management

The Sun implementation of the Java 1.4 environment has a sample provider named SunJCE that implements the interfaces in the `javax.crypto` package. Prior to 1.4, this provider needed to be separately downloaded and explicitly configured. This provider implements the following algorithms:

- The DES, Triple DES, and Blowfish ciphers using ECB, CBC, OFB, CFB, and PCBC modes, with optional PKCS #5 padding and key generation for the ciphers
- Password-based encryption, using PKCS #8, using MD5 and either DES or Triple DES
- Diffie-Hellman Key Exchange, plus key and parameter generation
- Two HMAC implementations, MD5HMAC and SHA1HMAC, which are based on the standard HMAC algorithm

Other Providers

In certain situations, you might need an algorithm not included in the SUN or SunJCE providers. Keep in mind that even if the stock providers contain the algorithms you need, there are good reasons to at least *try* another provider. Performance improvements are very significant, sometimes doubling the performance (in one case, it was so much faster, I thought the implementation was broken!).

Table 5.5 lists major providers. The Licensing column refers to licensing and availability status. Commercial providers are indicated by a *C*, while noncommercial, open-source, or free providers are indicated by an *N*. Some free providers are under the restrictive GNU or similar licensing for free projects but also have a commercial license as well.

Because providers are constantly improving and adding algorithms, we won't make a full comparison here. Among noncommercial providers, however, the Bouncy Castle has a very unrestrictive license and a full suite of algorithms.

Table 5.5 Third-Party Providers

AUTHOR	PRODUCT	LICENSING	HOME PAGE URL
Baltimore	KeyTools Crypto	C	www.baltimore.com
Certicom	SecurityBuilder	C	www.certicom.com
Cryptix Foundation Limited	Cryptix JCE	N	www.cryptix.org
Eracom	Jprov	C	www.eracom-tech.com
IAIK	IAIK-JCE	C	http://jcewww.iaik.at
ISNetworks	Pinatubo	C	www.isnetworks.com/pinatubo
Legion of the Bouncy Castle	Bouncy Castle	N	www.bouncycastle.org
Phaos	Phaos Crypto	C	http://phaos.com
RSA Security	Crypto/J	C	www.rsasecurity.com
Technical University of Darmstadt, Germany	cdcProvider	N/C	www.informatik.tudarmstadt.de/TI/Forschung/cdcProvider
Virtual Unlimited	BeeCrypt	N	http://virtualunlimited/products/beecrypt
WedgeTail	JCSI	N/C	www.wedgetail.com

Initializing Providers

To use the classes in `java.crypto`, you need to initialize the JCE, even the default Sun provided. One way is to edit the `${java_home}/lib/security/java.security` file and add a line such as:

```
security.provider.2=com.sun.crypto.provider.SunJCE
```

This is nice because once this file is set, the application does not need to know anything about JCE initialization. However, this requires another configuration file that requires maintenance and synchronization between the development and production versions.

The other method is to register the JCE dynamically from the application:

```
import java.security.*;
Provider sunjce = new com.sun.crypto.provider.SunJCE();
Security.addProvider(sunjce);
```

The only catch with this method is that you have to make sure that this snippet of code is executed before any calls to `javax.crypto` are done. Sometimes it can be hard to tell exactly when that might occur, so it should occur right at application start time. In addition, you'd like all this code in one place so you can test different JCE providers:

```
import java.security.*;
public class InitJCE {
     public static Provider jce = new
com.sun.crypto.provider.SunJCE();
     static {
          Security.addProvider(jce);
     }
     public static void init() {
          // NOP
     }
}
```

This funny code uses the Java class loader to initialize the JCE once and only once with virtually no overhead, no matter how many threads or times the `init` method is called. The first call to `init` loads the class `InitJCE`. Next, the Java class loader initializes the static variable, then calls the static initializer (the last part of the preceding class) to get the JCE up and running.

More naïve methods would include just adding the JCE in the `init` method. This certainly works, but in big applications, it might mean the same JCE gets repeatedly added. Other methods might use flags to load the JCE only once, but that would require synchronization (since the flag may be read and written simultaneously).

Writing Your Own Provider

Another option is implementing your own provider to provide your own algorithms or your own performance enhancements. Unfortunately, starting in Java 1.4, this is difficult because providers will only be recognized if they are digitally signed using a certificate from Sun Microsystems. You can certainly apply for a certificate, but it's a lot of work. Full instructions are presented with the software development kit (SDK).

No one really knows why this restriction is in place except Sun. It certainly makes the work of commercial provider implementers easier, since they only need to write one provider and not worry about import/export rules. The Java VM handles that for them. For the end user, the signing restrictions don't seem to add much value. One benefit is that it's harder to deploy "rogue" providers that secretly store or transmit keys, but that's a stretch.

Core Engine Classes

At the core of the Java Cryptography API are five main classes that directly correspond to cryptographic primitives:

- `MessageDigest` for cryptographic hashes.
- `MAC` for MACs and HMACs.
- `KeyAgreements` for key agreement protocols such as Diffie-Hellman.
- `Signature` for digital signatures.
- `SecureRandom` for generating cryptographically secure random numbers.

MessageDigest

The `MessageDigest` is the simplest of the core engine classes and provides a model for others. At its simplest, it does the following:

```
byte[] inputdata = // data to hash
MessageDigest md = MessageDigest.getInstance("MD5"); // or "SHA"
byte[] hash = md.digest(inputdata);
```

A more formal step-by-step approach is the following:

1. *Initialize.*

```
MessageDigest.getInstance(String algorithmName)
MessageDigest.getInstance(String algorithmName, String providerName);
MessageDigest.getInstance(String algorithmName, Provider p)
```

2. *Update.* Data can be fed in piecemeal using the update method. If you already have the entire message to digest, this step can be skipped:

```
void update(byte input);
void update(byte[] input)
void update(byte[] input, int offset, int length);
```

3. *Finalize.* If you have the entire message, the digest can be computed in one step, with a call to the `digest` method. Otherwise, any remaining data can be fed in here. You can also pass in a preexisting array. The digest size can be determined by `getDigestLength`.

```
byte[] digest(); // no more data
byte[] digest(byte[] input); // last chunk of data
int digest(byte[] ouptput, int offset, int length);
```

4. *Verify.* You can compare two digests by using the `java.util.Arrays.equals` method and passing in two `byte` arrays.

```
byte[] digest1 = //
byte[] digest2 = ;//
if (java.util.Arrays.equals(digest1, digest2)) { /* good */ }
else { /* bad  */ }
```

Digest Streams

The `java.security` package provides two stream classes that can automatically compute data flowing through the stream. Every byte read or written is also sent through an update call to the underlying message digest. When done, a call to the digest's `digest` method returns the digest.

The classes are very useful because many times objects and applications are already built that do reading or writing of streams. Instead of rewriting those classes to handle message digests, you can replace the native streams with the new `Digest` streams. This way, the existing classes work unchanged, and you can still get digests.

The input stream, `DigestInputStream`, extends `java.io.FilterInputStream`. It is useful for reading arbitrary amounts of (and possibly temporary) data while simultaneously computing a digest:

```
FileInputStream fis = new FileInputStream("a file");
MessageDigest md = MessageDigest.getInstance("SHA1");
DigestInputStream dis = new DigestInputStream(fis,  md)

// tricky way of read whole file
while (dis.read() != -1) {}

byte[] digest = md.final();
```

`DigestOutputStream` is similar, except it is a subclass of `FilterOutputStream`. This class is very useful for printing or sending files, and then sending a cryptographic checksum afterwards.

Both classes allow you to turn the digesting functionality on and off. This may be useful for skipping sections of a stream, such as when writing or reading header data:

```
void on(boolean onOrOff);
```

You can also retrieve or replace the underlying message digest object:

```
MessageDigest getMessageDigest()
void setMessageDigest(MessageDigest digest)
```

MAC

The `MAC` class is the least complicated of the core classes that use keys. Typically, the `MAC` class only uses a single secret key and no algorithm parameters. The SunJCE provider implements an `HMACSHA1` and `HMACMD5` MACs that are based on the standard HMAC algorithms with a choice of the underlying hash function. Depending on the provider, a `MAC` instance might be able to be *cloned*. This is actually useful, since it allows you to create a new object without using a key. In this case, you may wish to use the `reset` method to clear any previous data.

The steps for using the `MAC` class are as follows:

1. *Create*. First you must create a MAC object by using one of the getInstance factory methods:

   ```
   Mac.getInstance(String algorithmName)
   Mac.getInstance(String algorithmName, String providerName)
   Mac.getInstance(String algoirhtm, Provider provider)
   ```

2. *Initialize*. Before using the MAC object, you must initialize it with a key. You can also initialize with a key and the `AlgorithmParameterSpec` object; however, I don't know of any MAC implementation that uses one. To initialize the MAC object:

```
void init(Key key)
void init(Key key, AlgorithmParameterSpec spec)
```

3. *Update.* Updating the `MAC` object is exactly the same as for `MessageDigest`. If you have the entire message already, skip this section.

```
void update(byte input);
void update(byte[] input)
void update(byte[] input, int offset, int length);
```

4. *Finalize.* Computing the `MAC` is the same as it is for `MessageDigest`, except the final step method is the more common named `doFinal` instead of `digest`. The size of `MAC` can be computed with a call of `getMacLength`:

```
byte[] doFinal()
byte[] doFinal(byte[] input);
void doFinal(byte[] buffer, int offset, int length);
```

5. *Verify.* If you receive a MAC and wish to verify it, you follow the same step as in generation. The Mac.verify algorithm provides a convenience function:

```
byte[] macRecieved = //;
byte[] message = //;
Mac m = Mac.getInstance("HmacSHA1");
m.init(key)
byte[] macGenerated = mac.doFinal(message)
if (java.util.Arrays.equalls(macRecieved, macGenerated)) {
     // ok
} else {
     // invalid mac
}
```

SecureRandom

Although you were already introduced to `SecureRandom` in Chapter 4, we didn't discuss that it is an engine class. This just means that it also can be created using an ordinary constructor. In this case, the first provider is used to provide the instance, which is normally the SUN provider. The same algorithm can be created using:

```
SecureRandom.getInstance("SHA1PRNG", "SUN");
```

We have already seen how `java.util`'s `Random` class is completely inappropriate for cryptographic applications. To remedy this, `java.security` defines a new class, `SecureRandom`, which is a base class for cryptographic-strength random numbers. Many interfaces require or allow an optional `SecureRandom` instance.

Implementing Blum-Blum-Shub

As mentioned in Chapter 4, the Blum-Blum-Shub generator is *provably* strong. Implementing this is quite easy, but there are some quirks on how to do this in Java. Normally you add algorithms by using the provider architecture. However, the API for `SecureRandom` is very limited. You can't `init` the `SecureRandom` class and use algorithm parameters as you do for other classes. So there is no easy way of generating $n = pq$. You could use `setSeed` in a nontraditional way by having the first indicate the size of bytes of n, followed by the bytes of n, followed by the seed. But then you need to write an `AlgorithmParametersGenerator` class, pass the "encoded" parameters into the `setSeed` method, and then package the whole thing up as a provider—and even then it's not particularly the right solution.

Fortunately, unlike many of the other classes, the `SecureRandom` class is not final, so we can subclass it and implement everything we need. Doing this is certainly a hack, but no more of a hack than what was described previously, and it takes a lot less work. What follows is a skeleton of how to implement BBS and use the `BigInteger` class.

First, we need some methods that generate the primes that compose n. Each prime p must satisfy the condition $p = 3 \bmod 4$. And given a seed value x, one random bit is generated taking the least-significant bit of $x_{n+1} = x_n \bmod n$. The code is as follows:

```
public class BlumBlumShub extends SecureRandom
{
    public static final BigInteger two = BigInteger.valueOf(2L);
    public static final BigInteger three = BigInteger.valueOf(3L);
    public static final BigInteger four = BigInteger.valueOf(4L);

    public static BigInteger getPrime(int bits, SecureRandom rand)
    {
     BigInteger p;
     while (true) {
```

```
        p = new BigInteger(bits, 100, rand);
        if( p.mod(four).equals(three)) break;
    }
    return p;
  }

  public static BigInteger generateN(int bits, SecureRandom rand)
  {
    BigInteger n = getPrime(bits, rand);
    return n.multiply(getPrime(bits, rand));
  }
```

Now we need some constructors. If a seed isn't given, we'll just use the normal `SecureRandom` method of generating a seed. This can be replaced with another method scheme if you wish:

```
  public BlumBlumShub(BigInteger n) {
    this(n, SecureRandom.getSeed(n.bitLength() / 8));
  }

  public BlumBlumShub(BigInteger n, byte[] seed)
  {
    this.n = n;
    setSeed(seed);
  }

  public void setSeed(byte[] seedBytes)
  {
    // ADD: use hardwired default value for n
    BigInteger seed = new BigInteger(1, seedBytes);
    state = seed.mod(n);
  }
```

Another approach is hardwiring a value of *n*, possibly some of various sizes.

The actual random generation is handled by the following routines:

```
  public int getBit() {
    state = state.modPow(two, n);
    return (state.testBit(0) == true ? 1 : 0);
  }

  public byte getByte() {
    int b = 0;
    for (int i = 7; i >= 0; --i) {
        b |= (getBit() << i);
    }
    return (byte)b;
  }
```

The remaining methods, such as `nextInt`, `nextBytes`, and so on, all need to be written, but they are fairly trivial to implement by using the methods from Chapter 4, so we won't bother here. Another option is to have a parameter specifying the number of bits to use per iteration.

In practice, you'd generate a value for *n* and save it or encode it for future use. Here's a sample method to exercise the routines:

```
public static void main(String[] args) {
     SecureRandom r = new SecureRandom();
     System.out.println("Generating stock random seed");
     r.nextInt();
     System.out.println("Generating N");
     BigInteger n = generateN(512, r);
     byte[] seed = new byte[64];
     r.nextBytes(seed);
     BlumBlumShub bbs = new BlumBlumShub(n, seed);
     System.out.println("Generating 10 bytes");
     for (int i = 0 ; i < 10; ++i) {
         System.out.println((int)bbs.getByte());
     }
}
```

Ciphers

The `getInstance` method with ciphers works a bit differently than it does for other engine classes because the algorithm name is actually a transformation and must be in the form of either *cipher* or *cipher/mode/padding*. The first form is frequently used for stream ciphers like RC4 that don't have a mode or padding form or when a mode and padding is implied by the algorithm.

The SunJCE provider supports any combination of the transformations shown in Table 5.6.

Table 5.6 Algorithm/Mode/Padding Transformations Supported by the SunJCE Provider

ALGORITHM	MODE	PADDING
Blowfish	ECB	NoPadding
DES	CBC	PKCS5Padding
Triple DES	CFB*n*, where *n* is the block size to process the stream	
	OFBn	
	PCBC	

For instance, Blowfish/ECB/NoPadding completely specifies a valid transformation within the SunJCE provider. Other providers work similarly but may have other algorithms, modes, or padding schemes.

In addition to the previous transformation, SunJCE specifies two password-based encryption schemes as defined in PKCS #5: `PBEWithMD5AndDES` and `PBEWithMD5AndTripleDES`. These are specified as-is, without any slashes or references to modes or padding.

After a cipher instance is obtained, it must be initialized. An operation mode, or opmode, is required. This is a flag describing the operation—in this case whether the instance is encrypting or decrypting. It cannot do both. If you need to do both encrypting and decrypting, you need two `Cipher` object instances. Also required is a `Key` object (for symmetric ciphers, it's actually a `SecretKey` object) to provide the key used by the cipher algorithm.

Finally, you might need to pass in an `AlgorithmParameter` object. This object, as its name implies, specifies any algorithm-specific parameters, such as block size or number of rounds. It also will specify an initialization vector, if any. If you are using a simple cipher that doesn't have any parameters, you can specify the initialization vector in the generic `IVParameterSpec`. Otherwise, a spec object will have a placeholder for the initialization vector.

If you are encrypting and using a feedback mode, but you do not specify an initialization vector, one will be created randomly. This should be retrieved with a call to `getIV`. This method returns a `byte` array containing the vector. If desired, you can save this to either create a new `IVParameterSpec` or to use in another algorithm-specific `Spec` class.

Working with the Cipher class is done as follows:

1. *Create.* You start the creation process using one of the standard `Cipher.getInstance` methods.
2. *Initialize.* The initialization step is required and takes a mode ecrypting the operation, a key, and optionally an `AlgorithmParameter`, `AlgorithmParametersSpec`, or a `SecureRandom` instance. In addition:
   a. You need an opmode (e.g., `Cipher.ENCRYPT_MODE`, `Cipher.DECRYPT_MODE`). Key-wrapping modes are also available and are discussed later in the chapter.
   b. A `key` is required.
   c. *Optional.* If the cipher has any domain parameters such as number of rounds, these should be passed in with either the appropriate `AlgorithmParameters` or `AlgorithmParametersSpec` object.

d. *Optional.* A `SecureRandom` instance is optional. If needed, it will be used for generating initialization vectors or random padding bytes (if implemented). If a initialization vector is created, it can be retrieved using the `getIV` method.

The initialization code is as follows:

```
void init(int opmode, Key key)
void init(int opmode, Key key, SecureRandom rand)
void init(int opmode, Key key, AlgorithmParameter params)
void init(int opmode, Key key, AlgorithmParameter params,
          SecureRandom rand)
void init(int opmode, Key key, AlgorithmParameterSpec spec,
          SecureRandom rand)
```

3. *Update.* Data can be fed in incrementally or all at once. The incremental result is either returned in a new array or placed in an existing array. The result may be zero bytes if a full block has not been used. You can determine in advance how many bytes the result will contain with a call to `getOutputSize`:

```
// methods that update t
byte[] update(byte[] input);
byte[] update(byte[] input, int offset, int length);

// methods that update and return partial results
int update(byte[] input, int inputoffset, int inputLength,
           byte[] output);
int update(byte[] input, int inputOffset, int inputLength,
           byte[] output, int outputOffset);
```

4. *Finalize.* There are two forms of the `doFinal` method. The first accepts remaining input and returns a new `byte` array. The other form accepts remaining input, but the result is placed in an existing array, and the number of bytes is returned. The appropriate size of the output can be determined in advance by calling `getOutputSize`. If you pass in an array that is too small, a `ShortBufferException` is thrown, in which case you can create an appropriately sized new array and try the call again (the data is not lost). As a `doFinal` call is made, the object is reset:

```
// method that return result as new array
byte[] doFinal()
byte[] doFinal(byte[] input)
byte[] doFinal(byte[] input, int offset, int length);

// methods that place result in an existing array
int doFinal(byte[] output, int outputOffset);
```

```
int doFinal(byte[] input, int offset, int length,
            byte[] output);
int doFinal(byte[] input, int offset, int length,
            byte[] output, int outputOffset);
```

Additional Cipher-Related Objects

There are four additional helper objects based on the `Cipher` class to perform encryption on streams and serialized objects.

NullCipher

The `NullCipher` class implements a null or identity cipher, where the ciphertext is always the same as the plaintext. This is very useful for debugging applications when you don't want to change the arch. There is one catch, however. `NullCipher` cannot (with the SunJCE provider anyway) be created using the `getInstance` methods. It can only be created by using a regular constructor. For example:

```
if ( some debug condition ) {
     c = new NullCipher();
} else {
     c = Cipher.getInstance("regular algorithm");
}
```

`NullCipher` works identically to a normal cipher instance. All parameters are ignored.

Cipher Stream Classes

Input and output stream classes are provided that work similarly to the message digest stream except these streams do encryption. These classes are phenomenally useful in communication or networked applications. The entire application can be written using normal stream, and when that is debugged, the cipher streams can be added. This makes debugging much easier.

`CipherInputStream` extends `FilterInputStream`, and construction is similar to the `DigestInputStream`. Just specify an existing `InputStream` and a configured `Cipher` object. Any data read will either be encrypted or decrypted depending on how the `Cipher` object was configured. Encrypting an input stream may sound odd, but it could be used if you received unencrypted data (perhaps over a VPN or a secure channel) but want to store it an encrypted format.

`CipherOutputStream`, likewise, extends `FilterOutputStream`. Any data written will be either encrypted or decrypted.

In both cases it is very important to `close()` the stream when finished. If the cipher is a block cipher, the call to close will pad any remaining buffers. Likewise, when using a block cipher with `CipherOutputStream`, you should not call `flush()`, as it may prematurely pad the outgoing data in an inappropriate way.

Sealed Objects

`SealedObject` is a container class that stores an encrypted serialized version for the underlying object. It can be decrypted and reconstituted using the appropriate key or cipher.

Any object that implements the `java.io.serializable` interface, along with a properly initialized `Cipher` object, can be used to create a sealed object. Once sealed, the encrypted object can then be serialized for storage or transmission. For example:

```
public SealedObject(Serializable object, Cipher c)

Cipher c = Cipher.getInstance("Blowfish");
C.Init(Cipher.ENCRYPT_MODE, sKey);
String myObject = new String("This Is the secret data");
SealedObject so = new SealedObject(myObject, c);
// seralize so to get the bytes.
```

Given a sealed object, there are two ways of retrieving the original object. The first is using an appropriate initialized `Cipher` object with the correct key, parameters such as initialization vectors, and the mode set to `decrypt`. This has the advantage that keys are not explicitly used. You can use a preinitialized `Cipher` object and never have to know what the original key is. Following is the code to retrieve the object using the `Cipher` object:

```
SealedObject so = // retrieved from serialized bytes
Object getObject(Key key)

c.init(cipher.DECRYPT_MODE, key);
Try {
     String s = (String) so.getObject( c);
} catch (Exception e) {
     // TBD
}
```

The other method, shown in the following code, just uses a key. The sealed object stores all parameters for the cipher so that only a key is required for decryption. This method has the advantage that the caller does not need to know any parameters, such as an initialization vector, in order to unseal.

```
try {
     String s = (String) so.getObject(key);
} catch (Exception e) {
     // TBD
}
```

Recall that the `Key` class is provider-specific, although most should use standardized format. However, if the key is encoded in an unusual format, the `getObject` method can also take a `Provider` argument:

```
Object getObject(Key key, Provider prov)
```

Unfortunately, in Java 1.2 and 1.3, `SealedObject` has a nasty bug. If you installed the JCE as an *installed extension*, where the JCE JAR file is placed in the system library directly, then you are unable to unseal any class custom class the user created. The error manifests itself by a `ClassNotFound` exception even though the class is in your `CLASSPATH`. In this situation, you would be able to work with native Java classes, just not any of your own. This occurs because standard extensions use a different class loader than the one core Java uses, and are restricted to only loading system classes. A full analysis of the bug can be found on Sun's Bug Parade under bug number 4224921 (`http://developer.java.sun.com/developer/bugParade/bugs/4224921.html`).

If this error pops up unexpectedly, check to make sure the Java on the offending machine is configured in the same manner as all others. Chances are someone installed the JCE differently and that is causing the problems.

If you run into this problem, there are a few solutions:

- Do not install the JCE as an installed extension. Instead, explicitly specify the JAR files needed in the `CLASSPATH` variable (either an environment variable or on the command line). For JCE 1.2, it's very simple: You only need to add `jce-1_2-do.jar` (or `jce-1_2.jar` depending on your system). For 1.2.1 you need to link two files: `jce1_2_1.jar` and `sunjce_provider.jar`. Additional steps may need to be taken if you are using a `SecurityManager`. Full information can be in the INSTALL.html file from the provider distribution.
- Upgrade to Java 1.4. Since JCE is now part of the core of Java, `SealedObject` uses the regular class loader and this bug no longer exists.
- Don't use `SealedObject`. Instead, write a custom wrapper to handle encrypting a specific serialized object.

Signatures

The `Signature` engine class is used for working with digital signature algorithms. An object is created using the usual `getInstance` methods taking algorithms and optionally a provider source.

Following are the steps to create a signature object:

1. *Create.* Create a signature object using the standard `getInstance` calls. The standard names for signatures are:

   ```
   Signature.getInstance(String algorithm)
   Signature.getInstance(String algorithm, String provider)
   Signature.getInstance(String algorithm, Provider p)
   ```

2. *Initialize.* Initialization is a bit different. Depending if the goal is signing a message or verifying a signature, a different initialization routine is used:

   ```
   void initSign(PrivateKey key)
   void initSign(PrivateKey key, SecureRandom rand)

   void initVerify(PublicKey key)
   void initVerify(Certificate cert)
   ```

   In both cases you may need to set algorithm parameters:

   ```
   void setParameter(AlgorithmParameterSpec spec)
   ```

3. *Update.* The next step is to pass in the data that needs to be signed or updated. Data can be passed in all at once or a byte at time. The `update` methods can be called repeatedly. There is no `SignatureInputStream` that might automate this process (of course, we can write one).

   ```
   void update(byte b)
   void update(byte[] input)
   void update(byte[] input, int offset, int length)
   ```

4. *Finalize.* Once all the data has been feed in, the data can be signed. You can either receive the data in a new `byte` array or have it placed in a user-specified `byte` array. The result is an ASN.1 representation of two numbers, *r* and *s*, which is the standard format:

   ```
   byte[] sign()
   int sign(byte[], int offset, int length)
   ```

   For verification, just pass in the actual signature (encoded in ASN.1 format as the `sign` function does):

   ```
   boolean verify(byte[] signature)
   boolean verify(byte[] signature, int offset, int length)
   ```

SignedObject

`SignedObject` creates a digitally signed serialized encoding of an object. This is most useful for interthread or interapplication transmission of data.

Following are steps to create a signed object:

1. *Create.* A `SignedObject` needs a serializable object, a `PrivateKey`, and a `Signature` object. The `Signature` object doesn't need to be initialized:

   ```
   public SignedObject(Serializable object, PrivateKey key, Signature
   sigEngine)
   ```

2. *Transmit.* Serialize or transmit the object.
3. *Verify.* Verification is done by the following steps:
   a. Receive. Received or deserialized the signed objects.
   b. Verify the data by passing in a public key and a `Signature` object (does not need to be initialized):

   ```
   boolean verify(PublicKey verficationKey, Signature sig)
   ```

4. *Retrieve.* The underlying object is retrieved with:

   ```
   Object getObject();
   ```

Key Agreement Protocols

The Java API can handle key agreement protocols with any number of parties. Key agreements, while not difficult to implement, are the most complicated of the core classes because they implement a protocol between multiple parties as opposed to an algorithm that can be used by a single party. The SunJCE implements the Diffie-Hellman Key Agreement, which should be sufficient for most applications. The protocol is implemented as follows:

1. *Create.* The `KeyAgreement` class follows the standard factory `getInstance` method that takes an algorithm and optionally a provider. If an implementation is found, a new `KeyAgreement` object will be created:

   ```
   static KeyAgreement getInstance(String algorithm)
   static KeyAgreement getInstance(String algorithm, Provider p)
   ```

2. *Initialize.* Initialization requires a `Key`, typically a `PrivateKey`, optionally a source of randomness, and most likely an `AlgorithmParameterSpec` containing common parameters

agreed to in advance by all parties. For instance, Diffie-Hellman requires a `PrivateKey` and an `AlgorithmParameterSpec` containing the common parameters, the prime modulus *p* and the generator *g*. These parameters can be generated with `AlgorithmParameterGenerator` or directly specified with the class `DHParameterSpec`. The code is as follows:

```
void init(Key key, AlgorithmParameterSpec params)
void init(Key key, AlgorithmParameterSpec params, SecureRandom rand)
```

With some other algorithms (or providers), the `Key` may contain everything that is needed. In this case, you can use simplify cases.

```
void init(Key key);
void init(Key key, SecureRandom rand);
```

3. *Update* (do key agreement phases). Each party in the agreement receives a `Key` from others. These keys are pumped into the `doPhase`. A `boolean` flag is used to indicate that this is the last phase. With Diffie-Hellman with two parties, there is only one phase, so `doPhase` is called once with the flag set to false.

```
Key doPhase(Key key, boolean lastPhase)
```

4. *Finalize* (generate the secret). After each party has completed all phases, you can retrieve the shared secret by making a call to `generateSecret`. You can retrieve raw bytes or use a convenience call to create a `SecretKey` object.

```
byte[] generateSecret();
int generateSecret(byte[] sharedSecret, int offset)
SecretKey generateSecret(String algorithm);
```

Parameters, Keys, and Certificates

The Java API provides full support for creating, encoding, and converting any parameters, keys, or certificates for cryptographic operations. Unfortunately, the API is a bit confusing because the classes for parameters and keys have similar names, yet operate quite differently. In addition, the word *key* can sometimes means an abstract key that could be secret, public, or private, or other times it specifically means a secret key. Trying to reconcile the differences and inconsistencies is actually much harder and time-consuming than just learning the API directly.

Algorithm Parameters

With the exception of `MessageDigest` and `SecureRandom`, every engine class accepts an `AlgorithmParameterSpec` class in the `init` method. `Spec` classes are transparent representations of the data needed by the engine class. *Transparent* here means you have access to the individual elements that make up the object. Actually, `AlgorithmParameterSpec` is not a class, but an empty interface. A class implementing this interface signals that it contains parameters in a transparent form.

The Java API has:

```
DHGenParameterSpec
DHParameterSpec
DSAParameterSpec
IvParameterSpec
PBEParameterSpec
PSSParameterSpec
RC2ParameterSpec
RC5ParameterSpec
RSAKeyGenParameterSpec
```

Third-party providers may have additional `Spec` classes.

For most of the `Spec` classes, use is quite simple: Just create the `Spec` class as a regular object, filling in the parameters. For more complicated parameter types such as `DHParameterSpec` (for Diffie-Hellman Key Exchange) and `DSAParameterSpec` (for Digital Signature Algorithm) and others used for elliptic curve and other complicated cryptosystems, the parameters are very large numbers. These parameters are not keyed in. Instead, they are either retrieved from a file (or other data source) or generated by `AlgorithmParameterGenerator`.

AlgorithmParameters

`AlgorithmParameters` provides a way of encoding or decoding `AlgorithmSpecClasses` as an array of bytes. In other words, it provides a fancy way of serializing the data. The `AlgorithmParameter` class is an engine class that provides an encoded version of the `Spec` class. It does not allow access to the individual members directly, but instead provides access to an encoded version and information about the encoding with the following methods:

- `getAlgorithm`. Returns the algorithm name used in generating the parameters.
- `getEncoded`. Returns the raw encoded `byte` array representing the parameters.

- getFormat. Describes the format in which the encoded bytes are stored.
- getProvider. Returns the provider this object is associated with.

The AlgorithmParameter class uses the usual getInstance methods, but then it has two different ways of initialization depending on what you wish to do. The first type is for converting a Spec object into an array of byte. To do this, Initialize the object with the Spec class followed by a call to getEncoded:

```
void init(AlgorithmParameterSpec spec);
byte[] getEncoded();
byte[] getEncoded(String format);
```

Check with your provider about what formats they support. The SUN and SunJCE providers ignore the format parameter altogether.

The other initialization is for doing the reverse process—converting encoded parameters back into an AlgorithmParameterSpec, and initializing using the encoded bytes. This is followed by a call to getParameterSpec using the class as the argument:

```
void init(byte[] encodedparmeters)
void init(byte[] encodedparameters, String format)
AlgorithmParameterSpec getParameterSpec(Class paramSpec);
```

AlgorithmParameters and Cipher

As a convenience (or as an oddity), the Cipher class allows you to skip the conversion back into a AlgorithmParameterSpec and work directly with AlgorithmParameters. Here's an example:

```
byte[] encodedRC5Params = ...;
AlgorithmParameter ap = AlgorithmParmaeter.getInstance("RC5");
RC5ParameterSpec spec = (RC5ParameterSpec)
          ap.getParameterSpec(RC5ParameterSpec.class);
Cipher c = Cipher.getInstance("RC5");
c.init(mode, key, spec);
```

Or you can just do the following:

```
byte[] encodedRC5Params = ...;
AlgorithmParameter ap = AlgorithmParmaeter.getInstance("RC5");
Cipher c = Cipher.getInstance("RC5");
c.init(mode, key, ap);
```

which saves one line of code. The example uses RC5, which is not implemented in the SunJCE, but there aren't many examples you can do. This is more useful for DHEAS or Elliptic Curve Cryptosystems that have complicated domain parameters, but they don't have standard `Spec` classes either. A more realistic example would be using `DHParameterSpec`, but `KeyAgreement` doesn't allow initialization from `AlgorithmParameters` objects.

If this is confusing (and it is), it can all be summarized this way: If you have an `AlgorithmParameters` object, you can use it to initialize `Cipher`; otherwise, you'll have to convert it into a `Spec` object first.

AlgorithmParameterGenerators

Generating parameters is done with the `AlgorithmParameterGenerator` class. Oddly, this class only generates the `AlogithmParameter` objects. If you need a `Spec` object, you'll have to do a conversion. This may sound odd, but the logic here is that if you are generating parameters, you'll probably want to save them.

For every parameter type that needs to be generated, there is a matching `AlgorithmParameterSpec` class that specifies the parameters to generate the parameters. For instance, to generate parameters for the `DHParameterSpec`, you'd fill in the values for `DHGenParameterSpec`:

```
AlgorithmParameterSpec getParameterSpec(Class paramSpec)
```

Many public key algorithms require parameters that need generating from a random source. For instance, the Diffie-Hellman Key Exchange needs a random prime modulus of a certain bit size. The `AlgorithmParameterGenerator` class is another engine class that is designed for these tasks. The steps are as follows:

1. *Create*. As always, the `AlgorithmParameterGenertor` object is created by using a `getInstance` call.

   ```
   public static AlgorithmParameterGenerator getInstance(String
   algorithm)
   public static AlgorithmParameterGenerator getInstance(String
   algorithm, String provider)
   ```

2. *Initialize*. You have two choices here. For many algorithms, the only information needed is a size. What the size represents is algorithm-dependent, of course. However, most of them have a notion of it. Any additional parameters will be provided as default by the provider. The advantage here is that you can use different parameters and even different providers with no code changes. The downside is that size might mean different things and the default might be different.

For more complicated algorithms, you could create the correct AlgorithmParameterSpec object, fill in the appropriate values, and pass that into the init method. The advantage here is that you are not using any default and are self-documenting your code by explicitly describing every parameter. The downside is that you may not be able to switch providers or algorithms without making code changes.

```
public void init(int size)
public void init(int size, SecureRandom r)
public void init(AlgorithmParameterSpec spec)
public void init(AlgorithmParameterSpec spec, SecureRandom r)
```

3. *Generate*. After initialization, you can actually generate the parameters with a call to:

```
public AlgorithmParameters generateParameters()
```

4. *Convert*. This step isn't required, but the API for the most part only takes Spec objects, in which case you have to convert. You also need to convert if you wish to examine the parameters (or you might be able to view the encoded bytes; which might work depending on the format).

Keys

Working with keys in the Java Cryptography API isn't hard, but the naming scheme (and the native Sun documentation) isn't very clear. The terms *transparent* and *opaque* are used frequently but there are so many exceptions, it's not a useful concept. Likewise, the use of the word Key in the class names can have different meanings. In spite of this, the API isn't particularly hard. The interface Key provides three simple methods to provide access to key data. The entire interface is shown as follows:

```
public interface Key extends Serializable {
     public byte[] getEncoded();       // raw binary representation
     public String getAlgorithm(); // algorithm used to generate this key
     public String getFormat();    // format of binary representation
}
```

The getEncoded and getFormat methods return a *provider-specific* representation of the key. It's considered good manners for the provider to represent the key in a standard format, but where there are no standards, this allows providers to implement any scheme they might like.

There are no *public* classes that implement Key interface, so you cannot directly create an object with this interface. Instead objects implementing the Key interface are created or returned by method calls to engine classes.

There are three empty sub-interfaces, PublicKey, PrivateKey, and SecretKey, that are just used for typing Key objects. For RSA, DSA, and Diffie-Hellman algorithms, Java provides further subinterfaces that allow getting the individual components that make up the key (e.g., the modulus, the generators, etc). For instance, a private RSA key would be:

```
public interface RSAKey extends PublicKey {
     public BigInteger getModulus();
}

public interface RSAPrivateKey extends RSAKey {
     public getPrivateExponent();
}
```

The interface KeySpec signals that a class can accept individual components that make up a key. The Java API provides numerous classes implementing KeySpec and can be created using normal constructors. In other words, classes implementing KeySpec are provider-neutral data structures. As an example, RSAPrivateKeySpec is just:

```
public class RSAPrivateKeySpec implements KeySpec {
     public RSAPrivateKeySpec(BigInteger modulus, BigInteger
privateExponent);
     public BigInteger getModulus();
     public BigInteger getPrivateExponent();
     }
```

Notice that this class *does not* implement the RSAPrivateKey interface even though they have the same API. You can create an object that implements RSAPrivateKeySpec but not one with RSAPrivateKey.

This rather screwy system can partially be understood by knowing that KeySpec objects can represent keys that have encoding issues that are not ready for use in a Cipher or other object. For instance, the PBEKeySpec class defines a representation of a key or an encoding of a key. Likewise, the X509EncodedKeySpec and PKCS8EncodedKeySpec classes define a key, but it will need decoding before it can be used. So if a KeySpec can define an encoded key, what is the point of the key interface of getEncoded and getFormat? The idea is that those methods return provider-specific encoding, while the X509EncodedKeySpec and PKCS8EncodedKeySpec classes are explicitly known encodings.

Table 5.7 compares the different Key types.

Table 5.7 Comparison and Summary of Key, KeySpec, and EncodedKeySpec Types

	KEY	KEYSPEC	ENCODEDKEYSPEC
Type	Interface	Interface	Abstract class

Methods	`getEncoded`
	`getFormat`
	`getAlgorithm`
	Subinterfaces may define.
		None; empty interface.	Defined constructor and `getEncoded()` or `getFormat()`.

Creating	Must be done using an encoded `byte` array, or by another engine class.	Normal constructors.	Normal constructors.
Implementers	All implementing classes are private to the provider.	All implementing classes are public; many are defined in the Java API.	Only two subclasses: `X509EncodedkeySpec`. `PKCS8EncodedKeySpec`.
Usage in Cipher, Mac, and Signature classes	Can be used directly.	Cannot be used. Must be converted in a `Key` object before being used.	Must be converted to a `Key` object first.
Serializable	Yes.	No.	No.
Encoding	Provides a provider-specific encoding.	No encoding is given.	Already encoded.
Direct Access to Key components	Yes, if cast to the correct subinterface.	Yes.	No. Object must be converted into the appropriate algorithm-specific `KeySpec` class first.

The `Cipher`, `Mac`, `Signature`, and `Key` agreement classes expect objects to implement this interface. There are no public classes to implement the `Key` interface, and thus, a `Key` type cannot be created using a constructor. (Because `Key` is purely an interface, Sun documentation refers to this as "opaque," since you can't see the implementation. But this "opaque" is quite different from how parameters are represented.)

Secret Keys

Working with secret keys is much easier than working with public keys, mostly because secret keys only contain one component and don't have formal ways of external representation. The standard encoding of a secret key is simply as an array of bytes. Public keys are trickier, since a key may consist of many individual numbers.

`SecretKey` is a empty interface that extends the `Key` interface. It simply marks an object as containing an opaque secret key representation. Since it extends the `Key` interface, it inherits the `getAlgorithm`, `getEncoded`, and `getFormat` methods.

`SecretKeySpec` is a concrete base class that defines a transparent representation of a secret key. You can construct a secret using a constructor directly by using a `byte` array to define the raw key, as well as the standard algorithm name the key is for. For example:

```
public SecretKeySpec(byte[] key, String algorithm)
public SecretKeySpec(byte[] key, int offset, int len, String algorithm)
```

In addition, `SecretKeySpec` also implements the `SecretKey` interface.

```
public String getAlgorithm();
public byte[] getEncoded();
public String getFormat();
```

This is very useful, since the JCA almost exclusively uses `Key` or `SecretKey` in the API. But since `SecretKeySpec` implements the `SecretKey` interface, you can use it without doing any conversion, as you had to do with public key `KeySpec` objects.

Algorithm-Specific Key Specifications

Most secret keys have only one representation; for example, a 128-bit key is 128 bits, and `SecretKeySpec` works well in these cases. However, sometimes an algorithm may have multiple representations for a key, and at times you may want to perform an algorithm-specific test on a key. In these cases, you use an algorithm-specific KeySpec, just as you did with public keys. The JCA defines the Spec class for password-based encryption, DES, and Triple DES.

For password-based encryption, a password, a salt, and an iteration count generate the key. The PBEKeySpec defines password-based encryption; there is the PBEKeySpec that provides a transparent representation of the password used in generating the key:

```
public PBEKeySpec(char[] password); // constructor
public final char[] getPassword.
```

For DES and Triple DES, two Spec classes are provided: DESKeySpec and DESedeKeySpec. They also define a static method to test if raw bytes are parity-adjusted—that is, whether a single DES key is 56 bits or 64 bits. Since it's in a Spec object, it needs to be converted to a Key object for subsequent use in the API:

```
byte[] key = {(byte) 0x01, (byte) 0x02,  (byte) 0x03,...}
DESKeySpec dks = new DESKeySpec(byte); // may throw InvalidKeyException
    if wrong size or weak
SecretKeyFactory skf = SecretKeyFactory.getInstance("DES")
SecretKey sk = skf.generateKey()
```

Unless you are really uncertain about the source or integrity of a key, it's normally easier just to use SecretKeySpec and skip the subsequent KeyFactory step:

```
byte[] key = {(byte) 0x01, (byte) 0x02,  (byte) 0x03,...}
SecretKeySpec sks = new SecretKeySpec(key, "DES");
```

The two Spec classes also provide a static method to see whether or not the key is parity-adjusted. In the DES case this tests if is the key is 56 (not adjusted) or 64 bits (adjusted correctly). It is up to the provider to support both cases. For example:

```
public static boolean isParityAdjusted(byte[] key, int offset)
```

The DESKeySpec class also defines a static method to test if a key is weak:

```
public static boolean isWeak(byte[] key, int offset)
```

SecretKeyFactory and Key Conversion

If you are using the algorithm-specific key types, you need to convert the `KeySpec` object into a `Key` (or `SecretKey`) for use in the API. `SecretKeyFactory` provides the interface to do this translation. It works in much the same way as other engine classes.

First, you create an instance of the factory using `getInstance`, and then you convert algorithm-specific key specification into a `SecretKey`:

```
public final SecretKey generateSecret(KeySpec spec)
```

You can also convert a secret key into a particular `Keyspec` type:

```
public final KeySpec getKeySpec(SecretKey key, Class keyspec)
```

The following is almost exclusively used for PBE keys to retrieve the password:

```
PBEKeySpec spec = (PBEKeySpec)mysecretkeyfactory.getKeySpec(key,
PBEKeySpec)
char[] password =  spec.getPassword();
```

In other cases, you don't need the factory at all, since you can retrieve the raw bytes from the `SecretKey` object with a call to `getEncoded`. Converting back to the DES key specs is only useful if you are interested in the key length and the weak key checks those classes provide:

```
// will throw InvalidKeyException if DES key is wrong length or weak
DESKeySpec spec  = (DESKeySpec) mysecretkeyfactory.getKeySpec(key,
DESKeySpec);
```

Generating Secret Keys

The `KeyGenerator` class is responsible for generating secret keys (and not public/private keys, recall that is done by `KeyPairGenerator`). It is invoked in the standard way:

1. *Create.*

   ```
   public static KeyGenerator getInstance(String algorithm)
   public static KeyGenerator getInstance(String algorithm, String
   provider)
   ```

2. *Initialize.* Initialization is also standard; however, `KeyGenerator` has a new `init` method that just takes a `SecureRandom` instance, and the key size is set by a provider default value. It is not

recommended! It is always good practice to explicitly set the key size. The method that takes an `AlgorithmParameterSpec` is also not particularly useful.

```
public void init(int keysize)
public void init(int keysize, SecureRandom r)
public void init(SecureRandom r)
public void init(AlgorithmParameterSpec params, SecureRandom r)
```

3. *Finalize* (generate the key). Once everything is initialized, the key is generated with a call to generate key. The resulting `SecretKey` object can be used as is or the raw key bytes can be retrieved calling `getEncoded` from the object:

   ```
   SecretKey generateKey();
   ```

The following code sample demonstrates creating a DES key and passing it to a `Cipher` object.

```
KeyGenerator kg = KeyGenerator.getInstance("DES");
kg.init(56);
SecretKey sk = kg.generateKey();

Cipher c = Cipher.getInstance("DES/CBC/PKCSPadding");
c.init(Cipher.ENCRYPT_MODE, sk);
byte[] cipherText = c.doFinal("encrypt this".getBytes());
```

Public/Private Keys

Often public and private keys are handled together, such as when they are being generated. The `KeyPair` class aids here and is a container class holding a public and private key. Following is the entire interface:

```
public class KeyPair {
     public KeyPair(PublicKey pub, PrivateKey pri);
     public  Key getPublicKey();
     private Key getPrivate();
}
```

Generating Key Pairs

Key pairs are generated using the engine class `KeyPairGenerator` as follows:

1. *Create*. You create using the standard `getInstance` calls. The algorithm name is the name of the generation algorithm, not the algorithm

for keys are used for. Normally they are the same but a provider might implement two different RSA key generation algorithms: the normal `RSA` and perhaps another, `RSAStrongPrimes`.

2. *Initialize.* There are two ways to initialize. The simplest is just supplying a key size or security parameter. Any additional parameters will be the provider's defaults. The other way is to fully specify every parameter by passing in an `AlgorithmParameterSpec` object. The benefit with this method is that it's provider-independent:

```
public void initialize(int keysize)
public void initialize(int keysize, SecureRandom r)
public void initialize(AlgorithmParameterSpec params)
public void initialize(AlgorithmParameterSpec params, SecureRandom r)
```

3. *Generate.* The final key pair is generated with a call to:

```
public KeyPair generateKeyPair();
```

KeyFactory

If keys are coming from an outside source in a format not recognized by the provider, you'll have to manually create new `KeySpec` objects and then convert them to `Key` objects for use in the API. Likewise, if you are exporting `Key` objects in a format not supported by the provider, you'll have to convert them to `KeySpec` objects and manually extract the components. Using the `KeyFactory` class does this. (Recall that this functionality for algorithm parameters was in the `AlgorithmParameter` class. For keys this functionality was moved into its own class.)

`KeyFactory` is an engine class, and like all other engines you call the `getInstance` method with an algorithm and an optional provider:

```
public static KeyFactory getInstance(String algorithm)
public static KeyFactory getInstance(String algorithm, String provider)
```

Convert between a KeySpec and a Key Object

Convert the key spec to a public or private key using the appropriate method:

```
public PublicKey generatePublic(KeySpec keySpec)
public PrivateKey generatePrivate(KeySpec keySpec)
```

Convert between a Key Object and a KeySpec

If you are given a `Key` object and you want to extract the components or have it translated into standard key format (`EncodedKeySpec`), use the following method with the key and class of the specification you wish it translated to:

```
public KeySpec getKeySpec(Key key, Class keySpec)
```

Converting between Equivalent KeySpec Objects

Some keys are represented by two specifications: one that specifies the raw components and another using an encoded key specification. For instance, public DSA keys can be represented by their components by using `DSAKeySpec` or by using a certificate using `PKCS8KeySpec`. You convert between the two formats by first converting the original `Spec` into an intermediate `Key` format, and then converting that into the new `KeySpec`.

To convert between equivalent `KeySpec` objects:

```
KeySpec ks1 = Original Public DSA Key Spec;
KeyFactory kf = KeyFactory.getInstance("DSA");
PublicKey pk = kf.generatePublic(ks1);
PKCSEncodedKeySpec = (PKCSEncodedKeySpec) kf.getKeySpec(pk,
PKCSEncodedKeySpec);
```

Working with RSA

The RSA algorithm has a large number of key-related classes. While RSA key-related interfaces are opaque in the sense they are interfaces and the actual implementation is left to the provider, they provide specific methods to extract various components. So while the implementation may be unknown, you don't really care, since you can get the components in a standard form. It's rare you need to convert a `Key` object into a `KeySpec`. Figure 5.2 shows the hierarchy for RSA `Key` interfaces.

There are similar `KeySpec` classes; however, the layout is a bit different. Remember, `Spec` classes are concrete classes and are fully implemented with public constructors. The key-based classes are just abstract interfaces and cannot be directly created. Figure 5.3 shows the hierarchy for RSA `KeySpec` interfaces.

Encoding and Encrypting Keys

The Java API provides numerous methods for encoding and encrypting keys.

Key Wrapping

The `Cipher` class directly supports key wrapping; however, it is up to the provider to actually choose which algorithm is used and implement the wrapping algorithm. Key wrapping is specific to the cipher algorithm. A provider may implement one key-wrapping algorithm for Triple DES and another for AES, or it may use the same algorithm, or none at all.

To do key wrapping, you specify the cipher via `getInstance` as you normally would. During initialization, the mode must be either `Cipher.WRAP_MODE` or `Cipher.UNWRAP_MODE`, but otherwise it is identical to normal initialization.

Then there are two ways to actually do the key wrapping. The first uses the raw key bytes from `Key.getEncoded` and uses the `Cipher` object as you would for any other message.

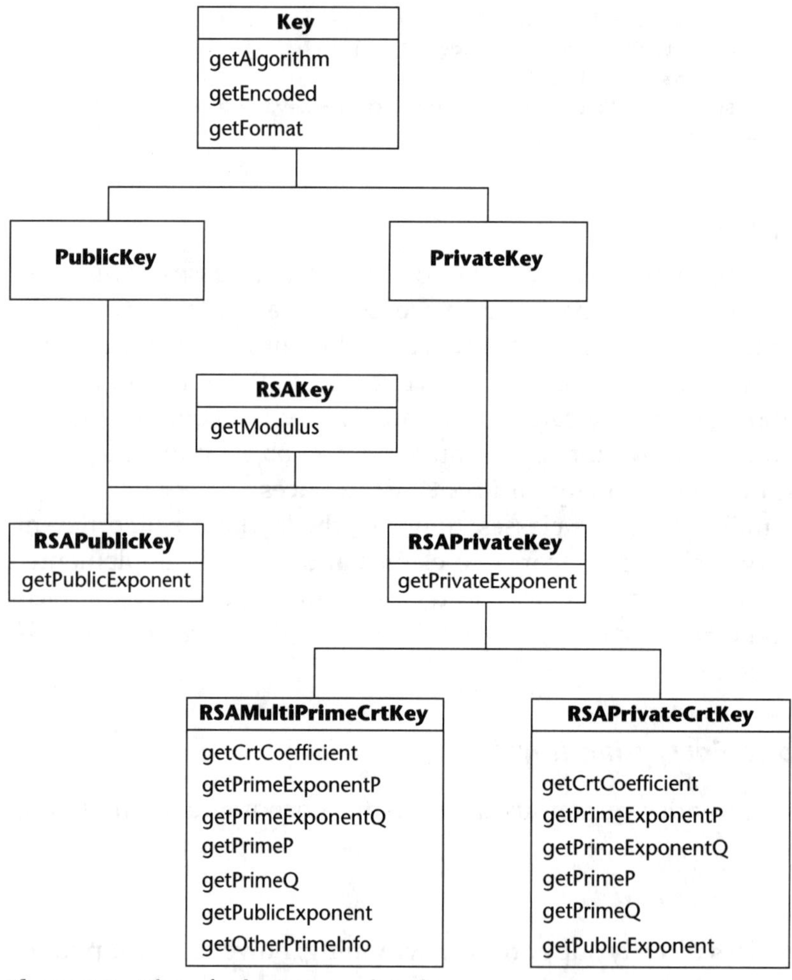

Figure 5.2 Hierarchy for RSA `Key` interfaces.

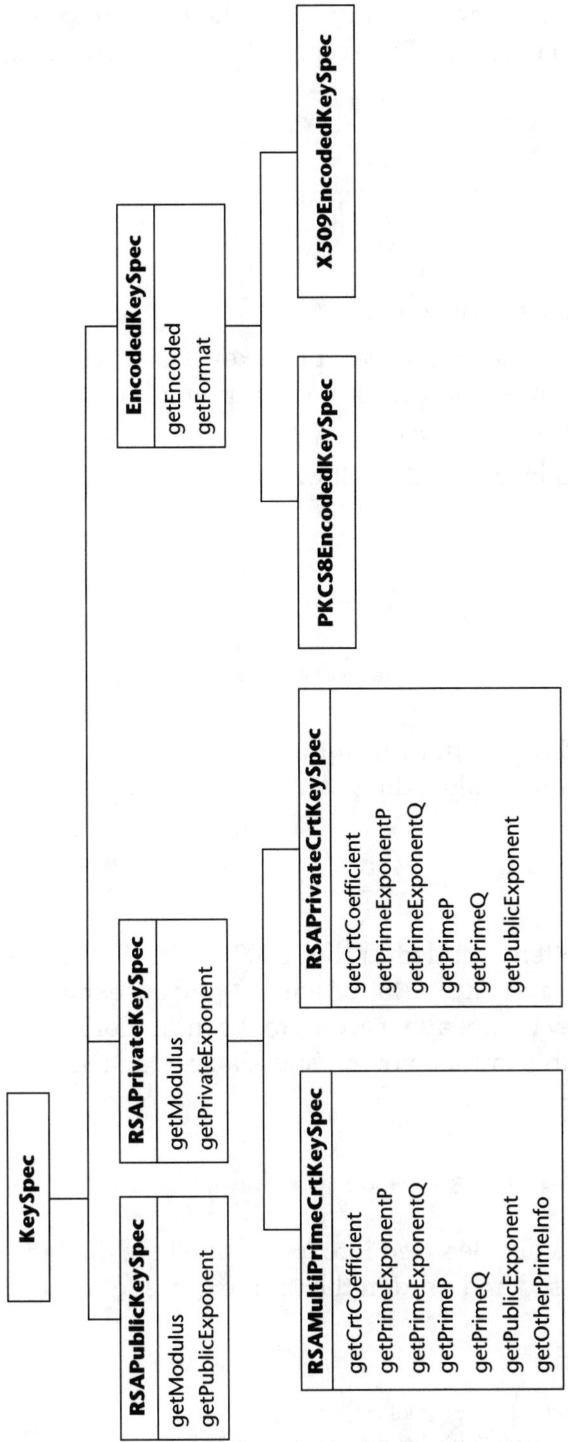

Figure 5.3 Hierarchy for RSA `KeySpec` classes.

The other method uses convenience functions that the `Cipher` object provides to work directly with keys and save some of the steps. Wrapping is especially easy:

```
byte[] wrap(Key key)
```

To unwrap, you need:

- The wrapped key bytes.
- The key for decrypting the wrapped bytes.
- The name of the algorithm the original wrapped key is to be used for (not the name of algorithm the key for key wrapping is used for). This can be extracted by `Key.getName`.
- The key type as specified by one of the following:

  ```
  Cipher.SECRET_KEY
  Cipher.PUBLIC_KEY
  Cipher.PRIVATE_KEY
  ```

  Then the call to:

  ```
  Key unwrap(byte[] wrappedKey, String wrappedKeyAlgorithm,
  int wrappedKeyType);
  ```

  provides the unwrapped key, with the resulting object `SecretKey`, `PublicKey`, or `PrivateKey` depending on the flag passed in.

X509 and PKCS8 Encodings

Public and private keys are often encoded in the X.509 or PKCS #8 standard. `X509EncodedKeySpec` and `PKCS8EncodedKeySpec` are explicitly known key encodings, but they do not allow access to the individual parameters. To convert a key into this format, you must use a `KeyFactory`:

```
RSAPublicKey k;
KeyFactory.getInstance("RSA");
X509EncodedKeySpec = kf.getSpec(X509EncodedKeySpec.class);
```

Likewise, an encoded key can be decoded into a format where the individual parameter can be accessed and used in the `Cipher` or `Signature` classes:

```
PKCS8EncodedKeySpec spec = ...;
KeyFactory kf = KeyFactory.getInstance("RSA");
RSAPrivateKey keypri = (RSAPrivateKey) kf.generatePrivate(spec);
```

Encrypted Formats

The EncryptedPrivateKeyInfo can be used to store an encrypted version of the key in provider-neutral way, based on the PKCS #8 format.

To encrypt:

1. Convert the key in a PKCS #8 format (technically the input into this can be any bytes).
2. Encrypt the key (preferably using a key-wrapping algorithm).
3. Create an EncryptedPrivateKeyInfo object, passing in the encrypted data, the name of algorithm, and AlgorithmParameters object if used.
4. Extract the bytes for storage:

```
Key key =                    // key for cipher
AlgorithmParameters ap = // ap for cipher, if any
String cipherName = // name of cipher;
Cipher c = c.getInstance(cipherName);
int mode = Cipher.ENCRYPT_MODE or  Cipher.WRAP_MODE;
c.init(mode,  key, /* ap, if used */)
byte[] encrypted = c.doFinal(pkcs8.getEncoded());

EncryptedPrivateKeyInfo epki =
       new EncryptedPrivateKeyInfo(ap, encrypted);
```

or

```
EncryptedPrivateKeyInfo epki =
       new EncryptedPrivateKeyInfo(name, encrypted);

byte[] encoded = epki.getEncoded();
```

To decrypt:

1. Create a EncryptedPrivateKeyInfo object using the encoded bytes.
2. Get the name of cipher algorithm by calling getAlgorithm.
3. Get the AlgorithmParameters if any.
4. Create a Cipher object with the previous values and the key.
5. Pass in the Cipher object and get the PKCS8EncodedKeySpec object:

```
EncryptedPrivateKeyInfo epki= new
EncryptedPrivateKeyInfo(encodedBytes);
Cipher c = Cipher.getInstance(epki.getAlgorithm);
AlgorithmParameters ap = epki.getAlgParameters();
```

```
int mode = Cipher.DECRYPT_MODE or Cipher.UNWRAP_MODE;
if (ap != null) {
      c.init(mode, key, ap);
} else {
      c.init(mode, key); // can't pass in null ap value
}
PKCS8EncodedKeySpec pkcs8 = epki.getKeySpec();
KeyFactory.getInstance ();
```

Summary

While the API is fairly large and has a number of inconsistencies, for day-to-day work only a small subset is typically used and is fairly straightforward. The main points to remember are:

- Even if you think you'll only use the SUN and SunJCE, create a `CryptoInit` class that will dynamically load any providers. This will aid in long-term management of your application.
- Likewise, create a SecureRandom `init` class (perhaps combined with `CryptoInit`). This will provide future flexibility.
- `AlgorithmParameter` objects are provider-specific encodings of parameters and are engine classes. They need to be converted into an `AlgorithmParameterSpec` object before being used in the API.
- Objects that implement the `Key` interface are provider-specific encodings of keys. These can be used directly in the API without being converted (with the exception if you are using multiple providers). `KeySpec` objects are mostly used for manually specifying key components and need to be converted into a `Key` object using `KeyFactory` (for public/private keys) or `SecretKeyFactory` (for secret keys, but rarely used).
- Secret keys can be specified using `SecretKeySpec`. This implements both `Key` and `KeySpec` and therefore does not need any conversion.

Small Message Encoding and Encryption

This chapter's focus is on small messages (typically under a few dozen bytes) most often used in cryptographic tokens or database fields. This type of encoding has very different requirements than the general long message encryption. For database work these steps can have significant implications on searches and indexing. Those issues will be covered in the next chapter.

Preprocessing

The goal of preprocessing is to transform the original data so that it can be either encrypted or encoded using a minimal amount of space.

Converting Digits into Bytes

Frequently, you will have a string consisting only of digits that needs to be encrypted, such as a credit card number. The easiest way is just using the ASCII bytes. This is certainly simple, but it's not very space efficient. For maximal space savings, you could parse the string as if it were an integer to create an `int`, `long`, or `BigIntegers`. If the string is only eight digits, you can use `Integer.parseLong`, or if it's up to 18 digits, you can use a `long` representation using `Long.parseLong`. For longer strings, you could use `BigInteger` to convert the value into an array of bytes. These methods provide the best compression, but they're also fairly expensive (or very expensive with `BigInteger`), since many multiplication calls need to be made. And the integer will probably need to be converted back into a string eventually as well.

Another option that falls between the two methods in terms of speed and space efficiency is using *binary-coded decimal encoding* (BCD). With this method, each decimal digit is naturally encoded into 4-bits—the character 0 is encoded into 0000_2, 1 becomes 0001_2, and so on. Thus, two decimal digits can be encoded into 1 byte. For instance, 39 is converted directly into hexadecimal format as `0x39`. The benefit of BCD is that you can convert one form into another very quickly and take up half as much space.

Following is a general-purpose BCD converter, where the input is arbitrary and could be an odd number of digits. If the input is fixed and known to have an even number of digits, the system can be altered to become even more efficient:

```
/** decimal digits to BCD **/
public static byte[] encode(String s)
{
 int i = 0, j = 0;
 int max = s.length() - (s.length() % 2);
 byte[] buf= new byte[(s.length() + (s.length() % 2))/2];
 while (i < max) {
     buf[j++] = (byte)((((s.charAt(i++) - '0') << 4) |
                 (s.charAt(i++) - '0')));
 }
 if ((s.length() % 2) == 1) { // If odd, add pad char
     buf[j] = (byte)((s.charAt(i++) - '0') << 4 | 0x0A);
 }
 return buf;
}

/** BCD to decimal digits string **/
public static String decode(byte[] b)
{
 StringBuffer buf = new StringBuffer(b.length * 2);
 for (int i = 0; i < b.length; ++i) {
     buf.append((char)(((b[i] & 0xf0) >> 4) + '0'));
     if ((i != b.length) && ((b[i]&0xf) != 0x0A)) // If not pad char
      buf.append((char)((b[i] & 0x0f) + '0'));
 }
 return buf.toString();
}
```

7-bit to 8-bit Compression

If you are either encrypting or encoding 7-bit data, such as plain ASCII or some other character encodings, you might want to compress the 7-bit data into 8-bits, providing a minimal savings of 14 percent—really a conversion from base 127 to base 256. (There is another benefit with encoding raw bytes in Java source code, which is described later in the chapter.)

The conversion code isn't pretty, but it is fairly compact. It assumes the input is a multiple of 7. If not, the decode process may add an extra `0x00` byte at the end. In practice, this isn't usually a problem, but if so, you could encode the length as the first byte. The code is as follows:

```
// From 7-bit to 8-bit
public static byte[] to8Bit(byte[] ba)
    {
     int len = ba.length;
     byte[] out = new byte[(len * 7) / 8];
     int i = 0;
     int inputOffset = 0;
     int outputOffset = 0;
     while (inputOffset < len - 1) {
         out[outputOffset++] = (byte)(((ba[inputOffset] & 0xff) >>> i) |
                                 (((ba[++inputOffset] & 0xff) << (7-i))));
         if (++i == 7) {
          i = 0;
          ++inputOffset;
         }
     }
     return out;
    }

public static byte[] to7Bit(byte[] ba)
    {
     int inputOffset = 0;
     int outputOffset = 0;
     int len = ba.length;
     byte[] out = new byte[(len % 7 == 0) ? (len * 8)/7 : (len * 8)/7 +
1];
     int lastBits = 0;
     int i = 0;
     while (inputOffset < len) {
         int b = ba[inputOffset] & 0xFF;
         out[outputOffset++] = (byte)(((b << i) | lastBits) & 0x7F);
         if (i == 7) {
          i = 0; lastBits = 0;
         } else {
          lastBits =  b >>> (7-i); ++inputOffset; ++i;
         }
         if (inputOffset == len)
```

```
        out[outputOffset] = (byte) lastBits;
    }
    return out;
}
```

General Compression and java.util.zip.Deflate

More general compression algorithms require a few hundred bytes before any space savings can be realized. Using these algorithms with less than the minimum will typically cause inflation.

In Java, the `Deflate` and `Inflate` classes from the `java.util.zip` package perform compression using the popular zLib algorithm (www `.gzip.org/zlib`). Unfortunately, these classes don't follow the model of the cipher classes.

To deflate or compress data:

```
import java.util.zip.*;

byte[] field = new byte[field_size];
Deflated d = new Deflater();
d.setInput(byte array of data);
d.finish();
int len = d.deflate(field);
if (!d.finished()) {
    // compressed data is too large for field
} else {
    // ok. len contains size of data
}
```

Inverting is done in a similar fashion, but the `deflate` method is replaced with `inflate`.

The Deflate class also allows various hints as to how to perform the compressions. There are two compression strategies: `Deflate.FILTER` is best for randomlike data, while `Deflate.HUFFMAN_ONLY` is probably best for textlike data.

In addition, there are parameters that control speed and compression size: from 1 to 9, where 1 is faster but may not have the best compression and 9 is slower but has the best compression. In practice, especially with short messages, the setting makes no difference.

The following code snippet allows you to experiment with the different settings. A command-line flag of -*N* is used with *N* being a digit that sets the compression level, and `-h` and `-f` sets Huffman or filtered strategies. The last argument is the data to compress. Below is source code and sample output of a program that allows you to experiment with the different settings:

```
java compress -h -9 'this is a test'
Input Length : 33
Output Length: 41
```

```
import java.util.zip.Deflater;
public class compress {

    public static boolean parsearg(Deflater d, String arg) {
     if (arg.startsWith("-")) {
         char c = arg.charAt(1);
         if (c >= '0' && c <= '9') {
          d.setLevel(c - '0');
         } else if (c == 'h') {
          d.setStrategy(Deflater.HUFFMAN_ONLY);
         } else if (c == 'f')  {
          d.setStrategy(Deflater.FILTERED);
         } else {
          throw new RuntimeException("Bad input");
         }
         return true;
     }  else {
         return false;
     }
    }

    public static void main(String[] args)
    {
     int i = 0;
     Deflater d = new Deflater();
     byte[] buffer = new byte[64];
     while (parsearg(d, args[i])) {++i; }
     System.out.println("Input Length: " + args[i].getBytes().length);
     d.setInput(args[i].getBytes());
     d.finish();
     while (d.finished() == false) {
         d.deflate(buffer);
     }
     System.out.println("Output Length: " + d.getTotalOut());
    }
}
```

Adding Check and Parity Bits

Adding parity or check bits to the data allows data integrity, and if enough bits are used, it allows for message authentication. The simplest form is to use a single-bit set such that the total number of one-bits (the *hamming weight*) in the message is an odd or even number. This only provides rudimentary checking and is useful for very small messages. The following code makes the computations using an `int` type but could just as easily be extended to a `long` type as well:

```
public class Parity {

    public static int hammingWeight(int val){
     int mask = 1;
     int count = 0;
     for (int i = 0; i < 32; i++) {
         if ((val & mask) != 0)
          count++;
         mask <<= 1;
     }
     return count;
    }

    public static boolean isOddParity(int val) {
     return ((hammingWeight(val) & 0x01) == 0x01);
    }

    //
    public static int makeOddParity(int val) {
     val <<= 1; // shift over by one
     if (!isOddParity(val)) {
         val |= 0x01; // set first bit
     }
     return val;
    }
}
```

A more sophisticated and secure approach is using multiple bits that come from a MAC function. If *k* bits are used, then there is a 2^{-k} chance that a randomly created message is considered valid; for instance, a 1 in 1,000 chance requires 10 check bits ($2^{10} = 1024$). You'll have to determine the appropriate number of bits depending on the message and its intended use; however, this scheme should only be used for "low-value" messages, since using a few dozen bits won't prevent serious attacks. For longer messages, you'll want to use much more of the full MAC value. Techniques for doing so are described in the next chapter.

MD5 is a good choice because it's a lot faster than SHA-1 and the additional security of SHA-1 isn't needed. A fair question is whether a cryptographic hash function is needed at all if only a few bits are being used from it. While it *may* be acceptable to use a generic hash function, it's probably not a good idea. Using a cryptographic hash function ensures that the check bits are fairly random and can't be predicted. The following code uses the `MAC` class. However, given the usage, it's all right to use

MessageDigest and Key and manually use an enveloping scheme (i.e., hash the key plus the long bytes) for efficiency:

```
import javax.crypto.Mac;
public class CheckBits {

    protected Mac mac;
    protected int bits;

    public CheckBits(Mac mac, int bits) {
     this.mac = mac;
     this.bits = bits;  // bits < 64
     this.mac.reset();
    }

    public long encode(long val) {
     // convert long value to byte array
     // Mac
     // convert first 8 bytes of output into a long value
long hashVal =
          ByteArray.toLong(mac.doFinal(ByteArray.fromLong(val)));

     // shift to get the right number of bits
     hashVal >>>= (64 - bits);

     return (val << bits) | hashVal;
    }

    public long decode(long val) {
     long origVal = val >>> bits;
     long encodedVal = encode(origVal);
     if (encodedVal != val) {
         throw new RuntimeException("Bad input");
     }
     return origVal;
    }
}
```

Small Message Encryption

Encryption is commonly used for long messages or transmissions. Encrypting small messages, such as those used in database or cryptographic tokens, has special requirements that are often overlooked. First, the standard modes of operation, such as the Cipher Block Chaining (CBC) mode, are really designed to encrypt many blocks, and key-wrapping algorithms are too expensive for general use. While the current trend in symmetric ciphers is to use 128-bit blocks, many times it's desirable to use 64-bit or even smaller blocks for database storage or for low-value messages.

Single-Block Encryption

For messages that can fit into a single block, the usual padding options apply. Hopefully, the message length is fixed. If so, then you can just pad using fixed values, such as 0x00s, or checksum bits from a hash of the data. Both work. The fixed-value scheme is obviously faster, while the checksum method provides a little data integrity.

Another technique is to pad by using random bits, but note that this will have significant implications for database indexing and searching.

n-Block Encryption

If possible, it's best to use a single block, but especially with 64-bit block ciphers, two (or more) blocks are sometimes needed to fully encrypt the message. Electronic Codebook (ECB) mode is normally not acceptable because of security concerns. The other traditional modes, however, aren't much better. The initialization vector is typically a null or fixed value, and the first block is basically in ECB mode, while the next block has some additional protection. Typically, the *n*th block depends on previous blocks and not on any subsequent blocks. This is fine for long messages, since one block is typically a small percentage of the message. For small messages, this "exposed" block is 50 percent or more of the total message.

This new mode, which we'll refer to as *n-block mode*, makes every block depend on every other using a similar method as CBC. For a two-block message, it's an enhanced CBC mode, but the IV is the hash of the second plaintext block. This scheme can be extended to any number of blocks, but of course becomes more expensive as the number of blocks grows. A three-block version is presented in Table 6.1.

Table 6.1 *n*-block Encryption Mode Using 2 and 3 Blocks

	2 BLOCKS	3 BLOCKS
Encryption	$C_1 = E_k(P_1 \oplus H(P_2))$ $C_2 = E_k(P_2 \oplus C_1)$	$C_1 = \text{encrypt}(P_1 \oplus \text{hash}(P_2 \parallel P_3))$ $C_2 = \text{encrypt}(P_2 \oplus C_1)$ $C_3 = \text{encrypt}(P_3 \oplus \text{hash}(C_1 \parallel C_2))$
Decryption	$P_2 = E_k(C_2) \oplus C_1$ $P_1 = D_k(C_1) \oplus \text{hash}(P_2)$	$P_2 = \text{decrypt}(C_2) \oplus C_1$ $P_3 = \text{decrypt}(C_3) \oplus \text{hash}(C_1 \parallel C_2)$ $P_1 = \text{decrypt}(C_1) \oplus \text{hash}(P_2 \parallel P_3)$

Very Small Message Encryption

As mentioned earlier in the chapter, if the message is quite small or can only take a few values, it's sometimes not desirable to use a full 64- or 128-bit block for encryption. The following systems can be used for small low-value data, since the small block size is inherently insecure and these methods are really obscuring the data. For small values like this, all this system is doing is generating a large dictionary, mapping plaintext to ciphertext.

XOR Tables

This system uses check bits as a key. First, assume the message is only n bits long and select $k \leq n$, the security parameter that corresponds to roughly a 1 in 2^k chance that a random ciphertext will decrypt to a valid plaintext. The next step is generating 2^k random n-bit values and storing them in an array. This can be done by setting up a `SecureRandom` instance with a specific seed, and then calling `nextInt` repeatedly and storing it into the array.

The parameters for this system are as follows:

- m, an n-bit message
- key, a secret key value
- k, the security parameter
- $mask$, a 2^k array containing random n-bit values

The encryption process is as follows:

1. index = k bits of H(m || key)
2. c = message ⊕ mask[index]
3. index || c

Decryption is similar:

1. $m = c$ ⊕ mask[index]
2. Check that index = k bits of H(m)

Small Codebooks

Block ciphers are actually codes that map one block to another. With a 64-bit block, explicitly listing the entire code makes the code too long, so algorithms that generate the mapping on the fly are used. For smaller blocks you can create the entire codebook. To do this, you generate a random permutation, as described in Chapter 4; then using this permutation, encryption is done just by doing a lookup:

```
c = code[m]
```

The reverse map can be computed by:

```
char[] codeinverse = new char[n];
for (int i = 0; i < code.length; ++i)
     codeinverse[code[i]] = (char)i;
```

Then decryption is done with:

```
m = codeinverse[c];
```

This works well for scrambling the original message, but it's not secure in the sense that any ciphertext converts into a valid plaintext. For some applications this may be just fine, but if you desire some additional checksum, you can create some checksum bits using a `hash` function and a key. Instead of using a real `hash` function, we'll just define one:

```
char[] hash = new char[n];
SecureRandom sr = SecureRandom(secretkeyseed)
for (int i=0; i < code.length; ++i)
     hash[i] = sr.nextInt(2^k);
```

Then given message m and k bits of security, the final output is:

```
code[m] << k | hash[m]
```

RC5-16/16

If you have access to an RC5 implementation, another option is to use RC5-16 that does encryption on 32-bit blocks. There are no published guidelines on the number of rounds to use, mostly because on such a small word size, it's inherently insecure. However, 16 rounds should be more than enough to sufficiently scramble the message.

Small Message Encoding

For general-purpose messages, you typically don't do much for encoding the raw, possibly encrypted data. It either is transmitted in raw binary format or occasionally in Base 64 (see text coming up), and that's about it. It's a different story for small messages, such as those being stored in the database or when the message is visible and possibly will be typed in by a customer or member of the product or service.

Encoding for Customer-Usable Data

Frequently you issue various numbers or messages to the customer that the customer may need to store or reenter on Web site or server, such as membership numbers, order IDs, tracking IDs, coupons, promotion codes, and other similar items. If you are starting a new service, you typically don't want to show "order id: 000001" on the invoice. Likewise, you don't want your competitors (or members) to know how many members there are. In addition, you may want to make the encoding as small as possible while limiting manual data entry errors. Overall, encoding customer-usable data has three components, expressed in the following questions:

1. What is capacity or range of number?
2. What should be the encoding?
3. Should check digits be added?

Capacity and Range

Many times the size of the message is fixed and mandated by a standard or existing application. But other times, you must select the size of the message. For instance, for an order number, a short type of 16 bits only holds 65,000 entries, which is too short. Using a full `int` type of 31 bits holds over 2 billion entries, which is probably too large for most applications. The full relationship between the size of the message in bits, the maximum value or capacity, and the encoded size using various bases is shown in Table 6.2. While encodings are discussed in the next section, the table shows that many times you can add capacity, since it doesn't change the final size of the encoded tokens. For instance, let's say you are encoding an order number, and since you are a small business, you expect 10 million orders will likely be more than enough for the lifetime of the business. Using the table, you see that you need 24 bits to represent the number and it encodes to 8 decimal digits. In this case, you might as well use 26 bits, since it also encodes to 8 decimal digits (but does require one more base 64 digit). However, if you can relax the requirement and get away with 23 bits, then the number encodes to 7 decimal digits.

Table 6.2 Relationship between Number Digits and Bit Length

BITS	CAPACITY	DIGITS BASE 10	DIGITS BASE 16	DIGITS BASE 32	DIGITS BASE 64
16	65 Thousand	5	4	4	3
17	131 Thousand	6	5	4	3
18	262 Thousand	6	5	4	3
19	524 Thousand	6	5	4	4
20	1.04 Million	7	5	4	4
21	2.1 Million	7	6	5	4
22	4.1 Million	7	6	5	4
23	8.3 Million	7	6	5	4
24	16 Million	8	6	5	4
25	33 Million	8	7	5	5
26	67 Million	8	7	6	5
27	134 Million	9	7	6	5
28	268 Million	9	7	6	5
29	536 Million	9	8	6	5
30	1.07 Billion	10	8	6	5
31	2.14 Billion	10	8	7	6
32	4.92 Billion	10	8	7	6

Selecting a Base Representation

You'd think that selecting the base to represent the number would be easy. Unfortunately, it's a bit more complicated than you might expect. Following is a rundown of the base representations:

- *Base 10.* This is the easiest, since it's all numbers and it's the most natural to work with. For small values, say, 20 to 30 bits, it's probably not unreasonable for a member to enter up to 10 digits—especially if the digits are formatted for easy reading by grouping or using dashes. Instead of 1234567890, printing 123-456-7890 is much easier (and it resembles a phone number, which people are used to processing). It also has the advantage that all the digits *sound* different (at least in English) and aren't easily confused on the phone. For machine applications in URLs or cookies, base 10 is almost never desired because it crowds out the more useful information in the Web browser. Browsers typically display the rightmost characters in the URL, which can obscure the first part of the URL that contains your company's name.

- *Base 16.* This is the standard format for encoding raw binary data, and it's a bit more compact than base 10. Base 16 is another good choice, except you should not use the traditional alphabet of 0 though 9, a through f for two reasons. First, there are quite a few words that can be spelled with a through f. The other reason is that using standard hexadecimal notation is a dead giveaway you are encoding a binary data, and that looks bad.
- *Base 32.* This isn't used very often, but its alphabet consists of the letters and six additional characters or digits.
- *Base 64.* This is the most compact, and you should always use it when encoding data for use in URLs and cookies. For large-message encoding, base 64 is fine; however, if the data is part of the URL or cookie, a slightly modified version of base 64 should be used.

The absolute simplest way of disguising the underlying number is by using a different alphabet for base 10. Instead of the numbers 0 through 9, you use different letters. The advantage is that the number can be converted very quickly to native form for processing. Using a different alphabet is quite simple. One consideration is again selecting a vowel-free alphabet to prevent the accidental spelling of words.

Selecting Base Alphabets

You don't need to use the native digits for a particular base. There are a few issues to consider, which we detail in this section.

Visual Confusion

Eliminating visual confusion is done be removing letters that look alike (such as, I versus J) or are similar to numbers (for example, 1 and I, and 0 and O). Using uppercase is preferred to using lowercase because these letters are less confusing to many people and they exhibit less symmetry that do the lowercase ones. This is important for people with dyslexia—for instance, b and d can be confused, but it's less likely with B and D.

Vowels and Spelling

If the public has to see or use the encoding, you might want to make sure the actual encoding doesn't spell something inadvertent. Using standard hexadecimal, lots of unpleasant words can be created: dead, beef, defaced. Using zero as an O and one as lowercase l (ell) allows others such as blood, flea, fleeced to be spelled. Granted, there are only at best a few dozen you don't want to use, so the odds of them occurring are low. But it only takes one to result in an irate customer, and depending on the possible application, a nice news story. The easiest way to solve this problem is choosing a new alphabet that is vowel-free.

Phonetic Issues

If the encoding is likely to be spoken over the phone lines, then it's best to pick an encoding that doesn't use letters than sound alike. This is not a trivial problem. In Japanese, new "phone speaking numbers" are used, since the original ones were confused too often.

For English, letters fall into six similar-sounding categories, noted in Table 6.3.

In addition:

- F, L, O, R do not have any similar-sounding letters.
- O does not sound like any other letters, but in printed form it may be confused with the number 0, depending on the typeface.
- H, while starting with an "ay" sound, has a hard "chuh" sound at the end that makes it unlikely to be confused with other letters.
- W is unique in that it is pronounced with two or three syllables, and the pronunciation can range from "dub yuh" to "double you."
- X is unlikely to be confused with S in normal situations unless the connection has dropouts.

Using these guidelines, you can create an alternate base 10 alphabet using letters that are unlikely to be confused on the telephone: F, L, R, H, K, Z, Y, N, S, and W.

With base 16 you must make some compromises, since there are not 16 letters that all sound different. You can extend base 10 with your pick of any five consonants, such as C, D, G, J, and X. An alternate base 16 representation still uses the numbers 0 through 9, plus five new letters. One option is F, H, Z, W, and Y, since they all look and sound different. One problem is the use of 0 and 1 (zero and one), which may be substituted for vowels. Dropping 0 and 1, we could create an alphabet using F, H, 2, 3, 4, 5, 6, 7, 8, 9, Z, W, Y, L, and N. However, mixing letters and numbers randomly can be difficult to read.

Table 6.3 English Letters that Sound Similar

SOUND	ENGLISH LETTERS
ay	A, J, K, and lesser H
ee	B, C, D, E, G, P, T, V, Z
eye	I, Y
e	M, N
oo	U, Q, and lesser W
Ending "ess" sound	S, X

Using Word-Based Encodings

An alternate idea is to skip numerical encoding and instead use actual *words* to encode the number. For instance, 0x65A3FE might be encoded using three words, such as "flex pear jump." Originally this was proposed for encoding secret keys (see RFC 2289) where 2,048 different words are used, with each word encoding 11 bits. Multiple words can be used to produce larger values. For 64-bit keys, this required six words, and the leftover two bits was used as minimal parity or as check bits. There is no reason why this can't be scaled up or down for other purposes and smaller messages.

The beauty of this system is that it's easy to speak the code over the telephone; it doesn't have the "code word spells something" problem, and it doesn't require nearly as much typing as you might think. You could have the person type out the entire words, but on a Web browser you can use the auto-complete function. In the United States, this is most commonly used for state drop-down lists when an address needs to be entered. Typing "M" once gives Maine, "M" twice gives Maryland, "M" three times gives "Massachusetts," and so on. For optimal usage, you'll want the word list to be roughly uniformly distributed. And using the Tab key to change "focus," you can enter a very large number very quickly with little chance of error. Again, using check digits, this can be verified on the client side as well. This can help eliminate member name scanning and member lockout attacks.

It's easiest to use a dictionary that is a power of 2, since converting back and forth into words just requires extracting the right set of bits from the message (by shifting and using an AND mask). Given a dictionary size and the number of words used to encode, Table 6.4 shows how many bits are encoded.

Table 6.4 Encoding Size Based on Dictionary Size and Number of Words

DICTIONARY SIZE	3 WORDS	4 WORDS	5 WORDS	6 WORDS
32	15	20	25	30
64	18	24	30	36
128	21	28	35	42
256	24	32	40	48
512	27	36	45	54
1,024	30	40	50	60
2,048	33	44	55	66

However, for user-interface purposes it might be better to use the *smallest* dictionary possible for encoding. Table 6.5 shows the size of the dictionary needed given a message size and the number of words you wish to use for encoding. Converting back and forth is just the same as doing a general base conversion, where the base is the size of the dictionary, as shown in the example code following Table 6.5.

Words themselves can be selected from RFC 2289. You can think of them yourself or use a Scrabble dictionary. SOGPODS, an international Scrabble society, has a list of three- and four-letter words available at `http://members.ozemail.com.au/~rjackman/`. According to this organization, there are exactly 952 three-letter words and 5,083 four-letter words, which should give you plenty of choices.

Table 6.5 Dictionary Size Requirements for Encoding a Message Using Multiple Words

	3 WORDS	4 WORDS	5 WORDS	6 WORDS
20 bits	102	32	16	11
21 bits	128	39	19	12
22 bits	162	46	22	13
23 bits	204	54	25	15
24 bits	256	64	28	16
25 bits	323	77	32	18
26 bits	407	91	37	21

Table 6.5 *(Continued)*

	3 WORDS	4 WORDS	5 WORDS	6 WORDS
27 bits	512	108	43	23
28 bits	646	128	49	26
29 bits	813	153	56	29
30 bits	1024	182	64	32
31 bits	1291	216	74	36
32 bits	1626	256	85	41

```
import java.util.*;
public class wordencode {
    public static final String[] dictionary = {"zero", "one", "two",
                                "three", "four", "five",
                                "six", "seven", "eight",
                                "nine"};

    public static final long size = (long)dictionary.length;

    public static final HashMap wordvalue = new HashMap();
    static {
     for (int i = 0; i < dictionary.length; i++) {
         wordvalue.put(dictionary[i], new Integer(i));
     }
    }

    public static long decode(String words)
    {
     long val = 0;
     StringTokenizer st = new StringTokenizer(words);
     while (st.hasMoreTokens()) {
         val *= size;
         Integer tmp = (Integer)wordvalue.get(st.nextToken());
         val += tmp.intValue();
     }
     return val;
    }

    public static String encode(long val, int numWords) {
     ArrayList list = new ArrayList();
     while (numWords-- > 0) {
         list.add(dictionary[(int)(val % size)]);
         val /= size;
```

```
        }

        StringBuffer buf = new StringBuffer();
        for (int i = list.size() -1; i >= 0; --i) {
            buf.append((String)(list.get(i)));
            buf.append(" ");
        }
        return buf.toString();
    }

    public static void main(String args[]) throws Exception
    {
        String encoded = encode(Long.parseLong(args[0]), 5);
        System.out.println(encoded);
        long val = decode(encoded);
        System.out.println(val);
    }
}
```

Phonetic Alphabets for Customer Service

Phonetic alphabets are used to avoid confusion when calling out letters. This is very useful in customer service applications when verifying names and encoded data over the telephone. The most common is the NATO version, as shown in Table 6.6, but dozen of other variants exist. A comprehensive collection is posted by Brian Kelk on his Web site at www.bckelk.uklinux.net/menu.html. But you can certainly make your own—after all, "whiskey" might not be the most appropriate choice of words for customer service applications.

Table 6.6 Standard NATO Phonetic Alphabet

Alpha	Hotel	Oscar	Victor
Bravo	India	Papa	Whiskey
Charlie	Juliet	Quebec	X-ray
Delta	Kilo	Romeo	Yankee
Echo	Lima	Sierra	Zulu
Foxtrot	Mike	Tango	
Golf	November	Uniform	

Mixed Bases and Alphabets

Occasionally, you may wish to have the number fit into a template where the last digit is a number but others are letters such as ddd-aaa-ddd or aaaaaaa-d or addddd (where *a* stands for *alpha*, and *d* for *numerical digit*). This typically is useful for printed materials, such as coupons and certificates, but has other uses as well:

- You may need to make the letter fit a certain size, but your encoding is too small (lucky you). If, however, you have that much extra space, consider adding more security bits.
- To make it look more official, incorporate more structure and avoid making the material look less like random junk. Keep in mind you want the material to be psychologically easier to read or identify, for instance, by having the first two "digits" be alphanumeric, while the rest are numeric digits.

Adding Check Digits

Check digits are additional digits added to the encoded message that provide a quick check to see if the number or message is correct and to determine if the user mistyped the entry. They differ from check *bits* previously described because they provide little security, but they do have useful properties in detecting common data entry errors.

Check digits typically can detect single-digit errors and transposition errors where digits are out of order (see Table 6.7, based on [Verhoelff1969], [WaPu1989], and [Schulz2001]). Cryptographically, check digits are insecure, since they are easy to generate and forge, but in Web-based and client/server applications, they are quite useful. Using a JavaScript implementation, the Web browser can quickly check to see the user provided valid input, without making a round-trip to the server.

Mathematically, the entire message including the check digits are used in a formula to determine validity. This formula can also be used for computing what the check digit should be. You can verify the message either by using the original check equation or by recomputing the check digit and comparing.

Table 6.7 Description and Frequency of Errors for Manual Data Entry of Digits

NAME	DESCRIPTION	PERCENTAGE
Single errors	a → b	60% to 95%
Omitting or adding a digit	c → cc cc → c	10% to 20%
Adjacent transpositions	ab → ba	10% to 20%
Twin errors	aa → bb	0.5% to 1.5%
Jump transpositions	acb → bca	0.5% to 1.5%
Jump twin errors	aca → bcb	Less than 1%
Phonetic errors (English)	a0 → 1a, a > 2 (e.g., 30 → 13)	0.5% to 1.5%

Mod 10

The previous mathematics are used in what is commonly known as the *modulus 10 or mod 10* check but formally known as the LUHN formula, a method created by a group of mathematicians in the late 1960s. This method detects all single-digit errors and all single transposition errors. It is most commonly used in credit card numbers (the last digits), such as Visa, MasterCard, Discover, and American Express. It is also used in the Canadian Social Insurance Number and the Sweden Personal Number.

The specification is in Annex B to ISO/IEC 7812, Part 1 and ANSI X4.13, but you don't need to look those up to know the formula:

$$\text{sum} = a_1 + f(a_2) + a_3 + f(a_4) + a_5 + f(a_6) + a_7 + \ldots + f(a_{n-1}) \bmod 10$$

where the function $f(x)$ is $2x$ if $x \leq 4$, and $2x - 9$ if $x \geq 5$. This function encodes by adding the two digits of the number $2x$. For instance, $2 \times 6 = 12$, so the value is $1 + 2 = 3$, which is the same thing as $2 \times 6 - 9$. Using this rather odd formula, the check formula is sum + check = 0 mod 10, and the check digit can be computed as, 0 if sum is 0; otherwise, 10 – sum:

```
public class mod10 {

    // computes the special sum function
    protected static int computeSum(String digits) {
     int val = 0;
     boolean odd = true;
     for (int i = 0; i < digits.length(); i++) {
         if (odd) {
          int c = digits.charAt(i) - '0';
          val += c;
```

```
                odd = false;
            } else {
                int c = 2 * (digits.charAt(i) - '0');
                if (c >= 10) {
                    val += c - 9;
                } else {
                    val += c;
                }
                odd = true;
            }
        }
        return val %  10;
    }

    // compute check digit
    public static int compute(String digits) {
        // error if even number of digits
        int val = computeSum(digits);
        if (val != 0) {
            val = 10 - val;
        }
        return val;
    }

    // compute check equation
    public static boolean verify(String digits) {
        // error if odd number of digits
        return ((computeSum(digits) % 10) == 0);
    }
}
```

UPC

The ubiquitous Universal Product Code (UPC) on consumer packaging was first invented by George J. Lauer and first used by the grocery industry in 1973 (see `http://members.aol.com/productupc/`). Interestingly, when UPCs were first printed, they did not even include the check digit, since the time to key in the extra digit was not deemed worthwhile (yes, in pre-optical scanner days, clerks had to manually key in every UPC in an order).

In the United States, UPC codes are 12 digits including the check digit; however, outside the United States, they are commonly 13 digits. The first digits (or first two digits) are a category code. The next five digits are a registered manufacturer code. The next five digits are an internal code for the product. For space-limited situations (such as on cans) and for very large manufactures, there is a compressed seven-digit format that strips out the extra zeros.

The scheme itself is a simplified version of the mod 10 check. All individual digits are added, but those in even positions are multiplied by 3 (called a 1-to-3 weighting), resulting in the check equation of:

$$\text{sum} + \text{check} = 0 \bmod 10$$

where $sum = a_1 + 3a_2 + a_3 + 3a_4 + a_5 + 3a_6 + \ldots + a_{n-1}$ mod 10. The check digit is 0 if the sum is 0; otherwise, 10 – sum.

The inventor says originally someone else proposed this to him, since they were convinced it would protect against "some bit representation errors." This certainly covers single-digit errors, but it was an unfortunate decision because transpositions where the digits differ by 5, or (1, 6) (2, 7) (3, 8),(4, 9)(5, 0), go undetected. There are 45 possible transposition errors (45 = 9 + 8 + 7 + 6 + 5 + 4 + 3 + 2 + 1), so this scheme detects 40/45 = 88.9 percent of them.

ABA Routing Numbers

Another system similar to the UPC check digit is used on the American Banking Association (ABA) routing numbers used on American checks. It's always nine digits. The first four are routing symbols for the Federal Reserve, the next four are the institution number, and the last digit is the check digit.

The check digit is computed as before but uses 3-7-1-3-7-1-3-7-1 for the weighting. It has the same transposition error detection rate as the UPC check digit.

ISBN

International Standard Book Number (ISBN) is a 10-digit number (including a check digit) that is used to uniquely identify books and periodicals at the point of sale. It uses a completely different scheme than those previously described. Given an ISBN number is $a_1 a_2 a_3 a_4 a_5 a_6 a_7 a_8 a_9 c_{10}$, the check equation is sum + check = 0 mod 11, where sum = $10a_1 + 9a_2 + 8a_3 + 7a_4 + 6a_5 + 5a_6 + 4a_7 + 3a_8 + 2a_9$ mod 11. Using this, check digit is 0 if sum is 0, or the letter X (for 10) if the sum value is 1; otherwise, the check digit is 11 – sum.

Verhoeff's Dihedral Group D_5 Check

The Dihedral Group D_5 is a group with 10 elements, but addition is defined very differently and is based on rotations of a pentagon. This group is not commutative, meaning the order of addition is important. For instance, 1 + 9 = 5, but 9 + 1 = 8. Table 6.8 defines the addition rules, with the first element chosen from the first column. Using this table, inverses can also be determined. For instance –4 = 1, since 1 + 4 = 1 + 4 = 0.

Verhoeff in 1969 used the properties of the group to create a very effective check digit that was used, among other places, for serial numbers on German banknotes (pre-euro) [Verhoeff1969]. Unlike other schemes, the weighting is both value- and position-based, using the matrix in Table 6.9 [for those more mathematically inclined, this matrix is generated by iterating the permutation (01589427)(36)]. The top row is the digit value, and the rows are digit position (mod 8).

Table 6.8 Dihedral Addition

+	0	1	2	3	4	5	6	7	8	9
0	0	1	2	3	4	5	6	7	8	9
1	1	2	3	4	0	6	7	8	9	5
2	2	3	4	0	1	7	8	9	5	6
3	3	4	0	1	2	8	9	5	6	7
4	4	0	1	2	3	9	5	6	7	8
5	5	9	8	7	6	0	4	3	2	1
6	6	5	9	8	7	1	0	4	3	2
7	7	6	5	9	8	2	1	0	4	3
8	8	7	6	5	9	3	2	1	0	4
9	9	8	7	6	5	4	3	2	1	0

Table 6.9. Permutation Array

P	0	1	2	3	4	5	6	7	8	9
0	0	1	2	3	4	5	6	7	8	9
1	1	5	7	6	2	8	3	0	9	4
2	5	8	0	3	7	9	6	1	4	2
3	8	9	1	6	0	4	3	5	2	7
4	9	4	5	3	1	2	6	8	7	0
5	4	2	8	6	5	7	3	9	0	1
6	2	7	9	3	8	0	6	4	1	5
7	7	0	4	6	9	1	3	2	5	8

Finally, the actual check equation is:

$$\text{check} + P(1, a_1) + P(2, a_2) + \dots + P(n \bmod 8, a_n) = 0,$$

where + is *dihedral* addition.

While it's a bit long to describe, coding this scheme is very quick:

```
// dihedral addition matrix A + B = a[A][B]
public static final int a[][] = {{0,1,2,3,4,5,6,7,8,9},
 {1,2,3,4,0,6,7,8,9,5}, {2,3,4,0,1,7,8,9,5,6}, {3,4,0,1,2,8,9,5,6,7},
 {4,0,1,2,3,9,5,6,7,8}, {5,9,8,7,6,0,4,3,2,1}, {6,5,9,8,7,1,0,4,3,2},
 {7,6,5,9,8,2,1,0,4,3}, {8,7,6,5,9,3,2,1,0,4}, {9,8,7,6,5,4,3,2,1,0}};

// dihedral inverse map, A + inverse[A] = 0
public static final int inverse[] = {0,4,3,2,1,5,6,7,8,9};

// permutation weighting matrix P[position][value]
public static final  int p[][] = {{0,1,2,3,4,5,6,7,8,9},
  {1,5,7,6,2,8,3,0,9,4}, {5,8,0,3,7,9,6,1,4,2}, {8,9,1,6,0,4,3,5,2,7},
  {9,4,5,3,1,2,6,8,7,0}, {4,2,8,6,5,7,3,9,0,1}, {2,7,9,3,8,0,6,4,1,5},
  {7,0,4,6,9,1,3,2,5,8}};

public static int compute(String digits) {
     int check = 0;
     for (int i = 0; i < digits.length(); ++i) {
         int c = digits.charAt(i) - '0';
         check = a[check][p[(i+1)%8][c]];
     }
     return inverse[check];
}

// assumes check digit first digit
public static boolean verify(String digits) {
     int check = 0;
     for (int i = 0; i < digits.length(); ++i) {
         int c = digits.charAt(i) - '0';
         check = a[check][p[i%8][c]];
     }
     return (check == 0);
}
```

This scheme catches all single and adjacent transposition errors, and about 95 percent of jump transposition, twin errors, and phonetic errors. The exact details of how and why this works can be found in [Schulz2001] (the author has published many other papers on check digit schemes).

Mod 11,10 and Mod 17,16

The ISO 7064 standard defines a number of check digit schemes. Most useful is the mod 11,10 check that produces a single check digit. According to the standard, this scheme catches all single substitutions, but misses 2.2 percent of transpositions, 9.3 percent of jump transpositions, 11 percent of double substitutions, and 10 percent of "other." In any event, this scheme is being used for labeling blood bags in Germany, and a hexadecimal version (mod 16,15) is being used in the International Standard Audiovisual Number (ISAN), which is somewhat similar to an ISBN number. The algorithm uses a combination of mod 10 and mod 11 computations; however, mod 10 is computed slightly differently—if a mod 10 computation results in 0, the number 10 is substituted. Following is the code for this scheme:

```
public static final int b = 10;
public static final f(int x) {
     int val = x % b;
     return (val == 0) ? b : val;
}
```

The scheme defines a recursive sequence using the message digits:

$$T_0 = 10$$
$$T_n = (2\ (\ f(T_{n-1} + a_n))\ \text{mod}\ 11$$

The check equation is simply $T_{n+1} = 1 \bmod 11$. The check digit is computed by $c_{n+1} = (11 - T_n) \bmod 10$.

The following algorithm is for base 10, but it could be easily extended for base 16 by changing the values for `b` and `b1`, and making an appropriate translation from characters to numbers. ISO 7064 defines other alphanumeric schemes such as mod 27,26, where characters A through Z are mapped to 0 to 25, and mod 37,36 maps the characters 0 – 9 to 0 to 9, and A – Z to 10 – 35.

```
public static final int b = 10;
public static final int b1 = 11;

// Minor optimization.  input x is never greated than 2*b
public static int f(int x) {
     if (x == 0) return b;
     if (x <= b) return x;
     return x-b;
}

public static int compute(String digits) {
     int t = 10;
     for (int i = 0; i < digits.length(); ++i) {
         int c = digits.charAt(i) - '0';
         t = (2 * f(t + c)) % 11;
     }
```

```
        return (b1 - t) % b;
    }

    public static boolean verify(String digits) {
        int t = b;
        for (int i = 0; i < digits.length(); ++i) {
          int c = digits.charAt(i) - '0';
          t = (f(t + c) * 2) % b1;
      }
      return (t % b == 1);
    }
```

Mod 97

The mod 97 scheme adds *two* check digits, but as a result, it catches just about all errors involving two digits. The main idea is to use a weighting using powers of 10 and using modulo 97 arithmetic. The number 97 is chosen because it's the largest two-digit prime number, and thus it forms a field. Fields are useful because every digit has an inverse.

There are many variations, with some done incorrectly. We'll describe the ISO 7064 version, formally known as mod 97,10, since it's the only version that is actually standardized and fully documented. According to the standard, this catches all single substitutions, along with adjacent and jump transpositions. It only misses 1 percent of double substitutions and 1 percent of "other" errors.

Instead of the previous check-digit algorithms that worked left to right, this technique does the opposite. Given an $(n + 1)$-digit decimal number $a_n...a_2c_1c_0$, the check equation is:

$$10^n a_n + 10^{n-1}a_{n-1} + ... + 10^3 a_3 + 10^2 a_2 + 10c_1 + c_0 = 1 \bmod 97$$

Alternatively, it can be expressed as:

$$D \times 100 + C = 1 \bmod 97$$

where D is the integer value of the string (e.g., "123" is 123) and C is the two-digit check number. For example, computing the check digits for "1234" is computed as $10^5 \times 1 + 10^4 \times 2 + 3 \times 10^3 + 4 \times 10^2 \equiv 16 \bmod 97$, so the check digit is $98 - 62 = 82$. The resulting value is 123482.

There are a number of tricks in computing this formula. First, if the number you are adding the check digits to is seven decimal digits or less, this scheme can done very quickly by just using basic arithmetic. It can be extended to 14 digits by using `longs` instead of `int` types:

```
public static int compute(String digits)
{
 int val = Integer.parseInt(digits) * 100;
 return ( 98 - val % 97);
}

public static boolean verify(String digits)
{
 int val = Integer.parseInt(digits);
 return  (val % 97 == 1);
}
```

The other trick doesn't need to explicitly compute powers of 10 (mod 97) or use a table of them, since we can write a very small algorithm that skips that computation all together. The trick is rewriting the number using Horner's Rule. Instead of viewing 1234 as $1 \times 10^3 + 2 \times 10^2 + 3 \times 10^1 + 4 \times 10^0$, the same number is expressed recursively using Horner's Rule as $((((1) \times 10) + 2) \times 10 + 3) \times 10) + 4$. Our algorithm just adds a few extra multiplications. For instance, the check digit for 1234 is computed by:

$$98 - ((((((1) \times 10) + 2) \times 10 + 3) \times 10 + 4) \times 10) \times 10) \bmod 97$$

The code is as follows:

```
public static int compute(String digits)
{
 int check = 0, c = 0;
 for (int i = 0; i < digits.length(); ++i) {
     c = digits.charAt(i) - '0';
     check = ((check + c) * 10) % 97;
 }
 return 98 - ((check*10) % 97); // need one more 10x
}

public static boolean verify(String digits)
{
 int check = 0, c = 0;
 int i = 0; // outside 'for' statement
 for (i = 0; i < digits.length()-1; ++i) {
     c = digits.charAt(i) - '0';
     check = ((check + c) * 10) % 97;
 }
 check += digits.charAt(i) - '0'; // last digit just added, no 10x
 return ((check % 97) == 1);
}
```

Table 6.10 Guidelines for Selection of an Appropriate Base Representation

APPLICATION	BASE
General, email, general encoding of binary data	Base 64
Encoding data in a URL or cookie	"URL-safe" Base 64
Specialized encodings, PostScript	Base 85
Java source code `byte` arrays	Base 128

Encoding for Machines and Customer-Visible Applications

When a message doesn't need to be manually keyed by a member or user but is still *publicly* visible, the choices are more clear-cut. You normally want to keep the encoding as small as possible.

When space is not a premium, or if the message is very short, base 10 or base 16 is perfectly fine. In other cases a more specialized encoding is needed. See Table 6.10.

Base 64

Base 64 is the standard binary data encoding, but yet again there are some wrinkles to using it. Since there are 64 different characters, the odds of a token spelling anything significant are quite low, and the token is normally transient, so it's not much of deal. Base 64 is commonly used to encode binary files. The question here is what alphabet to use; there are three standard variations.

uuencode

The "original" format is the uuencode format. It's primarily a leftover from early days with primitive keyboards that didn't have lowercase. See Table 6.11.

Unfortunately, it's only semistandardized and there are many variations.

Mime/Base 64 RFC 1521

This RFC defines a standard base 64 implementation and is commonly used to format binary files suitable for sending in email or posting to newsgroups. It's also standard to append a padding character '=' so the final result is a multiple of 4. In addition, it's customary to print no more than 76 base 64 characters per line. See Table 6.12.

Table 6.11 "Common" uuencode Base 64 Alphabet

`!"#$%&'()*+,./0123456789:;<=>?@ABCDEFGHIJKLMNOPQRSTUVWXYZ[\]^_

Table 6.12 Standard RFC 1521 Base 64 Alphabet

ABCDEFGHIJKLMNOPQRSTUVWXYZabcdefghijklmnopqrstuvwxyz0123456789+/

URL-Base 64

This encoding is fine for email, but it doesn't work for embedding data in a URL or Web cookie or for generating temporary filenames. The original base 64 is caught between multiple specifications and usages, and the characters +/= have other meaning or purposes. Reading through various specifications, you'll note that only ".-_*" are "safe" characters. In practice, the "." should be a safe character, but many proxies and Web servers interpret it as a filesystem reference (for instance, `http://www.cnn.com/./works` fine and adding dot-slash is frequently ignored).

Therefore, I normally use the substitution given in Table 6.13 so that the encoding can be used without fear in a URL.

Fast Implementation

Oddly, Sun does not include an implementation of Base 64 in the Java API. That's just as well, since we would have to modify it anyway to make it URL safe. The following implementation is very high performance—most unnecessary comparisons are eliminated by either using tables or by unrolling loops.

Table 6.13 Difference between the Standard and URL-Safe Base 64 Encoding

VALUE	STANDARD BASE 64	URL-SAFE BASE 64
62	+	- (dash)
63	/	_ (underscore)
pad	=	* (asterisk)

The first section defines the mappings between values and characters. To change this to standard base 64 encoding (for use with electronic mail or other applications), just change the values for `LETTER_62`, `LETTER_63`, `PAD_CHAR`:

```
public class Base64UrlSafe {
    /**
     * Character to use to pad blocks.
     * The spec is '=', but this code is using a '*' to be url friendly
     */
    public static final char PAD_CHAR = '*';

    /**
     * The letter 62.
     * The spec is '+', but here it is a '-' to be url friendly
     */
    public static final char LETTER_62 = '-';

    /**
     * The letter 63
     * The spec is '/', here it's '_' to be web friendly
     */
    public static final char LETTER_63 = '_';

    /**
     * Map used in encoding into base 64
     */
    protected static final char[] encodeMap = {
     'A', 'B', 'C', 'D', 'E', 'F', 'G', 'H', 'I', 'J', 'K', 'L',
     'M', 'N', 'O', 'P', 'Q', 'R', 'S', 'T', 'U', 'V', 'W', 'X',
     'Y', 'Z', 'a', 'b', 'c', 'd', 'e', 'f', 'g', 'h', 'i', 'j',
     'k', 'l', 'm', 'n', 'o', 'p', 'q', 'r', 's', 't', 'u', 'v',
     'w', 'x', 'y', 'z', '0', '1', '2', '3', '4', '5', '6', '7',
     '8', '9', LETTER_62, LETTER_63};

    /**
     * Map used in decoding base64 back into raw bytes
     */
    protected static byte[] decodeMap = new byte[256];
    static {
     for (int i = 0  ; i < 256 ; i++) decodeMap[i] = -1;
     for (int i = 'A'; i <= 'Z'; i++) decodeMap[i] =
           (byte)(i - 'A');
     for (int i = 'a'; i <= 'z'; i++) decodeMap[i] =
           (byte)(26 + i - 'a');
     for (int i = '0'; i <= '9'; i++) decodeMap[i] =
           (byte)(52 + i - '0');
     decodeMap[LETTER_62] = 62;
     decodeMap[LETTER_63] = 63;
```

The next step is encoding. The basic strategy is to read 4 bytes at a time and convert into a 32-bit integer and then successively shift to get 6-bit values. The leftovers are handled as a special case, which allows you to modify the behavior if you are encoding a fixed-sized message and do not want to use padding characters:

```
public static String encode(byte[] raw) {
     int end = raw.length;
     int slop = end % 3;
     char[] buf = new char[(slop == 0) ? (4*(end/3)) : (4*(end/3 + 1))];
     int i = 0, j = 0;
     end = end - slop;
     while (i < end) {
         int block = ((raw[i++] & 0xff) << 16) |
          ((raw[i++] & 0xff) << 8) | (raw[i++] & 0xff);

         buf[j++] = encodeMap[(block >>> 18) & 0x3f];
         buf[j++] = encodeMap[(block >>> 12) & 0x3f];
         buf[j++] = encodeMap[(block >>>  6) & 0x3f];
         buf[j++] = encodeMap[(block & 0x3f)];
     }
     if (slop == 2) {
         int block = ((raw[i++] & 0xff) << 16)
 | ((raw[i++] & 0xff) << 8);

         buf[j++] = encodeMap[(block >>> 18) & 0x3f];
         buf[j++] = encodeMap[(block >>> 12) & 0x3f];
         buf[j++] = encodeMap[(block >>>  6) & 0x3f];
         buf[j] = PAD_CHAR;
     } else if (slop == 1) {
         int block = (raw[i++] & 0xff) << 16;
         buf[j++] = encodeMap[(block >>> 18) & 0x3f];
         buf[j++] = encodeMap[(block >>> 12) & 0x3f];
         buf[j++] = PAD_CHAR;
         buf[j] = PAD_CHAR;
     }
     return new String(buf);
    }
```

The decode process works similarly:

```
public static byte[] decode(String base64String)
{
 char[] base64 = base64String.toCharArray();
 int pad = 0;
 int max = base64.length;
 if (max == 0) return new byte[0];
```

```
    for (int i = max - 1; base64[i] == PAD_CHAR; i--)  pad++;
    byte[] r = new byte[ max * 6 / 8 - pad];
    if (pad > 0) max = max - 4; // if padding, save last block
    int ri =0, i = 0;
    while ( i < max) {
        int block = (getValue(base64[i++]) << 18)
          | (getValue(base64[i++]) << 12)
          | (getValue(base64[i++]) << 6)
          | (getValue(base64[i++]));

        r[ri++] = (byte)((block >> 16) & 0xff);
        r[ri++] = (byte)((block >> 8) & 0xff);
        r[ri++] = (byte)(block & 0xff);
    }

    // now handle padding
    if (pad == 2) {
        int block = (getValue(base64[i++]) << 18)
          | (getValue(base64[i++]) << 12);
        r[ri++] = (byte)((block >> 16) & 0xff);
    } else if (pad == 1) {
        int block = (getValue(base64[i++]) << 18)
          | (getValue(base64[i++]) << 12)
          | (getValue(base64[i++]) << 6);
        r[ri++] = (byte)((block >> 16) & 0xff);
        r[ri++] = (byte)((block >> 8) & 0xff);
    }
    return r;
  }
```

The method getValue is a helper function to get the decoding value and make sure it's valid:

```
    protected static int getValue(char c) {
    byte x = decodeMap[c];
    if (x == -1) {
        throw new RuntimeException("Bad base64 character of value "
                                  + (int) c + " found in decode");
    }
    return x;
  }
```

Base 85

Base 85 is the most efficient reasonable encoding of binary data using standard printable characters by converting 4 bytes into 5 characters (an expansion percent of 1.20). Although there are 94 printable characters in ASCII, base 85 is used because:

- Base 84 encodes 4 bytes into 6 characters (expansion percent of 1.5).
- Bases 85 through 94 all return 5 characters given 4 bytes, (expansion percent of 1.20).
- The technical benefits of base 94 aren't apparent until you use a 13-byte block, which is encoded into 16 characters (expansion percent of 1.23).

In other words, base 85 is the smallest base that can encode a 1.20 expansion percent using a reasonable block size, and base 94's improvement of 3 percent over base 84 isn't worthwhile because the block size is too long. However, even though base 85 is more efficient in terms of memory compared to base 64, it's not commonly used, since it's much slower; it requires division in its implementation and the alphabet requires using "special" characters that can conflict with other encoding requirements. Even so, it can be useful in certain situations.

Following is a generic implementation that just converts 4 bytes into 5 characters and vice versa. The encoding of values from 0 to 84 into characters and back is also not given (see next sections on possible alphabet choices). The encoding process just consists of converting the bytes into a `long` value and then successively dividing to convert into base 85 digits. You can't use an `int` type, since it's signed, and we are using all 32 bits.

```
public class base84 {

    public static char[] encode(byte[] buf) {
     char[] result = new char[5];
     long val =  ((buf[0] & 0xffL) << 24) | ((buf[1] & 0xffL) << 16) |
         ((buf[2] & 0xffL) << 8) | (buf[3] & 0xffL);
     for (int i = 0; i < 5; i++) {
         result[5 - i] = GET_CHARACTER_FROM_VALUE(val % 85);
         val /= 85;
     }
    }

    public static byte decode(char[] buf) {
     long val = 0;
     for (int i = 0; i < 5; i++) {
         val += GET_VALUE_FROM_CHAR(buf[i]);
         val *= 85;
     }
     result[0] = (byte)(val >>> 24);
     result[1] = (byte)(val >>> 16);
     result[2] = (byte)(val >>> 8);
     result[3] = (byte)(val);
     return result;
    }
}
```

Table 6.14 Base 85 Alphabet and Unused Characters in PostScript Encoding

Used characters in numerical order	!"#$%&'()*+,./0123456789:;<=>? ABCDEFGHIJKLMNOPQRSTUVWXYZ[\]^ _`abcdefghijklmnopqrstuvwxyz
Unused characters	vwxyz{|}~

PostScript

The PostScript language most frequently used for printing is an all-ASCII language, and any binary data (such as images) must be converted in a base 85 encoding. Four bytes are processed at a time. It's easiest to interpret the 4 bytes as a single integer type. The result will be five numbers 0 to 84. They are converted into ASCII by adding 33 (0×21), so the final alphabet ranges from 0×21 to 0×76 (! to u in ASCII).

Table 6.14 lists used and unused characters in the base 85 alphabet with PostScript encoding.

There are three additional rules:

1. If the data block is all zeros, instead of converting into !!!!!, a single z is used. (the four zeros rule).
2. Output new line characters 0x0d at least once for every 80 characters output (i.e., the output lines must be less than 80 characters).
3. If the data isn't a multiple of 4 bytes, special rules are used to pad the ending. If there are *n* leftover bytes, append (4 – *n*) zero bytes, and convert the result into base 85 characters without using the "four zeros rule." Then output *n* + 1 characters, followed by an end-of-file marker "~>". This system produces an unambiguous way to remove padding.

Implementation is fairly simple, especially if you create your own variant that doesn't perform the four zeros rule or the final padding rule. Unfortunately, the alphabet covers all quoting characters and the backslash character, making this difficult to use as-is in a non-PostScript environment.

RFC 1738

RFC 1738 is an informational RFC (not a standard) that proposes a 20-character ASCII representation of 128-bit IPv6 using base 85. Its alphabet is different than the PostScript one and is shown in Table 6.15.

Table 6.15 RFC 1738 Base 85 Alphabet

Used printable characters in numerical order	`0123456789ABCDEFGHIJKLMNOPQRS TUVWXYZabcdefghijklmnopqrstuv wxyz!#$%&()*+-;<=>?@^_`{|}~`
Unused printable characters	`"`,./:[\]`

Base 128 and Java Source Encoding

A common chore in any computer language is specifying a large number of constant bytes. In Java, the problem is especially awkward, because the byte type is signed, while byte constants are normally specified as unsigned values from 0 to 255. How you specify the data in a Java source file has a huge impact on the resulting class file size. Knowing this is especially important when working with embedded systems and library design. To demonstrate, we'll compare various formats.

The first approach is to convert the unsigned values into signed values –128 to 127. The more natural approach is to use a cast operator:

```
public static byte[] b0 = {
0, 1,2,3, ..., 127,-128, -127, ..., -3, -2, -1};

public static final byte[] b1 = {
(byte)0, (byte)1, (byte)2, ..., (byte)253, (byte)254, (byte)255};
```

(You could just as well use hexadecimal notation instead of decimal.)

Another option would be using an `int` array to skip the casting. Much of the time, the bytes need to be converted into an integer anyway, so it might be better to store them this way:

```
public static final int[] b2 = {
   0, 1, 2, 3, 4, 5, 6, 7, 8, 9, ...,
   250, 251, 252, 253, 254, 255
};
```

Since we are just encoding bytes, one optimization would be to pack 4 bytes into one `int`. You would expect this to be roughly the same size as the `byte` array. This technique and those that follow require code to unpack the bytes, but it's minimal. While we are at it, we could also use packed longs as well:

```
public static final int b3[]= {
0x3020100, 0x7060504, 0xb0a0908, ..., 0xf7f6f5f4, 0xfbfaf9f8, 0xfffefdfc};

public static final long[] b4 = {
0x706050403020100L, .. .,  0xfffefdfcfbfaf9f8L};
```

Another technique uses the fact that the `char` type is unsigned 16-bit type and the `String` class can read embedded `chars` if they are escaping using the \u*XXXX* format, where *X* is a hex digit. This creates a fairly easy-to-read format. We'll compare this to a class that has an empty string:

```
public static final String b4 =
"\u0001\u0203\u0405\u0607\u0809\u0a0b\u0c0d\u0e0f\u1011" +
... "\ufcfd\ufeff";}
```

The final method is not at all obvious. Instead of using normal 8-bit bytes, we'll first convert the array to use base 128, and then convert that to a `String` representation. In other words, we'll end up with bytes that have the sign or high bit unset with values from 0 to 127. The entire encoding looks messy but is very compact:

```
public static String b5 =
"\000\002\b\030@ \001\003\007\020$P0\001C\006\016\036@\b!b\004" +
"\n\025,\\@\021CF\r\034:xx\001$\b\021#H\0241r\004J\024*V0ibe\013" +
"\0301dL!SFM\0338rhYC'\017\037?\000\005\0224\bQ\"F\016!J$i\022" +
"&M\034=\002\025JT)T*Y:\005+\026-[8uru\013X0bF\021+fl\0314iT-" +
"cVM[7pbI\033G.\035;wpeS7\017_>~~\001\f(p B\005\r\036D\030QbE" +
"\f\033:|\b2$I\023)V4y\022fL\0327rlis'P!E\016%ZTiS(S*]J5+W/aF" +
"\025;\026mZ6obM+w.^=}~\005\034XpaD\013\033>\f92eK\0317v|\031" +
"thR'S.mz5lY5of][wo`C\013\037N<9sgQ'W>\035{vn_C\017/~<zum_G\037" +
"_~}|{{ \017";
```

All of the source files were then compiled with `javac` using `-O -g:none` to eliminate any debug information; however, the results, listed in Table 6.16, are similar using other flags.

Table 6.16 Comparison of Various Method of Encoding Binary Data in Java Source Code

METHOD	SOURCE FILE SIZE	CLASS FILE SIZE	CLASS FILE OVERHEAD	BYTE REP SIZE	STORAGE PER BYTE
Raw `bytes`	1269	1845	193	1654	6.45
Casted `bytes`	2539	1845	193	1653	6.45

Table 6.16 *(Continued)*

METHOD	SOURCE FILE SIZE	CLASS FILE SIZE	CLASS FILE OVERHEAD	BYTE REP SIZE	STORAGE PER BYTE
Raw `ints`	1002	1974	193	1782	6.96
Packed `ints`	806	891	193	699	2.73
Packed `longs`	741	775	193	583	2.28
Packed `String`	916	563	185	350	1.37
Packed 7-bit `String`	610	479	185	294	1.15

The raw or casted `bytes` scheme used approximately 6.5 bytes to store one byte, and raw `int` scheme was worse, but certainly not as bad as you would expect. What is going on? It appears that raw constants are not compiled into their native form but instead are represented in some other neutral format. In other words, each numeric constant is effectively treated and stored as an object type. The packed integer scheme is better, but only by a factor of 2, not a factor of 4 as expected, and the packed `long` scheme improved the matter modestly. Packed `String`'s odd result is explained by the fact that Java stored string constants in class files using UTF-8 encoding, which is a variable-length encoding where characters with a value over 127 may be encoded using 2, 3, or even 4 bytes. Finally, the packed 7-bit `String` is the champion, coming close to the perfect score of 1. The 7-bit representation thwarts the UTF-8 expansion.

Generating Source Code

The first step in using this encoding transforms a normal 8-bit `byte` array into an encoded 7-bit format, using the `to7Bit` routine given earlier. After that the new 7-bit array must be converted into source code. The following routine does this by creating a Java `String` using a huge if-then-else statement (this could also be done with a `switch` statement). The output of this function then gets pasted into your final source file. In the end, your final class should look something like this:

```
public class AClass
{
   protected static String ps = "7-bit packed string representation";
   protected static byte[] origByte[] =
   ByteUtil.to8Bit(ps.getBytes());

}
```

```
public static final char bs = '\\'; // backslash
public static String makeJavaSourceFrom7Bit(byte[] ba)
{
 StringBuffer buf = new StringBuffer("String XXX = \\\n\"");
 int lineCount = 0;
 int i = 0;
 int len = ba.length;
 while (i < len) {
     int b = ba[i] & 0xff;
     if (b == '\b') { // backspace
      lineCount+=2; buf.append(bs);     buf.append('b');
     } else if (b == '\t') { // tab
      lineCount+=2; buf.append(bs);     buf.append('t');
     } else if (b == '\n') { // newline
      lineCount+=2; buf.append(bs);     buf.append('n');
     } else if (b == '\f') { // formfeed
      lineCount+=2; buf.append(bs);     buf.append('f');
     } else if (b == '\r') { // carriage return
      lineCount+=2; buf.append(bs);     buf.append('r');
     } else if (b  < 32) { // other control characters
      lineCount += 4; buf.append(bs); buf.append('0');
      if (b < 8) { // add leading zero
          buf.append('0'); buf.append((char)(48 + b));
      } else {
          String octalRep = Integer.toString(b, 8);
          buf.append(octalRep);
      }
     } else if (b == '\"' || b == bs) {
           lineCount += 2; buf.append(bs); buf.append((char)b);
     } else { // ordinary printable characters
      lineCount++; buf.append((char)b);
     }
     if (lineCount > 59) { // line wrap at 60 characters
            lineCount = 0;     buf.append("\" +\n\"");
     }
     ++i;
     }
     if (lineCount != 0)
        buf.append("\";\n");

 return buf.toString();
}
```

Application and Data Architecture

Now that we know how to encode and encrypt data, both in theory and in implementation, it's time to actually start using it in an application. In this chapter we discuss:

- Storing sensitive information in a database.
- Secret key and memory management.
- Working with passwords.
- Logging sensitive information.
- The design and application of cryptographic tokens.
- Performing financial calculations.

Database Architecture for Encrypted Data

In a perfect world, data in the database would never need to be encrypted. There would be no curious employees, network and firewalls would be configured to keep others out, and the operating system and related applications would never have faults. In the real world, we know this to be false, and in the end, the last defense against data theft is by encrypting sensitive data.

In designing a database that stores sensitive information, we have some basic goals:

- *Minimize the collection of unneeded sensitive and personally identifiable information.* At its simplest, this means not collecting data you don't need. Other techniques include quantization of the data, or lumping the data in a pool, such as using an age range instead of a birthday or using a metropolitan area instead of an address, and so on.
- *Eliminate the need for decryption as much as possible.* If you do need to collect sensitive information, you want store it in such a way that minimizes the number of time it needs decrypting. If you collect a credit card number, do you really need to show the entire card number back to the user? Or will just showing part of the credit card do? Many times sensitive information is used initially then stored for archival reasons. Separating this type of "use-once" data can aid in security by moving the data (even if it's encrypted) off the online high-performance database and into a secondary database. This type of data can be stored using a public key cipher as well.
- *Protect against mass theft of data.* Through extraordinary means, someone will always be able to steal small amounts of data. The real goal is preventing mass or bulk decryption of your data. Solving this problem involves segmenting the data or using multiple keys for encrypting the data. This means each piece of encrypted data will have a secondary field indicating what key is used. Even if you choose not to implement multiple keys, this still aids in security by allowing you to change keys (or perform *key rolling,* where old data is decrypted and re-encrypted with a new key). This is extremely important in case of a security breach.
- *Minimize storage costs.* A side goal is to keep storage costs down. Even in the age of cheap disks, you still want to keep the tables and fields small so network traffic is reduced and to load as much data as possible in memory caches. This can be done by using small block sizes ciphers, minimizing extraneous padding, and ensuring the table design separates seldom-used encrypted data from more commonly used plaintext data.

Designing a database architecture that involves encrypted fields isn't really much different than designing a database with encryption. The following questions first must be asked:

- What is being collected?
- What is it being used for? Is it part of a required operation, or is it for marketing purposes?
- Is the item used once, then stored?
- How often is the item used?
- Is it read frequently?
- Is it written frequently?
- Does the data need to be used in real time or in bulk?
- Does the data need to be shared with another entity?
- What is the size of the data (fixed field or free-form)?
- What queries (if any) might you expect to run (for daily reporting, marketing, customer service, administration, etc.)? How often will they be run?
- Is the data sensitive, or can it be combined with other data to be personally identifiable?
- Are there any uniqueness constraints or required indexing?

It's a lot to keep track of; however, you need to know most of the information anyway as part of designing the database. If this is a new database, you won't get all the answers correct, but having a good understanding of how the data is being used makes a big difference.

The most important question is "Does the data need to be encrypted?" If the data isn't needed for core operations but only for marketing purposes, you might be able to make a substitution or quantization with the data so it's not personally identifiable.

Selecting a Cipher

Before selecting a cipher, you'll need to know whether the data can be stored outside the main database.

Secret or Public?

One of the most important criteria in selecting a cipher is the frequency of read and write operations of the database field. If the field is frequently updated, the choice is clear: Secret key ciphers are the only way to go. If the same application needs to read and write, the benefits of the public key system are defeated because the application has both keys. Likewise, if the field is frequently decrypted in real-time, public key systems are likely to be too slow. If the data is write-once and is seldom used, then using a public key cipher is an option. Elliptic curve systems are highly preferred, since they are faster and have a much smaller block size than RSA systems.

Cipher Selection

As always, selecting a cipher involves not just selecting the encryption algorithm but also the padding type and the appropriate mode of operation.

Cipher. For secret key ciphers the main choice is between 64-bit and 128-bit block ciphers. The main benefit of smaller block size is space savings in the database, but if that's not a concern, you can just use a 128-bit block such as Advanced Encryption Standard (AES) for everything. If you are comfortable using two different ciphers, you can use a 64-bit block cipher (e.g., Blowfish) for small data and use the 128-bit cipher for larger data. For public key ciphers, the choice is whatever you feel most comfortable with. If you have a solid elliptic curve implementation, this might be optimal, since it has a smaller block size. However, RSA is also perfectly acceptable, and implementations are much more available and uniform. In addition, with RSA you might be able to piggyback hardware accelerator cards, normally used for SSL.

Padding. For general-purpose secret key encryption, PKCS #7 is fine. For fixed-size data, a more advisable choice it to use checksum bits or bytes.

Mode of operation. Ideally, you like to encrypt whatever you have in one block, since it saves time and space, and eliminates the question of what mode to use. For "long" text messages, the choice is CBC mode, but for smaller messages there are some options. For example, say the data in question is between 64 and 128 bits. The choices are (in order of security):

- Two 8-byte blocks using ECB mode. Each block is separately encrypted.
- Two 8-byte blocks using CBC mode and a fixed or null initialization vector. The second block depends on the first block.
- Two 8-byte blocks using the two-block mode described in Chapter 6. Here each encrypted block depends on the other one.
- One 16-byte block. This is the most secure. Each ciphertext byte depends on each byte of the plaintext.

An attack using ECB mode might work like this. Suppose an attacker had access to the database, and knew you were using ECB mode. That might sound far-fetched, but surely there are many employees that could do this. To make the example easy, let's say the data is exactly 128 bits so there is no padding. The attacker visits the Web site, signs up for the service, and enters the sensitive data. The attack now has two plaintext messages and two ciphertext messages. The registration process could be repeated, and the attacker could collect many pairs of plaintext and ciphertext this way. Then the attacker goes in the backdoor and scans the database looking for matches with the known ciphertext collected. With some luck, the attacker finds a match. (Obviously, an element of luck would be needed; given that the match is 64 bits, finding matches is a tall order unless the data has some specific structure or can only take certain values. The probability of two matches is an even taller order.) While a match isn't interesting in itself, decrypting everything is. CBC mode doesn't help that much, since we can assume the attacker knows the fixed initiation vector. Our attacker can now determine only the first block. The second block is more secure and, depending on other issues, may not be by much.

Using a 128-bit block solves all these problems. Using a different IV for each encryption also solves this problem, but this is an expensive solution. You must generate the random byte, which takes time. More importantly, however, you have to store the IV.

Data

Each type of data that needs to stored has its own special cases on how it should be encrypted for best usage and storage.

Passwords

Standard practice is to store a MAC'ed version of the password. An ordinary hash is useful, but it allows for a dictionary attack.

The obvious downside to this scheme is that the password can never be recovered. This may create issues in the customer service organizations, since they cannot directly assist the user. Instead, a new password must be generated.

The other downside is future migration to another platform that will certainly use a different authentication scheme. Then you would need to write custom authentication to first probe the new system, and if that fails, probe the old system, and then prompt the user for a new password. This is not a pleasant process, and more than few consultants are making some nice income implementing these types of conversions.

The ideal system is to MAC and store the password in the standard format in the high-availability database, and then store an encrypted version using a public key in a secondary database. The write-only database field is just used in case of future migration or storage. While many public key ciphers have huge block sizes, this shouldn't be much of an issue, since we are storing this in a secondary database. This database could even be a log file that just records the user ID, the date, and the password. This log can be replayed to regenerate passwords for whatever reason. The matching private key should be stored very securely. Ideally, you'd burn it onto a CD and let the CTO or even the CEO store it. The system or database administrators have no need to access the passwords.

Challenges and Responses

Challenges must be encrypted. Just knowing what the question is can provide significant hints for an attacker. The overhead of the encryption and decryption should be very low because challenges are rarely used.

The choice of encrypting or MAC'ing the response is harder. Using a MAC is technically ideal, but this option has some operational difficulties. First are customer service issues. If you have phone support, the customer service representative will have to take the response over the phone and type it in. If encrypted, the representative can make a judgment call on whether or not they got the right response. Depending on your model, one could be more desirable than another.

The other issue is matching responses. If you use a MAC, you should strip out any white space and punctuation, and convert to all upper- or lowercase. This drastically reduces the input space, but it still should be secure because you used a keyed hash instead of a pure hash. Of course, you also want to reduce the number of false negatives. Ideally, you'd like a fuzzy hash that could handle common typing errors such as transposition; however, that might be more trouble than it's worth for such a seldom-used event. The issue of being future-compatible using MACs still applies. You might want to have an encrypted log of events.

Using encryption solves the customer service issues but requires a decryption process (which you want to minimize if at all possible) and you still would have a matching issue. However, you can refine the matching process and implement fuzzy matching schemes as time goes by. With a MAC you get one chance to get it right.

So while using a MAC is technically best, the human issues typically make it easier for some customer service issues.

Payment, Credit Card, and Other Account Numbers

If you are storing credit card numbers in your data, they must be encrypted, as shown in Table 7.1.

Cleartext Using the Last Four, First Four

An alternative is showing the first four digits (eBay uses this). Actually, using the first four digits is more secure against determining the entire credit card number, but it leaks personal information. So, in sum, the trade-off is that while using the first four numbers is more secure, personal information is leaked on the account and the number is not particularly unique, which can be a problem when more than one card is used. The last four numbers are not as secure, but are more common and may work better when more than one card is being displayed.

If you use the first four numbers, when displaying the number to the member, consider showing the expiration date as well to aid in uniquely identifying the card. Many times people will enter two different cards that were issued by the same bank (one is an ATM card, the other a credit card), meaning that both card numbers will start with the same digits. However, it's unlikely that both cards will have the same expiration date.

Expiration Date

The expiration date information for a credit card can be month/year or month/day/year. This is considered sensitive information and should be encrypted.

Table 7.1 Structure of Common Credit Card Numbers

CARD TYPE	PREFIX	LENGTH
Visa	4	16
MasterCard	51 to 55	16
American Express	34, 37	15
Discover	6011	16
JCB	3	16
	2131, 3000	15

CV2

With the CV2 (card verification value) system, an additional three digits are typically printed on the back of the credit card. This scheme is most popularized by Citibank, although other companies use it as well. This number doesn't show up on card imprints, billing statements, or order/invoices. The algorithm matching the card to the CV2 is only known by the issuing bank. The CV2 is used frequently by online systems as proof that the user has possession of the card.

If your payment gateway doesn't use CV2, don't collect it. If your payment gateway does use it, and if, for instance, you get a lower fee for using it, you should go ahead. However, you should not store it for many reasons, including the following:

1. You will fail any security audit done by a financial institution.
2. It creates a liability.
3. You have no use for it.

The fact that you used a CV2 in the authorization step will certainly be recorded by the payment gateway. If you feel you want the CV2 values accounted for, it's all right to store a flag saying you collected it.

Storing the Number

The naïve way of storing the credit card number is encrypting a string of 16 decimal numbers. Since credit card numbers are used in a mathematical way and converting to a true integer is time-consuming, you would just encrypt the entire card number in one database field and store the plaintext of the last four digits in another field. Depending on the algorithm, the encrypted card might be one or two blocks.

For simplicity, say the card is stored in one block. You start out with 16 encrypted digits. This drops immediately to 12 because the last four digits are in the clear. The first digit determines if the card is Visa, MasterCard, American Express, or Discover (4, 5, 3, 6), respectively. For Visa and MasterCard, the first 6 digits are a bank identification number that determines the issuing bank or financial institution. Considering that most credit cards are issued by only a few institutions, the first four digits might really only have a few hundred values. If someone targets a particular institution or bases his or her deductions on geography, there might be fewer than 10 possibilities. So now we have approximately 10^7. But given a six-digit bin number and the last four digits, only five digits are uniquely determined, since the checksum will determine the seventh digit. So using the last four digits and the properties of the credit card, an attacker really only has

10^6 or 100,000 possible choices of what the actual card might be. With a large database, an attacker may be able to infer the complete card number. To solve these weaknesses, the first step is to encode the number efficiently. Instead of storing the decimal digits, you first convert them to binary coded decimal (BCD). This squeezes a 16-digit number into a 64-bit block. This has a number of advantages:

- It saves space in the database, allowing for more internal caching.
- The card can be encrypted with one iteration of a 64-bit cipher such as Blowfish. The overhead for encrypting another block is much greater than converting it into BCD.
- It reduces the amount of the structure the plaintext has. While BCD does have some structure, it's a lot less than using 7-bit ASCII codes for digits.

(You could also convert into an integer, but that is a slow process and doesn't add much to the value of using BCD.)

However, this doesn't solve the basic security problem that we just aren't encrypting very much data. The solution varies depending on how big a block size the cipher is.

64-Bit Blocks

If you are using Blowfish or another 64-bit block cipher (hopefully, not DES), the trick is to just not encrypt the last four digits. This completely eliminates the partial plaintext attack possibility, since there is no encrypted text to compare against. However, it does mean that if you need the complete credit card, you need to read two fields, decrypt and convert back to decimal, and then concatenate them both. While a bit annoying, it doesn't cost much, and the whole mess can safely be hidden under an API. Also, actually using the full credit card is rare after the initial authorization, so you shouldn't need to do this very often anyway.

Now you have a 6-byte credit card being stored. What to do with those last 2 bytes? Since it's so small, it's probably safe to leave them as zeros; however, other options include:

- *Adding random bits.* This certainly works; however, it may make searching very difficult (see the next section).
- *Adding the expiration date.* The expiration date fits perfectly. The 4 bits holds 0 to 16, ideal for a month representation, 5 bits for a day representation (if needed, 0 through 31), and the remaining 7 bits is enough to represent 2000 to 2127, which should be enough for your

application. (See the information on expiration dates coming up.) You don't want to use this method if you are storing the expiration date in the clear.

- *Adding a checksum or check digits.* Using a full-blown hash such as MD5 or SHA-1 is a bit much for so little data.

128-Bit and Larger Blocks

With a 128-bit block cipher such as AES, there are more options. You can encrypt a full 16-digit number in ASCII without preprocessing or encoding.

Expiration Dates

While expiration dates are not particularly sensitive, they do give an attacker some hints as to what credit cards even to try and decrypt. Since it's rare that expiration dates need to be read frequently, it's best to encrypt them.

Social Security Number (U.S.)

While the Social Security Number (SSN) is commonly used as the identification number on everything from driver's licenses to health insurance cards, it is sensitive information and should be treated as such. If you must collect it, you really do not need to show it again on the public site.

Ideally, you won't need to show the number back to the end user, *ever.* If you must show anything, show the *last* three digits. The first three digits determine where the Social Security card was issued and has a strong correlation to birth location. Even using the last few digits isn't recommended, since they are frequently used for authentication by other services (in other words, even knowing the last four digits may help someone access a service).

Birthdates and Birthdays

The birthdate or birthday of a member is considered personally identifiable information. The threat is not so much the birthdate itself, but how it can be combined with other information to aid in identity theft and fraud.

This field is a bit tricky, since marketing will absolutely want access to this data—if not for direct marketing purposes, at least for market demographic information. Encrypting this information makes database queries difficult.

The trick here to give marketing what they want, but without using personal identifiable information. Marketing, advertisers, and sponsors rarely care about the *exact* age but instead about age groupings. For instance, rather than "this many are 25 years old, this many 26, this many 27," they usually look at "z many in the range 25 to 30." Instead of asking for an exact age, could having them select an age bracket work instead? This would be converted into a birth year bracket for the database, which can be stored unencrypted as well.

Another scenario is that perhaps you need to collect birthdays for marketing purposes or for a birthday promotion of some type. Again, do you need to know the exact date or is a range good enough? No matter what the application is, it's very unlikely that the exact date is needed. Whatever promotion is planned, it's probably going to be mailed or emailed a few weeks before the event in bulk with other people who have similar birthdays. Therefore, why not just collect the month, and a day range, such as 1 to 10, 11 to 20, 21 to 31, or 1 to 14, 15 to 31? Or is just the month acceptable?

This abstraction has a side benefit. The member is much more likely to answer honestly if he or she feels the information isn't personally identifiable. If you must collect the birthday and year (say, for a financial application), it's likely the date will be used initially for some application and then it will sit there. The solution is to encrypt it and then segment it for marketing.

Last Name

While it sounds a bit crazy, encrypting the last name of the member is not a bad idea. It provides the ultimate in privacy, since an attacker with access to the database will only have anonymous entries. Many times, even knowing whether or not someone is a member can be sensitive; the attacker will surely pick out high-profile names.

Most applications collect the name but don't actually use it for anything except for direct mail or back-end nonreal-time processes. The first name can be left in plaintext for personalization. The only catch is the difficulty indexing successfully for any customer service queries, since people often forget their usernames.

Searching, Indexing, and Constraints

Encrypted fields present some challenges for searching, indexing, and database uniqueness constraints, especially when you are using multiple keys, multiple initialization vectors, or probabilistic encodings such as OAEP. However, with a little work, the obstacles can be overcome, but there's quite a cost.

Before embarking on this, make sure you really need to index the value in the first place. For instance, do you need to look up a transaction by credit card number, or can you look it up by the date, dollar amount, and last four digits? Occasionally, you might need to make an ad hoc search to look up a problem. Don't optimize for these cases. Doing a table scan and decrypting every entry, while somewhat painful, isn't as bad you think.

Constraints, on the other hand, are a more difficult problem to solve, which we will look at next.

Removing Randomness

For using OAEP or multiple initialization vectors, unfortunately, there is nothing we can do that preserves the same level of security as the encryption. The problem is that our plaintext input space is too small. True, a hash is invertible, but it's possible it just creates a table. Let's use Social Security numbers as an example. At most, we know there are 10^9 possible values. This is approximately 2^{30}, and we've previously seen that brute-force attacks on 2^{55} are very doable. So an attacker can simply create a massive lookup table, hashing every possible value and comparing to the existing hashes in the database. So our hashes would have to be at least as secure as our encryption.

The next obvious step is use a MAC with a secret key. The problem here is that to be useful we can only use one key, which again is less secret than our system of multiple keys.

The only choice here, and it's not perfect, is for the "random" bits (used in OAEP or the IV) not to be random, but determined by the data to be encrypted. The model of OAEP is that the bits are truly random. Using a nonrandom IV isn't as terrible, but it does give hints about the encrypted data, which is not a good thing.

Deterministic Key Selection

The next issue is to remove randomness from the key selection. During encryption it's easiest to just randomly select a key; however, this creates the problem for indexing and constraints, since the same data will have different encrypted representations.

To solve this problem, we need to use indirection using a key lookup table. Instead of directly specifying a key, we specify a table index. The table is then mapped to keys. Determining the table index doesn't need to be extravagant. Using the first or last byte or doing a mod check on the sum of the bytes will work fine.

The big downfall of this scheme is that it requires extremely careful key and table management. It will require a mature operational environment to get it right.

Adding a key without a table lookup was an easy process. You added a key to the pool and it was used. In this case, you add a key as well, but you add it to the key table. This involves scanning for the old key table, decrypting with the old key, then reencrypting with the new key. You cannot "retire" keys; you can only delete them by replacing one table index with another key, which, again, will require a full scan. This process is a bit hairy, so you might have to take the database offline to do it successfully.

Indexing and Hashing

If you are using the deterministic key selection process, then indexing is easy, since it's based on both the encrypted value and the key index. Indexing encrypted fields can be done, but it involves some security trade-offs. The idea is to store a hash of the sensitive value in the database along with the encrypted field. The hash really functions as cipher, except there is no inverse option. Using a 160-bit hash, even after hashing all possible credit values (10^{16}), the probability of collision is practically nothing. The problem is that you are susceptible to dictionary attacks, because the number of input messages is relatively small. You could just hash every possible credit card value and then compare it against what is in the database. This would be a lot more efficient than trying to break the cipher, even a weak one such as DES. Or you could use MACs with secret keys, but that defeats the purpose of using a hash in the first place. The other problem is that a 160-bit hash is larger than the encrypted field. As a result the hash is more secure than the data being hashed.

To fix this problem and so save space, you can cripple the hash by making it smaller. First off, you might as well use MD5 since it's faster. The second issue is to convert a 128-bit hash into something much smaller. Given that there is only $10^{16} \approx 2^{55}$ possible credit cards, we want a hash value much smaller than 55 bits. We want the hash to lose information in order to prevent dictionary attacks. In other words, we want collisions! A hash size of only 32 bits is a good start, since given the input space 2^{55}, this means each hash corresponds to 8.4 million possible credit card values ($2^{55} / 2^{32} = 2^{23} \approx 8.4 \times 10^6$). A hash size of 40 bits means each hash corresponds to 33,000 different cards. If an attacker with a dictionary makes a match, all the attacker knows is the card is one of thousands—in other words, he or she knows nothing. For Social Security numbers there are only $10^9 \approx 2^{30}$ possible values, so a good choice here is using 16-bits for the hash.

Converting an MD5 hash into a smaller hash can be done in two ways. The first is just taking the first bytes as needed. This works; however, it's considered better form to use the entire hash by XORing the first bytes with the later bytes:

```
md[0] ^= md[4]  ^ md[8];
md[1] ^= md[5]  ^ md[9];
md[2] ^= md[6]  ^ md[10];
md[3] ^= md[7]  ^ md[11];
```

Now the first four bytes (32-bits) contain the hash using the entire MD5 output. This may need to be converted into an `int` type depending on your database (some databases don't allow indexing on raw binary data).

The collisions are a double-edged sword: They are good because the hash is losing information, but now you must expect and manage collisions in database operations. Doing a search based on the hash may turn up multiple values. You will need to decrypt each one in turn to find the correct value unless some other context is used. While not optimal, it's a lot better than having no index and doing a full table scan.

Uniqueness Constraints

Again, using deterministic keys makes uniqueness easy. Data will be unique for an encrypted data and the key index. Failing this, you'll have to add even more fields to the database (so make sure you really need the uniqueness constraint).

The uniqueness scheme extends the indexing process from the previous section and involves implementing the hash table in the database. Instead of just storing the hash, you are now storing the hash and another index for resolving collisions. First, you implement a constraint on both fields (if your database does not support this, you'll have to merge both items into one field). When you need to write data, write the hash and a value of 0. Write the value for the hash resolver index. If the database reports that its constraint is being violated, you'll have to look up all values with the same hash value, decrypt them, and check to see if there is a match. If there is no match, set the hash resolver value to an unused value, and try the write again. That's not particularly pleasant, but it should not happen very often. Most of these fields such as credit cards and Social Security numbers are "write-once," so even if it is somewhat expensive, it should be a small percentage of the total load on your system, and then you may or may not get a collision. If it's a 32-bit hash, you can expect collisions starting with $2^{16} \approx 65{,}000$ entries because of the birthday paradox discussed in Chapter 2. Over time how many collisions will there be? If the hash size is h bits longs, and given 2^n hash values (and $n < h$), then you can estimate the number of collisions with 2^{2n-h+1} (using the expected number of collisions is also a test of randomness; see [Knuth98] for details on the collision test). Using a 32-bit hash, the values are computed in Table 7.2 (for a 40-bit hash, divide the results by 256). Thus, hash collisions aren't much of a problem until many millions of records are entered, and even then it's a small percentage of the total.

Asymmetric Data Usages

Often, data stored has asymmetrical usages. It's written once, but rarely if ever displayed to the member again, and occasionally a back-office process needs to reference it. An example is the Social Security number. Financial sites must collect it in order to send tax statements, but other than that, it is not really used. The member doesn't really need to see it again. The member's Social Security number also rarely changes. Likewise with credit card numbers: It's stored once, but then never fully displayed to the member again. The rest of the usage is done in the back office.

Table 7.2 Expected Number of Collisions Using a 32-bit Hash

NUMBER OF HASHES	EXPECTED NUMBER OF COLLISIONS
$1.774 \times 2^{16} \approx 116261$	1
$2^{17} = 131072$	2
$2^{18} = 262144$	8
$2^{19} = 524{,}288$	32
$2^{20} \approx$ 1 Million	128
$2^{21} \approx$ 2 Million	512
$2^{22} \approx$ 4 Million	2048
$2^{23} \approx$ 8 Million	8192
$2^{24} \approx$ 17 Million	32768
$2^{25} \approx$ 34 Million	131072
$2^{26} \approx$ 67 Million	524288

There are two techniques to really lock down this type of data. The first is to replicate the data to another database instance, then delete the data on the primary database, preferably on another machine, separated by a firewall. If anyone penetrates the security on the public system, the truly valuable data is stored on another network and is not accessible. The attacker may be able to see the limited amount of data that hasn't been replicated yet, but that is minimal compared to the entire database.

The other technique is to use public key encryption. Here, the data is encrypted with the public key and the public applications do not have private key.

The trick to make this work is to store the encrypted data in another column so the database can optimize the layout for the more common read case. If you store a 1,000-byte field in the main column, the database will likely cache that data even though the public applications only write to it once. The customer service and operation scripts are located on a different network and contain the private key and read or write the data as appropriate.

Null Values and Database Applications

Database fields are commonly specified as a numeric type or a null value (indicating unset). The numeric class wrappers are a natural way of modeling this type of relationship, since they are objects and can either be null or contain a numeric value. Unfortunately, working with numeric types is at best awkward and is a fairly expensive way to test for a null value. An object must then be created, and then garbage must be collected for what should be a very simple test. Another disadvantage is the developer or use of the database API must convert back and forth between the wrappers and the raw type. Again, it is a lot of typing for a very small check. For instance, say your database API is something like the following:

```
void setField(Integer x)
Integer getField();
```

Then to set values you have to do something like:

```
int x = // some value
setField(new Integer(x));
```

Getting values is worse:

```
Integer val = getField();
int x;
if (val != null) // do something
```

```
else x = val.intValue();

int val = getField().valueOf()
```

To remove the use of objects, you could write auxiliary methods:

```
void setField(int x);
void setFieldAsNull();
int getField() throws NullPointerException
```

The last method will throw an exception if the field value is null. That might be okay when the field is occasionally null, but it then forces the caller to catch exceptions at every time.

An alternate way of removing the use of the object is to have the raw types themselves signal if they are null or not. For most applications a 32-bit signed integer can represent numbers much larger than what is truly needed. If so, we can use one of the bits to indicate that the value is null. Floating-point numbers can signal that they are null by using the special value of "infinity." These ideas are encapsulated in the following utility class:

```
public class NullUtil {

    public static final int NULL_INT = (1 << 31);
    public static final long NULL_LONG = (1 << 63);
    public static final float NULL_FLOAT =  1.0f/0.0f;
    public static final double NULL_DOUBLE = 1.0/0.0;

    public static boolean isNull(int x) {
          return x == NULL_INT; }
    public static boolean isNull(long x) {
          return x == NULL_LONG;}
    public static boolean isNull(float x) {
          return x == NULL_FLOAT; }
    public static boolean isNull(double x) {
          return x == NULL_DOUBLE;}
    public static int valueOf(Integer x) {
          return (x == null) ? NULL_INT : x.intValue();}
    public static long valueOf(Long x) {
          return (x == null) ? NULL_LONG : x.longValue();}
    public static float valueOf(Float x) {
          return (x == null) ? NULL_FLOAT:  x.floatValue();}
    public static double valueOf(Double x) {
          return (x == null) ? NULL_DOUBLE: x.doubleValue();}
}
```

Now our API can be:

```
void setField(int x) {
if (NullUtil.isNull(x)) // store a null value
else // store regular value
}
int getField() {
          // get value from db.
          if (value == null)
return NullUtil.NULL_INT;
          else, return value;
}
```

This pushes most of the ugliness behind the API instead of in front of it. The downside is that this system doesn't force the caller to check for null values. If the floating-point value is null, and the caller does any computations with it, the final result will be infinity (on the other hand, it's quite easy to tell if someone didn't check). For integer types, it's not as easy to tell. If any computation is greater than `NULL_INT` (which is a very large number), then you can suspect someone received a null value and didn't check it.

The right model of handling null values will depend on your application and whether you use null within your database. You may wish to use a hybrid system, which combines both techniques described.

Secure Memory Management in Java

One of Java's main benefits as a programming language is that memory management is handled automatically. Memory is allocated, and when an object is no longer being used its memory is marked for reuse. Periodically, a garbage collection "wakes up" and looks for objects no longer being used and marks their memory as being free for future use. Normally, this is just fine. However, for sensitive data this has a few problems. To begin with, you don't know when an object is actually "unused," when the garbage collection wakes up and finds an unused object, when the memory is actually reused, or when the original data is overwritten. The garbage collector only marks the memory as free; it doesn't clear it. In time, new objects may overwrite the memory. Ultimately, this means that "hostile VMs" that don't respect object boundaries, remote debuggers, or memory snoopers can peer into a running program and extract data. Worse, the whole program could be put into swap space on the disk.

The main problem is with the `String` type. Unlike other languages, the Java `String` is *immutable*—once set, it cannot be changed. If a change or subset is needed, a new object is created. The `StringBuffer` class allows direct access to the underlying characters, but you don't have complete control over the internal buffer. For fundamental types, and arrays with fundamental types, you *do* have direct access to the data. Given an array of `chars` or `bytes`, you can zero out or clear the actual characters.

We can speed along the process by setting an obsolete object to a `null` value. This explicitly makes it clear to the garbage collector that an object is no longer is use. This certainly helps, but it doesn't solve the problem because the memory isn't actually cleared. When the garbage collection does reap the object, it first calls the `finalize` method that is inherited from the `Object` class. Normally, this method doesn't do anything, but you can override it to release any resources or clear memory.

Putting this all together, we can create "safe" `byte` and `char` array classes.

Smart Array Classes

When working with keys, it's important to clear out the data when it's not needed anymore. To do this, you need to be careful when passing array types in and out of methods. At first glance the following code look perfectly fine:

```
class Aclass {
     private byte[] aKey
     public void setKey(byte[] key) {
         aKey = key;
     }
     byte[] getKey() {
               return myKey;
     }
     void printKey() {// print the key}
}
```

However, it has some serious problems.

```
Aclass myclass = new Aclass();
byte[] myKey = {(byte) 1, (byte) 2, (byte) 3, (byte) 4}
myclass.setKey(myKey);
...
// caller is now done with key.  Clears it
Arrays.fill(myKey, (byte) 0);

// later the key is needed, and retrieved from the aclass
aclass.printKey() ;  // key is not 1,2,34, but instead all zeros
```

The problem is the class does not "own" the key data, only a reference to it. Anyone, anywhere holding a reference to the array can change the internal private variable. These problems are certainly not unique to Java. Many C++ and especially C programmers are painfully aware of the who-owns-the-data issue. Somehow, partially because of the ease of Java, these issues seem to get overlooked. In any event, to solve this problem, you should clone the array, so the object owns the data, as in the following:

```
public void setKey(byte[] key) {
          aKey = (byte[]) key.clone();
}
```

A similar problem occurs with the `getKey` method. Ideally, once the key is set within an object, there is no need to retrieve it. But if it must be done, be aware that the caller can change the state of the key if you are returning a reference to an interface object. An example of this would be:

```
byte[] thekey = aclass.getKey();
Arrays.fill(thekey, (byte) 0);
aclass.printKey(); // internal key is all zeros
```

Again to fix this, you can return a clone of the internal data:

```
// caller owns results
public byte[] getKey() {
          return (byte[]) akey.clone();
}
```

Many times these issues are recast in a different format:

```
public void getKey(byte[] result) {
          result = (byte[]) akey.clone();
}
```

This makes it clearer that the caller owns the result. These two methods do the same thing, and it's a matter of preference which one you choose.

Ideally, you can construct your object model so sensitive data is write-once and then let the object do all the messy work: The fewer references and copies floating around the better. One way of doing this is by making the object a "drop box" for data. The caller "deposits" the data into the object and then doesn't have the data any more:

```
// caller's copy of the data is destroyed.
public void setKey(byte[] key) {
          aKey = (byte[]) key.clone();
          Arrays.fill(key, (byte) 0);
}
```

Using finalizers we can make it so the data is cleared whenever the object is no longer needed. In addition, we should allow the user of an object to explicitly clear the sensitive information:

```
public void clearKey() {
     if (akey != null) {
          Arrays.fill(akey, (byte) 0);
          akey = null;
     }
}

public finalize() {
     clearKey();
}
```

Whenever the object is no longer needed, the object's memory will eventually be released so it can be used again. Instead of the array being marked as free space, it's now also zeroed out.

Finally, if you are concerned about snooping and data being stored on swap space, you can also encrypt or obscure the data when it's not being used. Using full encryption can certainly be used, but then, of course, you have the problem of dealing with another key. Another approach that obscures the data is using a mask function that generates random bytes and XORs the array for encryption and decryption. The following example uses the ordinary Random function, which normally you don't want to use because it does not generate cryptographically secure numbers. In this application, however, it's acceptable—plus it's very simple and very fast. If the goal is just making it so a casual snooper can't peer into memory and swap space and see keys and passwords, this will work. (A discussion of working with SecureRandom is coming up in the chapter.)

```
private void doMask(byte[] a, long seed) {
          Random r = new Random(seed);
          seed = r.nextLong();
          byte[] mask = new byte[a.length];
          r.nextBytes(mask);
          int max = mask.length;
          for (int i = 0; i < max; ++i) {
                    akey[i] = a[i] ^ mask[i];
                    mask[i] = 0; // clear the mask
          }
}
```

Now the `set` and `get` functions can call this to obscure the underlying data. A *random long* is a seed value for the `Random` class and functions as the key for the encryption and decryption. This works well, since using a native type as a key is much easier to manage than an object or an array:

```
private long seed; // the 'secret key'

public void setKey(byte[] key) {
          Random r = new Random();
          seed = r.nextLong();    // make a seed.  This is the "key"

          akey = (byte[])  key.clone();
          Arrays.fill(key, (byte) 0) ; //Optional.
                                         Clear the callers copy.
          byte[] result = (byte[]) akey.clone();
          doMask(result, seed);
}

//
// caller owns the result.  Caller must clear the array when finished
//
public byte[] getKey() {
          byte[] result = (byte[]) akey.clone();
          doMask(result, seed);
          return result;
}
```

Char Arrays

Working with `char` arrays instead of `byte` arrays is no different, except if you are working on obscuring the data. The `Random` class doesn't have a convenient way of generating an array of random numbers (or chars). Recall that a `char` type is 16 bits, so if you are using pure ASCII data (such as commonly used for passwords), meaning no accented characters or Asian languages, then you can just `XOR` the least-significant bit (LSB) of the `char` value

If you are just using ASCII values (7-bit), then technically there is a problem, since the most-significant bit (MSB) of a `char` will always be 0, so you know every other random value. Alternatively, you can just XOR the LSB of the `char`:

```
akey[i] = (char)(a[i] ^ (mask[i]&0xff))
```

If you *are* using Unicode data, the entire `char` value should be obscured. You can do this by creating a mask twice as long and using 2 bytes to create a `mask` character:

```
private void doMask(char[] a, long seed) {
        Random r = new Random(seed);
        seed = r.nextLong();
        byte[] mask = new byte[a.length * 2];
        r.nextBytes(mask);
        int max = mask.length;
        for (int i = 0, j = 0; i < max; ++i) {
                akey[i] = (char)(a[i] ^
                      ((mask[j++] & 0xff)<< 4) | (mask[j++] & 0xff)));
                mask[i] = 0; // clear the mask
        }
}
```

Using SecureRandom

`SecureRandom` wasn't used previously because the object actually contained the seed value. The quality of the randomness doesn't matter, since the key is right there. To make the class more secure (if needed), you can pass in the seed value in the `get` and `set` calls, and not store the seed in the object. For general use this is a bit clumsy, but the result really will be more secure. You can also use the object as a lightweight `SealedObject` class, or you could be even more secure and pass in a password (in `char` arrays) and a `byte` array for the seed, but this is approaching overkill. Using a `long` type as a key also has some advantages; it's passed by value and it's easy to clear and reset. Using a `long` type is effectively a 64-bit key, which is certainly enough for this application—temporary short-term storage memory and swap file protection. For long-term storage, consider using `SealedObject` and a real cipher.

Secret Key Management

The hardest part of any security architecture is the management of secret keys. Most discussions on secret key management come in two flavors. The first is using *secure hardware* with tamperproof fittings and epoxied microchips. Most of these solutions are quite old, originating in pre-public key days. For the average commercial user, these "solutions" are worthless. The second type of discussion is completely abstract and also doesn't amount to much.

Public key management is a completely different story and mostly involves indexing keys to *identities* (e.g., people) by using directories and so forth. Lots of literature has been published on this subject, and numerous commercial products exist for public key management. There really is no need to roll your own system, especially since these key management packages are bundled with some security application such as encrypted email. Java also provides a simple `CertificateStore` class for this purpose. In addition, Java provides a `KeyStore` class for storing private and secret keys. However, I've found it to be more trouble than it's worth for purely secret key management.

Secret Key Data

While Java provides a simple `Key` class that stores basic key information, an application-level class needs quite a bit more data to decide whether or not the key is valid, as well as basic auditing and troubleshooting. At a minimum, a key needs:

- The key itself
- An alias or index for the key
- The algorithm that the key is used for
- The category or domain the key should be used for
- The time the key was created
- The time the key was modified (deleted, retired, or otherwise modified)
- Optionally, information to store about who created or modified the key for auditing purposes
- Optionally, any algorithm parameter data

A simple key implementation is as follows:

```
import javax.crypto.SecretKey;
import java.util.Date;
public class SecretKeyData implements Key, KeySpec
{
    public static final int KEY_ACTIVE  = 0;
    public static final int KEY_RETIRED = 1;
    public static final int KEY_DELETED = 2;

    protected int    status;
    protected String index;
    protected byte[] keybytes;
    protected String algorithm;
    protected Date   startDate;
    protected Date   endDate;

    public SecretKeyData(byte[] key, String algorithm, String index,
                         Date startDate, Date endDate, int status)
```

```
    {
          this.keybytes = (byte[])key.clone();
          this.algorithm = algorithm;
          this.index = index;
          this.status = status;
          this.startDate = startDate;
          this.endDate = endDate;
    }

    public byte[] getEncoded() {
          return (byte[]) keybytes.clone();
    }

    public String getFormat()    {return "RAW"; }
    public String getAlgorithm() {return algorithm;}
    public String getIndex()     {return index;}
    public int    getStatus()    {return status;}
    public void   setStatus(int status) {this.status = status;}

    public void clearKey() {
          if (keybytes != null) {
              for (int i = 0; i < keybytes.length; ++i)
                    keybytes[i] = 0;
              keybytes = null;
          }
    }

    public void finalize() { clearKey(); }
}
```

Following are some important aspects of this code:

- This class implements `Key` and `KeySpec`, so it can be used directly in the Java `crypto` classes (another option would be to extend `SecretKeySpec`).
- `getEncoded` returns a copy of the internal key array instead of passing a reference to it. This prevents the caller from altering the key.
- The `finalize` method clears the internal key array.

The key status flags indicate how the key may be used. `KEY_DELETED` means the key cannot be used for any purpose and only exists for archival reasons. `KEY_RETIRED` means the key can be used for decryption, but not for encryption. This state is useful when you are trying to change keys in use in the database. `KEY_ACTIVE` means the key can used for both encryption and decryption.

Key Generation

For basic application and database work, keys aren't generated very frequently, and when they are generated, it is done "in private," so the randomness requirement is nearly as great as when session keys are generated. There are really two systems for creating keys.

A randomly generated key is basically just that—given a random source, you create an array of bytes as the key. The random source requirements are normally pretty basic if keys are generated once a month or so. The previous method has the downside of being forced to manage a variety of keys. Depending on your application, you might be managing hundreds or thousands of keys, which isn't particularly practical.

One other technique is to derive keys from a master key. There isn't much in the way of standards on this, but most schemes involve using a hash function, such as using a counter:

$$K_0 = \text{"master" key}$$
$$K_n = \text{HMAC}(K_0 \,||\, n)$$

Or you could iteratively use a hash function, $H^n(K)$, which means repeating the hash code $H^2(K) = H(H(K) \,||\, \text{Counter})$ or `H(H(K))` or `MAC(MAC(K))` or some similar scheme.

The good points about this system is that a client needs only a master key and generates any key that it might need. The downside is that you really have to guard that key, because if someone steals it, he or she can decrypt not only past messages but also *any future messages*. However, there are a lot of advantages. One is that you can perform key management without knowing anything about the keys themselves. You can add, delete, or retire keys just by referring to their index. When needed, the keys will be generated on the fly. Another advantage is that you can never delete keys by mistake. You can mark keys as being deleted, but if you find out that you really do need that key, it's easily retrievable by a simple computation.

Key Encryption

The keys themselves certainly need to be encrypted. The choice is whether to generate a single key file and encrypt that or use a plaintext version where only the keys are encrypted (possibly using a key-wrapping algorithm) and with the auxiliary data in the clear. There are advantages and drawbacks to both.

The solitary encrypted file is easy to implement; you can use a `SealedObject` class and store the serialized bytes. The downside to serialization is that it's a bit tricky to upgrade if you make changes to the `Key` class. It might be better to store the keys in a text format in columns, or XML-based format that is very explicit on how the data is stored (this can be done by implementing a custom serialization procedure as well).

Storing key data in plaintext with only the actual key bytes being encrypted is a bit harder to implement, but it has the advantage that key management can be done *without* actually seeing what the keys are. Keys can be added, deleted, or queried without compromising the keys themselves. The downside is that without careful controls, anyone can see how you have encrypted data. Technically this shouldn't make any difference, but it's definitely better not to advertise your security methods.

Storage

The next issue is where should the key records be held. There really only are three places it can go: the main database, the filesystem, or a remote machine. The correct solution is the one that best plays to your organization's strengths. If security is already being handled by the database group, then the key should probably go into the database. Likewise, if security is being handled by the networking and main operations group, then using a remote machine is probably best.

Storing the keys in the main database that holds the encrypted data has a lot of advantages. The database is frequently "three-M'ed"—that is, mirrored, managed, and monitored—so basic file integrity is already covered. Queries on keys are trivially done with SQL (assuming the auxiliary data is left unencrypted). The real downside is concern about access to the database and its security and who is managing the keys. Many times network and machine operations and database operations are two completely different groups, each with different security policies. If the database group is not in charge of managing the keys, it might be best not to store them in the database. This really depends on your organization. The other problem is if the database goes down, so do the keys. Many times the keys will be used in situations where the database is not involved, so this creates a dependency when there shouldn't be.

Another option is storing the key file on the local machine. I personally don't like this system, since it allows an attacker something to chew on. It also has the problem of managing and synchronizing multiple files. Another option would be storing the keys on a shared partition, but that has its own set of management and security issues.

The last option is storing the key remotely and having the application request the keys over the network. This has the advantage that there is one place for the keys and the key server is a self-contained entity; it can be monitored as needed. The downside is this is a new service to manage. Key requests should only come from known hosts on the production network and reject requests from elsewhere (including development). If the database group is in charge of security, then clearly this is probably not the best solution. There are multiple ways of actually sending the keys, including Java's Remote Method Invocation (RMI) or HTTP (both can operate over SSL as well). HTTP has the advantage that the server can be a stock Web server that is well known and has numerous access control and logging facilities. RMI is very nice since the implementation is fairly simple (if you are already familiar with it). The downside to RMI is that access control and logging is weak. In either case, a *key server* should be made available (and is easy to install) for development purposes. In both cases, I prefer sending the encrypted keys over an encrypted channel (SSL or a roll-your-own Diffie-Hellman), since it prevents network snoopers from even seeing what is being sent in the first place.

Key Access and Distribution

We have keys; we have encrypted keys; the next step is to grant access to those keys. The keys themselves are used in two places. One place is by the key operation or key administration—whatever the group is called that decides new keys need to be generated or deleted. The other is by the application that uses the keys for cryptographic purposes. In other words, there is a natural separation between read and write access, which is perfect for asymmetric encryption. But there is a bit of a twist. The public and private keys *both* are kept secret. The public key for encrypting the key file is secret so only the administrator can update the key file. The private key file is used by the application to decrypt the key file and certainly must be kept secret. Using this system, a public key encrypts a key file, and a password decrypts a private key that decrypts the file that contains keys to decrypt data in the database.

If you don't want to use public key techniques, a similar type of result can be done using two key files: a master and a slave. The master file creates the slave file every time it is updated and is encrypted using a different key. It's not quite as elegant, but it does work.

To be secure, this system requires a human sitting down at the computer typing in a password when the application starts to begin the decryption process. Unfortunately, there really isn't any way getting around that. You could try to work around these requirements by "hiding" the master key in source code, memory, or a file, but no method is truly secure. This is especially true with Java, since the class files are so easy to disassemble to re-create reasonable source code. Someone who gained access to your class files would only disassemble everything and then search for "Cipher" in the output. The whole process would take seconds.

The pain can be lessened by some of the techniques in the next section.

Using Keys with Ciphers and MACs

Now that we have discussed key generation, key storage, and key transport, it's time to put the keys to work. First and foremost, hanging on to the keys, even in memory, is dangerous and should be avoided. The other problem is that the time to set up a cipher can be quite expensive. Instead of setting up `Cipher` objects for one-time use, a much more efficient way is to create a array or hash of `Cipher` objects all configured for encryption or decryption or a MAC operation.

Following is a sample just for initialization for encryption. This can easily be extended and can be done just using more if-then-else statements, so a single class can handle either encryption, decryption, or MACing, In any event, you'll end up with three different objects, one for encryption, one for decryption, and one for MAC functions. After being initialized, the secret keys can be erased.

```
public class IndexedCrypto
{

    protected HashMap map;

    public IndexedCrypto.(SecretKeyData[] skd)
    {
            this.map = new HashMap();
            for (int i = skd.length -1; i >= 0; --i) {
                if (skd[i].getStatus() == SecretKeyData.KEY_DELETED)
                     continue;
                try {
                 Cipher c;
            String alg = skd[i].getAlgorithm();
            if (alg.equalsIgnoreCase("null")) {
                c = new NullCipher();
            } else {
                c = Cipher.getInstance(alg);
            }
            //
            // MAY NEED MORE COMPLICATED CHECKS TO
            // HANDLE ALGORITHM PARAMETERS
            //
            // just check for ECB mode, if not
            // use a null IV.  This works for DES, Triple DES, and Blowfish
            //
```

```
            if (alg.indexOf("ECB") >= 0) {
                c.init(Cipher.ENCRYPT_MODE, skd[i]);
            } else { // not ECB mode default to null IV
                IvParameterSpec ivs =
                 new IvParameterSpec(new byte[8]);
                c.init(cmode, skd[i], ivs);
            }

            map.put(skd[i].getIndex(), c);
           } catch (Exception e) {
            throw new RuntimeException("Error -- " + e);
           }
       }
  }

      public byte[] doFinal(byte[] data, String i)
      {
       try {
           Cipher c = (Cipher) map.get(i);
           if (c == null)
            throw new RuntimeException("Bad index -- " + i);
           return c.doFinal(data);
       } catch (Exception e) {
           throw new RuntimeException("Error -- " + e);
       }
      }
  }
```

For decrypting, the process is simple. You receive the ciphertext and the key index from the database and pass them directly to the `doFinal` call. Likewise for MAC verification. However, for encryption and MAC generation, you need to get a key index. If you have an algorithm for generating the index, you'll need to add it. If you are just using random key indexes, you'll have to do some type of code like this:

```
IndexedCrypto encrypt = ....; // create and initialize
byte[] plaintext = ... ;// plaintext
int index = Random.nextInt(ic.length()); // regular random is ok, just
want uniform distribution
byte[] ciphertext = encrypt.doFinal(plaintext, index);
// save ciphertext and index to database.
```

That can be a bit clunky. One aid is to make a data structure that models the relationship between the plaintext and ciphertext:

```
public class EncryptedData
{
    public EncryptedData() { index = -1 };
```

```
    public byte[] plaintext;
    public byte[] ciphertext;
    public String   index;

    public void finalize() {
     if (plaintext != null) {
         for (int i= plaintext.length; i >= 0; --i) plaintext[i] = 0;
         plaintext = null;
     }
    }
}
```

Then the doFinal can be modified to take this object. If the index is –1, then a random index (or whatever algorithm you decide) may be used:

```
IndexedCrypto encrypt = ....; // create and initialize
String plaintext = ... ;// plaintext
EncryptedData ed = new EncryptedData();
ed.plaintext = plaintext.getBytes();
encrypt.doFinal(ed);
// save ed.ciphertext and ed.index to the database.

ed.index = // from db
ed.ciphertext = // from db
decrypt.doFinal(ed);

ed.plaintext contains the data.
```

This makes the code a bit more self-documenting. In practice, you'll probably put wrappers around various data types to make the work even more transparent. If you never work with byte arrays, it probably makes sense to use wrappers to make the converted form String to byte[] invisible. A more complex example would be to do the following:

```
public CreditCardEncryptor(...) {
     encrypt = new IndexedCrypto(KeyRequest.request("cc-db"));
     decrypt = new IndexedCrypto(...);
     r = new Random();
}
public EncrypedData encrypt(String cc) {
     EncryptedData ed = new EncryptedData();
     ed.index = r.nextInt(encrypt.length()); // or maybe some other scheme
     ed.plaintext = BCD.encode(cc);
     encrypt.doFinal(ed);
     return ed;
}

public String decrypt(EncryptedData ed) {
```

```
        decrypt.doFinal(ed);
        return BCD.decode(ed.plaintext);
    }
```

Passwords

Closely related to keys are passwords. We saw in Chapter 2 how to turn a password into a key. Frequently, the entire security of the system is tied to a password that allows the secret keys to be decrypted so the whole application can be used. In addition, passwords are by far the most common method of authentication for Web-based services.

Startup Passwords

A crucial part of application security is a password that is required for the application to start. Normally this password is used to decrypt a key file.

For Abstract Window Toolkit (AWT) GUI applications, you can create a window to collect the password that prints a "*" when a character is pressed, but if you read a password from a stream or from the console, as is the case with most server applications, it's trickier. You might be tempted to use `BufferedReader` and `getLine()`. This certainly works, but then the password is represented as a `String`. And as mentioned, I don't like keys and password in "immutable" form, since they linger in memory or in swap space for an unknown amount of time.

Much preferred is to read the stream a character at a time and store the result in a `char[]` array. In the Java 1.4 JCE documentation, Sun provides a function that reads one character at a time. However, if you use it for reading passwords, you'll get this disturbing display:

```
>password: ThisIsMyPassword
```

In other words, the password is displayed or echoed to the screen. There is no simple work around to this. Sun is aware of the issue, but it isn't keen on fixing it, since as it turns out, creating a universal mechanism to handle various terminal functions is extremely nontrivial. In general, Java is terrible about handling console and system functions.

I've tried working around the limitation. Here's what *doesn't* work:

- *Handing the password reading to another application (shell, Perl, etc.).* Unfortunately, Java thinks it owns the console input and gets upset when another application steals it. Normally, this results in Java crashing.

- *Bootstrapping by collecting the password first, then invoking the Java application with the password.* Passing it in by environment variable puts the password into the system. Passing it in on the command line (either -D flag on the command line) puts it into the process list and can be retrieved with the right combinations of `ps` parameters (Unix) or in the Task Manager (Windows). Encrypting the password with a public key and having the Java application decrypt with a private key doesn't work, since how would you protect the private key?
- *Waiting for Sun to fix this.* This bug has been in effect since 1.0, and Sun doesn't appear to be particularly interested in fixing it, since reading from the console is a very platform-dependant thing. Here are some hacks that work around the Java limitation but ultimately do not solve the problem:
  - *Turn off character echoing altogether.* For simple applications or for server applications, this is the simplest workaround. Just type "`stty -echo;` *`cmd`*" and you are all set. This does not work on Windows (but it will work on Cygwin). The application can echo the input, but since Java buffers console input, you won't see the echoing until the user presses Enter. This option is not particularly useful.
  - *Bite the bullet and write the application using AWT.* If the end user is already using Windows or X, this is not a problem. But if the application needs to be terminal-based (perhaps it's for a remote management or administration), then this isn't going to work.

Another approach is running the application in a telnet session and controlling echoing using telnet session codes. Typically, telnet is something you want to turn off because it's insecure. However, the advantage is that the telnet protocol negotiates between a server and client a common set of functionality. When that is done, you typically have a very standard console that behaves in a very predictable way and has the ability to turn on and off character echoing. You then start the application (and maybe push it into the background), start a mini-server listening on one port, and then wait. Next, you telnet to that particular port, and the application runs like a normal console application. Using various control characters, you can turn on console echoing when a password is being entered. In addition, there are other commands to create various "windows" and "menus" just using text characters (1980s style). It's very handy and very portable. The downside is that you must simulate the normal flow of telnet protocol, which is a bit tricky and fairly long. The source code is presented on the Web site. Following is a portion:

```
> java TelnetAppTest &
Waiting to connect on port 3000....
> telnet localhost:3000
Connected!
Enter username: nickg
Enter password: (blank)
```

Member Names and Passwords

Unlike an internal application where you have full control over the security design, a public service presents trade-offs based on threat attempts (for instance, what particular threats are you protecting against?) and on the value of service.

Following are some considerations when setting up guidelines for member names and passwords:

Customer ease of use and user interface. Requiring members to enter a 50-character password, for example, is likely to drive potential members away.

Customer service model and costs. If you are staffing a telephone-based customer support model, the issue of lost passwords can get very expensive.

Roll member names and passwords in total security assessment. Keep in mind that passwords are just one element of a total security assessment.

One important aspect that is easy to forget is that many users will be accessing your service from public terminals such as a local library or Internet café. Outside the United States, Internet cafés are frequently the primary way people access the Internet.

While member names and passwords aren't directly related to cryptography, for Internet and database applications, they are the primary way of authentication. However, it's done incorrectly so often that it's worth reviewing.

Selecting Passwords

For internal use, password selection is normally taken quite seriously and a password or phrase is used with a variety of characters and numbers. Password selection by the members of your service is a different story altogether. There is a trade-off between convenience, customer service costs, and security. Members, of course, will want a short, easy-to-remember password. You want secure passwords, but don't want customers to start calling up customer care because they've forgotten their passwords.

Table 7.3 provides some guidelines regarding password restrictions.

The threat here is not that someone will do a dictionary attack online. This is thwarted easily by implementing a "three-strikes" rule. After three bad attempts the account is either locked, requiring the user to call customer service, or forcing the user to use password recovery.

The problem here is that the more rules you impose, the more likely the member will pick a password he or she will forget.

Member Login, Success and Failure

On a bad attempt, you should not identify to the user what the specific problem is. It would be quite easy for someone to scan the space of usernames and get either an estimate of your member base or use the list for subsequent attacks.

The login scheme should be as follows:

- Upon an unsuccessful login attempt, a message is returned that reads, "I'm sorry the username or password is invalid. Please try again."
- After three strikes, the computer notifies the person attempting to log in that the account is either invalid or that it has been deactivated.

Table 7.3 Common Password Restrictions

RESTRICTION	REASON
Minimum length	Prevent trivial passwords.
Maximum length	Prevent very long passwords either because of database storage costs or to reduce the chance the member will enter the password incorrectly, or for visual user interface issues (size of password box).
Require numbers	Increase password space.
Require upper- and lowercase letters	Increase password space.
Password must not in be dictionary	Prevent easy-to-guess or easy-to-crack passwords.
Shifts of username (for example, "fred" -> "redf")	Prevent easy-to-guess or easy-to-crack passwords.
Reversals of user names (such as, "fred" -> "dref"	Prevent easy-to-guess or easy-to-crack passwords.

In all cases, you should give the member an opportunity to do a member name or password lookup.

More sophisticated systems might show the total number of attempts, the total number of different usernames tried, and so forth. All of these are helpful in securing the system, but none of them are foolproof, since you can't count on the cookies working and you really don't know who is probing your system.

With a valid member name, an attacker can quickly lock out a user (or get their password). Annoying for the user? Yes, but well-scaled up, an attack locking a substantial portion of the member base can have a devastating impact to the business.

One way of enhancing security is, on the welcome screen, to announce to the user his or her last login (or logout) time measured in days. This can help the member audit his or her account usage and check if someone else logged on with his or her information.

Changing Passwords and Challenges

When the user wishes to change (or in some cases view) sensitive information, the password, or challenges, it's good practice to require them to reauthenticate. You don't want someone walking off from a public terminal and have another person jump in and change a lot of data.

The quick way is to check the last authentication time, and if it's within a certain time period, allow the user to perform the operation. If it's not, the user will have to reauthenticate.

Web-Based Password Entry

Originally, BasicAuth was the method used to enter member names and passwords. It's still useful for simple applications; however, the data is transferred in the clear (well, just about—it's in base 64).

Most modern applications now do logon using a form along with cookies. This has proven most flexible in terms of user interface and for flexibility. More information on using cookies for authentication is given later in the chapter.

When designing this system, always give the member the opportunity to log in securely under SSL, even if your application doesn't run under SSL normally. This allows the password to be securely transmitted, even if the authentication cookie is returned in the clear. You'll find that 99.9 percent of the time users won't use the option, but it's still a very good idea. The first reason is that the 0.1 percent who do care, care about it greatly. Second, it shows that you are serious about security (even if your members aren't).

For high-security applications, of course, you don't have a choice; you will authenticate under SSL.

Generating New Passwords

Ideally, you are storing a keyed hash of the password, and if the member loses the password, he or she is presented with a challenge and then forced to enter a new password. But perhaps the existing system is storing encrypted versions, or for whatever reason, you don't like unrecoverable passwords.

The next problem is when members forget their username or account number. The safer option is to physically mail users their account information. This is normally done by financial institutions. For less sensitive sites, the issue is then customer convenience, and it's common practice to email the member a new password.

While the last practice is not ideal, the trade-off is security versus losing a customer or having the customer call in, which is expensive for such a routine operation. Actually sniffing the wire to retrieve these emails can certainly be done, but it is only possible in specific situations. An ill-intentioned employee could set up a sniffer that scans for packets or emails with the words "account" and "password" at the entire site. The odds of this happening need to be reconciled with the customer costs. The fact is until some type of standard Web identity or wallets are in place, members find having a password emailed to them very convenient.

Eventually you will run into a case where a member's password needs to be reset, often because they locked themselves out with bad attempts and a challenge wasn't implemented. In this case what temporary password do you send them? Sending random junk consisting of upper- and lowercase letters and numbers is clearly an option, but it's not very friendly. Ordinary humans have a hard time reading "hG6Tys8UA" and then typing it. Also, you run the risk of the member making three bad attempts again, resulting in another call to the customer service or, worse, the user just abandoning the service altogether and going somewhere else.

Another way of generating passwords is to use multiple short words concatenated together, such as "ZeroFlexGray." This technique is similar to the message encoding technique described in the previous chapter. Using a dictionary of 2,048 words, each word corresponds to 11 bits of security. Three words correspond to a randomly generated password of six characters, and four words is roughly eight characters. The added benefit is that these passwords are also easily communicated over the telephone.

Member Names

Member name scanning is a problem. For instance, you can count on an account being named "jsmith" in just about every service. One way around this problem is to give the user a member name instead of letting the user choose it.

I've seen pre-assigned member names as short as 6 numeral digits, and they appear to be issued in a near sequential manner. If the service issues member lockout when the incorrect password is entered, a distributed denial of service attack could disable every account in under an hour.

One option is to invert the member-name password process by either generating a multiple-word username with some high check digit or security code to eliminate guessing. Depending on the system and how the dictionary is selected, you could also have the member select his or her name from a word list. In this case, you'll want the drop-down lists to be randomized, so members don't get lazy and select words from the top of the list. An additional technique is to have different categories of words, and users could select word lists they preferred. "Fruits and vegetables," "flowers," and "animals" are some that come to mind.

In addition, there is really no reason to limit word lengths to three or four letters. The only issue is efficiently encoding this in the HTML page.

The big problem with this scheme is that nobody wants to restrict member choice in usernames. However, it's not that uncommon for many people to be restricted already, since someone else already has the same username.

Logging

An area that frequently gets overlooked for leakage of sensitive information is from errors and logging. Scanning the log file is often a very handy way of gaining information on the system. Frequently, developers will leave useful information or error information present.

When designing encrypted logs, be sure to consult with operations staff or whomever will be using the logs to understand their needs. Ask them what the log contains and what type of restrictions need to be placed on it for security purposes. Answers can be as follows:

- Preventing unauthorized people from easily reading and monitoring the log files
- Preventing unauthorized people from gaining any log information
- Preventing only sensitive information from being read

The sensitive data is frequently transient, does not have a long useful lifetime, and in many cases is of low value to begin with. In addition, logging needs to be nearly invisible and cannot be a drain on system resources. Because of this, you *might* choose to relax many of the security requirements you would normally use for long-term storage. For secret key ciphers, this may mean using ECB mode and using the fastest (reasonable) cipher available. For public key cipher, this can mean using a smaller-than-normal key size to speed the process up.

Embedded-Encryption Logging

One option for logging is embedding the encrypted data in the plaintext message. This is tricky, since you have specified a key entry and then the encrypted data in a base 64 (or other ASCII) format. Another option is to use a public key cipher. This can eliminate the key index issue. New public keys can be referenced by using the data of the log file. Most of the time the log will be read immediately, analyzed, then archived, so long-term key storage isn't much of an issue.

If you are using mixed logging and a public key cipher, be aware of the potential for denial-of-service attacks by someone using your service and intentionally doing a process that causes a log. If you are using 2048 bits of security using RSA, this can be an expensive process.

Fully Encrypted Log Files

The other option is to fully encrypt every entry. The benefit is that it's fairly easy to write tools that copy the standard Unix tools or to develop bulk decrypters.

Encryption using the symmetric cipher has to be done in a particular way. A stream cipher is definitely the easiest to use, but you'll have to find a provider that supports RC4 (ArcFour) or a similar cipher. Then all you do is a successive series of update calls to the `Cipher` object.

If you wish to use a block cipher, the choice depends on how secure you wish the log file to be. For lower security, you'll want to select the fastest cipher (probably Blowfish) and use ECB mode. For more security, you should use CBC mode. Do not use a padding mode; instead, you'll have to pre-pad the log message in advance. This needs to be done to make sure the update call encrypts the entire message instead of waiting for more input to fill an entire block. The code sample presents a skeleton for doing encrypted logging. Certainly, you won't hardwire a secret key! (And I haven't had a chance to examine the new Java logging API.) Logging should have an invisible performance impact, so you really want to prevent needless copying of strings and arrays. It first encrypts the entire message, then encrypts a padding array. This array just contains padding characters and a newline at the end. For instance, if the block size is 8 bytes, and the message has three leftover characters, `padding[3]` will contain four spaces and a newline so the last block is complete. The `doFinal` method is never called in this case, since the logger is making sure there are no leftover characters.

```
public class EncryptedLogger {

    protected byte[][] padding;
    protected char padChar = ' ';
    protected Cipher c;
    protected int size;  // blocksize in bytes for cipher

    public EncryptedLogger() throws Exception {

     // replace with real initialization
     c = Cipher.getInstance("Blowfish/ECB/NoPadding");
     byte[] keybytes = {1,2,3,4,5,6,7,8};
     SecretKeySpec sks = new SecretKeySpec(keybytes, "Blowfish");
     c.init(Cipher.ENCRYPT_MODE, sks);

     size = c.getBlockSize();

     // this initializes padding
     // array is (padchars) + '\n'
     padding = new byte[size][];
     char[] paddingchars = new char[size];
     paddingchars[0] = '\n';
     for (int i = 1; i < size; i++) {
         padding[size - i] = new String(paddingchars, 0, i).getBytes();
         paddingchars[i-1] = padChar;
         paddingchars[i] = '\n';
     }
     padding[0] = new String(paddingchars, 0, size).getBytes();
    }

    public void log(String message) {
        byte[] e1 = c.update(message.getBytes());
     byte[] e2 = c.update(padding[message.length() % size]);

     // send both e1 and e2 to log file
     System.out.print("Message  Length : " + message.length());
     System.out.println(", Encrypted Length: " +
                          (e1.length + e2.length));
    }
```

```
    // cmd line test of interface.
   public static void main(String[] args) throws Exception{
    EncryptedLogger logger = new EncryptedLogger();
    for (int i = 0; i < args.length; i++) {
        logger.log(args[i]);
    }

   }
}
```

Public Key Logging

You could use raw symmetric ciphers to do the encrypting, but then you would have key management issues. The key used could be encoded into the filename so the utilities to decrypt the log know which key to use.

Another technique is to use a public key cipher. The beauty is that the public key can be read from a configuration file and does not need to be kept secret. The tools to read the log can be kept on a separate machine and have access control. To do this, you'll need to:

- Write out start date.
- Write out the number of bytes.
- Know the symmetric cipher, mode, and padding used.
- Write out the encrypted asymmetric block.

As an example, the header of the log file might look as follows:

```
# Log started on March 13, 2001 04:00:00 by app foobar by user@machine1

key = logkey1
blocksize = 128
cipher=Blowfish/ECB/NoPadding
// 128 bytes of an  asymetric cipher block
// log follows, encrypted in symmetric cipher
```

Split Log Files

The other option is to use two log files: one for general-purpose messages and another for sensitive information.

For example, the common log entry might look like this:

```
12367674 WARNING Problem with credit card.  See reference Id 126372
```

While the matching sensitive log entry (encrypted) looks like this:

```
12367679 INFO  Credit card 4000 0000 0000 0000 failed authorization
```

Network-Based Logs

One solution to storing logs on the local machine is to send all log messages to a *log server* on another machine. The syslog application and protocol is the most common example of this (note that many implementations truncate the log message if it is too long). Many syslog applications can route messages based on severity or state to another process, and this can make the job of encrypting sensitive data a bit easier. If the network traffic scares you, a secure version using Diffie-Hellman Key Exchange or SSL can be implemented. Even though the log data is being sent to a "secure" machine, the sensitive information still must be encrypted. Sensitive information should never be stored on disk without being encrypted first, to prevent general misuse and to prevent the data from being in the clear when archived.

Cryptographic Tokens and Applications

A cryptographic token is an encoded MAC that contains additional information on the key used to compute the MAC, expiration, and other data. It's used to protect small messages from being altered or used as key for another application. We'll demonstrate a simple implementation at the end of the section.

Token Design

The token itself consists of a few basic fields, and if desired, expiration information. The token itself may or may not contain the actual message that is being protected. A token normally contains the following information:

Security bits. Someone trying to generate a fraudulent token using b bits can expect on an average random attempt to need 2^{b-1} attempts to find a valid entry. What the security size is depends on the application. Normally the result is adjusted a bit or two to make the complete token size is a multiple of 8 bits so it can fit cleanly into a `byte` array.

Security parameter. If you are developing a system where multiple tokens are used, you'll want to specify how many security bits (or bytes) are expected. Typical is 4 bits, which provides plenty of room (e.g., 0 = 20 bits, 1 = 16 bits, etc.).

Version bits. You should always use 1 bit for a version control. For long-term use, 2 bits is even better.

Key index bit. Two bits should be used for referencing the key. This gives you a total of four different keys to work with. For the application, this should be acceptable. If you are working with multiple partners, you may also have to add domain bits or partner ID bits as well.

Expirations and Time Quantization

If desired, expiration dates (and times) can be efficiently encoded into the token as well. There are three methods for doing so. The first is just using the version information or the key information and matching that to internal rules to see if the token is expired or not.

Second, time expiration can also explicitly be added to the token by using a code for representing days, months, and year. Typical is an 11-bit representation:

- 5 bits for day (0 to 32)
- 4 bits for month (0 to 15)
- 2 bits for year, so 0 = 2002, 1 = 2003, 2 = 2004, 3 = 2005

The third technique is to specify a "relative" expiration that allows for much finer granularity for expiration time. The relative method uses number of seconds since some base point. To-the-second resolution typically isn't needed. The `java.lang.System.currentTimeMillis()` returns the number of milliseconds since January 1, 1970 GMT. You certainly don't need to keep track of time in the past, and you certainly don't need millisecond resolution. In fact, you don't usually even need hour resolution. The other issue to consider is the final date. If it's made too soon, then everything expires prematurely, but if it's too distant, you are wasting bits. Typically, you make a trade-off between the resolution and the bit size. The guiding factoring is making the entire token by a multiple of 8 bits, and the time resolution is normally the first item to be adjusted.

Given a set number of bits, the resolution, you can do a quick estimation of $(years \times 365 \times 24 \times 60 \times 60) / (2^{bits} - 1)$. A more detailed analysis is found in Table 7.4. Making these calculations in Java is a bit roundabout because of internationalization requirements.

You could also use the "default" locale, but it's best to explicitly use UTC (GMT) time. If you are developing and deploying on a single machine, it's no problem. However, it's not uncommon for some machines to be misconfigured with an incorrect locale or time zone (normally, one might be set to the local time, while another is at UTC). It shouldn't make any difference in practice, but it's just one more source of errors. To eliminate this, do all computations with an explicit time zone.

Java frowns on using the "standard" abbreviations for time zones, such as EST for "Eastern Time Zone" in North America, instead preferring a different style based on the continent and a major city. EST is specified under Java by "America/NewYork." A list of available time zone identifiers can be found by writing a small program that does the following:

```
String[] zones = java.util.TimeZone.getAvailableIDs();
for (int i = 0; i < zones.length; ++i) {
    System.out.println(zones[i]);
}
```

Table 7.4 Resolution in days:hours:minutes

	1 YEAR	2 YEARS	3 YEARS	4 YEARS	5 YEARS
5 bits	11:18:35	23:13:10	35:07:45	47:02:20	58:20:55
6 bits	05:19:03	11:14:06	17:09:09	23:04:12	28:23:15
7 bits	02:20:59	05:17:58	08:14:56	11:11:55	14:08:53
8 bits	01:10:22	02:20:43	04:07:04	05:17:25	07:03:46
9 bits	00:17:09	01:10:18	02:03:25	02:20:35	03:13:43
10 bits	00:08:34	00:17:08	01:01:42	01:10:16	01:18:49
11 bits	00:04:17	00:08:34	00:12:51	00:17:08	00:21:24
12 bits	00:02:09	00:04:17	00:06:26	00:08:34	00:10:42
13 bits	00:01:05	00:02:09	00:03:13	00:04:17	00:05:21
14 bits	00:00:33	00:01:05	00:01:37	00:02:09	00:02:41
15 bits	00:00:17	00:00:33	00:00:49	00:01:05	00:01:21
16 bits	00:00:09	00:00:17	00:00:25	00:00:33	00:00:41

Creating the Security Bits

One thing to be aware of in creating the MAC is that you aren't just MAC'ing the main payload, but all of your header bits also need to be MAC'ed. The easy way is just call `Mac.update` with the main payload, then call `Mac.doFinal` by passing in the final bytes of the header.

The other way, which is sometimes more useful (especially for debugging purposes), is to create a new payload string that explicitly describes all of the fields. For instance, if the message is "transfer=$100.00" using a key ID of 1, version of 0, you'd actually MAC "transfer=$100.00&keyid=1&version=0" (or equivalent).

URL Tokens

A common use for cryptographic tokens is protecting URLs from being altered or tampered with. This can have applications for protecting data and session. Another use is to protect static content and using the token as an authentication tag.

Tamper-Evident URLs

A typical application of cryptographic tokens is to ensure that a URL query string portion has not been altered. For instance, say you are running a promotion. In the offer email, you ask people to click on a special URL in order to get 10 percent off the total purchase:

```
myapp.jsp?couponcode=1234
```

You don't want people to arbitrarily change the coupon code or do parameter scanning determining all possible codes. Frequently, the URL links to a page that then describes the offer. I find this type of problem frequently. Users can just change the URL and scan all the available offers. Some businesses might find this perfectly acceptable, since the point is to get users to try the service. In other cases, this is a disaster. Adding a token at the end of the URL prevents anyone doing parameter scanning and URL tampering, since the application will know by checking the token that the URL was altered.

The other main use is secure communication with different parts of the Web application. Most Web applications have limited states, and using a cookie for one-time use isn't ideal because cookies can be turned off and it's a bit heavyweight. And cookies cannot be bookmarked either.

In all cases, using a cryptographic token is needed. Here the payload is the query string of the URL. You pass in `couponcode=1234` and out comes `couponcode=1234&mac=7DTUHGA`. You'd then create the full or partial URL by adding the hostname and path:

```
http://myhost/myapp.jsp?couponcode=1234&mac=7DTUHGA
```

I typically put the MAC on *every* query string unless I have a reason not too. Sometimes you do not want a MAC, since another partner may wish to link to your site without using one. In all cases, it's a good idea to have some internal flag to turn off MAC checking. Sometimes the Q&A team will want to tweak the parameters without the pain of actually using the application.

To decode, you retrieve the query string and do the following checks:

1. Check that the `&mac=` tag is at the end of the query string.
2. Check that duplicate `mac` tags are not present.
3. Then, split the query string into the original part and the `&mac=...` part.
4. Extract the actual MAC from the `&mac=...` part.
5. Recompute the MAC.
6. Verify that it's equal to what you received.
7. If valid, then check expiration, if any (you always check expiration after you know the MAC is valid).

Protecting Static Content

Of course, the previous scheme only works when there is a script processing the data. For static content, you could put the document in question as part of the query string and protect that:

```
/a/directory/myapp.cgi?doc=/other/directory/myfile.html&mac=...
```

The application would then read and send the file. This works, but it looks ugly and somewhat hides what the document in question is. A seldom-used feature of the CGI protocol is the `PATH` function. Here:

```
/a/directory/app/another/directory/myfile.html
```

If part of the path in the URL is a CGI-enabled application, the application is invoked with the `PATH` variable set to `/another/directory/myfile.html`. With this you can do the following:

```
/a/directory/myapp/YWTSHA2A/another/directory/myfile.html
```

For creating the token, you'd pass in the static directory path `/another/directory/myfile.html` as the payload. For verification you just extract the MAC from the beginning of the URL and continue.

This looks a bit cleaner, but the MAC will push the filename out.

A Simple URL MAC Implementation

To illustrate the ideas from the previous section, a simple URL MAC is presented:

```
$ java SimpleMac '...myapp.cgi?offer=1234'
...myapp.cgi?offer=1234&mac=ABAqtXQZR2TY

...myapp.cgi?offer=1234&_version=0&_keyid=0&_security=7&
                _reserved=0&_expYear=0&_expMonth=0
```

Our layout will use the first byte to store 2 bits for version, 2 bits for a key ID, 2 bits for security ID, and 2 bits reserved for future use. The second byte will contain 4 bits containing the number of years since 2002 and 4 bits for the month. The start of the class defines a number of constants. I chose the security bits to correspond to 7, 10, 13, and 16 bytes from an HMAC which should provide a wide variety of token lengths. The numbers are chosen so that the hash bytes and the header bytes (2) are a multiple of 3, so no padding is needed when it is encoded using base 64.

The constructor takes an array of `byte` arrays for keys. This is probably not how you'd want to do this in production but it works as a demonstration. Using those keys, we create an array of `MAC` instances. The constructor also takes a default value for the key ID and security parameter, so you don't always have to specify it when performing a MAC. The source for the first part of the implementation is as follows:

```
import javax.crypto.*;
import javax.crypto.spec.*;
import java.util.*;
import java.security.*;

public class SimpleMac {

    protected final int MAX_KEYS = 4;
    protected Mac[] mac = new Mac[MAX_KEYS];
    protected final String MAC_ALG = "HmacSHA1"; // name of HMAC alg
    protected final String MAC_TAG = "&mac="; // tag to use in URL
    protected final int YEAR_START = 2002; // year to start counting
from
    protected final int YEAR_BITS = 4; // size of field
    protected final int YEAR_LAST = YEAR_START + (1 << 4) -1;
```

```
    protected final int MAC_HEADER = 2; // header info is two bytes
    protected final int[] SECURITY = {7,10,13,16} ; // number of bytes
of security
    protected final int reserved = 0;  // preset
    protected final int version = 0;   // preset

    protected int defaultKeyId;
    protected int defaultSecId;


    public SimpleMac(int defaultKeyId, int defaultSecId, byte[][]
keybytes)
    {
     this.defaultKeyId = defaultKeyId;
     this.defaultSecId = defaultSecId;

     try {
         for (int i = 0; i < MAX_KEYS; i++) { // check range
          if (keybytes[i] != null) {
              mac[i] = Mac.getInstance(MAC_ALG);
              mac[i].init(new SecretKeySpec(keybytes[i], MAC_ALG));
          }
         }
     } catch (NoSuchAlgorithmException e) {
         System.out.println(e);
         throw new RuntimeException("Unable to load Mac Instance of '" +
MAC_ALG + "'");
     } catch (InvalidKeyException e) {
         throw new RuntimeException("Bad key");
     }

    }
```

Following is code that actually creates the token. It can take the plain URL, and optionally the key ID, the security ID, and expiration. If the expiration is "0," then the token has "no expiration."

```
public String mac(String url) {
     return mac(url, defaultKeyId, defaultSecId, 0, 0);
}

public String mac(String url, int year, int month) {
     return mac(url, defaultKeyId, defaultSecId, year, month);
}

public String mac(String url, int keyid, int secid, int year, int month)
{
     // if year+month=0, then no expiration
     if ((year + month != 0) && ((year < YEAR_START
```

```
            || year > YEAR_LAST || month < 0 || month > 11)))
        throw new RuntimeException("bad expiration");

    String message = new String(url + "&_version=" + version +
                "&_keyid=" + keyid + "&_security=" + SECURITY[secid] +
                "&_reserved=" + reserved + "&_expYear=" + year +
                "&_expMonth=" + month);


    byte[] macraw = mac[keyid].doFinal(message.getBytes());

    byte[] token = new byte[SECURITY[secid] + MAC_HEADER];
    token[0] = (byte)((version << 6) | (keyid << 4) |
                      (secid << 2) | reserved);
    if (year + month != 0) {
        token[1] = (byte)(((year - YEAR_START) << 4) | month);
    }
    System.arraycopy(macraw, 0, token, 2, SECURITY[secid]);
    return new String(url + MAC_TAG + Base64UrlSafe.encode(token));
  }
```

Unmac performs a number of checks to make sure the incoming URL has the right format. Then it decomposes the token into various pieces, then recomputes the MAC bytes. Finally, it checks to see if the value is expired. If all is well, the caller will receive the original message plus all of the internal token values. The code is as follows:

```
public String unmac(String urlmac) {

    // check for mac;
    int i = urlmac.indexOf(MAC_TAG);
    if (i == -1) throw new RuntimeException("NO MAC" + urlmac);

    // make sure it's the only one!
    int j = urlmac.lastIndexOf(MAC_TAG);
    if (j == -1 || j != i)
        throw new RuntimeException("Multiple Macs!" + urlmac);

    // take the payload
    String urlnomac = urlmac.substring(0, i);

    // extract the MAC
    if (i + MAC_TAG.length() > urlmac.length()) {
        throw new RuntimeException("Truncated Mac");
    }
    String macString = urlmac.substring(i+MAC_TAG.length());


    // Base64 decode
```

```
        byte[] token = Base64UrlSafe.decode(macString);

        // get bits
        int iversion = (token[0] & 0xC0) >>> 6; // could check version here
        int ikeyid = (token[0] & 0x30)  >>> 4;
        int isecid = (token[0] & 0x0C) >> 2;
        int ireserved = (token[0] & 0x03);

        if (iversion != this.version)
            throw new RuntimeException("bad version");

        if (token.length != (SECURITY[isecid] + MAC_HEADER))
            throw new RuntimeException("MAC truncated or tampered");

        int iexpyear= ((token[1] & 0xf0) >> 4) + YEAR_START;
        int iexpmonth = (token[1] & 0x0f);
        if (token[1] == 0) iexpyear = 0; // no expiration was actually
used.

        // compute message
        String message = new String(urlnomac + "&_version=" + iversion +
            "&_keyid=" + ikeyid + "&_security=" + SECURITY[isecid] +
            "&_reserved=" + ireserved + "&_expYear=" + iexpyear +
            "&_expMonth=" + iexpmonth);
        // compute mac
        byte[] computed = mac[ikeyid].doFinal(message.getBytes());

        // compare macs
        for (i = 0; i < SECURITY[isecid]; i++) {
            if (computed[i] != token[i+ MAC_HEADER]) {
             throw new RuntimeException("MAC INVALID!");
            }
        }

        // check expiration
        if (iexpyear != 0) {
            Calendar cal = Calendar.getInstance();
            if ((iexpyear <  cal.get(Calendar.YEAR)) || ((iexpyear ==
cal.get(Calendar.YEAR)) &&
                (iexpmonth < cal.get(Calendar.MONTH)))) {
             throw new RuntimeException("MAC EXPIRED");
            }
        }
        return message;
    }
```

Fast Query String Parsing

URLEncode and URLDecode are very slow functions, mostly because they are very general and need to handle various character-set encoding issues.

But for most URLs, you don't need this type of generality. Since you'll be both reading and writing the data, you'll be using a consistent character set. Following are two drop-in replacements (add them to your packages).

The following uses the fast lookup table instead of programming the assumptions. The main improvement for `URLEncoder` is the assumption that only ASCII (values 0 to 127) is used in the encoding process. This allows it to work with `char` arrays that are very fast. Normally this assumption is acceptable, but if not, consider using the alternate version, `encodeGeneral`, which first converts the data to your native character encoding. It uses a `String` buffer instead of a `char` array to hold output, since you can't predict output size. If you know you are using a character encoding such as ISO-8859-1 (for American and Western European languages), then you know each character is represented as 1 byte and could optimize and use `char` arrays again.

```
public class URLEncoder {
    /**
     * Used in encoding unsafe characters
     */
    protected static final char[] hexChars =
    {'0', '1', '2', '3', '4', '5', '6', '7', '8', '9',
     'A', 'B', 'C', 'D', 'E', 'F'};

    protected static char[] encodeMap = new char[256];
    static {
     for (int i = 0  ; i <= 255; i++)  encodeMap[i] = (char) 0 ;
     for (int i = 'A'; i <= 'Z'; i++)  encodeMap[i] = (char) i ;
     for (int i = 'a'; i <= 'z'; i++)  encodeMap[i] = (char) i ;
     for (int i = '0'; i <= '9'; i++)  encodeMap[i] = (char) i ;
     encodeMap[' '] = '+';
     encodeMap['.'] = '.';
     encodeMap['-'] = '-';
     encodeMap['_'] = '_';
     encodeMap['*'] = '*';

    }

    /**
     * Assume input string only contains unicode characters from [0,255]
     * If not, an ArrayOutOfBoundsException will occur
     *
     */
    public static String encode(String s) {
     char c, ec;
     char[] ca = s.toCharArray();
     int len = s.length();
     char[] buf = new char[len * 3];
     int bi = 0;
```

```
        for (int i = 0; i < len; i++) {
            c = ca[i];
            ec = encodeMap[c];
            if (ec == (char)0) {
             buf[bi++] = '%';
             buf[bi++] = hexChars[( c & 0xf0) >> 4];
             buf[bi++] = hexChars[( c & 0x0f)];
            } else {
             buf[bi++] = ec;
            }
        }
        return new String(buf, 0, bi);
       }

       /**
        * No assumption on what input s.  Converted to local
        * Use string buffer since we can't predict how many bytes
        * will be used.  Some character encodings are stateful.
        */
       public static String encodeGeneral(String s) {
        byte[] ba = s.getBytes();
            int len = ba.length;
        char c; byte b;
        StringBuffer buf = new StringBuffer();
        for (int i = 0; i < len; i++) {
            b = ba[i];
            c = encodeMap[b & 0xFF];
            if (c == (char)0) {
             buf.append('%');
             buf.append(hexChars[((b & 0xf0) >> 4)]);
             buf.append(hexChars[ (b & 0x0f)]);
            }
        }
        return buf.toString();
       }
   }
```

The matching `URLDecode` is similar, as shown in the following. This uses a fast map for both mapping the general character and mapping hex characters to values. The version below assumes the pre-encoded input is ASCII for optimum speed. If it's not, convert the variable `buf` to be a `byte` array, and convert the `(char)` casts to `(byte)` casts.

```
   public class URLDecoder {

       /**
        *  Fast mappings of encoded values to original values
        *  Fast hex digit to value conversions by means of table as well
        */
```

```
    protected static char[] decodeMap = new char[256];
    protected static byte[] hexDecode = new byte[256];
    static {
for (int i = 0  ; i <= 255; i++) { decodeMap[i] = (char)-1;
  hexDecode[i] = (byte)i;}
     for (int i = 'A'; i <= 'Z'; i++) decodeMap[i] = (char)i;
     for (int i = 'a'; i <= 'z'; i++) decodeMap[i] = (char)i;
     for (int i = '0'; i <= '9'; i++) decodeMap[i] = (char)i;
     for (int i = '0'; i <= '9'; i++) hexDecode[i] = (byte)(i-'0');
     for (int i = 'A'; i <= 'F'; i++) hexDecode[i] = (byte)(i-'A'+10);
     for (int i = 'a'; i <= 'f'; i++) hexDecode[i] = (byte)(i-'a'+10);
     decodeMap['+'] =  ' ';
     decodeMap['.'] =  '.';
     decodeMap['-'] =  '-';
     decodeMap['_'] =  '_';
     decodeMap['*'] =  '*';
    }


public static String decode(String s)
      throws InvalidFormatException
    {

     byte hi, lo;
     int len = s.length();
     char[] buf = new char[len];
     int ci = 0;
     for (int i = 0; i < len; i++) {
         char c = s.charAt(i);
         if (c == '%') {
          if (i + 2 < len) {
              hi = hexDecode[s.charAt(++i)];
              lo = hexDecode[s.charAt(++i)];
              if (hi == -1 || lo == -1) {
               throw new InvalidFormatException("Bad hex number '" +
                    s.charAt(i-2) + s.charAt(i-1) + "' at position " +
                    Integer.toString(i-2), s);;
              }
              buf[ci++] = (char)((hi << 4) | lo);
          } else {
              throw new InvalidFormatException("Truncated hex digit at
position " + i, s);
          }
         } else {
          char foo = decodeMap[c];
          if (foo == -1) {
              throw new InvalidFormatException("Bad character encoding
of '" + c + "' at position " + i, s);
          } else {
              buf[ci++] = foo;
```

```
            }
          }
        }
        return new String(buf, 0, ci);
      }
  }
```

The last optimization is to convert a hash table of name-value pairs into an appropriate query string format:

```
name1=value1&name2=value2....
```

Encoding is fairly straightforward, but decoding is a tad tricky, as shown in the following. The natural way of doing this is by using `StringTokenizer` to parse for "&" and so on. However, `StringTokenizer` is *slow*. One Web application I was working on was spending a full 50 percent of its time in `StringTokenizer` parsing the query string.

```
import java.util.*;
public class URLFormEncode {

    /**
     * Converts a Map to an x-www-form-encoded string
     *
     * @param map  Input map to convert.  It is assumed that key names
are
     *    It is assumed the keys in the map are pure alphanumeric
     *     [a-zA-Z0-9.-_*].  Values can contain any characters.
     *
     * @returns String  x-www-form-encoded string
     *
     */
    public static String encode(Map map) {
     StringBuffer buf = new StringBuffer();
     Iterator iter = map.keySet().iterator();
     boolean first = true;
     String key;
     while (iter.hasNext()) {
         key = (String)(iter.next());
         if (!first) {
          buf.append('&');
         }
         buf.append(key);
         buf.append('=');
         buf.append(URLEncoder.encode((String)(map.get(key))));
         first = false;
     }
```

```
    return buf.toString();
   }

   /**
    * Assumptions
    *    keys are pure ascii, and are not urldecoded
    *    values are urldecoded.
    * @param s A x-www-form-encoded string
    * @returns Map
    * @throws InvalidFormatException if the input is not in the right
format
    *    or if a key appears twice.
    */
   public static Map decode(String s)
    throws InvalidFormatException
   {
    if (s == null) return null;
    s = s.trim();
    HashMap map = new HashMap();
    if (s.length() == 0) {
        return map;
    }
    int start = 0;
    int len = s.length();
    while (start < len - 1) {
        String key, value;
        int end = s.indexOf('=', start);
        if (end == -1) throw new InvalidFormatException("Unable to find
value for key", s);
        key = s.substring(start, end);
        if (map.containsKey(key)) {
         throw new InvalidFormatException("Key '" + key + "' appears
twice in input", s);
        }
        start = end + 1;
        end = s.indexOf('&', start);
        if (end == -1) {
         value = s.substring(start);
         start = len;
        } else {
         value = s.substring(start, end);
         start = end + 1;
        }
        map.put(key, URLDecoder.decode(value));
    }
    return map;
   }
}
```

URL Encryption

While it's not ideal, sometimes sensitive information must be passed in URL. Normally you never want to do this, but sometimes it's a very easy data interchange format. Unfortunately, the URL will be logged in numerous places. To prevent this, the entire query string must be encrypted.

Depending on the context, you might be able to infer the key identifier—in this case, the query string—in its entirety. There are two different ways of doing URL encryption, each with various advantages and disadvantages.

In the first, the entire URL is encrypted: `kid=keyed&payload=&mac=`. The MAC is checked, then using the `payload` and `kid`, you decrypt the payload into another query string. This is then passed off as the real query string.

If you can determine what the key is (by, for instance, knowing what script uses this key), then the second option is to MAC the query string, then encrypt. This has the advantage of being "more mysterious." The query string is just base 64 material.

Very Short URLs

When sending URLs in electronic mail, it's often a good idea to make sure the total length of the URL is less than 72 characters to make sure it doesn't get wrapped. Wrapped URLs frequently don't work in email.

Even modest domain names and path names can eat up half of that, leaving 30 to 40 characters for any information in the query string. Add a MAC to that, and you have less than 20 characters, which doesn't leave much room for any information.

One way around this limitation is to store the "real" query string in a database, and put the index to that query string into the URL. For instance, `http://some-company/youapp.jsp?offer=12345&mac=UTGHGYT`. Doing a lookup in the database will then return the `true` query string: `memberid=1278643&offervalue=12345&expiration=10-20-2002 &onetime=true`.

The advantage of having this indirection is that you can test the direct version without having to use the database. Then, at production time, the existing code is just wrapped with the code to parse the incoming URL and do a database lookup.

This allows for one-time offers and unsharable coupons. During the lookup you can mark the offer as being used or check that the offer belongs to the member.

Cookie Tokens

Cookies are programmatically almost identical to URLs and use the same format for the payload, but there are some important differences. First, you should always MAC cookies. With URL, it's somewhat optional, depending on the URL.

Detecting Cookie Capability

Using client-side code such as JavaScript can detect if the browser accepts cookies, by setting and retrieving a cookie. This, of course, depends on having JavaScript working and may not be portable.

Another technique is to use a cookie checker script. It works like this:

1. The client registers with the service.
2. If no cookie is present, have the application issue a cookie and redirect back itself using a URL `hasCookie=1` flag in the MAC'ed URL.
3. The application should see a cookie and the `hasCookie` flag in the URL. It can then proceed normally.
4. If the `hasCookie` flag is present and no cookie is found, then an error page can be issued.

Cookies and Authentication

By default, a cookie set on an SSL session will be reused for a non-SSL session. This is a security problem, since someone can sniff out the insecure cookie and then reuse it to gain access to the secure sections of the site.

This problem can be solved by setting a special flag in the cookie: `secure=1`. With this the SSL cookie stays on the SSL. This prevents cookie sniffers, but then the entire session has to stay in SSL, which is computationally expensive and, depending on the content, unnecessary. This problem can be solved so the user can go to SSL and non-SSL sites in a safe manner all under the same session. Conceptually, it's not particularly hard and the general outline is given below:

1. Initial registration or sign-on occurs on an SSL protected page.
2. After a successful sign-on, a secure session cookie is issued.
3. The member can then visit any SSL protected sites.

4. If the member visits a non-SSL page, the application sees that a session cookie is missing, so it redirects to the auth application (under SSL).
5. The auth application under SSL knows the member is validated because a valid cookie has been received. The auth application then redirects to itself under plain HTTP with a MAC'ed URL indicating that an insecure session cookie should be issued and then redirects to the final destination.
6. The auth application (not under SSL) receives the MAC'ed URL, issues a session cookie, and redirects to the final destination.

If someone steals the insecure cookie, that person can only access insecure parts of the site. If somehow the cookie is inserted into the secure site, it will be rejected, since it will not be of the correct form.

Tokens for Access Control

Note that none of these systems are foolproof and all will quickly crumble if the source code is available. This is the case of *any* client application using a shared key. To repeat: There is no such thing as a secure client using a shared key. The goal is to make cracking the system by average people laborious enough that they don't bother, or to make it hard enough so you make most of your income before it gets cracked. The simple way is just give the customer the key. However, that can be posted on the Internet, which is obviously a security risk.

Shared key systems are based on distributing content or tokens using a single key among multiple parties, but not conspicuously distributing the key to them to unlock the content.

It works like this:

1. The server distributes content, encrypted with key k (and a hash checksum for integrity).
2. The client obtains encrypted content and wishes to view it.
3. The client sends his or her *identifier* (such as serial number) to the server.
4. The server computes the client-specific unlock code based on the identifier and issues it to the client.
5. The client decrypts content using a key created by XOR'ing the identifier with the specific unlock code from the server.

Buy-on-Demand Systems

It's much easier to encrypt what needs protecting once and issue each customer a unique serial number. Then to unlock the data, the customer enters his or her number. The unlock code service takes that and computes a special key, which, combined with the serial number, produces the correct key. The process is as follows:

1. Customer's Serial Number (Encoded) CSN
2. Data Encrypted With Key X (and checksum)
3. SN $\oplus$ UC = KEY
4. UC = SN $\oplus$ KEY
5. Send Encoded(A) to the customer

Of course, this system can be broken quickly by examining the code that actually does the unlocking, but that's true of any system that relies on a common key. The hope is that it's sufficiently difficult to "keep honest people honest." Most people won't bother with tracking down unlock codes, especially in a business environment.

To make this system feasible, you'll want to generate serial numbers that are sufficiently large that include significant internal and external check digits. Internal *check bits* are derived from taking part of a MAC. These are used to determine the validity of the token. The external check digit is strictly for detecting quickly whether or not the user made a typo. In addition, you will want to use a unique encoding that prevents obvious visual analysis.

Multiple Key Systems

Of course, the most secure solution would be to deliver to each customer a separate specially built copy using unique keys. Besides giving the release engineer a heart attack, this system is tough to manage. You would need to keep track of a customer's serial number, know the product that was delivered, and be able to regenerate the keys. If you can handle it, this *is* a secure system. The other obvious downside is that if the content is large, creating encrypted copies takes time and is resource-intensive. This makes it difficult to produce large quantities of CDs, for example, since there is master copy. For online delivery, doing this on demand can really slow down the server. To mitigate this, you can have one machine create a pool of encrypted copies, and the service can just pick up copies as needed.

Trials and Expirations

You can use a registration license to implement network and CPU restrictions. In both cases, some type of license server is required. For a CPU restriction, the server must reside locally on the machine, and of course, the network license server is located on the network. The application cannot start if it cannot make contact with the server. At the end of the application, it unregisters itself with the server.

Another technique is to have the application write a unique token based on the user's ID (or name) to a common location. The application can start if the number of tokens present in the current directory is less than the threshold. These tokens can even have an expiration attached to them, so if an application dies, it doesn't indefinitely hold a license. Other tricks involve the application periodically refreshing the token to make sure it doesn't expire or to replace any tokens that might have been mistakenly deleted.

Since these tokens are stored on the filesystem and not desired for public consumption, they don't have to be pretty, but they should only contain characters that are "typeable" and should be of reasonable length.

Decimal and Monetary Computations

Financial computations are in some ways similar to cryptographic operations. Frequently, you must work with low-level bit operations (indirectly), and there are issues of encoding and storage. Also, such issues are not the systems programmers' expertise.

Doubles and Floats

There is a reason COBOL and PureBasic (used in point-of-sale systems) are still around. Very few languages natively and easily handle financial computations in a sane manner. Using the simple example program:

```
public class test {
    public static void main(String args[]) {
      Iint step = 0;
     for (float i = 0; i < 1.0; i += 0.1) {
         System.out.println("Step " + step + ": " +i);
         step++;
     }
    }
}
```

we get the following results:

```
Step 0: 0.0
Step 1: 0.1
Step 2: 0.2
Step 3: 0.3
Step 4: 0.4
Step 5: 0.5
Step 6: 0.6
Step 7: 0.70000005
Step 8: 0.8000001
Step 9: 0.9000001
```

This problem still occurs even if we double precision. In fact, the problem is worse, and the loop even has an extra step:

```
Step 0: 0.0
Step 1: 0.1
Step 2: 0.2
Step 3: 0.30000000000000004
Step 4: 0.4
Step 5: 0.5
Step 6: 0.6
Step 7: 0.7
Step 8: 0.7999999999999999
Step 9: 0.8999999999999999
Step 10: 0.9999999999999999
```

This occurs because powers of 10 can't exactly equal powers of 2, so some truncation and rounding occurs to make a base 10 value fit into a base 2 value (precisely, there are no integers $x, y > 1$ such that $2^x = 10^y$). Over time, these errors add up and can cause strange results. Because of this, the float and double type should *never* be used in monetary computations.

BigDecimal

The `BigDecimal` class offers arbitrary precision decimal arithmetic that solves many of the rounding problems encountered when using machine arithmetic. It's the floating-point equivalent of `BigInteger`, but it has a much more limited set of functions: abs, add, min, max, multiply, negate, and subtract work as you would expect them to. Division is a bit different, since rounding must be involved. For instance 1/3 isn't represented as a fraction, so you must decide how many digits to preserve.

A `BigDecimal` object consists of two parts: an *unscaled* value and a scale. The number has the value $unscaled/10^{\text{scale}}$. Addition and subtraction operations result in a new value that uses the largest scale of the two. For example, a number with a scale of 1 added to another number with a scale of 4 is again, another number with a scale of 4. For example:

```
0.1 + 0.0001 = 0.1001
```

Multiplication results in a new value with a scale being the sum of the type arguments. Again, scale –1 multiplied by a scale –4 results in scale –5:

```
0.1 × 0.0001 = 0.00001
```

Division works a bit differently, since it can result in a *repeating decimal* value such as 1/3 = 0.333333. . . . Because of this, the `division` method requires an argument to set a scale value and a rounding mode to chop off the result at a certain precision.

A number can be "rescaled" by calling the `setScale` method. This also can take a rounding mode when precision is being lost.

Construction is done by passing in a string representation of the number. The number's scale is the number of digits or precision to the right of the decimal point. Printing `BigDecimal` types is done with the `toString` method. It will always print exactly *scale* number of digits after the decimal point. For money computations, you'll want to scale down the value.

The key to accurate financial computations is to *never* use the `double` type. Any numeric type that might need to be used should be stored and retrieved as a *string* so it can be fed back into a `BigDecimal` type with no loss of precision.

Rounding

`BigDecimal` has eight different rounding modes, as described in Table 7.5, but by default, you'll just want to use `ROUND_HALF_EVEN`. It has good statistical properties and is used in most financial computations. It is also known as "banker's rounding" or "unbiased rounding." Other types include:

- `ROUND_UNNECCESSARY`. This enforces that the computation doesn't need rounding and that the computation is exact. If rounding does need to occur, an `ArthimeticException` is thrown.
- `ROUND_DOWN`. This truncation is mostly used for converting decimal values into integer types.
- `ROUND_CEILING` and `ROUND_FLOOR`. These can be used for interval computations, when you're not concerned so much with an exact answer, but that it lies in a certain interval.

- ROUND_UP, ROUND_HALF_UP, ROUND_HALF_DOWN. These are commonly used when you are working with existing or legacy systems, such as accounting packages, cash registers, and point-of-sale systems.

BigDecimal and Mathematics

The BigDecimal class has proven to be controversial, since it has a limited selection of mathematical functions and in practice it's a bit clumsy to use. Even relatively common financial values, such as mortgage payments that require exponents and logarithms, cannot easily be computed with the stock implementation. There is also a complete lack of formatting methods. IBM has been actively working to get BigDecimal overhauled as part of JSR 13 (www.jcp.org/jsr/detail/13.jsp), but as of Java 1.4, it still looks a long way off. However, you don't have to wait for Sun to fix BigDecimal. It's standard on IBM's JVM and is available at www2.hursley.ibm.com/decimalj.

Table 7.5 Rounding Modes for BigDecimal

ROUNDING TYPE	DESCRIPTION
ROUND_CEILING	Rounding mode to round toward positive infinity; positive numbers are rounded up, while negative numbers involve truncation.
ROUND_DOWN	Round toward zero. This is truncation for both positive and negative numbers.
ROUND_FLOOR	Round toward negative infinity. Negative numbers are round down, while positive numbers involve truncation.
ROUND_HALF_DOWN	Round toward nearest neighbor unless both neighbors are equidistant, then ROUND_DOWN.
ROUND_HALF_EVEN	Round toward nearest neighbor unless both neighbors are equidistant, in which case, round toward the even neighbor.
ROUND_HALF_UP	Round toward nearest neighbor unless both neighbors are equidistant, in which case, ROUND_UP.
ROUND_UNNECESSARY	Assert that the requested operation has an exact result; hence, no rounding is necessary.
ROUND_UP	Round away from zero.

BigDecimal Alternatives and Wrappers

For applications that have limited memory or applications that are very high speed, you can implement an alternative of `BigDecimal` using native integers. Our preceding example programs could be reimplemented as:

```
public class test {
    public static void main(String[] args) {
     for (int i = 0; i == 100; i += 10) {
          String s = Integer.toString(i)
          System.out.println(s.substring(0,2) + "." + s.substring(3,2));
      }
    }
}
```

In practice, you'll want to use many more digits than just two. The native `long` type can hold approximately 18 decimal digits, which can be portioned out as needed.

A completely opposite approach is using a commercial wrapper around the `BigDecimal` class specifically for monetary computations. The most notable is `Money` and related classes from RogueWave (`www.roguewave.com/`), which makes common operations much more convenient and can handle such things as formatting and currency conversion. By default, they use a scale of 16 for monetary computations.

Usage and Storage

To key to using `BigDecimal` (or equivalents) successfully is to always store and retrieve decimal numbers as strings and never use the `double` type for intermediate steps.

Most databases have a `NUMERIC` or similar type that allows you to store decimal values with a fixed, but arbitrary, precision. Frequently, there is also a `MONEY` type that can be useful, but typically only has four decimal places of precision. That is just fine for final results, but it isn't enough for intermediate results.

Java Cryptography Class Reference

This class reference covers every class from the following:

- java.security
- java.security.interfaces
- java.security.cert
- java.security.spec
- javax.crypto
- javax.crypto.interfaces
- javax.crypto.spec

In addition, a few classes that are commonly used in cryptographic applications are from:

- java.lang
- java.math
- java.util
- java.security.cert

The classes are listed alphabetically by class name, ignoring the package name (e.g., `Cipher`, not `javax.crypto.Cipher`). Within each class section, the method and fields are organized in the following order:

1. Constants or "public static type" constants.
2. Static methods.
3. Constructors.
4. Instance or concrete methods.
5. Abstract methods.

AlgorithmParameterGenerator (java.security)

This engine class is for generating appropriate parameters for use in `Cipher`, `Signature`, and `KeyAgreement` classes. Primary uses for this class are for generating common parameters for the Diffie-Hellman key agreement and other discrete logarithm-based cryptosystems. To use, first create an instance using the standard `getInstance` methods. Initialize using either a generic "size in bits" value or with the specific `AlgorithmParameterSpec` object. Then send a call to `generateParameters`, which will return the `AlgorithmParameter` instance. The result is useful for storage, but for use in a cryptographic algorithm, the object needs to be converted into `AlgorithmParameterSpec` for subsequent use in the API with a call to `getParameterSpec`.

The SUN and SunJCE providers implement a DSA and DiffieHellmen generator, respectively.

```
package java.security;
public class AlgorithmParameterGenerator
{
    // Static Methods
    public static AlgorithmParameterGenerator getInstance(String alg)
           throws NoSuchAlgorithmException;
    public static AlgorithmParameterGenerator getInstance(String algorithm,
           String provider) throws NoSuchAlgorithmException,
           NoSuchProviderException;
    public static AlgorithmParameterGenerator getInstance(String algorithm,
           Provider p) throws NoSuchAlgorithmException;
    public final AlgorithmParameters generateParameters();

    // Instance Methods
    public final AlgorithmParameters generateParameters();
    public final String getAlgorithm();
    public final Provider getProvider();
    public final void init(int size);
    public final void init(AlgorithmParameterSpec genParamSpec) throws
           InvalidAlgorithmParameterException;
    public final void init(int size, SecureRandom rand);
    public final void init(AlgorithmParameterSpec genParamSpec,
           SecureRandom rand) throws
           InvalidAlgorithmParameterException;
}
```

AlgorithmParameterGeneratorSpi (java.security)

This abstract class is for provider authors who must create a concrete instance of this class for use by `AlgorithmParameterGenerator`. End users and applications never need to use this class.

```
package java.security;
public abstract class AlgorithmParameterGeneratorSpi
{
    // Constructors
    public AlgorithmParameterGeneratorSpi();

    // Abstract Methods
    protected abstract AlgorithmParameters engineGenerateParameters();
    protected abstract void engineInit(int size, SecureRandom rand);
    protected abstract void engineInit(AlgorithmParameterSpec genParamSpec,
          SecureRandom rand) throws InvalidAlgorithmParameterException;
}
```

AlgorithmParameters (java.security)

This engine class is used to convert `AlgorithmParameterSpec` objects into an encoded representation for storage or transmission. The conversion algorithm name (normally similar to the underlying cryptographic algorithm the parameters are used for) is passed into the `getInstance` method. Converting a `Spec` object into bytes is done by calling `init` with the `Spec` object followed by `getEncoded`. Converting bytes back into a `Spec` is done by calling `init` with the encoded bytes, followed by `get- ParameterSpec` with the appropriate class object.

```
package java.security;
public class AlgorithmParameters
{
     // Constructors
     protected AlgorithmParameters(AlgorithmParametersSpi paramSpi,
     Provider p, String algorithm);

     // Static Methods
     static AlgorithmParameters getInstance(String algorithm)
           throws NoSuchAlgorithmException;
     static AlgorithmParameters getInstance(String algorithm,
           String provider) throws NoSuchAlgorithmException,
           NoSuchProviderException;
     static AlgorithmParameters getInstance(String algorithm, Provider p)
           throws NoSuchAlgorithmException;

     // Instance Methods
     final String getAlgorithm();
     final byte[] getEncoded() throws IOException;
     final byte[] getEncoded(String format) throws IOException;
```

```
    final AlgorithmParameterSpec getParameterSpec(Class paramSpec)
        throws InvalidParameterSpecException;
    final Provider getProvider();
    final void init(AlgorithmParameterSpec paramSpec)
        throws InvalidParameterSpecException;
    final void init(byte[] params) throws IOException;
    final void init(byte[] params, String format) throws IOException;
    final String toString();
}
```

AlgorithmParameterSpec (java.security.spec)

Objects that implement this empty interface contain representations of parameters used in cryptographic algorithms.

```
package java.security.spec;
public interface AlgorithmParameterSpec
{
    // Implemented By: DHGenParameterSpec, DHParameterSpec,
    //                 DSAParameterSpec, IvParameterSpec,
    //                 PBEParameterSpec, PSSParameterSpec,
    //                 RC2ParameterSpec, RC5ParameterSpec,
    //                 RSAKeyGenParameterSpec

}
```

AlgorithmParameterSpi (java.security)

This is the internal API used by provider authors to implement a digital signature algorithm that works with the `AlgorithmParameters` engine class. End users and applications never need to use this class.

```
package java.security;
public abstract class AlgorithmParametersSpi
{
    // Constructors
    public AlgorithmParametersSpi();

    // Abstract Methods
    protected abstract byte[] engineGetEncoded() throws IOException;
    protected abstract byte[] engineGetEncoded(String format)
        throws IOException;
    protected abstract AlgorithmParameterSpec engineGetParameterSpec
        (Class paramSpec) throws InvalidParameterSpecException;
    protected abstract void engineInit(AlgorithmParameterSpec paramSpec)
        throws InvalidParameterSpecException;
    protected abstract void engineInit(byte[] params) throws IOException;
    protected abstract void engineInit(byte[] params, String format)
        throws IOException;
    protected abstract String engineToString();
}
```

BadPaddingException (javax.crypto)

This exception is only thrown by the `Cipher.doFinal` method during decryption if the underlying data is improperly padded or malformed.

```
public class BadPaddingException extends GeneralSecurityException
{
     // Hierarchy :  GeneralSecurityException, Exception, Throwable
     // Implements:  Serializable
     // Thrown By :  Cipher.doFinal, CipherSpi.doFinal
     //              SealedObject.getObject

     // Constructors
     public BadPaddingException();
     public BadPaddingException(String msg);
}
```

BigDecimal (java.math)

`BigDecimal` implements arbitrary precision floating-point arithmetic. Objects can be created by passing in a string representation of a floating-point number or by using a native type (although this is not recommended). A number is represented internally using an unscaled value and a scale representing the number $unscaled \times 10^{scale}$. Addition and subtraction produce a new `BigDecimal` with a scale the larger of the two arguments. Multiplication of two numbers produces a new `BigDecimal` with a scale set to the product of the two scale values. Since division may not have a finite representation, you must specifically set a scale (precision) value and a rounding mode, normally with `ROUND_HALF_EVEN`. A number can be rescaled and rerounded at any time with a call to `setScale`. The `toString` method produces a string representation of the number with *scale* decimal numbers after the decimal point, as well as with trailing zeros added if needed. Only simple arithmetic functions are provided in the core API, but for more advanced versions, see an alternative version from IBM (www.alphaworks.ibm.com/tech/bigdecimal).

```
package java.math;
public class BigDecimal extends Number implements Comparable
{
     // Implements: Serializable, Comparable

     // Constants
     public static final ROUND_CEILING
     public static final ROUND_DOWN;
     public static final ROUND_FLOOR;
     public static final ROUND_HALF_DOWN
     public static final ROUND_HALF_EVEN
     public static final ROUND_HALF_UP
     public static final ROUND_UNNECESSARY
     public static final ROUND_UP;

     // Static Methods
     public static BigDecimal valueOf(long val);
     public static BigDecimal valueOf(long unscaledVal, int scale);
```

```
    // Constructors
    public BigDecimal(BigInteger val);
    public BigDecimal(String val);
    public BigDecimal(double val);
    public BigDecimal(BigInteger unscaledval, int scale)

    // Instance Methods
    public BigDecimal abs();
    public BigDecimal add(BigDecimal val);
    public int compareTo(BigDecimal val);
    public BigDecimal divide(BigDecimal val, int roundingMode);
    public BigDecimal divide(BigDecimal val, int scale, int roundingMode)
    public BigDecimal max(BigDecimal val);
    public BigDecimal min(BigDecimal val);
    public BigDecimal movePointLeft(int n)
    public BigDecimal movePointRight(int n)
    public BigDecimal multiply(BigDecimal val);
    public BigDecimal negate();
    public int scale()
    public BigDecimal setScale(int scale)
    public BigDecimal setScale(int scale, int roundingMode)
    public int signum();
    public BigDecimal subtract(BigDecimal val)
    public BigInteger toBigInteger()
    public BigInteger unscaledValue()
}
```

BigInteger (java.math)

The BigInteger class supports arbitrary large integers and basic operations on them. An instance can be created by using a string representation of an integer (in any base), a native type, or from an array of bytes. The `toByteArray` method returns a *signed* representation of the number, where the leading (most-significant) bit is 0 if the number is positive, or 1 if the value is negative. This has the consequence that if the number of bits is a multiple of 8, the array will have an extra byte that only contains the sign bit. This signed array can be used to construct another `BigInteger`, but for other applications, this extra byte will have to be removed or ignored. An unsigned `byte` array can be used to create a `BigIntger` by passing in a sign value, 1, 0, –1 for positive, zero, or negative values, along with the raw bytes. Random number, random prime, and primality testing are supported. The static method `probablePrime` will generate an integer where the probability of being prime is $1 - 2^{-100}$. Another constructor allows you to specify the certainly value, and the instance method `isProbablyPrime` can test an existing value, also with a user-specified certainly value of $1 - 2^n$ (*n* should be 100 in virtually all applications).

```
package java.math;
public class BigInteger extends Number implements Comparable
{
    // Implements: Comparable, Serializable

    // Constants
    public static final BigInteger ONE;
    public static final BigInteger ZERO;
```

```
    // Static Methods
    public static BigInteger valueOf(long val);
    public static BigInteger probablePrime(int bitLength, Random r);

    // Constructors
    public BigInteger(String val);
    public BigInteger(byte[] val); // requires sign bit
    public BigInteger(String val, int radix);
    public BigInteger(int signum, byte[] magnitude); // unsigned
    public BigInteger(int numBits, Random rand); // random number
    public BigInteger(int bitLength, int certainty, Random r);

    // Instance Methods
    public BigInteger abs();
    public BigInteger add(BigInteger val);
    public BigInteger and(BigInteger val);
    public BigIntger andNot(BigIntger val);
    public int bitCount(); // for postive values, this hamming weight
    public int bitLength(); // minimal number of bits representation
    public BigInteger clearBit();
    public int compareTo(BigInteger val)
    public int compareTo(Object val)
    public BigInteger divide(BigInteger val);
    public BigInteger[] divideAndRemainder(BigInteger val);
    public boolean equals(Object o)
    public BigInteger flipBit(int n)
    public BigInteger gcd(BigInteger val);  // GCD(abs(this), abs(val))
    public int getLowestBitSet(); // index of first 1 bit.
    public boolean isProbablePrime(int certainty);
    public long longValue();
    public BigInteger max(BigInteger val);
    public BigInteger min(BigInteger val);
    public BigIntger mod(BigInteger n);  // (this mod n)
    public BigInteger modInverse(BigInteger n); // (this^-1 mod n)
    public BigInteger modPow(BigInteger exp, BigInteger n); (this^exp mod n)
    public BigInteger multiply(BigInteger val);
    public BigInteger negate();
    public BigInteger not();
    public BigInteger or(BigInteger val);
    public BigInteger pow(int exponent);
    public BigInteger remainder(BigInteger val);
    public BigInteger setBit(int n);
    public BigInteger shiftLeft(int n);
    public BigInteger shiftRight(int n);
    public int signum();
    public BigInteger subtract(BigInteger val);
    public boolean testBit(int n)
    public byte[] toByteArray();
    public String toString();
    public String toString(int radix);
    public BigInteger xor(BigInteger val);
}
```

CertificateFactory (java.security.cert)

This class is used to generate certificates, certificate revocation lists (CRLs), and certificate paths/chains from a stream. The `getInstance` methods take the name of the certificate format most commonly using the standard name of X.509. These certificates should be in a DER encoding using either raw bytes or with base-64 encoding, along with the standard certificate headers and footers. After a certificate is read, the result from `generateCertificate` will be a `X509Certificate` object. If a stream contains multiple certificates, you can either read all of the certificates at once using a `generate-Certificates` (plural) call. In either case, the entire input stream will be consumed reading the first certificate unless the input stream supports the mark and reset methods (such as `BufferedInputStream`). The situation is the same when reading CRLs. For details regarding CertPaths, see the Java Certification Path API Programmer's Guide, included with the SDK documentation.

```
package java.security.cert;
public class CertificateFactory
{
    // Static Methods
    static final CertificateFactory getInstance(String type)
          throws CertificateException;
    static final CertificateFactory getInstance(String type, Provider p)
          throws CertificateException, IllegalArgumentException;
    static final CertificateFactory getInstance(String type,
          String provider) throws CertificateException,
          NoSuchProviderException;

    // Instance Methods
    public final Certificate generateCertificate(InputStream is)
          throws CertificateException;
    public final Collection generateCertificates(InputStream is)
          throws CertificateException;
    public final CertPath generateCertPath(InputStream is)
          throws CertificateException;
    public final CertPath generateCertPath(InputStream is,
          String encoding) throws CertificateException;
    public final CertPath generateCertPath(List certificates)
          throws CertificateException;
    public final CRL generateCRL(InputStream is) throws CRLException;
    public final Collection generateCRLs(InputStream is)
          throws CRLException;
    public final Iterator getCertParthEncodings();
    public final Provider getProvider();
    public final String getType();
}
```

Cipher (javax.crypto)

At the core of the cryptography API is the `Cipher` class, which provides encryption and decryption services. Like all other engine classes, the `Cipher` object can only be created with a call to `Cipher.getInstance` using a transformation string and a provider. The transformation can be in one of two formats: *algorithm/mode/padding* or just a single word with no slashes *transformation.*

The JCA/JCE specifies standard names that should be portable between different providers, although there is no requirement that the provider actually implement all of the algorithms. The transformation strings are case-insensitive.

Block ciphers, shown in Table A.1, are composed using the algorithm/ mode/padding. Those names followed by an asterisk in the table are implemented in the stock SunJCE provider.

Support for password-based encryption is specified using `PBEWith`*`Hash`*`And`*`Cipher`*. The SunJCE provider implements two versions: `PBEWithMD5AndDES` and `PBEWithHmac-SHA1AndDESede`. Both imply a mode of CBC and padding of PKCS5Padding and cannot be overridden. For stream ciphers the only standard name is RC4, but Sun does not provide an implementation.

After creation, the `Cipher` must be initialized to do either encryption or decryption by passing in `ENCRYPT_MODE` or `DECRYPT_MODE` as the first argument to `init`. In addition to the mode, the `Cipher` object must be initialized with a key and optionally a source of randomness via a `SecureRandom` instance. Depending on the algorithm, an `AlgorithmParameter` or `AlgorithmParameterSpec` object may also need to be part of the initialization step. Frequently, the appropriate `Spec` object will contain a field for an initialization vector. If no such field or `Spec` class exists, an initialization vector can be specified using a generic `IVParameterSpec` object; otherwise, one will be generated randomly and be retrieved with a call to `getIV`.

Input data, for any mode, is fed into the `Cipher` object using one of the many varieties of the `update` method, and it may return output bytes. When all data is submitted, `doFinal` returns the final `byte` array. You can check the length of a result in advance with a call to `getOutputLength`.

Starting in Java 1.4, the `Cipher` class also provides a means for *key wrapping*, or encrypting a key using another key. For wrapping, you initialize a `Cipher` object using the mode of `WRAP_MODE` along with the key and algorithm desired for encryption, followed by a call to `wrap` with the `Key`. The result is a `byte` array containing the wrapped key. To unwrap, you similarly initialize a `Cipher` object using `UNWRAP_MODE`. This passes into the unwrap method the wrapped key bytes, the algorithm the original key is used with, along with a key type of `SECRET_KEY`, `PUBLIC_KEY`, or `PRIVATE_KEY`. The result is the appropriate `Key` object containing the original key.

Table A.1 Block Ciphers

CIPHER	MODE	PADDING
AES	None*	NoPadding*
Blowfish*	ECB*	PKCS5Padding*
DES*	CBC*	SSL3Padding
Triple DES*	CFB*or CFB*n**	OAEPWith*Hash*And*MGF*Padding
RC2, RC5	OFB* or OFB*n**	
RSA	PCBC*	

*implemented in the stock SunSCE provider

```
package javax.crypto;
public class Cipher
{
     // Constants
     public static final int DECRYPT_MODE;
     public static final int ENCRYPT_MODE;
     public static final int PRIVATE_KEY;
     public static final int PUBLIC_KEY;
     public static final int SECRET_KEY;
     public static final int UNWRAP_MODE;
     public static final int WRAP_MODE;

     // Static Methods
     public static final Cipher getInstance(String transformation)
           throws NoSuchAlgorithm, NoSuchPaddingException;
     public static final Cipher getInstance(String transformation,
           Provider p) throws NoSuchAlgorithm, NoSuchPaddingException,
           NoSuchProviderException;

     // Instance Methods
     public final String getAlgorithm();
     public final int getBlockSize();
     public final byte[] getIV();
     public final AlgorithmParameter getParameters();
     public final Provider getProvider();
     public final byte[] doFinal() throws IllegalStateException,
           IllegalBlockSizeException, BadPaddingException
     public final byte[] doFinal(byte[] input)
           throws IllegalStateException, IllegalBlockSizeException,
           BadPaddingException
     public final int doFinal(byte[] output, int outputOffset)
           throws IllegalStateException, IllegalBlockSizeException,
           BadPaddingException
     public final byte[] doFinal(byte[] input, int inputOffset,
           int inputLen) throws IllegalStateException,
           IllegalBlockSizeException, BadPaddingException
     public final int doFinal(byte[] input, int inputOffset, int inputLen,
           byte[] output) throws IllegalStateException,
           IllegalBlockSizeException, BadPaddingException
     public final int doFinal(byte[] input, int inputOffset, int inputLen,
           byte[] output, int outputOffset) throws IllegalStateException,
           ShortBufferException, IllegalBlockSizeException
     public final ExemptionMechanism getExemptionMechanism()
     public final int getOutputSize(int inputLen)
           throws IllegalStateException;
     public final void init(int opmode, Key key) throws InvalidKeyException;
     public final void init(int opmode, Key key, SecureRandom rand)
           throws InvalidKeyException
     public final void init(int opmode, Key key, AlgorithmParameter params)
           throws InvalidKeyException, InvalidParameterException;
     public final void init(int opmode, Key key, AlgorithmParameter params,
           SecureRandom rand) throws InvalidKeyException,
           InvalidParameterException;
     public final void init(int opmode, Key key, AlgorithmParameterSpec
           spec, SecureRandom rand) throws InvalidKeyException,
           InvalidParameterException;
     public final byte[] update(byte[] input) throws IllegalStateException;
```

```
    public final byte[] update(byte[] input, int inputOffset,
          int inputLen) throws IllegalStateException;
    public final int update(byte[] input, int inputOffset, int inputLen,
          byte[] output) throws IllegalStateException,
          ShortBufferException
    public final int update(byte[] input, int inputOffset, int inputLen,
          byte[] output, int outputOffset) throws IllegalStateException,
          ShortBufferException;
    public byte[] wrap(Key key);
    public Key unwrap(byte[] wrappedKey, String algorithm,
          int wrappedKeyType)
}
```

CipherInputStream (javax.crypto)

`CipherInputStream` provides a transparent means of automatically encrypting or decrypting an input stream. To create, you pass in the `InputStream` to parse, along with a fully configured `Cipher` object. After that the object behaves similarly to a normal `FilterInputStream` object. If the underlying cipher is a *block* cipher, be sure to close the stream when finished to make sure whatever padding is used is handled promptly by the `Cipher` object.

```
package javax.crypto;
public class CipherInputStream extends java.io.FilterInputStream
{
    // Ancestry: FilterInputStream, InputStream

    // Constructors
    public CipherInputStream(InputStream is, Cipher c);
    protected CipherInputStream(InputStream is);

    // Instance Methods
    public int available() throws IOException
    public void close() throws IOException;
    public boolean markSupported()
    public int read() throws IOException
    public int read(byte[] b) throws IOException
    public int read(byte[] b, int offset, int length) throws IOException
    public long skip(long n) throws IOException
}
```

CipherOutputStream (javax.crypto)

This class provides a transparent means of writing an output stream that is automatically encrypted or decrypted. To create, you pass in the `OutputStream` and a fully configured output stream. After that the object behaves similarly to a `FilterOutputStream` object. If a block cipher is being used, do not use the `flush` method, since it will prematurely pad and corrupt the output stream. In addition, be sure to explicitly close the stream when finished to force any final padding to be written.

```
package javax.crypto;
public class CipherOutputStream extends java.io.FilterOutputStream
{
     // Ancestry: FilterOutputStream, OutputStream

     // Constructors
     public CipherOutputStream(OutputStream os, Cipher c);
     protected CipherOutputStream(OutputStream os);

     // Instance Methods
     public void close() throws IOException
     public void flush() throws IOException
     public void write(byte[] b) throws IOException;
     public void write(byte[] b, int offset, int length) throws IOException
     public void write(int b) throws IOException
}
```

CipherSpi (javax.crypto)

This class provides a service provider interface. For end users and applications this class is never directly used; instead, they use the `Cipher` class. For providers wishing to implement a transformation, a concrete class must implement each of the interfaces that follow. Unlike other factory classes, ciphers are parameterized using *algorithm/mode/padding* or a single transformation (either default values for mode and padding are provided or they do not apply). A provider has the option of providing separate classes for each combination of *algorithm/mode/padding* or can provide generic *algorithm//, algorithm/mode/,* and *algorithm//* classes. In the latter cases, the mode and padding are set by `engineSetMode` and `engineSetPadding`. It is then up to the class to call upon its own generic mode and padding functionality. When the `Cipher` object's `getInstance` method is called with *algorithm/mode/padding*, the factory checks registration in the following order:

1. algorithm/mode/padding
2. algorithm/mode
3. algorithm//padding
4. algorithm

If the `getInstance` method was called with just *algorithm* (no slashes), then an exact match is checked for and no additional checking for modes or padding is done. If no provider was specified, the next provider (if any) will be searched. If no match is found, `NoSuchAlgorithmException` is thrown.

```
package javax.crypto;
public abstract class CipherSpi
{

     // Constructors
     public CipherSpi();

     // Abstract Methods
     protected abstract byte[] engineDoFinal(byte[] input, int inputOffset,
           int inputLen) throws IllegalBlockSizeException,
           BadPaddingException;
```

```
    protected abstract byte[] engineDoFinal(byte[] input, int inputOffset,
          int inputLen, byte[] output, int outputOffset) throws
          IllegalBlockSizeException, BadPaddingException,
          ShortBufferException;
    protected abstract int engineGetBlockSize();
    protected abstract byte[] engineGetIV();
    protected abstract int engineGetOutputSize(int inputLen);
    protected abstract AlgorithmParameter engineGetParameters();
    protected abstract void engineInit(int opmode, Key key,
          SecureRandom rand) throws InvalidKeyException;
    protected abstract void engineInit(int opmode, Key key,
          AlgorithmParameterSpec spec, SecureRandom rand)
          throws InvalidKeyException, InvalidAlgorithmParamterException;
    protected abstract void engineSetMode(String mode)
          throws NoSuchAlgorithmException;
    protected abstract void engineSetPadding(String padding)
          throws NoSuchPaddingException;
    protected abstract byte[] engineUpdate(byte[] input, int inputOffset,
          int inputLen);
    protected abstrct int engineUpdate(byte[] input, int inputOffset,
          int inputLen, byte[] output, int outputOffset)
          throws ShortBufferException;
}
```

Collections (java.util)

This class has a variety of static functions for manipulating `Collection` types such as lists and sets. Of particular note is the `shuffle` method. Unfortunately, it only works on `List` types and there is no efficient way of converting a native array (e.g., `int[]`) into a `List`. In this case, you must use custom code similar to the following routine:

```
int a[] = ...;                // array to shuffle
java.util.Random r = ...;     // random source
for (int i = a.length; i >= 1; --i)  {
     int j = r.nextInt(i);
     // swap a[i] and a[j]
     int tmp = a[i]; a[i] = a[j]; a[j] = tmp;
}
```

```
package java.util;
public class Collections
{
     // Static Methods
     public static void shuffle(java.util.List list);
     public static void shuffle(java.util.List list, Random rand);
     /*... and many others */
}
```

DESedeKeySpec (javax.crypto.spec)

This class provides a transparent representation of a three-key 168-bit DES-EDE (Triple DES) key. The constructors assume the key is 24 bytes (three 64-bit DES keys). This class also provides a static method, `isParityAdjusted`, to test if a key is 24 bytes and is parity-adjusted (each byte has an odd number of one-bits). To use this class for encryption, it must be converted to a `Key` representation. The easiest way is using `new SecretKeySpec(tdeskey.getKey())`, although you could also use `SecretKeyFactory`.

```
package javax.crypto.spec
public class DESedeKeySpec implements KeySpec
{

     // Constants
     public static int DES_EDE_KEY_LEN; // in bytes

     // Static Methods
     public static boolean isParityAdjusted(byte[] key, int offset);

     // Constructors
     public DESedeKeySpec(byte[] key) throws InvalidKeyException
     public DESedeKeySpec(byte[] key, int offset) throws InvalidKeyException

     // Instance Methods
     public byte[] getKey();
}
```

DESKeySpec (javax.crypto.spec)

This class provides a transparent representation of the DES key. Both constructors assume a DES key is 8 bytes (64-bits) and tests to make sure the key is not weak and has proper parity (each byte has an odd number of one-bits). If not, an `InvalidKeyException` is thrown. These tests are also implemented as static methods, `isParityAdjusted` and `isWeak`. To use this class for encryption, you must convert it to a `Key` representation. The easiest way is using `new SecretKeySpec(deskey.getKey())`, although you could also use `SecretKeyFactory`.

```
package javax.crypto.spec;
public class DESKeySpec implements KeySpec
{
     // Constants
     public static int DES_KEY_LEN; // in bytes

     // Instance Methods
     public static boolean isParityAdjusted(byte[] key, int offset)
     public static boolean isWeak(byte[] key, int offset)


     // Constructors
     public DESKeySpec(byte[] key) throws InvalidKeyException
     public DESKeySpec(byte[] key, int offset) throws InvalidKeyException

     // Instance Methods
     public byte[] getKey();
}
```

DHGenParameterSpec (javax.crypto.spec)

This class is used to create common domain parameters for use in the Diffie-Hellman Key Exchange Protocol (as defined in the PKCS #3), using `AlgorithmParameterGenerator`. The resulting `AlgorithmParameters` object can be used in the `KeyAgreement` class with an algorithm name of "DiffieHellman." Normally these parameters are generated once by a certain authority and distributed by interested parties. The parameters themselves can be reused and do not need to be kept secret.

```
to create parameters or a DHParameterSpec object for use in the
package javax.crypto.spec;
public class DHGenParameterSpec implements AlgorithmParameterSpec
{
     // Constructors
     public DHGenParameterSpec(int primeSizeBits, int expononetSizeBits);

     // Instance Methods
     public int getExponentSize();
     public int getPrimeSize();
}
```

DHParameterSpec (javax.crypto.spec)

This `AlgorithmParameterSpec` object defines the parameters used in the Diffie-Hellman key exchange protocol as defined in the PKCS #3 standard. The number of bits for the private value may optionally be specified; otherwise, the provider will use a default value of its own choosing.

```
package javax.crypto.spec;
public class DHParameterSpec implements AlgorithmParameterSpec {

     // Constructors
     public DHParameterSpec(BigInteger p, BigInteger g);
     public DHParameterSpec(BigInteger p, BigInteger g, int l);

     // Instance Methods
     public BigInteger getG(); // base generator
     public BigInteger getP(); // prime modulus
     public int getL();        // number of bits for private value
}
```

DHKey (javax.crypto.interfaces)

An object implementing this interface is a provider-based key used in the Diffie-Hellman Key Exchange Protocol. The interface also provides a standard way of accessing the common parameters used in the key exchange.

```
public interface DHKey
{
     // Implementors: DHPublicKey, DHPrivateKey

     DHParameterSpec getParams();
}
```

DHPrivateKey (javax.crypto.interfaces)

This interface provides access to the public key components of a provider-based key used in the Diffie-Hellman Key Exchange Protocol.

```
public interface DHPrivateKey extends DHKey, PrivateKey
{
     // Implements: DHKey, Key, PrivateKey, Serializable

     BigInteger getX() ; // private value;
     DHParameterSpec getParams(); // from DHKey
}
```

DHPrivateKeySpec (javax.crypto.spec)

This is a transparent or concrete implementation of a private key used in the Diffie-Hellman key agreement. To use this is in the `KeyAgreement` class, you need to convert this object into a `Key` object by using `KeyFactory`. The primary use of this object is directly creating a key manually or importing a key from legacy or encoded source, instead of dynamically generating keys with `KeyPairGenerator.getInstance("DH");`.

```
package javax.crypto.spec;
public class DHPrivateKeySpec implements KeySpec
{
     // Constructors
     public DHPrivateKeySpec(BigInteger x, BigInteger p, BigInteger g);

     // Instance Methods
     public BigInteger getG(); // base generator
     public BigInteger getP(); // prime modulus
     public BigInteger getX(); // private value
}
```

DHPublicKey (javax.crypto.interfaces)

This interface provides access to the public key components of a provider-based key used in the Diffie-Hellman Key Exchange Protocol.

```
public interface DHPublicKey extends DHKey, PublicKey
{
```

```
    // Implements: DHKey, Key, PublicKey, Serializable

    BigInteger getY() ; // public value;
    DHParameterSpec getParams(); // from DHKey
}
```

DHPublicKeySpec (javax.crypto.spec)

This is a transparent or concrete implementation of a public key used in the Diffie-Hellman key agreement. To use this in the `KeyAgreement` class, you need to convert this object into a `Key` object by using `KeyFactory`. The primary use of this object is directly creating a key manually, or importing a key from legacy or encoded source, instead of dynamically generating keys with `KeyPairGenerator.getInstance("DH");`.

```
package javax.crypto.spec;
public class DHPublicKeySpec implements KeySpec
{
    // Constructors
    public DHPublicKeySpec(BigInteger y, BigInteger p, BigInteger g)

    // Instance Methods
    public BigInteger getG(); // base generator
    public BigInteger getP(); // prime modulus
    public BigInteger getY(); // public value
}
```

DigestException (java.security)

While the Sun documentation states this is a "generic message digest exception," in practice this is only thrown by one method for one reason: when `MessageDigest.doFinal` receives an array that is too small to hold the digest results. In practice this is equivalent to the `ShortBufferException`.

```
package java.security;
public class DigestException extends GeneralSecurityException
{
    // Hierachy   : GeneralSecurityException, Exception, Throwable
    // Implements: Serializable
    // Thrown By  : MessageDigest.digest, MessageDigestSpi.digest

    public DigestException();
    public DigestException(String mesg);
}
```

DigestInputStream (java.security)

This provides automatic digesting of an input stream as bytes are read. You create this by passing in an `InputStream` to process, along with a fully initialized `MessageDigest` object. You can selectively turn digesting on or off by setting the on method appropriately. This may be useful for skipping header or trailers in files.

```
package java.security;
public class DigestInputStream extends FilterInputStream
{
     // Ancestry: FilterInputStream, InputStream

     // Constructors
     public DigestInputStream(InputStream is, MessageDigest digest);

     // Instance Methods
     public MessageDigest getMessageDigest();
     public void on(boolean on);
     public int read() throws IOException;
     public int read(byte[] b, int off, int length) throws IOException;
     public void setMessageDigest(MessageDigest digest);
     public String toString();
}
```

DigestOuputStream (java.security)

This class automatically computes a message digest as bytes are written to an `OutputStream`. To create, you pass in the output stream and a fully constructed `MessageDigest` object. You can selectively turn digesting on or off by setting the on method appropriately. This may be useful for skipping header or trailers in files.

```
package java.security;
public class DigestOutputStream extends FilterOutputStream
{
     // Ancestry: FilterOutputStream, OutputStream

     // Constructors
     public DigestOutputStream(OutputStream os, MessageDigest digest);

     // Instance Methods
     public MessageDigest getMessageDigest();
     public void on(boolean on);
     public void setMessageDigest(MessageDigest digest);
     public String toString();
     public void write(int b) throws IOException;
     public void write(byte[] b, int off, int length) throws IOException;
}
```

Double (java.lang)

This provides an object wrapper around a native `double` type. This is most useful for passing double into `java.util` collections or other APIs that require an `Object`. The methods `doubleToLongBits` and `doubleToRawLongBits` both convert the double into a 64-bit integer, preserving the double's internal structure. The difference between the two versions is the former represents NaN (not a number) by a single value, while the later version doesn't do any sanitizing and returns any numeric data that may be present. The method `isNaN` is the only way to test a native double for NaN. Using the == operator with a NaN double is always false.

```
package java.lang;
public class Double extends Numeric implements Comparable
{
     // Implements: Serializable, Comparable

     // Constants
     public static final double MAX_VALUE;
     public static final double MIN_VALUE;
     public static final double NaN;
     public static final double NEGATIVE_INFINITY;
     public static final double POSITIVE_INFINITY;

     // Static Methods
     public static final double isInfinite(double val)
     public static final boolean isNan(double val)
     public static long doubleToLongBits(double val);
     public sttaic long doubleToRawLongBits(double val);
     public static double longBitsToDouble(long val);
     // more...
}
```

DSAKey (java.security.interfaces)

An object implementing this interface is a provider-based key used in the Digital Signature Algorithm (DSA). The interface also provides a standard way of accessing the common parameters used in the signature algorithm.

```
package java.security.interfaces;
public abstract interface DSAKey
{
     // Subinterfaces: DSAPrivateKey, DSAPublicKey

     public DSAParams getParams();
}
```

DSAKeyPairGenerator (java.security.interfaces)

This provides an interface for generating DSA key pairs. This provides a means of generating key pairs without using an `AlgorithmParameters` object. Typically this is used by:

1. Calling `KeyPairGenerator`'s `getInstance` method using "DSA" as the algorithm.
2. Casting the result to `DSAKeyPairGenerator`.
3. Using one of the DSA specific initialization methods.

Of particular instance is the second form of the `initialize` method. It takes:

- The modulus length in bits. The length must be a multiple of 8 between 512 and 1024, inclusive.
- Determining if new parameters are generated. If the flag is false, *precomputed* values may be used. If no precomputed values are available for the modulus length, an exception is thrown.
- A source of randomness, a `SecureRandom` instance.

```
package java.security.interfaces;
public interface DSAKeyPairGenerator
{
    public void initialize(DSAParams params, SecureRandom rand)
          throws InvalidParameterException;
    public void initialize(int modLenInBits, boolean genParams,
          SecureRandom rand) throws InvalidParameterException;
}
```

DSAParameterSpec (java.security.spec)

This provides a parameter specification for the DSA using the `BigInteger` class. This specification can be explicitly created using the constructor, or it can be generated from `AlgorithmParamaterGenerator` using the DSA. The `Signature` class uses these parameters for implementing the DSA.

```
public class DSAParameterSpec implements AlgorithmParameterSpec, DSAParams
{
     // Constructors
     public DSAParameterSpec(BigInteger p, BigInteger q, BigInteger g);

     // Instance Methods
     public BigInteger getG(); // base
     public BigInteger getP(); // prime
     public BigInteger getQ(); // subprime
}
```

DSAParams (java.security.interfaces)

This provides an interface for accessing common parameters of the DSA.

```
package java.security.interfaces;
public abstract interface DSAParams
{
    public BigInteger getG(); // base
    public BigInteger getP(); // prime
    public BigInteger getQ(); // subprime
}
```

DSAPrivateKey (java.security.interfaces)

An object implementing this interface is a provider-based private key used in the DSA and provides access to its components.

```
public interface DSAPrivateKey implements DSAKey, PublicKey
{
    // Superinterfaces: DSAKey, Key, PrivateKey, Serializable

    public BigInteger getX(); // private value
    public DSAParams getParams(); // from DSAKey
}
```

DSAPrivateKeySpec (java.security.spec)

This provider-independent class implements a private key for use with the Digital Signature Algorithm, as specified in the FIPS 182 standard. Before this class can be used with the `Signature` class, it must be converted using `KeyFactory.getInstance("DSA")` to produce key-based objects.

```
public class DSAParameterSpec implements AlgorithmParameterSpec, DSAParams
{
    // Constructors
    public DSAParameterSpec(BigInteger x, BigInteger p, BigInteger q,
          BigInteger g);

    // Instance Methods
    public BigInteger getG(); // base
    public BigInteger getP(); // prime
    public BigInteger getQ(); // sub-prime
    public BigInteger getX(); // private key value
}
```

DSAPublicKey (java.security.interfaces)

Objects implementing this interface are a provider-based public key used in the Digital Signature Algorithm and provide access to the key's components.

```
package java.security.interfaces;
public interface DSAPublicKey implements DSAKey, PublicKey
{
    // Superinterfaces: DSAKey, Key, PublicKey, Serializable

    public BigInteger getY(); // public key value
    public DSAParams getParams(); // from DSAKey
}
```

DSAPublicKeySpec (java.security.spec)

This provider-independent class implements a private key for use with the Digital Signature Algorithm, as specified in the FIPS 182 standard. Before this class can be used with the `Signature` class, it must be converted using `KeyFactory.getInstance("DSA")` to produce a key-based object.

```
package java.security.spec;
public class DSAPublicKeySpec implements KeySpec
{
    // Constructors
    public DSAPublicKeySpec(BigInteger y, BigInteger p, BigInteger q,
          BigInteger g);

    // Instance Methods
    public BigInteger getG(); // base
    public BigInteger getP(); // prime
    public BigInteger getQ(); // sub-prime
    public BigInteger getY(); // public key value
}
```

EncodedKeySpec (java.security.spec)

This is the base class for key specifications that are encoded in an explicitly known format (such as X.509 or PKCS #8). To access the individual parameters, you must convert to an appropriate `Key` or `KeySpec` class using `KeyFactory` or `SecretKeyFactory`.

```
package java.security.spec;
public abstract class EncodedKeySpec implements KeySpec
{
    // Subclasses: X509EncodedKeySpec, PKCS8EncodedKeySpec

    // Constructors
    public EncodedKeySpec(byte[] encodedKey);

    // Instance Methods
    public byte[] getEncoded();

    // Abstract Methods
    public abstract String getFormat();
}
```

EncryptedPrivateKeyInfo (javax.crypto)

This class packages encrypted data with any parameters used during the encryption process into an encoded `byte` array as defined in PKCS #8. This is most commonly used to store encrypted private keys. To use, you pass in the encrypted `byte` array and the `AlgorithmParameters` object. If no parameters are used, you pass in the name of the encryption algorithm instead. The final `byte` array containing the combined data is retrieved using `getEncoded`. Conversely, given the encoded data, you can retrieve the algorithm and parameters used for encryption and create an appropriate `Cipher` object for decryption (along with the `Key` that is stored elsewhere). If the encrypted data contains a `PKCS8EncodedKeySpec`, you can directly retrieve the key by passing in an initialized `Cipher` object to `getKeySpec`.

```
package javax.crypto;
public class EncryptedPrivateKeyInfo
{
     // Constructors
     public EncryptedPrivateKeyInfo(AlgorithmParameters algParams,
          byte[] encryptedData) throws NoSuchAlgorithmException
     public EncryptedPrivateKeyInfo(byte[] encoded) throws IOException
     public EncryptedPrivateKeyInfo(String algorithm,
          byte[] encryptedData) throws NoSuchAlgorithmException

     // Instance Methods
     public String getAlgorithm()
     AlgorithmParameters getAlgorithmParameters()
     byte[] getEncoded();
     byte[] getEncryptedData();
     PKCS8EncodedKeySpec getKeySpec(Cipher c)
          throws InvalidKeySpecException
}
```

ExemptionMechanism (javax.crypto)

This engine class, first appearing in Java 1.4, provides a mechanism for blocking or overriding access to encryption by implementing one of the following generic algorithms:

KeyEscrow. KeyEscrow provides an alternative means of decryption to be used by authorized personnel under prescribed conditions. Escrow may be different than recovering in that the alternative means of the decryption may not need or know what the primary key was.

KeyRecovery. A method of recovering or recalling a key used in encryption in case the unthinkable happens: a key of password is lost using traditional means.

KeyWeakening. A method of reducing the effective length of a key by either escrowing or allowing for recovery of *part* of the key.

This class also implements a special finalize mechanism that ensures the internal representation of the key is cleared once the object has no more references to it.

Sun does not provide a concrete implementation.

```
package javax.crypto;
public class ExemptionMechanism
{
     // Static Methods
     public static ExemptionMechanism getInstance(String mechanism)
          throws NoSuchAlgorithmException
     public static ExemptionMechanism getInstance(String mechanism,
          String provider) throws NoSuchAlgorithmException, NoSuchProvider
```

```
    public static ExemptionMechanism getInstance(String mechanism,
          Provider p) throws NoSuchAlgorithmException,
          IllegalArgumentException

    // Instance Methods
    public byte[] genExemptionBlob() throws IllegalStateException,
          ExemptionMechanismException
    public int genExemptionBlob(byte[] output)
          throws IllegalStateException, ExemptionMechanismException,
          ShortBufferException
    public int genExemptionBlob(byte[] output, int outputOffset)
          throws IllegalStateException, ExemptionMechanismException,
          ShortBufferException
    public String getName()
    public int getOutputSize(int inputLen) throws IllegalStateException
    public Provider getProvider()
    public void init(Key key) throws InvalidKeyException,
          ExemptionMechanismException
    public void init(Key key, AlgorithmParameters params)
          throws InvalidKeyException, InvalidAlgorithmParameterException,
          ExemptionMechanismException
    void init(Key key, AlgorithmParametersSpec params)
          throws InvalidKeyException, InvalidAlgorithmParameterException,
          ExemptionMechanismException
    boolean isCryptoAllowed(Key key) throws ExemptionMechanismException
}
```

ExemptionMechanismException (javax.crypto)

This is a generic exception indicating a problem with an `ExemptionMechanism` instance.

```
package javax.crypto;
public class ExemptionMechanismException extends GeneralSecurityException {
    // Hierarchy : GeneralSecurityException, Exception, Throwable
    // Implements: Serializable
    // Thrown By : various methods from ExceptionMechanism and
    //             ExemptionMechanismSpi

    public ExemptionMechanismException();
    public ExemptionMechanismException(String msg);
}
```

ExemptionMechanismSpi (javax.crypto)

This is the internal API used by provider authors to implement a key escrow, key weakening, or key recovery algorithm. This API works with the `ExemptionMechanism` engine class. End users and applications never need to use this class.

```
package javax.crypto;
public abstract class ExemptionMechanismSpi
{
```

```
    // Constructors
    public ExemptionMechanismSpi();

    // Abtract Methods
    protected abstract byte[] engineGenExemptionBlob() throws
          ExemptionMechanismException
    protected abstract int engineGenExemptionBlob(byte[] output,
          int outputOffset) throws ExemptionMechanismException,
          ShortBufferException
    protected abstract int engineGetOutputSize(int inputLen)
    protected abstract void engineInit(Key key)
          throws InvalidKeyException, ExemptionMechanismException
    protected abstract void engineInit(Key key,
          AlgorithmParameters params) throws InvalidKeyException,
          ExemptionMechanismException, InvalidAlgorithmParameterException
    protected abstract void engineInit(Key key,
          AlgorithmParametesSpec spec) throws InvalidKeyException,
          ExemptionMechanismException, InvalidAlgorithmParameterException

}
```

GeneralSecurityException (java.security)

This is the base class for all exceptions the `java.security` and `javax.crypto`, along with their subpackages. It is not explicitly thrown. For cryptographic applications there are two special cases: `java.security.ProviderException`, which inherits from `java.lang.RuntimeException`, and `java.security.InvalidParameterExcepts` subclasses `java.lang.IllegalArgumentException`.

```
package java.security;
public class GeneralSecurityException extends Exception
{
    // Ancestry: Exception, Throwable
    // Thrown By: none, only subclasses are thrown

    GeneralSecurityException();
    GeneralSecurityException(String msg);
}
```

IllegalBlockSizeException (javax.crypto)

This exception signals that data being fed to a block cipher is not the right size. During encryption, this happens when `NoPadding` has been specified and the plaintext data does not fill a block. During decryption, this occurs when the ciphertext ends prematurely and does not fill a block.

```
package javax.crypto;
public class IllegalBlockSizeException extends GeneralSecurityException
{
    // Thrown By: Cipher.doFinal, SealedObject.SealedObject
```

```
    IllegalBlockSizeException();
    IllegalBlockSizeException(String msg);
}
```

IllegalStateException (java.lang)

This exception is thrown when a method has been invoked on an engine object (e.g., `Cipher`) that has been created but not initialized.

```
package java.lang;
public class IllegalStateException extends RuntimeException
{
    // Thrown By: most methods from engine classes

    IllegalStateSizeException();
    IllegalStateSizeException(String msg);
}
```

Integer (java.lang)

This provides a wrapper class around the native `int` type for use in APIs that expect an `Object` type, such as the `java.util` collections. It also provides a number of useful static methods for parsing and printing integer types.

```
package java.lang;
public class Integer extends Numeric implements Comparable
{
    // Constants
    public static final int MAX_VALUE;
    public static final int MIN_VALUE;

    // Static Methods
    static int parseInt(String s) throws NumberFormatExceptions;
    static int parseInt(String s, int radix) throws NumberFormatException;
    static String toBinaryString(int n);
    static String toHexString(int n);
    static String toOctalString(int n);
    static String toString(int n);

    // other instance methods not listed
}
```

InvalidKeyException (java.security)

This exception is thrown when a key is invalid. This can occur when:

- The key was intended for a different algorithm than the one it was passed to.
- The key is null or empty.

- The key is too short or too long.
- The provider determined that a key is "weak."
- The key's encoding is unknown or invalid.

```
package java.security;
public class InvalidKeyException extends KeyException
{
     // Hierarchy :  KeyException, GeneralSecurityException, Exception,
     //              Throwable
     // Implements:  Serializable
     // Thrown By :  Cipher.init, DESedeKeySpec.DESedeKeySpec,
     //              DESKeySpec.DesKeySpec, ExemptionMechanism.init,
     //              KeyAgreement.generateSecret, KeyAgreementSpi.init,
     //              KeyFactor.translateKey, Mac.Iinit, MacSpi.init,
     //              SealedObject.getKey,SecretKeyFactory.translateKey,
     //              Signature.initSign, Signature.initVerify,
     //              SignedObject.SignedObject, SignedObject.verfiy

     InvalidKeyException();
     InvalidKeyException(String msg);
}
```

InvalidKeySpecException (java.security.spec)

This exception indicates that a `KeySpec` object is invalid. This can happen when a particular `KeySpec` type is expected but a different type was received (e.g., `KeyFactory` was configured for RSA but received a DSA `KeySpec` object).

```
package java.security;
public class InvalidKeySpecException extends GeneralSecurityException
{
     // Hierarchy :  GeneralSecurityException, Exception, Throwable
     // Implements:  Serializable
     // Thrown By :  KeyFactory.generatePublic, KeyFactory.generatePrivate,
     //              PKCS8EncodedKey.getKeySpec, KeyFactory.getKeySpec,
     //              SecretKeyFactory.generateSecret,
     //              SecretKeyFactory.getKeySpec

     InvalidKeySpecException();
     InvalidKeySpecException(String msg);
}
```

InvalidParameterException (java.security)

This exception is thrown when an invalid `AlgorithmParameters` object is passed to a `Cipher` or `DSAKeyPair` instance. This most often occurs when a `Cipher` object was created using one algorithm, but parameters for a different algorithm were passed in.

```
package java.security;
public class InvalidAlgorithmParameterException extends
GeneralSecurityException
{
    // Hierarchy :  GeneralSecurityException, Exception, Throwable
    // Implements:  Serializable
    // Thrown By :  Cipher.init, DSAKeyPair.initialize, KeyGenerator.init,

    InvalidAlgorithmParameterException();
    InvalidAlgorithmParameterException(String msg);
}
```

InvalidParameterSpecException (java.security.spec)

This exception is thrown when an `AlgorithmParameterSpec` object is invalid; mostly likely because of the wrong type of object being passed in or because the individual parameters themselves contain invalid values.

```
package java.security.spec;
public class InvalidParameterSpecException extends GeneralSecurityException
{
    // Hierarchy :  GeneralSecurityException, Exception, Throwable
    // Implements:  Serializable
    // Thrown By :  AlgorithmParameters.init,
    //              AlgorithmParameters.getParameterSpec

    public InvalidParameterSpecException();
    public InvalidParameterSpecException(String msg);
}
```

IvParameterSpec (javax.crypto.spec)

This is a generic parameter `Spec` class that represents an initialization vector used by a particular mode of operation (e.g., CBC) for a cipher. This class is used by simple unparameterized cipher algorithms such as DES and Blowfish to pass in an initialization vector to Cipher.init, since they do not have specific `AlgorithmParmaeterSpec` classes. More complicated ciphers that have other parameters do *not* use this class, but have their own `ParameterSpec` object that includes a field for an initialization vector. See `RC5ParameterSpec` as an example.

```
package javax.crypto.spec;
public class IvParameterSpec implements AlgorithmParameterSpec
{
    // Constructors
    IvParameterSpec(byte[] iv)
    IvParameterSpec(byte[] iv, int offset, int length)

    // Instance Methods
    byte[] getIV()
}
```

Key (java.security)

An object implementing the Key interface is a provider's representation of a cryptographic key, and it provides standard methods to retrieve the algorithm name, the encoded bytes, and a format of the encoding. How a key is encoded or what format is used is provider-specific, although it should be fairly consistent between providers.

```
package java.security;
public interface Key implements Serializable
{
    // Subinterfaces: DHPrivateKey, DHPublicKey, DSAPrivateKey,
    //     DSAPublicKey, PublicKey, RSAMultiPrimePrivateCrtKey,
    //     RSAPrivateCrtKey, RSAPublicKey, SecretKey

    // Implemented By: SecretKeySpec

    String getAlgorithm();
    byte[] getEncoded();
    String getFormat();
}
```

KeyAgreement (javax.crypto)

This class provides an API for multiparty key agreement protocols, most commonly the Diffie-Hellman Key Exchange. You create the object by using the standard name of DH. Each party uses the same AlgorithmParameterSpec for initialization. Then each party executes a doPhase (with the lastPhase set to true on the last step) and shares the result with others. At the end, each party will be able to compute the shared secret value using the generateSecret method. A fully working example of two- and three-party Diffie-Hellman can be found in Appendix F of the JCE API Specification and Reference included in the Java 1.4 SDK documentation.

```
package javax.crypto;
public class KeyAgreement
{
    // Static Methods
    static final KeyAgreement getInstance(String algorithm)
        throws NoSuchAlgorithmException;
    static final KeyAgreement getInstance(String algorithm,
        String provider) throws NoSuchAlgorithmException,
        NoSuchProviderException;
    static final KeyAgreement getInstance(String algorithm, Provider p)
        throws NoSuchAlgorithmException;

    // Instance Methods
    Key doPhase(Key key, boolean lastPhase) throws InvalidKeyException,
        IllegalStateException;
    byte[] generateSecret() throws IllegalStateException;
    int generateSecret(byte[] sharedSecret, int offset)
        throws IllegalStateException, ShortBufferException;
    SecretKey generateSecret(String algorithm)
        throws IllegalStateException, NoSuchAlgorithmException,
        InvalidKeyException;
```

```
    public String getAlgorithm();
    public Provider getProvider();
    public void init(Key key) throws InvalidKeyException;
    public void init(Key key, AlgorithmParameterSpec spec)
         throws InvalidKeyException, InvalidAlgorithmParameterException;
    public void init(Key key, SecureRandom rand)
         throws InvalidKeyException;
    public void init(Key key, AlgorithmParameterSpec spec,
         SecureRandom rand) throws InvalidKeyException,
         InvalidAlgorithmParameterException;
}
```

KeyAgreementSpi (javax.crypto)

This is a service provider interface for those implementing a key agreement algorithm for use in a provider. End users and applications never should use this interface.

```
package javax.crypto;
public abstract class KeyAgreementSpi
{
    // Constructors
    public KeyAgreementSpi();

    // Abstract Methods
    protected abstract Key engineDoPhase(Key key, boolean lastPhase);
    protected abstract byte[] engineGenerateSecret()
         throws IllegalStateException;
    protected abstract SecretKey engineGenerateSecret()
         throws IllegalStateException, NoSuchAlgorithmException,
         InvalidKeyException;
    protected abstract int engineGenerateSecret(byte[] sharedSecret,
         int offset) IllegalStateException, ShortBufferException;
    protected abstract engineInit(Key key, SecureRandom rand)
         throws InvalidKeyException;
    protected abstract void engineInit(Key key,
         AlgorithmParameterSpec spec, SecureRandom rand)
         throws InvalidKeyException;
}
```

KeyException (java.security)

This exception is not thrown but provides a base class for other key exceptions.

```
package java.security;
public class KeyException extends GeneralSecurityException
{
    // Hierarchy :  GeneralSecurityException, Exception, Throwable
    // Subclasses:  InvalidKeyException, KeyManagementException,
    //              KeyStoreException
```

```
    // Implements:  Serializable
    // Thrown By  :  none, base class for other key related exceptions

    public KeyException();
    public KeyException(String msg);
}
```

KeyFactory (java.security)

`KeyFactory` is an engine class primarily used for converting pubic or private keys represented in a `KeySpec` object (using legacy sources or manually created) into a provider-based `Key` object so they can be used with `Cipher`, `Mac`, `Signature`, or `KeyAgreement` classes. It can be used to do the reverse process of converting a `Key` object into a `KeySpec` object, normally `X509EncodedKeySpec` or `PKCS8EncodedKeySpec` format.

Like other engine classes, `KeyFactory` is not constructed directly but instead uses one of the static `getInstance` methods that take an algorithm name and optionally a provider. There is no initialization step. A `KeySpec` object can be converted to a `PrivateKey` or `PublicKey` using `generatePublic` or `generatePrivate`, respectively. Conversely, a `Key` object can be converted into a `KeySpec` using the `getKeySpec` method.

A `Key` object is *provider-based*, and different providers may use different internal representation. The `translate` method takes a `Key` issued by one provider and converts into the current provider's format. It also allows the current provider to perform various checks (e.g., minimal size, format, encoding, weakness) on the key before actually using it for cryptographic operations.

The SUN provider implements a `KeyFactory` for DSA, and SunJCE implements `DiffieHellman`.

```
package java.security;
public class KeyFactory
{
    // Static Methods
    public static KeyFactory getInstance(String algorithm)
          throws NoSuchAlgorithmException;
    public static KeyFactory getInstance(String algorithm,
          String provider) throws NoSuchAlgorithmException,
          NoSuchProviderException;
    public static KeyFactory getInstance(String algorithm,
          Provider p) throws NoSuchAlgorithmException;

    // Instance Methods
    public final PrivateKey generatePrivate(KeySpec keySpec)
          throws InvalidKeySpecException;
    public final PublicKey generatePublic(KeySpec keySpec)
          throws InvalidKeySpecException;
    public final String getAlgorithm();
    public final KeySpec getKeySpec(Key key, Class keySpecClass)
          throws InvalidKeySpecException;
    public final Provider getProvider();
    public final Key translateKey(Key key) throws InvalidKeyException;
}
```

KeyFactorySpi (java.security)

This is the base class for service providers implementing algorithms for use with `KeyFactory`. End users and applications never need to use this class directly.

```
package java.security;
public abstract class KeyFactorySpi
{
     // Constructors
     public KeyFactorySpi();

     // Abstract Methods
     protected abstract PrivateKey engineGeneratePrivate(KeySpec spec)
           throws InvalidKeySpecException
     protected abstract PrivateKey engineGeneratePublic(KeySpec spec)
           throws InvalidKeySpecException
     protected abstract KeySpec engineGetKeySpec(Key key,
           Class keySpecClass) throws InvalidKeySpecException
     protected abstract Key engineTranslateKey(Key key)
           throws InvalidKeyException;
}
```

KeyGenerator (javax.crypto)

This engine class provides a provider-specific way of generating *secret* keys for a particular algorithm (public/private key pairs are generated using `KeyPairGenerator`). The initialization step will accept either `AlgorithmParameterSpec` object or just a key size, where any additional parameters (if any) will be the provider's defaults.

```
package javax.crypto;
public class KeyGenerator
{
     // Static Methods
     public final static KeyGenerator getInstance(String algorithm)
           throws NoSuchAlgorithmException;
     public final static KeyGenerator getInstance(String algorithm,
           String provider) throws NoSuchAlgorithmException,
           NoSuchProviderException;
     public final static KeyGenerator getInstance(String algorithm,
           Provider p) throws NoSuchAlgorithmException;

     // Instance Methods
     public final Provider getProvider();
     public final SecretKey generateKey();
     public final String getAlgorithm();
     public final void init(int keysize);
     public final void init(int keysize, SecureRandom rand);
     public final void init(SecureRandom rand);
     public final void init(AlgorithmParameterSpec spec)
           throws InvalidParameterException;
     public final void init(AlgorithmParameterSpec spec, SecureRandom rand)
           throws InvalidParameterException;
}
```

KeyGeneratorSpi (javax.crypto)

This is the internal API used by provider authors to implement key generation algorithms. This API works with the `KeyGenerator` engine class. End users and applications never need to use this class.

```
package javax.crypto;
public abstract class KeyGeneratorSpi
{
     // Constructors
     public KeyGeneratorSpi();

     // Abstract Methods
     protected abstract SecretKey engineGenerateKey();
     protected abstract engineInit(AlgorithmParamtersSpec params,
           SecureRandom rand);
     protected abstract engineInit(int keysize, SecureRandom rand);
     protected abstract engineInit(SecureRandom rand);
}
```

KeyManagementException (java.security)

This is a placeholder exception that is not thrown by any method in the core Java API. It is designed for future or third-party development of more descriptive key management problems such as key expiration.

```
package java.security;
public class KeyManagementException extends KeyException
{
     // Hierarchy :  KeyException, GeneralSecurityException, Exception,
     //              Throwable
     // Implements:  Serializable
     // Thrown By :  none

     public KeyManagementException();
     public KeyManagementException(String msg);
}
```

KeyPair (java.security)

This class is just a container holding a public and private key.

```
package java.security;
public class KeyPair implements Serializable
{
     // Constructors
     public KeyPair(PublicKey publicKey, PrivateKey privateKey);
```

```
    // Instance Methods
    public PrivateKey getPrivate();
    public PublicKey getPublic();
}
```

KeyPairGenerator (java.security)

`KeyPairGenerator` is an engine class for generating key pairs for public key algorithms (secret keys are generated by `KeyGenerator`). Initialization can be done in an "algorithm-independent" manner where all that is specified is a key size (typically in bits) and any additional parameters will be set to provider-specific defaults. Alternatively, you can specify all parameters explicitly in an algorithm-dependant manner using the appropriate `AlgorithmParameterSpec`. After initialization, a call to `genPair` returns a `KeyPair` object.

The SUN provider implements a key pair generator for DSA keys. If the modulus is 512, 768, or 1024, precomputed values for *p*, *q*, and *g* are used (if the modulus is a different value, the new parameters are generated). This provider also implements a generator for RSA keys, but no precomputed values are used. The SunJCE provider can generate Diffie-Hellman key pairs using the standard name of `DiffieHellman`.

```
package java.security;
public abstract class KeyPairGenerator extends KeyPairGeneratorSpi
{
    // Static Methods
    public static KeyPairGenerator getInstance(String algorithm)
          throws NoSuchAlgorithmException;
    public static KeyPairGenerator getInstance(String algorithm,
          String provider) throws NoSuchAlgorithmException,
          NoSuchProviderException;
    public static KeyPairGenerator getInstance(String algorithm,
          Provider p) throws NoSuchAlgorithmException;
    // Instance Methods
    public final KeyPair genKeyPair();
    public KeyPair generateKeyPair();
    public String getAlgorithm();
    public final Provider getProvider();
    public void initialize(int keysize);
    public void initialize(AlgorithmParameterSpec params)
          throws InvalidAlgorithmParameterException;
    public void initialize(int keysize, SecureRandom rand);
    public void initialize(AlgorithmParameterSpec params,
          SecureRandom rand) throws InvalidAlgorithmParameterException;
}
```

KeyPairGeneratorSpi (java.security)

This is the internal API used by provider authors to implement public/private key pair generators. This API works with the `KeyPairGenerator` engine class. End users and applications never need to use this class.

```
package java.security;
public abstract class KeyPairGeneratorSpi
{
    public KeyPairGeneratorSpi();
    public abstract KeyPair generateKeyPair();
    public abstract void initialize(int keysize, SecureRandom rand);
    public void initialize(AlgorithmParameterSpec params,
          SecureRandom rand) throws InvalidAlgorithmParameterException;
}
```

KeySpec (java.security.spec)

This empty interface is used to group and provide type safety for classes representing transparent or explicitly known representations of a key. Objects implementing this interface can be created using normal constructors, but they cannot be used in `Cipher`, `MAC`, `Signature`, or `KeyAgreement` classes without first being converted into a provider-based `Key` object (using `KeyFactory` or `SecretKeyFactory`). The exception is `SecretKeySpec`, which inherits from both `Key` and `KeySpec` and can be used directly.

```
package java.security.spec;
public abstract interface KeySpec
{
     // Implemented By: DESedeKeySpec, DESKeySpec, DHPrivateKeySpec,
     //     DSAPrivateKeySpec, DSAPublicKeySpec, EncodedKeySpec,
     //     PBEKeySpec, RSAPrivateKeySpec, RSAPublicKeySpec, SecretKeySpec

     // empty
}
```

KeyStore (java.security)

The `KeyStore` engine class provides an interface for persistent key and certificate storage. It's most useful for private keys and certificates, but it can work with secret keys as well. Keys and certificates are indexed by an *alias* that was specified at storage time. The key store is loaded or saved by providing an input or output stream and a password to encrypt the keys.

The SunJCE provider implements a proprietary key store named `JCEKS`. The SUN provider also implements a key store, `JKS`, but the encryption of private keys is much weaker and not recommended.

```
package java.security;
public class KeyStore
{
     // Static Methods
     public static final String getDefaultType();
     public static KeyStore getInstance(String type)
          throws KeyStoreException;
     public static KeyStore getInstance(String type, String provider)
          throws KeyStoreException, NoSuchProviderException;
```

```
    public static KeyStore getInstance(String type, Provider p)
        throws KeyStoreException;

    // Instance Methods
    public final Enumeration aliases() throws KeyStoreException;
    public final boolean containsAlias(String alias)
        throws KeyStoreException;
    public final void deleteEntry(String alias) throws KeyStoreException;
    public final Certificate getCertificate(String alias)
        throws KeyStoreException;
    public final String getCertificateAlias(Certificate cert)
        throws KeyStoreException;
    public final Certificate[] getCertificateChain(String alias)
        throws KeyStoreException;
    public final Date getCreationDate(String alias)
        throws KeyStoreException;
    public final Key getKey(String alias, char[] password)
        throws KeyStoreException, NoSuchAlgorithmException,
        UnrecoverableKeyException;
    public final Provider getProvider();
    public final String getType();
    public final boolean isCertificateEntry(String alias)
        throws KeyStoreException;
    public final boolean isKeyEntry(String alias)
        throws KeyStoreException;
    public final void load(InputStream is, char[] password)
        throws IOException, NoSuchAlgorithmException,
        CertificateException;
    public final void setCertificateEntry(String alias, Certificate cert)
        throws KeyStoreException;
    public final void setKeyEntry(String alias, byte[] key,
        Certificate[] chain) throws KeyStoreException;
    public final void setKeyEntry(String alias, Key key, char[] password,
        Certificate[] chain) throws KeyStoreException;
    public final int size() throws KeyStoreException;
    public final void store(OutputStream os, char[] password)
        throws KeyStoreException, IOException, NoSuchAlgorithmException,
        CertificateException;
}
```

KeyStoreException (java.security)

This exception is thrown when a problem with a KeyStore object occurs.

```
package java.security;
public class KeyStoreException extends KeyException
{
    // Hierarchy :  KeyException, GeneralSecurityException, Exception,
    //              Throwable
    // Implements:  Serializable
    // Thrown By :  most methods from KeyStore

    public KeyStoreException();
    public KeyStoreException(String msg);
}
```

KeyStoreSpi (java.security)

This is the internal API used by provider authors to implement key storage algorithms. This API works with the `KeyStore` engine class. End users and applications never need to use this class.

```
package java.security;
public abstract class KeyStoreSpi
{
     // Constructors
     public KeyStoreSpi();

     // Abstract Methods
     public abstract Enumeration engineAliases();
     public abstract boolean engineContainsAlias(String alias);
     public abstract void engineDeleteEntry(String alias)
          throws KeyStoreException;
     public abstract Certificate engineGetCertificate(String alias);
     public abstract String engineGetCertificateAlias(Certificate cert);
     public abstract Certificate[] engineGetCertificateChain(String alias);
     public abstract Date engineGetCreationDate(String alias);
     public abstract Key engineGetKey(String alias, char[] password)
          throws NoSuchAlgorithmException, UnrecoverableKeyException;
     public abstract boolean engineIsCertificateEntry(String alias);
     public abstract boolean engineIsKeyEntry(String alias);
     public abstract void engineLoad(InputStream is, char[] password)
          throws IOException, NoSuchAlgorithmException,
          CertificateException;
     public abstract void engineSetCertificateEntry(String alias,
          Certificate cert) throws KeyStoreException;
     public abstract void engineSetKeyEntry(String alias, byte[] key,
          Certificate[] chain) throws KeyStoreException;
     public abstract void engineSetKeyEntry(String alias, Key key,
          char[] password, Certificate[] chain) throws KeyStoreException;
     public abstract int engineSize();
     public abstract void engineStore(OutputStream os, char[] password)
          throws IOException, NoSuchAlgorithmException,
          CertificateException;
}
```

Long (java.lang)

The `Long` class provides an object wrapper around the `long` native type for use with APIs that expect an `Object` type, such as the `java.util` collections. In addition, the class provides many methods to parse and create `long` types from strings using various base representations.

```
package java.lang;
public class Long extends Number implements Comparable
{
     // Constants
     public static final long MAX_VALUE;
     public static final long MIN_VALUE;
```

```
    // Static Methods
    public static long parseLong(String s, int radix)
          throws NumberFormatException
    public static String toBinaryString(long val);
    public static String toOctalString(long val);
    public static String toHexString(long val);
    public static toString(long val);
    public static toString(long val, int radix);

    // constructors and instance methods not listed
}
```

Mac (javax.crypto)

This class provides an interface to generate Message Authentication Codes and works similarly to `MessageDigest`, except that it requires initialization with a `Key` or a `AlgorithmParameterSpec` (rare) object. The stock SunJCE provider has two implementations: HMACMD5 and HMACSHA, which are based on the RFC 2104 specification.

```
package javax.crypto;
public class Mac
{
    // Static Methods
    public static final Mac getInstance(String algorithm)
          NoSuchAlgorithmException
    public static final Mac getInstance(String algorithm, String provider)
          throws NoSuchAlgorithmException, NoSuchProviderException
    public static final Mac getInstance(String algorithm, Provider p)
          throws NoSuchAlgorithmException

    // Instance Methods
    Object clone();
    byte[] doFinal() throws IllegalStateException;
    byte[] doFinal(byte[] input) throws IllegalStateException;
    void doFinal(bye[] output, int offset, int length)
          throws IllegalStateException, ShortBufferException;
    String getAlgorithm();
    int getMacLength();
    Provider getProvider();
    void init(Key key) throws InvalidKeyException;
    void init(Key key, AlgorithmParameterSpec spec)
          throws InvalidKeyException, InvalidAlgorithmParameterException;
    void reset();
    void update(byte input) throws IllegalStateException;
    void update(byte[] input) throws IllegalStateException;
    void update(byte[] input, int offset, int length)
          throws IllegalStateException;
}
```

MacSpi (javax.crypto)

This is the internal API used by provider authors to implement Message Authentication Code (MAC) algorithms. It works with the `Mac` engine class. End users and applications never need to use this class.

```
package javax.crypto;
public MacSpi
{
     // Constructors
     public MacSpi();

     // Abstract Methods
     Object clone();
     protected abstracted byte[] engineDoFinal()
     protected abstracted int engineGetMacLength()
     protected abstract void engineInit(Key key,
           AlgorithmParameterSpec spec) throws InvalidKeyException,
           InvalidAlgorithmParametersException
     protected abstract void engineReset()
     protected abstract void engineUpdate(byte input)
     protected abstract void engineUpdate(byte[] input, int offset,
           int length)
}
```

MessageDigest (java.security)

This is an engine class that provides cryptographic-quality message digests. Data being hashes, and the hash itself is always a `byte` array. Like all engine classes, using the static `getInstance` method creates an object. After creation, data can be fed in using one of the various `update` methods. The digest is computed and the object is reset after a call to `final`. The size of the digest can be determined using the `getDigestLength` method. This class also provides a static convenience method, `isEqual`, to compare two hashes for equivalence, and it is functionally identical to `java.util.Array.equals(byte[] a, byte[] b)`. A `MessageDigest` object may or may not be able to be cloned, depending on the provider's implementation.

The stock SUN provider implements MD5 and SHA-1.

```
package java.security;
public abstract class MessageDigest extends MessageDigestSpi
{
     // Static Methods
     public static boolean isEqual(byte[] digesta, byte[] digestb);
     public static MessageDigest getInstance(String algorithm)
           throws NoSuchAlgorithmException;
     public static MessageDigest getInstance(String algorithm,
           String provider) throws NoSuchAlgorithmException,
           NoSuchProviderException;
```

```
    public static MessageDigest getInstance(String algorithm, Provider p)
          throws NoSuchAlgorithmException;

    // Instance Methods
    public Object clone() throws CloneNotSupportedException;
    public byte[] digest();
    public byte[] digest(byte[] input);
    public int digest(byte[] buf, int offset, int length)
          throws DigestException;
    public final String getAlgorithm();
    public final int getDigestLength();
    public final Provider getProvider();
    public void reset();
    public String toString();
    public void update(byte input);
    public void update(byte[] input);
    public void update(byte[] input, int offset, int length);
}
```

MessageDigestSpi (java.security)

The implementation may or may not choose to implement the clone method. If not, it should explicitly throw the `CloneNotSupportedException`.

```
package java.security;
public abstract class MessageDigestSpi
{
    // Constructors
    public MessageDigestSpi();

    // Abstract Methods
    public Object clone() throws CloneNotSupportedException;
    protected abstract byte[] engineDigest();
    protected int engineDigest(byte[] buf, int offset, int length)
          throws DigestException;
    protected int engineGetDigestLength();
    protected abstract void engineReset();
    protected abstract void engineUpdate(byte input);
    protected abstract void engineUpdate(byte[] input, int offset,
          int length);
}
```

NoSuchAlgorithmException (java.security)

This exception is thrown by an engine class's `getInstance` method with a request for an algorithm that does not exist.

```
package java.security;
public class NoSuchAlgorithmException extends GeneralSecurityException
{
    // Hierarchy :  GeneralSecurityException, Exception, Throwable
    // Implements:  Serializable
```

```
    // Thrown By :  all "getInstance" methods, CipherSpi.engineSetMode,
    //              EncryptedPrivateKeyInfo.EncryptedPrivateKeyInfo,
    //              KeyStore.getKey, KeyStore.load
    //              KeyStore.store, KeyAgreement.generateSecret,
    //              SealedObject.getObject

    public NoSuchAlgorithmException();
    public NoSuchAlgorithmException(String msg);
}
```

NoSuchPaddingException (javax.crypto)

Ciphers can be specified as a string in the form of *algorithm/mode/padding*. If the provider does not recognize the padding specifier, this exception is thrown.

```
package javax.crypto;
public class NoSuchPaddingException extends GeneralSecurityException
{
    // Hierarchy :  GeneralSecurityException, Exception, Throwable
    // Implements:  Serializable
    // Thrown By :  Cipher.getInstance, CipherSpi.engineSetPadding

    public NoSuchPaddingException();
    public NoSuchPaddingException(String msg);
}
```

NoSuchProviderException (java.security)

This exception is thrown from an engine class's `getInstance` method when the specified provider could not be found.

```
package java.security;
public class NoSuchProviderException extends GeneralSecurityException
{
    // Hierarchy :  GeneralSecurityException, Exception, Throwable
    // Implements:  Serializable
    // Thrown By :  all "getInstance" methods

    public NoSuchProviderException();
    public NoSuchProviderException(String msg);
}
```

NullCipher (javax.crypto)

The `NullCipher` works like the `Cipher` class, except that it does not do any transformation of the original text—the output text is identical to the input text for any mode (e.g., encryption, decryption) All parameters are ignored and the block size is set to 1 byte, so there are no issues involving padding. In addition, this class can only be created using its constructor and cannot be created using the usual `Cipher.getInstance` methods. This class is most useful for testing and debugging applications.

```
package javax.crypto;
public class NullCipher extends Cipher
{
     // Constructors
     public NullCipher();

     // Instance Methods
     // all methods from Cipher carry over
     // all parameters are ignored
}
```

PBEKey (javax.crypto.interfaces)

An object implementing this interface is a provider-based implementation of a key for password-based encryption (PBE), as defined in the PKCS #5 standard. The actual key bytes from `getEncoded` is from the PBE algorithm of hashing the password and salt a number of times. The `salt` and `iterationCount` values are not considered secret and can alternatively be specified using `PBEParameterSpec`.

```
public interface PBEKey extends SecretKey
{
     // Superinterfaces: Key, SecretKey, Serializable

     int getIterationCount();
     char[] getPassword();
     byte[] getSalt();
     byte[] getEncoded(); // from Key
}
```

PBEKeySpec (javax.crypto.spec)

This provides a key specification for password-based encryption based on the PKCS #5 standard. You can directly create an object using the constructors, but it must be converted into a `PBEKey` for use in `Cipher` or `Mac` using `SecretKeyFactory`. When finished using the object, you should explicitly call `clearPassword` to clear internal memory. The `salt` and `iterationCount` values are not considered secret and can alternatively be specified using `PBEParameterSpec`.

```
package javax.crypto.spec;
public class PBEKeySpec implements KeySpec
{
     // Constructors
     public PBEKeySpec(char[] password);
     public PBEKeySpec(char[] password, byte[] salt, int iterationCount);
     public PBEKeySpec(char[] password, byte[] salt, int iterationCount,
          int keyLength);
```

```
    // Instance Methods
    public void clearPassword();
    public int getIterationCount();
    public int getKeyLength();
    public char[] getPassword();
    public byte[] getSalt();
}
```

PBEParameterSpec (javax.crypto.spec)

This class provides a parameter specification for password-based encryption, as described in PKCS #5. Note that the password is not part of the *parameter* specification, and the salt and iteration count can be public.

```
package javax.crypto.spec;
public class PBEParameterSpec implements AlgorithmParameterSpec
{
    // Constructors
    public PBEParameterSpec(byte[] salt, int iterationCount);

    // Instance Methods
    public Int getIterationCount();
    public byte[] getSalt();
}
```

PKCS8EncodedKeySpec (java.security.spec)

This class implements a private key encoded in the PKCS #8 format (occasionally, this encoding is also used for secret keys). Use `KeyFactory` to convert an encoded key into a `Key` object for use by `Cipher`, `Signature`, or `KeyAgreement` classes.

```
package java.security.spec;
public class PKCS8EncodedKeySpec extends EncodedKeySpec
{
    // Implements: KeySpec

    // Constructors
    public PKCS8EncodedKeySpec(byte[] encodedKey);

    // Instance Methods
    public byte[] getEncoded();
    public final String getFormat();
}
```

PrivateKey (java.security)

An object implementing this interface is a provider-based private key, as opposed to a public or secret key. The interface itself does not contain any methods or fields and is used strictly for grouping and type safety.

```
package java.security;
public abstract interface PrivateKey implements Key
{
     // Implements: Key, Serializable

     // Subinterfaces: DHPrivateKey, DSAPrivateKey,
     //     RSAMultiPrimePrivateCrtKey,
     //     RSAPrivateCrtKey, RSAPrivateKey

     // empty
}
```

Provider (java.security)

A provider maps "names" into classes that implement algorithms—specifically, in the case of the JCA and JCE, cryptographic algorithms. Normally, the only use for this class is to register a provider with the `Security` object. Consult your provider's documentation on how to create this object.

Also, a provider can be referenced indirectly in most engine class's `getInstance` method by using a provider's name.

```
package java.security;
public abstract class Provider extends java.util.Properties
{
        // Hierarchy : java.util.Properties, Hashtable, Dictionary
        // Implements: Serializable, Cloneable, Map

        // Instance Methods
        public synchronized void clear();
        public synchronized Set entrySet();
        public String getInfo();
        public String getName();
        public double getVersion();
        public Set keySet();
        public synchronized void load(InputStream is) throws IOException;
        public synchronized Object put(Object key, Object value);
        public synchronized void putAll(Map m);
        public synchronized Object remove(Object key);
        public String toString();
        public Collection values();
}
```

ProviderException (java.security)

This exception is thrown when an internal error happens within a provider, possibly when some resource could not be found. This exception extends `RuntimeException` and is therefore unchecked.

```
package java.security;
public class ProviderException extends RuntimeException
{
```

```
    // Hierarchy :  RuntimeException, Exception, Throwable
    // Implements:  Serializable
    // Thrown By :

    public ProviderException();
    public ProviderException(String msg);
}
```

PSSParameterSpec (java.security.spec)

This provides a `Spec` class for the RSAASSA-PSS signature scheme as defined in the PKCS #1 standard and equivalent IFSSA scheme (using ISSP-RSA, IFVP1, and EMSA4) as defined in IEEE 1363a.

```
package java.security.spec;
public class PSSParameterSpec implements AlgorithmParameterSpec
{
    // Constructors
    public PSSParameterSpec(int saltLen);

    // Instance Methods
    public int getSaltLength();
}
```

PublicKey (java.security)

An object implementing this interface is a provider-based public key, as opposed to a private or secret key. The interface itself does not contain any methods or fields and is used strictly for grouping and type safety.

```
package java.security;
public abstract interface PublicKey implements Key
{
    // Superinterfaces: Key, Serializable
    // Subinterfaces: DHPublicKey, DSAPublicKey, RSAPublicKey

    // empty
}
```

Random (java.util)

The `Random` class provides the main interface in Java for producing random numbers. While the quality of the number is not useful for cryptographic purposes, the API is also used in `SecureRandom`. A `Random` instance can be created using a constructor and a seed value. If the same seed is used, the same sequence of "random" numbers will be generated. If no seed value is present, the current system time is used. The seed can be reset at any time using another long value using the setSeed method. The nextDouble method returns a uniformly distributed number from 0 (inclusive) to 1 (exclusive), while nextGausian returns unbounded double using a Gaussian or normal (bell curve) distribution. The nextInt method returns a random 32-bit value over the entire range of value for the int type (positive and negative), while nextInt(int *n*) returns a random integer from 0 to $n - 1$.

```
package java.util;
public class Random implements Serialable
{
     // Subclasses: SecureRandom

     // Constructors
     public Random()
     public Random(long seed)

     // Instance Methods
     public boolean nextBoolean()
     public void nextBytes(byte[] bytes)
     public double nextDouble()
     public float nextFloat()
     public double nextGaussian()
     public int nextInt();
     public int nextInt(int n)
     public long nextLong()
     public void setSeed(long seed);
}
```

RC2ParameterSpec (javax.crypto.spec)

This class provides a provider-independent data structure containing the parameters used in the RC2 cipher consisting of the key length (in bits) and optionally an initialization vector, and it should be used when initializing a Cipher object.

The standard SUN and SunJCE providers do *not* have an implementation of the RC5 cipher. This class is primarily for use with commercial provider packages from RSA Security or its licensees.

```
package javax.crypto.spec;
public class RC2ParameterSpec implements AlgorithmParameterSpec
{
     // Constructors
     public RC2ParameterSpec(int effectiveKeyBits)
     public RC2ParameterSpec(int effectiveKeyBits, byte[] iv)
     public RC2ParameterSpec(int effectiveKeyBits, byte[] iv, int offset)

     // Instance Methods
     public getEffectiveKeyBits()
     byte[] getIV()
}
```

RC5ParameterSpec (javax.crypto.spec)

This class provides a transparent representation of a RC5 cipher including a version, rounds, word size, and optionally an initialization vector if the cipher is used in a feedback mode (such as CBC).

The standard SUN and SunJCE providers do not have an implementation of the RC5 cipher. This class is primarily for use with commercial provider packages from RSA Security or its licensees.

```
package javax.crypto.spec;
public class RC2ParameterSpec implements AlgorithmParameterSpec
{
    // Constructors
    public RC5ParameterSpec(int version, int rounds, int wordSize)
    public RC5ParameterSpec(int version, int rounds, int wordSize,
          byte[] iv)
    public RC5ParameterSpec(int version, int rounds, int wordSize,
          byte[] iv, int offset)

    // Instance Methods
    public getRounds()
    public byte[] getIV()
    public Int getVersion()
    public Int getWordSize()
}
```

RSAKey (java.security.interfaces)

An object implementing this interface is a provider-based key using either an RSA signature or a cipher algorithm. The key may be public or private, and it may be used for either encryption or signature algorithms. This interface also provides common access to the shared modulus value.

```
package java.security.interfaces;
public interface RSAKey
{
    // Subinterfaces: RSAMultiprimePrivateCrtKey, RSAPrivateCrtKey,
    //     RSAPrivateKey, RSAPublicKey

    public BigInteger getModulus();
}
```

RSAKeyGenParametersSpec (java.security.spec)

An `AlgorithmParameterSpec` for generating RSA key pairs. The key size is specified in bits, and a `BigInteger` is used to specify the public exponent.

```
package java.security.spec;
public class RSAKeyGenParameterSpec implements AlgorithmParameterSpec
{
    public RSAKeyGenParameterSpec(int keySizeBits,
          BigInteger publicExponent);
    public int getKeysize();
    public BigInteger getPublicExponent();
}
```

RSAMultiPrimeCrtKeySpec (java.security.spec)

This class specifies a provider-independent RSA MultiPrime private key using a Chinese remainder theorem (CRT) representation as defined in the PKCS #1 standard. Any primes beyond the first two are specified in a list of `RSAOtherPrimeInfo` objects.

Note: The stock SUN and SunJCE providers do not implement the RSA algorithm for encryption, and the MultiPrime algorithm is patented by the RSA Security. This class is provided to standardize third-party implementations.

```
package java.security.spec;
public class RSAMultiPrimePrivateCrtKeySpec extends RSAPrivateKeySpec
{
     // Constructors
     public RSAMultiPrimePrivateCrtKeySpec(BigInteger modulus,
           BigInteger publicExponent, BigInteger privateExponent,
           BigInteger primeP, BigInteger primeQ, BigInteger primeExponentP,
           BigInteger primeExponentQ, BigInteger crtCoefficient,
           RSAOtherPrimeInfo[] otherPrimeInfo);

     // Instance Methods
     public BigInteger getCrtCoefficient();
     public RSAOtherPrimeInfo[] getOtherPrimeInfo();
     public BigInteger getPrimeExponentP();
     public BigInteger getPrimeExponentQ();
     public BigInteger getPrimeP();
     public BigInteger getPrimeQ();
     public BigInteger getPublicExponent();
     public BigInteger getPrivateExponent(); // from RSAPrivateKeySpec
     public BigInteger getModulus(); // from RSAPrivateKeySpec
}
```

RSAMultiPrimePrivateCrtKey (java.security.interfaces)

This interface provides access to the components of a provider-based private RSA key using the MultiPrime algorithm. Prime components beyond the first two are represented in the `RSAOtherPrimeInfo` array.

```
package java.security.interfaces;
public abstract interface RSAMultiPrimePrivateCrtKey
      implements RSAPrivateKey
```

```
{
    // Superinterfaces: Key, PrivateKey, RSAKey, RSAPrivateKey,
    //                  Serializable

    public BigInteger getCrtCoefficient();
    public RSAOtherPrimeInfo[] getOtherPrimeInfo();
    public BigInteger getPrimeExponentP();
    public BigInteger getPrimeExponentQ();
    public BigInteger getPrimeP();
    public BigInteger getPrimeQ();
    public BigInteger getPublicExponent();

    public BigInteger getPrivateExponent(); // from RSAPrivateKey
    public BigInteger getModulus(); // from RSAKey
    public String getAlgorithm();   // from Key
    public byte[] getEncoded();     // from Key
    public String getFormat();      // from Key
}
```

RSAOtherPrimeInfo (java.security.spec)

This represents an additional prime, exponent, and coefficient value for use with a private key using the RSA MultiPrime algorithm, as defined in the PKCS #1 standard.

```
package java.security.spec;
public class RSAOtherPrimeInfo
{
    // Constructors
    public RSAOtherPrimeInfo(BigInteger prime, BigInteger primeExponent,
          BigInteger crtCoefficient)

    // Instance Methods
    public BigInteger getCrtCoefficient()
    public BigInteger getExponent()
    public BigInteger getPrime()
}
```

RSAPrivateCrtKey (java.security.interfaces)

This interface provides access to the components of a provider-based private RSA key using the Chinese remainder theorem representation.

```
package java.security.interfaces;
public abstract interface RSAPrivateCrtKey implements RSAPrivateKey
{
    // Superinterfaces: Key, PrivateKey, RSAKey, RSAPrivateKey,
    //                  Serializable

    public BigInteger getCrtCoefficient();
    public BigInteger getPrimeExponentP();
    public BigInteger getPrimeExponentQ();
```

```
    public BigInteger getPrimeP();
    public BigInteger getPrimeQ();
    public BigInteger getPublicExponent();
    public BigInteger getPrivateExponent(); // from RSAPrivateKey
    public BigInteger getModulus(); // from RSAKey
    public String getAlgorithm();   // from Key
    public byte[] getEncoded();     // from Key
    public String getFormat();      // from Key
}
```

RSAPrivateCrtKeySpec (java.security.spec)

A private key specification for the RSA algorithm using the Chinese remainder theorem format with `BigIntegers`.

```
package java.security.spec;
public class RSAPrivateCrtKeySpec extends RSAPrivateKeySpec
{
    // Constructors
    public RSAPrivateCrtKeySpec(BigInteger modulus,
        BigInteger publicExponent, BigInteger privateExponent,
        BigInteger primeP, BigInteger primeQ, BigInteger primeExponentP,
        BigInteger primeExponentQ, BigInteger crtCoefficient);

    // Instance Methods
    public BigInteger getCrtCoefficient();
    public BigInteger getPrimeExponentP();
    public BigInteger getPrimeExponentQ();
    public BigInteger getPrimeP();
    public BigInteger getPrimeQ();
    public BigInteger getPublicExponent();
    public BigInteger getModulus(); // from RSAPrivateKeySpec
    public BigInteger getPrivateExponent(); // from RSAPrivateKeySpec
}
```

RSAPrivateKey (java.security.interfaces)

This interface provides access to the private exponent of a provider-based private `RSA key`. The key itself may be used for either encryption or signature algorithms.

```
package java.security.interfaces;
public abstract interface RSAPrivateKey implements PrivateKey, RSAKey
{
    // Superinterfaces: Key, PrivateKey, RSAKey, Serializable

    public BigInteger getPrivateExponent();

    public BigInteger getModulus(); // from RSAKey
    public String getAlgorithm();   // from Key
    public byte[] getEncoded();     // from Key
    public String getFormat();      // from Key
}
```

RSAPrivateKeySpec (java.security.spec)

This provider-independent class implements a private key used in the RSA algorithm, using the common but slow *private exponent* and *modulus* representation. Decryption using a key in this form is 4 times slower than one specified using `RSAPrivateKeyCrtSpec`. Before it can be used with the `Cipher` and `Signature` classes, it must be converted to a `Key` object using `KeyFactory.getInstance("RSA")`. This class is primarily used for specifying a key directly, either manually or from a legacy source. RSA key pairs may be generated using the `KeyPairGenerator` engine class. *Note:* Sun provides an implementation for the RSA signature algorithms in the SUN provider (see `Signature` for details), but there is no implementation for RSA encryption.

```
package java.security.spec;
public class RSAPrivateKeySpec implements KeySpec
{
     // Implements: Serializable

     // Constructors
     public RSAPrivateKeySpec(BigInteger modulus,
           BigInteger privateExponent);

     // Instance Methods
     public BigInteger getModulus();
     public BigInteger getPrivateExponent();
}
```

RSAPublicKey (java.security.interfaces)

This interface provides access to the public exponent of a provider-based public RSA key. The key itself may be used for either encryption or signature algorithms.

```
package java.security.interfaces;
public abstract interface RSAPublicKey implements PublicKey, RSAKey
{
     // Superinterfaces: Key, PublicKey, RSAKey, Serializable

     public BigInteger getPublicExponent();
     public BigInteger getModulus(); // from RSAKey
     public String getAlgorithm();   // from Key
     public byte[] getEncoded();     // from Key
     public String getFormat();      // from Key
}
```

RSAPublicKeySpec (java.security.spec)

This class provides a provider-independent public key used with the RSA algorithm. Before using with `Cipher` and `Signature` classes, you must convert it into a `Key` object using `KeyFactory.getInstance("RSA")`. This class is primarily used for specifying a key directly, either manually or from a legacy source. RSA key pairs may be generated using the KeyPairGenerator engine class. *Note:* Sun provides an implementation for the RSA signature algorithms in the SUN provider (see Signature for details), but there is no implementation for RSA encryption.

```
package java.security.spec;
public class RSAPublicKeySpec implements KeySpec
{
     // Constructors
     public RSAPublicKeySpec(BigInteger modulus,
           BigInteger publicExponent);

     // Instance Methods
     public BigInteger getModulus();
     public BigInteger getPublicExponent();
}
```

SealedObject (javax.crypto)

A *sealed object* is an encrypted serialized representation of an object. To create a new SealedObject, you use the object to "seal" and a fully initialized Cipher object to perform the encryption. The resulting object can be serialized for transmission or storage (or left as-is). To reconstitute, you deserialize to re-create a SealedObject. (There is no constructor using the serialized array of bytes.) The original object can be retrieved with getObject using either an initialized Cipher object or just the appropriate key.

Prior to Java 1.4, there were errors in sealing objects that are not part of the Java core APIs.

```
package javax.crypto;
public class SealedObject implements Serializable
{
     // Constructors
     public SealedObject(Serializable object, Cipher c)
           throws java.io.Exception, IllegalBlockSizeException;

     // Instance Methods
     public final String getAlgorithm();
     public final Object getObject(Key key)
           throws java.io.Exception, ClassNotFoundException,
           InvalidKeyException
     public final Object getObject(Cipher c)
           throws IOException, ClassNotFoundException
     public final Object getObject(Key key, Provider p) throws IOException,
           ClassNotFoundException, NoSuchAlgorithmException,
           InvalidKeyException;
}
```

SecretKey (javax.crypto)

An object implementing this interface is a provider-based representation of a secret key, as opposed to a public or private key. The interface itself does not contain any methods or fields. It is used strictly for grouping and type safety.

```
package javax.crypto;
public abstract interface SecretKey extends Key
{
     // Implementors:  SecretKeySpec

     // no new methods

     public abstract String getAlgorithm(); // from Key
     public abstract byte[] getEncoded();   // from Key
     public abstract String getFormat();    // from Key
}
```

SecretKeyFactory (javax.crypto)

The SunJCE provides instances for converting a `KeySpec` object into a `Key` object so it can be used in `Cipher` or `MAC` classes. The primary use of `SecretKeyFactory` is converting a `PBEParameterSpec` object into `PBEKey`. You can convert most other secret key `KeySpec` objects into `Key` objects just by creating a new `SecretKeySpec` object (which implements `Key` and `KeySpec`) by using the raw bytes `new SecretKeySpec(otherKeySpec.getEncoded())`.

```
package javax.crypto;
public class SecretKeyFactory
{
     // Static Methods
     public static final SecretKeyFactory getInstance(String algorithm)
           throws NoSuchAlgorithmException;
     public static final SecretKeyFactory getInstance(String algorithm,
           Provider p) throws NoSuchAlgorithmException,
           NoSuchProviderException
     public final SecretKey generateSecret(KeySpec spec)
           throws InvalidKeySpecException;

     // Instance Methods
     public final String getAlgorithm();
     public final KeySpec getKeySpec(SecretKey key, Class keySpecClass)
           throws InvalidKeySpecException;
     public final Provider getProvider();
     public final SecretKey translateKey(SecretKey key)
           throws InvalidKeyException;
}
```

SecretKeyFactorySpi (javax.crypto)

This internal API is used by provider authors and works with the `SecretKeyFactory` engine class. End users and applications never need to use this class.

```
package javax.crypto;
public abstract class SecretKeyFactorySpi
{
     // Constructors
     public SecretKeyFactorySpi();

     // Abstract Methods
     protected abstract SecretKey engineGenerateSecret(KeySpec keySpec)
           throws InvalidKeySpecException;
     protected abstract KeySpec engineGetKeySpec(SecretKey spec,
           Class keySpecClass) throws InvalidKeySpecAlgorithm;
     protected abstract SecretKey engineTranslateKey(SecretKey key)
           throws InvalidKeyException;
}
```

SecretKeySpec (javax.crypto.spec)

This class specifies secret keys for use in simple ciphers in a provider-independent form. A call to `getEncoded` returns the raw bytes, and `getFormat` returns RAW. `SecretKeySpec` implements both the `Key` and `KeySpec` interfaces, so it can be used interchangeably without going through a factory.

You use this class primarily for cipher and transformations that do not take any parameters or have any encoding issues, such as Blowfish (technically, Blowfish is parameterizable but in practice, this is not done). DES and DES-EDE (Triple DES) keys can use this specification too, but they have their own classes (`DESKeySpec` and `DESedeKeySpec`) that handle the parity and weak-key issues.

See `RC5ParameterSpec` for an example of symmetric key specification that takes parameters in addition to the raw key.

```
package javax.crypto.spec;
public class SecretKeySpec implements KeySpec, SecretKey
{
     // Implements: Key, KeySpec, SecretKey, Serializable

     // Constructors
     public SecretKeySpec(byte[] key, int offset, int len,
           String algorithm)
     public SecretKeySpec(byte[] key, String algorithm)

     // Instance Methods
     public String getAlgorithm()
     public byte[] getEncoded()
     public String getFormat()
}
```

SecureRandom (java.security)

SecureRandom is an engine class for generating cryptographic-quality (i.e., unpredictable) random or pseudorandom numbers. Unlike all other engine classes, SecureRandom may also be directly created using common default constructors. In this case, the first implementation in the highest rank provider is used, typically the SUN provider using SHA-1 PRNG algorithm that is based on the IEEE 1363 recommendation. This algorithm may take several seconds to "seed" itself using an internal process.

SecureRandom inherits from java.util.Random and extends the API with a nextByte method that returns a user-selected number of random bytes. It also has a static method getSeed that generates "truly random" bytes for use in seeding other generators. Likewise, the setSeed method has been extended to allow the seed to be an array of bytes.

```
package java.security;
public class SecureRandom extends Random
{
      // Constructors
      public SecureRandom();
      public SecureRandom(byte[] seed);

      // Static Methods
      public static byte[] getSeed(int numBytes);
      public static SecureRandom getInstance(String algorithm)
            throws NoSuchAlgorithmException;
      public static SecureRandom getInstance(String algorithm,
            String provider) throws NoSuchAlgorithmException,
            NoSuchProviderException;
      public static SecureRandom getInstance(String algorithm, Provider p)
            throws NoSuchAlgorithmException;

      // Instance Methods
      public byte[] generateSeed(int numBytes);
      public final Provider getProvider();
      public synchronized void nextBytes(byte[] bytes);
      public synchronized void setSeed(byte[] seed);
      public void setSeed(long seed);
      public boolean nextBoolean();
      public void nextBytes(byte[] bytes);
      public double nextDouble(); // double in [0.0, 1.0)
      public float nextFloat();
      public double nextGaussian();
      public int nextInt();       // full range
      public int nextInt(int n); // 0 to n-1
      public long nextLong();
}
```

SecureRandomSpi (java.security)

This is the internal API used by provider authors to implement random or pseudorandom number generators that works with the SecureRandom engine class. End users and applications never need to use this class.

```
package java.security;
public abstract class SecureRandomSpi implements Serializable
{
     // Constructors
     public SecureRandomSpi();

     // Abstract Methods
     protected abstract byte[] engineGenerateSeed(int numBytes);
     protected abstract byte[] engineNextBytes(byte[] bytes);
     protected abstract byte[] engineSetSeed(byte[] seed);
}
```

Security (java.security)

The `Security` class is used to dynamically add, remove, and query cryptographic providers. You can add providers ad hoc or install them in an ordered preference. An alternate means of adding providers statically is editing the `${java-home}/jre/lib/security/java.security` file.

In Java 1.2 and 1.3, the SUN provider was installed by default. In Java 1.4, the SunJCE provider was also added by default.

```
package java.lang;
public class Security
{
     // Static Methods
     public static int addProvider(Provider p);
     public static String getAlgorithmProperty(String algName,
           String propName);
     public static Set getAlgorithms(String serviceName);
     public static String getProperty(String key);
     public static synchronized Provider getProvider(String name);
     public static synchronized Provider[] getProviders();
     public static Provider[] getProviders(String filter);
     public static Provider[] getProviders(Map m);
     public static synchronized int insertProviderAt(Provider p,
           int position);
     public static synchronized void removeProvider(String name);
     public static void setProperty(String key, String datum);
}
```

ShortBufferException (javax.crypto)

This exception indicates that the buffer provided for output is too short for the requested operation. This can happen with the `doFinal` method from the `Cipher`, `MAC`, and `MessageDigest` classes that place the result in a user-specified array.

```
package javax.crypto;
public class ShortBufferException extends GeneralSecurityException
{
```

```
    // Hierarchy :  GeneralSecurityException, Exception, Throwable
    // Implements:  Serializable
    // Thrown By :  Cipher.doFinal, Cipher.update,
    //              ExemptionMechanism.genExemptionBlob,
    //              KeyAgreeement.generateSecret,
    //              Mac.doFinal

    public ShortBufferException();
    public ShortBufferException(String msg);
}
```

Signature (java.security)

The `Signature` class provides an API to compute and verify digital signatures. Like all other engine classes, an instance is created with a call to `getInstance` with an algorithm and, optionally, a provider. Initialization depends whether the instance will be used to sign a document or to verify one. Initialization for signing is done with `initSign` and by passing in a private key and, optionally, a `SecureRandom`. For verification, you use `initVerify` with either a `PublicKey` or `Certificate`. You may also need to set additional parameters for the algorithm using `setParameters`. Once the object is properly configured, data is fed in using repeated calls to `update`. Once complete, `sign` produces a digital signature. Alternatively, `verify` returns `true` or `false` if the signature verified correctly.

The SUN provider implements the Digital Signature Algorithm as specified in FIPS 186-2 using the names `SHA1withDSA`, `MD2withRSA`, `MD5withRSA`, and `SHA1withRSA`, as described in PKCS #1.

```
package java.security;
public class Signature extends SignatureSpi
{
    // Static Methods
    public static Signature getInstance(String algorithm)
          throws NoSuchAlgorithmException;
    public static Signature getInstance(String algorithm, String provider)
          throws NoSuchAlgorithmException, NoSuchProviderException;
    public static Signature getInstance(String algorithm, Provider p)
          throws NoSuchAlgorithmException;

    // Instance Methods
    public Object clone() throws CloneNotSupportedException;
    public final String getAlgorithm();
    public final AlgorithmParameters getParameters();
    public final Provider getProvider();
    public final void initSign(PrivateKey privateKey)
          throws InvalidKeyException;
    public final void initSign(PrivateKey privateKey, SecureRandom rand)
          throws InvalidKeyException;
    public final void initVerify(PublicKey publicKey)
          throws InvalidKeyException;
    public final void initVerify(Certificate certificate)
          throws InvalidKeyException;
```

```
    public final void setParameter(AlgorithmParameterSpec spec)
          throws InvalidAlgorithmParameterException;
    public final byte[] sign() throws SignatureException;
    public final int sign(byte[] outbuf, int offset, int length)
          throws SignatureException;
    public String toString();
    public final void update(byte b) throws SignatureException;
    public final void update(byte[] input) throws SignatureException;
    public final void update(byte[] input, int offset, int length)
          throws SignatureException;
    public final boolean verify(byte[] signature)
          throws SignatureException;
    public final boolean verify(byte[] signature, int offset, int length)
          throws SignatureException;
}
```

SignatureException (java.security)

This generic exception indicates a problem with a call to a `Signature` object.

```
package java.security;
public class SignatureException extends GeneralSecurityException
{
    // Hierarchy :  GeneralSecurityException, Exception, Throwable
    // Implements:  Serializable
    // Thrown By :  most methods in Signature, SignedObject.SignedObject
    //              SignedObject.verify

    public SignatureException();
    public SignatureException(String msg);
}
```

SignatureSpi (java.security)

This is the internal API used by provider authors to implement a digital signature algorithm that works with the `Signature` engine class. End users and applications never need to use this class.

```
package java.security;
public abstract class SignatureSpi
{
    // Constructors
    public SignatureSpi();

    // Instance Methods
    public Object clone() throws CloneNotSupportedException;
    protected abstract Object engineGetParameter(String param)
          throws InvalidParameterException;
    protected AlgorithmParameters engineGetParameters();
    protected abstract void engineInitSign(PrivateKey privateKey)
          throws InvalidKeyException;
```

```
    protected void engineInitSign(PrivateKey privateKey, SecureRandom
          rand) throws InvalidKeyException;
    protected abstract void engineInitVerify(PublicKey publicKey)
          throws InvalidKeyException;
    protected void engineSetParameter(AlgorithmParameterSpec spec)
          throws InvalidAlgorithmParameterException;
    protected abstract void engineSetParameter(String param, Object value)
          throws InvalidParameterException;
    protected abstract byte[] engineSign() throws SignatureException;
    protected int engineSign(byte[] outbuf, int offset, int length)
          throws SignatureException;
    protected abstract void engineUpdate(byte b)
          throws SignatureException;
    protected abstract void engineUpdate(byte[] input, int offset,
          int length) throws SignatureException;
    protected abstract boolean engineVerify(byte[] sigBytes)
          throws SignatureException;
    protected boolean engineVerify(byte[] sigBytes, int offset,
          int length) throws SignatureException;
}
```

SignedObject (java.security)

`SignedObject` provides a digitally signed serialized object. To create, you pass in the object to sign, along with a private key and `Signature` object (need not be initialized). The resulting `SignedObject` can be left as-is or serialized and deserialized. To verify the signature, you pass in a `PublicKey` and a `Signature` object to the `verify` method, then retrieve the original object using `getObject`.

```
package java.security;
public class SignedObject implements Serializable
{
    // Constructors
    public SignedObject(Serializable object, PrivateKey signingKey,
          Signature signingEngine) throws IOException,
          InvalidKeyException, SignatureException;

    // Instance Methods
    public String getAlgorithm();
    public Object getObject() throws IOException, ClassNotFoundException;
    public byte[] getSignature();
    public boolean verify(PublicKey verificationKey,
          Signature verificationEngine) throws
          InvalidKeyException, SignatureException;
}
```

System (java.lang)

This class contains many methods, but the method `arrayCopy` is frequently used in cryptography code. It makes a system call to directly copy array values instead of using a `for` or equivalent loop. While the API takes an `Object` type, only native array types are actually allowed (e.g., `int[]`, `long[]`).

```
package java.lang;
public final class System
{
    // Static Methods
    public static void arrayCopy(Object input, int inputOffset,
          Object output, int outputOffset, int length);
    public static void currentTimeMillis();
    /* ... and many others */
}
```

UnrecoverableKeyException (java.security)

This exception is only thrown from `KeyStore.getKey` when a key is not retrievable from the key store.

```
package java.security;
public class UnrecoverableKeyException extends GeneralSecurityException
{
    // Hierarchy :  GeneralSecurityException, Exception, Throwable
    // Implements:  Serializable
    // Thrown By :  KeyStore.getKey

    public UnrecoverableKeyException();
    public UnrecoverableKeyException(String msg);
}
```

X509Certificate (java.security.cert)

This class provides various means for extracting fields from an X.509-encoded certificate.

```
package java.security.cert;
public abstract class X509Certificate
{
    // Static Methods
    // Instance Methods
    public List getExtendedKeyUsage() throws CertificateParsingException;
    public Collection getIssuerAlternativeNames()
          throws CertificateParsingException;
    public X500Principal getIssuerX500Principal();
    public Collection getSubjectAlternativeNames()
          throws CertificateParsingException;
    public X500Principal getSubjectX500Principal();

    // Abstract Methods
    public abstract void checkValidity()
          throws CertificateExpiredException,
          CertificateNotYetValidException;
```

```
    public abstract void checkValidity(Date date)
          throws  CertificateExpiredException,
          CertificateNotYetValidException;;
    public abstract int getBasicConstraints();
    public abstract Principal getIssuerDN();
    public abstract boolean getIssuerUniqueID();
    public abstract boolean[] getKeyUsage();
    public abstract Date     getNotAfter();
    public abstract Date getNotBefore();
    public abstract BigInteger getSerialNumber();
    public abstract String getSigAlgName();
    public abstract byte[] getSigAlgParams();
    public abstract byte[] getSignature();
    public abstract Principal getSubjectDN();
    public abstract boolean[] getSubjectUniqueID();
    public abstract byte[] getTBSCertificate()
          throws CertificateEncodingException;
    abstract int getVersion();
}
```

X509EncodedKeySpec (java.security.spec)

This class defines a key encoded with the X.509 specification in a raw `byte` array. Many different public key algorithms can normally use a key encoded this way, but it is up to the provider to support this encoding. An object of this type can be converted into a `PublicKey` class or another `KeySpec` class to extract individual key components.

```
package java.security.spec;
public class X509EncodedKeySpec extends EncodedKeySpec
{
    // Implements: KeySpec

    // Constructors
    public X509EncodedKeySpec(byte[] encodedKey);

    // Instance Methods
    public byte[] getEncoded();
    public final String getFormat();
}
```

REFERENCES

General Cryptography References

These general references provide a broad overview of cryptography and are all good places to start.

Schneier, Bruce. *Applied Cryptography.* New York: John Wiley & Sons, Inc., 1995.

This book really popularized cryptography when it came out, and it's still a great resource. It's very readable and doesn't involve much in the way of mathematics. The C source code provided (on the Web site or CD-ROM) covers basic reference implementations.

Menezes, Alfred J., Paul C. van Oorschor, and Scott A. Vanstone. *Handbook of Applied Cryptography.* Boca Raton, Florida: CRC Press, 1997.

This monster is nearly 800 pages and covers virtually every cryptographic subject (with the big exception of ECC). Much more comprehensive than *Applied Cryptography,* this book includes extensive research notes at the end of every section. If you are new to cryptography, it's probably the *second* book you want, since it's so large and a bit overwhelming. If you already have a good background, this is the book to get. The 1,276-entry bibliography is an excellent way to jump into the forefront of cryptography. Highly recommended.

Stinson, Douglas R. *Cryptography Theory and Practice.* Boca Raton, FL: CRC Press, 1995.

This might be the best place to start to find more about cryptography. Unlike the previous sources listed, which may be overwhelming, this book presents a very clear, straightforward approach that can be read and studied sequentially. It contains all the basics, but especially good are examples in linear and differential analysis on DES. The book also contains a number of more advanced topics. The only topic missing is ECC.

Implementation of Public Key Crytography

IEEE Standard P1363-2000

If you are implementing any public key algorithm or want definitive information, this standard is surprisingly good. The only problem is that all the algorithms (both cryptological and mathematical) are decomposed into very small units, so it can be hard stepping back and getting the big picture. For instance, you won't understand anything about how ECC works, but you will know how to implement it correctly. Again, highly recommended.

Rosen,Michael *Implementing Elliptic Curve Cryptography.* Greenwich, CN: Manning Press, 1999.

This book provides a very straightforward approach for implementing a complete elliptic curve package using C.

Numerical Algorithms

Knuth, Donald E. *The Art of Computer Programming.* Vol. 2, *Seminumerical Algorithms.* 3d ed. Boston: Addison Wesley Longman, 1998.

You mean you don't own this already? This has an excellent section on what *random* means and various usage of random algorithms, as well as number representation and computer arithmetic.

Crandall, Richard and Carl Pomerance. *Prime Numbers: A Computational Perspective.* New York: Springer-Verlag, 2000.

A new book, from two experts in the field. If you are obsessed with prime numbers, factoring, large number algorithms, computer arithmetic, and other topics, this is the book to get.

Rukin, Andrew, et al. "A Statistical Test Suite for Random and Pseudorandom Number Generators for Cryptographic Applications." NIST Special Publication SP-800-22. With Special Revisions. May 15, 2001. Published online at http://csrc.nist.gov/rng/SP800-22b.pdf

This along with Knuth's *Seminumerical Algorithms*, is the place to learn about testing for randomness.

Cryptographic Standards

There are six primary sources for standards that are frequently referenced. Many of the standards are referential and duplicates of others.

NIST FIPS

The National Institute of Standards and Technology (NIST) of the American government works on designing standards for common things such as weights and measures or fire suppression equipment. It also produces standards for information processing for the federal government that, in turn, leads to de facto corporate standards. The standards are issued Federal Information Processing Standards (FIPS) documents and are available at www.itl.nist.gov/fipspubs/index.htm.

Although not formal standards, the NIST also produces numerous "special publications," mostly regarding security basics (see Table 1). Worth investigating, these may be found at http://csrc.nist.gov/publications/nistpubs/index.html. The three shown in Table 2 are especially useful for cryptography.

Table 1 Select NIST FIPS Standards Relating to Cryptography

STANDARD	TITLE	YEAR
FIPS 81	DES Modes of Operation	1980
FIPS 140-2	Security Requirements for Cryptographic Modules	2001
FIPS 180	Secure Hash Standard (SHS)	1997
FIPS 181	Automated Password Generator	1993
FIPS 186-2	Digital Signature Standard (DSS)	2000
FIPS 196	Entity Authentication Using Public Key Cryptography	1997
FIPS 197	Advanced Encryption Standard (AES)	2001

Table 2 Select Special Publications from NIST

SPECIAL PUBLICATION	TITLE	YEAR
NIST SP 800-20	Modes of Operation Validation System for the Triple Data Encryption Algorithm (TMOVS): Requirements and Procedures	2000
NIST SP 800-22	A Statistical Test Suite for Random and Pseudorandom Number Generators for Cryptographic Applications	2000
NIST SP 800-38A	Recommendation for Block Cipher Modes of Operation – Methods and Techniques	2001

IETF RFC

The Internet Engineering Task Force issues many Request for Comment, or RFC, documents regarding various aspects of Internet design and engineering. Some of the RFCs are standards, while other are informational. The documents are free from `www.ietf.org/rfc.html` and are normally cached in many other places. Selected RFCS are listed in Table 3.

Table 3 Selected RFCs Relating to Cryptography

STANDARD	TITLE	YEAR
RFC 1319	The MD2 Message-Digest Algorithm	1992
RFC 1320	The MD4 Message-Digest Algorithm	1992
RFC 1321	The MD5 Message-Digest Algorithm	1992
RFC 1750	Recommendations for Randomness	1994
RFC 1751	A Convention for Human-Readable 128-bit Keys	1994
RFC 1760	The S/KEY One-Time Password System	1995
RFC 2040	The RC5, RC5-CBC, RC5-CBC-Pad, and RC5-CTS Algorithms	1996
RFC 2104	HMAC: Keyed-Hashing for Message Authentication	1997
RFC 2202	Test Cases for HMAC-MD5 and HMAC-SHA-1	1997
RFC 2268	A Description of the RC2(r) Encryption Algorithm	1998
RFC 2289	A One-Time Password System	1998
RFC 2459	Internet X.509 Public Key Infrastructure, Certificate and CRL Profile	1999

Table 3 *(Continued)*

STANDARD	TITLE	YEAR
RFC 2510	Internet X.509 Public Key Infrastructure Certificate Management Protocols	1999
RFC 2511	Internet X.509 Certificate Request Message Format	1999
RFC 2628	Simple Cryptographic Program Interface	1999
RFC 3161	Internet X.509 Public Key Infrastructure: Time-Stamp Protocol	2001
RFC 3217	Triple-DES and RC2 Key Wrapping	2001
RFC 3218	Preventing the Million Message Attack on Cryptographic Message Syntax	2002

PKCS (RSA)

To accelerate the adoption of public key cryptography, RSA issued their own standard documents on public key cryptosystems (see Table 4), called Public Key Cryptosystem Standards (PKCS), before "formal" standards bodies emerged. Most of these standards are now incorporated into other, more formal standards; however, they are still frequently referenced since they are free and publicly available (unlike some others). They can be downloaded from RSA Security's Web site at `www.rsasecurity.com/rsalabs/pkcs/index.html`.

Table 4 PKCS Standards

STANDARD	TITLE	CURRENT VERSION	YEAR
PKCS #1	RSA Cryptography Standard	2.1	2001
PKCS #3	Diffie-Hellman Key Agreement Standard	1.4	1993
PKCS #5	Password-Based Cryptography Standard	2.0	1999
PKCS #6	Extended-Certificate Syntax Standard	1.5	1993
PKCS #7	Cryptographic Message Syntax Standard, Extensions added 1997	1.5	1993, 1997
PKCS #8	Private-Key Information Syntax Standard	1.0	1993

(continues)

Table 4 PKCS Standards *(Continued)*

STANDARD	TITLE	CURRENT VERSION	YEAR
PKCS #9	Selected Object Classes and Attribute Types	2.0	2000
PKCS #10	Certification Request Syntax Standard	1.7	2000
PKCS #11	Cryptographic Token Interface Standard	2.11	2001
PKCS #12	Personal Information Exchange Syntax	1.0	1999
PKCS #15	Conformance Profile Specification	1.0	2000

Notes:
PKCS #2 and #4 were incorporated into PKCS #1.
PKCS #13 is a placeholder for an ECC future standard, but it is unlikely RSA will actually issue one, since IEEE 1363 already exists.
PKCS #14 was never issued.

IEEE 1363

The IEEE 1363-2000 standard for public key cryptography is *the* reference for implementing those systems. It is maintained by leading cryptographers and is comprehensive in its treatment, with clear, thorough algorithm implementation and discussion.

The one downside to this standard is that all algorithms are decomposed into reusable "primitives," which are combined to produce complete systems. For implementation, this is ideal, but it does make it a bit difficult to understand what a particular algorithm is actually doing, since it's composed of many parts with odd names, such as IFFSA.

A companion IEEE 1363a is a compendium of new and supplemental techniques not listed in IEEE 1363. Eventually, 1363 and 1363a will be merged into a new standard. Both 1363 and 1363a are highly recommended if you decide to implement any public key algorithm. (IEEE algorithm standards are shown in Table 5.) Copies of the standard (final and works in progress) may by available online at `http://grouper.ieee.org/groups/1363/`. If not, it's really worth buying the final standard from `http://standards.ieee.org/`.

Table 5 Algorithm coverage in IEEE 1363 standards

STANDARD NAME	SELECTED ALGORITHMS
IEEE 1363-2000	RSA: Key and prime generation
	Elliptic curves: Parameter generation for both binary and prime variants, coordinate representation, and transformation
	Digital signatures
	Random masks generation
IEEE 1363a (draft)	Encryption: Diffie-Hellman (DHAES) and Elliptic Curve Encryption
IEEE-1363.1 (in progress)	Lattice-based public key cryptographic techniques
IEEE-1363.2 (in progress)	Password-based techniques

ANSI/ABA X9 standards

Unfortunately, like most large private standards bodies, the standards are not freely available from the American National Standards Institute (ANSI). Until recently, they were also difficult just to obtain. Public libraries don't often stock them because of limited interest and expense (which can run a few dollars *per page*), but if you live in a large city, the main library or (if one exists) a specialized business library may have some of them. Fortunately, individuals can now buy the standards directly from the Web in PDF format from `www.x9.org`. Be aware that some of the older standards don't offer much more than just listing the algorithm and then listing pages and pages of test values (e.g., SHA-1). Some of the ANSI X9 standards are shown in Table 6.

ISO Standards

Like the ANSI standard, standards from the International Standards Organization (ISO) are not freely available. Table 7 shows some of the more pertinent standards.

Table 6 Selected X9 Standards

STANDARD	TITLE
X9.30.1-1997 X9.30.2-1997	Public Key Cryptography for the Financial Services Industry–Part 1: The Digital Signature Algorithm (DSA); Part 2: The Secure Hash Algorithm (SHA-1)
X9.31-1998	Digital Signatures Using Reversible Public Key Cryptography for the Financial Services Industry (rDSA)
X9.42-2001	Public Key Cryptography for the Financial Services Industry: Agreement of Symmetric Keys Using Discrete Logarithm Cryptography
X9.52-1998	Triple Data Encryption Algorithm Modes of Operation
X9.55-1997	Public Key Cryptography for the Financial Services Industry: Extensions to Public Key Certificates and Certificate Revocation Lists
X9.57-1997	Public Key Cryptography for the Financial Services Industry: Certificate Management
X9.69-1998	Key Management Extensions
X9.71-2000	Keyed Hash Message Authentication Code (MAC)
X9.8-1995	Banking: Personal Identification Number Management and Security–Part 1: PIN Protection Principles and Techniques; Part 2: Approved Algorithms for PIN Encipherment
X9 TG-3-1997	Pin Security Compliance Guideline (free download)
X9.63-2001	Public Key Cryptography for the Financial Services Industry, Key Agreement and Key Transport Using Elliptic Curve Cryptography
X9.80-2001	Prime Number Generation, Primality Testing and Primality Certificates
X9.84-2001	Biometric Information Management and Security

Table 7 Selected ISO Standards

STANDARD	TITLE
ISO 7064:1983	Data Processing–Check Characters Systems
ISO 8731-1:1987 ISO 8731-2:1992	Banking–Approved Algorithms for Message Authentication Part 1: DEA Part 2: Message Authenticator Algorithm
ISO 9564-1:1991 ISO 9564-2:1991	Banking–Personal Identification Number Management and Security Part 1: PIN Protection Principles and Techniques Part 2: Approved Algorithm(s) for PIN Encipherment
ISO/IEC 9979:1999	Information Technology–Security Techniques–Procedures for the Registration of Cryptographic Algorithms
ISO/IEC 9796-1:1999 ISO/IEC 9796-2:1997 ISO/IEC 9796-3:2000	Information Technology–Security Techniques–Digital Signature Schemes Giving Message Recovery Part 1: General Part 2: Mechanisms Using a Hash Function Part 3: Discrete Logarithm-based Mechanisms
ISO/IEC 9797-1:1999	Information Technology–Security Techniques–Message Authentication Codes (MACs) Part 1: Mechanisms Using a Block Cipher
ISO/IEC 9798-1:1997 ISO/IEC 9798-2:1999 ISO/IEC 9798-3:1998 ISO/IEC 9798-4:1999 ISO/IEC 9798-5:1999	Information Technology–Security Techniques–Entity Authentication Part 1: General Part 2: Mechanisms Using Symmetric Encipherment Algorithms Part 3: Mechanisms Using Digital Signature Techniques Part 4: Mechanisms Using a Cryptographic Check Function Part 5: Mechanisms Using Zero-knowledge Techniques
ISO/IEC 10116:1997	Information Technology–Security Techniques–Modes of Operation for an *n*-bit Block Cipher

(continues)

Table 7 Selected ISO Standards *(Continued)*

STANDARD	TITLE
ISO/IEC 10118-1:2000 ISO/IEC 10118-2:2000 ISO/IEC 10118-3:2000 ISO/IEC 10118-4:2000	Information Technology–Security Techniques–Hash Functions Part 1: General Part 2: Hash Functions Using an *n*-bit Block Cipher Part 3: Dedicated Hash Functions Part 4: Hash Functions Using Modular Arithmetic
ISO 11568-1:1994 ISO 11568-2:1994 ISO 11568-3:1994 ISO 11568-4:1998 ISO 11568-5:1998 ISO 11568-6:1998	Banking–Key Management (Retail) Part 1: Introduction to Key Management Part 2: Key Management Techniques for Symmetric Ciphers Part 3: Key Lifecycle for Symmetric Ciphers Part 4: Key Management Techniques Using Public Key Cryptosystems Part 5: Key Lifecycle for Public Key Cryptosystems Part 6: Key Management Schemes
ISO/IEC 11770-1:1996 ISO/IEC 11770-2:1996 ISO/IEC 11770-3:1996	Information Technology–Security Techniques–Key Management Part 1: Framework Part 2: Mechanisms Using Symmetric Techniques Part 3: Mechanisms Using Asymmetric Techniques
ISO/IEC 13888-1:1997 ISO/IEC 13888-2:1998 ISO/IEC 13888-3:1997	Information Technology–Security Techniques–Non-repudiation Part 1: General Part 2: Mechanisms Using symmetric techniques Part 3: Mechanisms Using asymmetric techniques
ISO/IEC 14888-1:1998 ISO/IEC 14888-2:1998 ISO/IEC 14888-3:1998 ISO/IEC 14888-3/Cor1:2001	Information Technology–Security Techniques–Digital Signatures with Appendix Part 1: General Part 2: Identity-based Mechanisms Part 3: Certificate-based Mechanisms
ISO/IEC 15408-1: 1999 ISO/IEC 15408-2: 1999 ISO/IEC 15408-3: 1999	Information Technology–Security Techniques–Evaluation Criteria for IT security Part 1–Introduction and General Model Part 2–Security Functional Requirements Part 3–Security Assurance Requirements
ISO/IEC 17799:2000	Information Technology–Code of Practice for Information Security Management

Research Papers

Finding research papers used to mean making a trip to the library. Today there are two main sources for cryptographic papers:

ResearchIndex. The NECI Scientific Literature Digital Library (`http://citeseer.nj.nec.com/cs`)

Advances in Cryptography, 1981–1997. Electronic proceeding and Index of the CRYPTO and EUROCRYPT conferences 1981 to 1997. Springer-Verlag, 2000.

Unfortunately, a large number of cryptography papers are not available from ResearchIndex. That's where *Advances in Cryptography* comes in. Springer-Verlag packaged on a CD 800 papers from the CRYPTO and EUROCRYPT conferences from 1981 to 1997. All are presented in PDF format. Quality varies, since they were scanned in. A title and author index are both online and in a book format. This will save you some painful trips to the local university trying to find the original articles.

References

[Baudron1999] Baudron, O., et al. "Report on the AES Candidates." *Proceedings from the Second Advanced Encryption Standard Candidate Conference,* National Institute of Standards and Technology (NIST), March 1999.

[BeCaKr1996] Bellare, M., R. Canetti, and H. Krawczyk. "Keying Hash Functions for Message Authentication." *Advances in Cryptology.* CRYPTO '96, pp. 1–15, 1996.

[BiKu1998] Biryukov, A. and E. Kushilevitz. "Improved Cryptanalysis of RC5." *Advances in Cryptography.* Proceedings of EUROCRYPT '98. Springer-Verlag, 1998.

[BlBlSh1986] Blum, L., M. Blum, and M Shub. "A Simple Unpredictable Pseudo-random Number Generator." *SIAM Journal on Computing*. vol. 15, no. 2, 1986.

[Boneh1999] Boneh, D. "Twenty Years of Attacks on the RSA Cryptosystem." *Notices of the American Mathematical Society*. vol. 46, 1999.

[Boneh2001] Boneh, D. "Simplied OAEP for the Rabin and RSA Functions." *Crypto 2001: Lecture Notes in Computer Science.* vol. 2139, Springer-Verlag, pp. 275–291, 2001.

[BoDu1998] Boneh, D. and G. Durfee. "Cryptanalysis of RSA with Private Key d Less Than $N^{0.292}$." *IEEE Transactions on Information Theory.* vol. 46, no. 4, pp. 1339–1349, July 2000.

[BoJoNg2000] Boneh, D., A. Joux, and P. Q. Nguyen. "Why Textbook ElGamal and RSA Encryption are Insecure." *Advances in Cryptology.* AsiaCrypt 2000. Springer-Verlag, 2000.

[BoVe1998] Boneh, D. and R. Venkatesan. "Breaking RSA May Be Easier Than Factoring." In Proceedings EUROCRYPT '98, *Lecture Notes in Computer Science.* vol. 1233, Springer-Verlag, pp. 59–71, 1998.

[Boyko1999] Boyko, Victor. "On the Security Properties of OAEP as an All-or-Nothing Transform." *Advances in Cryptography.* Crypto '99. Springer-Verlag pp. 503–518, 1999. See `http://link.springer.de/link/service/series/0558/tocs/t1666.htm` for details.

[CaRo1997] Caronni, G. and M. Robshaw, "How Exhausting Is Exhaustive Search?" *RSA Laboratories' CryptoBytes.* vol. 2, no. 3, pp. 1–6, 1997.

[ChJo1998] Chabaud, F. and A. Joux. "Differential Collisions in SHA-0." Crypto '98 Proceedings, 1998.

[DaGoVn1993] Daemen, J., R Govaerts, and J Van-Dewalle. "Weak Keys for IDEA." *Advances in Cryptology*. CRYPTO '93. pp. 223 and 231, 1994.

[DaLaPo1993] Damgard, I., P. Landrock, and C. Pomerance. "Average Case Error Estimates for the Strong Probable Prime Test." *Mathematics of Computation.* vol. 61, pp. 177–194, 1993.

[DeBo1994] den Boer, B., and A. Bosselaers. "Collisions for the Compression Function of MD5." *Advances in Cryptology*, Proceedings of EUROCRYPT '93, LNCS 765. T. Helleseth, Ed., pp. 293–304, Springer-Verlag, 1994.

[Dobbertin1995] Dobbertin, H. and Alf Swindles Ann. *CryptoBytes. vol.* 3, no. 1 (Autumn 1995). Available from RSA Security.

[ElGamal1985] elGamal, T., "A Public-Key Cryptosystem and a Signature Scheme Based on Discrete Logarithms," *Advances in Cryptography: Proceedings of CRYPTO '84.* pp 10–18. Springer-Verlag, 1985.

[Feistel1973] Feistel, H. "Cryptography and Computer Privacy." *Scientific American.* vol. 288, pp. 15–23, May 1973.

[FuSiSmFe2001] Fu, K., E. Sit, K. Smith, and N. Feamster. "Dos and Don'ts of Client Authentication on the Web." in Proceedings of the 10th USENIX Security Symposium, Washington, DC, August 2001.

[KaYi1998] Kaliski, B. S. Jr and Y. L. Yin. "On the Security of the RC5 Encryption Algorithm." *RSA Laboratories Technical Report TR-602*, version 1.0, September 1998.

[KeScFe1999] Kelsey, J., B. Schneier, and N. Ferguson. "Yarrow-160: Notes on the Design and Analysis of the Yarrow Cryptographic Pseudorandom Number Generator." *Sixth Annual Workshop on Selected Areas in Cryptography*, Springer-Verlag, August 1999.

[KeScWaHa1998] Kelsey, J., B. Schneier, D. Wagner, and C. Hall. "Cryptanalytic Attacks on Pseudorandom Number Generators." *Fast Software Encryption. Fifth International Workshop Proceedings* (March 1998), Springer-Verlag, pp. 168–188, 1998.

[Kocher1996] Kocher, P. "Timing Attacks on Implementations of Diffie-Hellman, RSA, DSS, and Other Systems." *Lecture Notes in Computer Science*, Crypto '96, vol. 1109, pp. 104–113. Springer-Verlag, 1996.

[Knuth1998] Knuth, D. E. *The Art of Computer Programming.* Vol. 2, *Seminumerical Algorithms.* 3d ed. Boston: Addison Wesley Longman, 1998.

[LaMa1990] Lai, X. and J. Massey. "A Proposal for a New Block Encryption Standard." *Advances in Cryptology.* EUROCRYPT '90, pp. 389–404. Springer-Verlag, 1990.

[LaMaMu1991] Lai, X., J. Massey, and S. Murphy. "Fast Software Encryption." *Lecture Notes in Computer Science.* vol. 809, pp. 1–17. Springer-Verlag, 1993.

[Lipmaa1998] Lipmaa, H. "IDEA: A Cipher for Multimedia Architectures?" in *Selected Areas in Cryptography '98*. Stafford Tavares and Henk Meijer, Eds. vol. 1556 of *Lecture Notes in Computer Science*, pp. 253–268, Springer-Verlag, 1998.

[MaNi1998] Matsumoto, M. and T. Nishimura. "Mersenne Twister: A 623-dimensionally Equidistributed Uniform Pseudorandom Number Generator." *ACM Transactions on Modeling and Computer Simulation:* Special Issue on Uniform Random Number Generation, 1998.

[Multiprime] Compaq. "Cryptography using Compaq Multiprime Technology in a Parallel Processing Environment." 2000. Unpublished. Available at `http://nonstop.compaq.com/docs/IO/4523/ATT/ESSCPTTB.pdf`

[PrVa1996] Preneel, B. and P. Van Oorschot. "On the Security of Two MAC Algorithms." *Advances in Cryptology*. EUROCRYPT '96, pp. 19–32, 1996.

[RiShAd1978] Rivest, R.L., A. Shamir, and L.M. Adleman. "A Method for Obtaining Digital Signatures and Public-Key Cryptosystems," *Communications of the ACM*, v21, n2, Feb 1978, pp 120–126.

[RiSi1999] Rivest, R. L. and R. D. Silverman. "Are 'Strong' Primes Needed for RSA?" Unpublished. Available from `http://theory.lcs.mit.edu/~rivest`.

[Rivest1995]Rivest, R. L. "The RC5 Encryption Algorithm." *Fast Software Encryption. Lecture Notes in Computer Science.* vol. 1008, pp 86–96. Springer-Verlag, 1995.

[Schneier1994] Schneier, B. "Description of a New Variable-Length Key, 64-Bit Block Cipher (Blowfish)" *Fast Software Encryption. Cambridge Security Workshop Proceedings* (December 1993). pp. 191–204. Springer-Verlag, 1994.

[ScKeWhWaFe1999] Schneier, B., J. Kelsey, D. Whiting, D. Wagner, and N. Ferguson. *The Twofish Encryption Algorithm: A 128-Bit Block Cipher*. New York: John Wiley & Sons, 1999.

[Schulz2001] Schulz, R.-H. "Check Character Systems and Anit-symmetric Mappings." *Computational Discrete Mathematics*, LNCS 2122, pp 136–147, 2001.

[Vaudenay1996] Vaudenay, S. "On the Weak Keys in Blowfish." *Fast Software Encryption*. Third International Workshop Proceedings, pp. 27–32. Springer-Verlag, 1996.

[Verhoelff1969] Verhoeff, J. "Error Dectecting Decimal Codes. Mathematical Centre Tract." vol 29, *The Mathematical Centrum*, Amsterdam, 1969.

[WaPu1989] Wagner, N. R. and P. S. Putter. "Error Detecting Error Decimal Digits." *Communications of the ACM*. vol. 32, no. 1, January 1989.

[Wiener1990] Wiener, M. "Cryptanalysis of Short RSA Secret Exponents." *IEEE Transactions on Information Theory*. vol. 36, no. 3, pp. 553–558, 1990.

[Wiener1996] Wiener, M. J. "Efficient DES Key Search." Reprinted in *Practical Cryptography for Data Internetworks*. W. Stallings, ed., pp. 31–79. Washington, DC: IEEE Computer Society Press, 1996.

[Wiener1997] Wiener, M. J. "Efficient DES Key Search: An Update." RSA Laboratories' *CryptoBytes*. vol. 3, no. 2, pp. 6–8.

Index

SYMBOLS

A

B

E

N

U

V

W